The Sociology of Work:

Structures and Inequalities

STEVEN P. VALLAS
Northeastern University

WILLIAM FINLAY
University of Georgia

AMY S. WHARTON
Washington State University

New York   Oxford
OXFORD UNIVERSITY PRESS
2009

Oxford University Press, Inc., publishes works that further Oxford University's
objective of excellence in research, scholarship, and education.

Oxford   New York
Auckland   Cape Town   Dar es Salaam   Hong Kong   Karachi
Kuala Lumpur   Madrid   Melbourne   Mexico City   Nairobi
New Delhi   Shanghai   Taipei   Toronto

With offices in
Argentina   Austria   Brazil   Chile   Czech Republic   France   Greece
Guatemala   Hungary   Italy   Japan   Poland   Portugal   Singapore
South Korea   Switzerland   Thailand   Turkey   Ukraine   Vietnam

Published by Oxford University Press, Inc.
198 Madison Avenue, New York, New York 10016
http://www.oup.com

Oxford is a registered trademark of Oxford University Press

Library of Congress Cataloging-in-Publication Data
Vallas, Steven P. (Steven Peter), 1951–
The sociology of work : structures and inequalities / Steven P. Vallas,
William Finlay, Amy S. Wharton.
p. cm.
ISBN 978-0-19-538172-6 (alk. paper)
1. Work—Sociological aspects. I. Finlay, William. II. Wharton,
Amy S. III. Title.
HD4904.V28 2009
306.3′6—dc22

                                                2008039378

Printing number: 9 8 7 6 5 4 3 2 1

Printed in the United States of America
on acid-free paper

Contents

Preface

The sociology of work and occupations is one of the larger and more influential of specialization in the discipline. Its concerns have been at the heart of sociology since its very establishment, and they have remained centrally important parts of the field. Yet those of us who teach the sociology of work have often had to make especially difficult choices when it comes time to submit our book orders. How can we best convey the substance of the field to newcomers—to undergraduates generally, to majors in sociology in particular, and to graduate students (among others) needing to grasp the field as a whole? Selecting useful readings for these audiences has often been a labored task. Using original monographs, or selected articles and chapters, has the advantage of immersing students in the original research—but relying on these specialized works often makes it difficult for students to grasp the broader conceptual principles that bind the field together. Using textbooks has an obvious advantage, for they can indeed convey the core principles and themes that inform the sociology of work. Yet textbooks in the sociology of work have typically wound up sacrificing the specifically *sociological* content of the field—that is, the theoretical principles and conceptual moorings that distinguishes

its approach from that of kindred disciplines such as management theory or industrial and organizational psychology. On the one hand, we have sociology as Babel. On the other, simply sociobabble. Not an ideal situation either way.

This text was written in an effort to transcend this dilemma. Put simply, we have written a textbook that seeks to convey the excitement of discovery that stems from close engagement with particular findings, yet does so in ways that remain faithful to the overarching principles and intellectual rigor that define sociology as a distinct discipline in its own right. In short, here (we hope) is a textbook written as if sociological thinking mattered. A corollary benefit of our approach will be the stimulation of discussion and debate among our fellow scholars, who may (we again hope) will derive benefit from the book as well.

Practicing what we preach, we have adopted a division of intellectual labor in which our respective interests and expertise complement one another, providing strengths that would be difficult for lone scholars to achieve. The result is a volume that is distinct in several respects. First, reflecting our sense that discussion of historical developments is indispensable for any serious understanding of work, employment, and social inequality, we have sought to discuss key historical issues that are too seldom given emphasis in books such as this, such as Luddism, the role of gender in the industrial revolution, or the rise and decline of the workers' movement. Without some understanding of economic, labor, and social history, students simply cannot grasp the choices (and the dangers) that contemporary developments imply. Second, we have sought to transcend the ironic tendency to ghettoize discussion of gender, which inevitably suffers when it is sequestered within isolated chapters. We therefore weave issues of gender inequality into our discussion at multiple points of the analysis, from the rise of the factory system to management occupations, access to the professions, to debates over work and family.

A third point is that the book does not refrain from introducing complex theoretical or methodological issues. We devote chapters to theoretical approaches that have informed the field, with treatment of both classical and contemporary views of work and paid employment. We also devote a chapter to the research methods and data sources that are employed within the sociology of work, the better to equip students to understand the findings the volume presents. Finally, we have sought to do these things in an engaging, lively manner that draws on contemporary events to illustrate the many points of applicability which sociological thinking enjoys. Let the readers be the judge.

We have incurred many personal and professional debts in the writing of this book, and we wish to thank Claude Tewles, who instigated this project, and Sherith Pankretz, Marianne Paul, and Chase Billingham, along with various reviewers, editors, and research assistants who are too numerous (or too anonymous!) to single out for thanks.

PART I

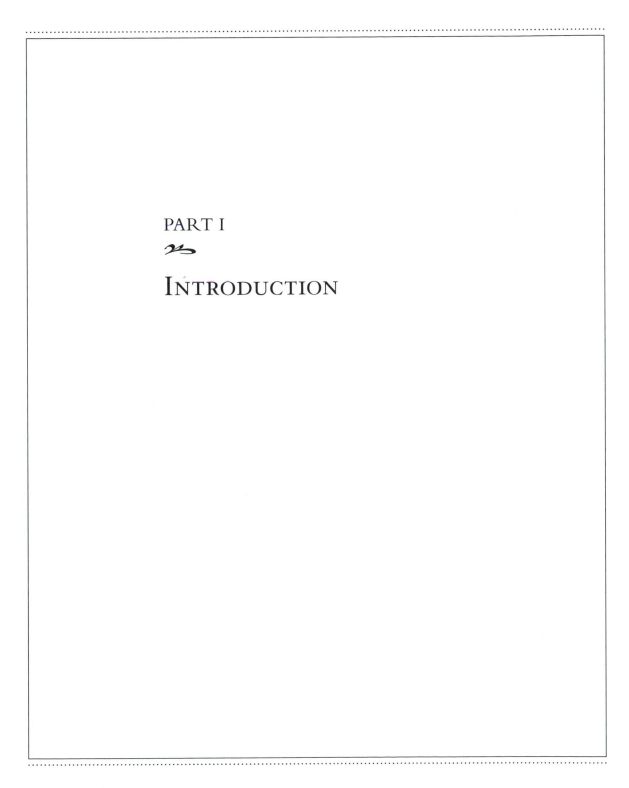

Introduction

Chapter 1

The Sociology of Work: An Invitation

Concerns about the shuttering of American factories and the disappearance of middle-class jobs. Debates in the U.S. Congress over the rights of women alleging discrimination in their paychecks. Reports about a "culture of corruption," first at such major financial corporations as Enron, Qwest, and HealthSouth, and now at major commercial lending institutions. Acrimony over the outsourcing of once-secure white-collar jobs in engineering, finance, and other professions, as work is shifted to India and other offshore sites. It is difficult nowadays to avoid the topic of "work" in one or another form. This should not be surprising: From its very establishment, political, business, and religious leaders have extolled the virtues of hard work. Immigrants, seeking a better life, have often flocked to U.S. shores in hopes of finding better jobs; they continue to do so today. The sitdown strikes in the 1930s were a pivotal event in American social history, through which industrial workers—a previously marginalized class—gained not only the wages but also the public admiration that helped them join mainstream society. Perhaps the most enduring symbol of the women's movement to date has been Rosie the Riveter, an iconic figure who symbolized women's ability to do manual work

as well as any man. And of course, for many people today, the pursuit of a college education has a practical significance in addition to its intellectual one: a college degree—much like the frontier during earlier periods in U.S. history—promises to open up a path to fulfilling working lives for millions of young people today.

Thus it is not difficult to understand why people should be concerned about the nature of work. What *is* surprising, however, is how few of us take work seriously as an object of study in its own right. This book aims to fill that gap. It invites the reader to look again at the meanings and orientations that people bring to bear on work, at the organizational structures that surround us at work, and at the forms of social interaction we sustain with managers and our fellow employees. The book is written in the belief that these are vital aspects of our lives, whose importance too often outstrips our understanding of them. Developing the principles, theories, and knowledge that make up the sociology of work, we hope to deepen our appreciation for the myriad ways in which work and employment affect our lives, our identities, and the societies in which we live.

Of course, social scientists have long studied the workplace, doing so from several different vantage points. Industrial and organizational psychologists have developed much research on employees' personalities and on the factors that affect motivation, job satisfaction, and job performance. Labor historians have explored shifts in the structure and meaning of work, focusing especially on the impact of industrial capitalism on workers' lives. Economic anthropologists have developed a rich corpus of research focused on the meanings of work within many cultures, especially less developed ones. And labor economists have amassed an impressive body of knowledge about how markets and social influences combine to affect levels of pay and productivity and even decisions about how economic transactions should be shaped.

These are all important and worthy areas of study. They tell us a great deal about the forces that impinge on the workplace, and for this reason we draw on these perspectives at several points throughout this book. Yet we do so in an effort to capture aspects of workplace life that these disciplines often neglect and which we believe are especially fateful for both individuals and the groups in which they live. We have in mind a series of issues and themes that are the province of the specifically *sociological* approach toward work, which focuses on the informal norms and values that workers establish on the job and that lend work meaning in their eyes; the workings of organizational structures and the different forms that managerial authority assumes; and differences in the work situations faced by employees in varying occupations, whether in managerial and professional jobs or in routine clerical, manual, and service occupations. The sociology of work also studies the distribution of opportunity among different groups of workers,

exploring how, when, and why job rewards are unequally allocated along the lines of gender, race, ethnicity, or nationality. The sociology of work approaches all of these themes in a dynamic fashion, asking how the workplace is changing in the wake of new digital technologies, innovative forms of work organization, rising concerns about work and family, and continuing debates about equal employment rights. These and other topics provide the central threads that unite the sociology of work and define its unique perspective toward the social and cultural dimensions of workplace life. They provide the themes we pursue in this book.

These themes are far from idle concerns. As will be discussed, although the sociology of work is based on academic theories and research, for several generations now the field has sought to contribute to the lives of individuals, groups, organizations, and the wider society and polity. Thus, for aspiring professionals or managers, an understanding of the informal underside of work organizations, of how diversity might be handled on the job, or how job ladders impinge on one's hopes for advancement within a given firm can all provide practical knowledge that has direct relevance to one's career aspirations. (The literature is filled with real-life instances in which managers and professionals underestimated the importance of social and cultural factors and suffered as a direct result.) In civic terms, too, the sociology of work can help one grasp a number of key issues that are hotly debated in political contests and debates. One has only to think of issues such as gender disparities in pay, the influx of immigrant workers into jobs previously held by native-born workers, debates over the fairness of hundred-million-dollar severance packages for CEOs (or, at the opposite end of the economic structure, the situation of the working poor) to see what we mean. Finally, and in more intellectual terms, the sociology of work promises to deepen our understanding of the human condition, exploring the ways in which the nature of our jobs affects our identities, values, and ideals. Exploring how work has been organized and distributed and how contemporary forces are transforming work organizations better equips us to make choices, both as individual citizens and as a society writ large.

In this introductory chapter, we sketch out the major principles that underlie the sociological study of work. Then, in Chapter 2, we present the major perspectives on which researchers have relied, both in classical and contemporary debates.

The Primacy-of-Production Thesis

References to the fundamental nature of work for human life can be found in works as different as the Bible, Adam Smith's *Wealth of Nations*, and Marx and Engels's *Communist Manifesto*. Drawing on a long history of theological and philosophical thinking about work, conservative thinkers and managers today often speak about the overarching significance of the work ethic—and the destructive impact of government support on the individual's sense of self-reliance and self-fulfillment. Sociologists of work agree with much of this thinking, though in very specific ways, and hold that the work that people do is "fateful" for their social lives more generally. This is what is sometimes meant by the "primacy-of-production thesis"—an important axiom which holds that the productive relations into which people enter

as they set about making ends meet have decisive effects on their individual and social lives. At the *individual* level, the notion is obvious: Especially in modern industrial societies, what we do for a living not only determines what we earn; in addition, it defines us in other people's eyes, "placing" us in relation to other people in ways that affect our friendship networks, our selection of appropriate marital partners, and even our self-esteem and physical well-being. At the more *collective* level, the notion here is that the structural arrangements that societies make while adapting to their environments will have far-reaching effects on the social order as a whole. It is in this sense that sociologists contend that work is a creative act in a double sense: In making our external world, we at the same time make ourselves, both as individuals and as collectivities.

The Impact of Work on the Individual

One of the first generations of sociologists to study work systematically coined the term "master status" to refer to the pivotal role that occupations play in defining us in the eyes of others. This is, after all, why the first question strangers ask us about ourselves is "What do you do?" or "Where do you work?" (For students, the equivalent is often "What's your major?"—a precursor, perhaps, to one's eventual occupational tie.) In an earlier historical period, the equivalent question might have asked about one's kin or village of origin. Now, in the wake of industrial capitalism, one's place within the labor market has become the defining characteristic of the person, conferring on us certain levels of prestige and levels of access to scarce opportunities. Experimental research indicates that our occupational roles strongly affect how other people perceive us, leading them to attribute certain characteristics to us that we may in fact lack. Thus, in a study by Humphrey (1985), it was found that in a laboratory setting, people who were randomly assigned to perform "managerial" jobs were more likely to be perceived as intelligent and as having leadership ability than were similar people who were assigned to perform "clerical" jobs. Apparently the role we play at work presents us in a particular light, affecting the characteristics that people attribute to us as individuals.

Research also suggests that the jobs we hold affect our perceptions of the world around us. This point emerged early in the development of the field, as in Lieberman's (1956) classic study of factory workers, which gathered a wealth of data on the levels of education, experience, and attitudes toward management found among 2,000 factory employees in the Midwest. Two years after his initial survey, more than 100 of his respondents had been promoted to jobs as supervisors, allowing Lieberman to devise an interesting comparison. He constructed two "matched" groups of respondents, contrasting the newly promoted supervisors with workers who had reported identical levels of experience, ability, and attitudes at the outset of the study but who had *not* been promoted to supervisory jobs. The author found that workers who had come to hold positions with authority developed very different attitudes toward management, toward the company's incentive pay plan, and toward their fellow employees from those held by workers who had stayed in nonsupervisory jobs. In other words, holding a position of authority at work dramatically changed the world views of those involved. The same point emerges in a more recent study by the Harvard sociologist Michele Lamont (1992). Interviewing middle-class employees in distinct

regions of both France and the United States, she finds that people whose jobs are located within commercial and market contexts tend to place a much greater value on material success and possessions as the basis for evaluating their fellow citizens than do employees in other occupations and industries. These findings, which are robust and replicated in many studies, suggest that *the job shapes the person* in deep and abiding ways quite beyond what we might suspect.

Work also embeds us within social networks of one or another sort. Indeed, evidence suggests that one's occupational position affects the friendships we form, the people we date, the leisure activities we tend to embrace, and even the people we are inclined to choose as mates (Jackman and Jackman 1983). By and large we choose as associates (or intimates) those who share many of our attitudes, backgrounds, and affiliations, often forming friendship networks on the basis of the organizations and institutions to which we are attached. This is one important reason why the friendship networks a classical musician develops are likely to be very different from those of a corrections officer, for example, even if they earn approximately the same level of pay.

Work also reaches into one's health. This point has been found repeatedly in studies of the linkage between occupational position and both physical and mental well-being. Thus, in an early study by a Swedish epidemiologist, Palmore (1971) sought to identify those factors that most strongly affected individual longevity. He began by administering physical examinations to a sample of subjects, gathering data about their medical histories and social behaviors such as smoking and drinking. He had the foresight to ask about their levels of job satisfaction.

A follow-up stage of data collection conducted several years later revealed that the single strongest predictor of his subjects' longevity was their level of job satisfaction at time one. Similar findings were reported in studies by Karasek (1979, 1981), which found that factory and office employees whose jobs combined two characteristics—low levels of autonomy and high quantitative demands—had significantly greater rates of coronary heart disease as a result. A recent study of French workers conducted by Cambois (2004) even found that job mobility (or the lack of it) had a pronounced effect on mortality rates: Especially among men, mobility into a higher status job contributed on average to a longer life, while workers who were stuck in place or downwardly mobile tended to die at higher rates.

The effects of the job on mental health have also been much studied, with results again suggesting how the job shapes the person. In a pioneering study of manual workers in Detroit, Kornhauser (1965) found that respondents who performed machine-paced tasks exhibited far higher levels of depression, poor self-esteem, and hostility toward others than did similar workers who enjoyed greater autonomy at work. Workers seemed to suffer from a sense that their lives were being wasted, with few significant gains to show for the tedium of their jobs. As some critics pointed out, this study was limited in certain respects: Since it was based on data gathered from a single point in time, workers may have had poor mental health to begin with and may have been "selected into" unrewarding jobs for lack of any alternative. Put differently, the point remained that it might have been the "person that shapes the job." To address precisely this question, Kohn and Schooler (1983) used a statistically rigorous method of analysis to separate out the causal effects that flow in each direction. Studying nationally representative samples of Americans (and later, workers in other nations as well), they drew two important conclusions in their study: First, while people with certain personality attributes did tend to cluster within certain jobs, the impact of the job on the person was more than twice as pronounced as the reverse. Second, the longer the person held a given job, the stronger the effect it had on his or her personality and well-being. Kohn and Schooler later found that the occupational conditions one encounters on the job also affect one's intellectual functioning and even one's values as a parent. Clearly, work reaches deep into one's personality, health, and self-concept.

The Impact of Work on Societies

We are trained to think of ourselves as self-reliant, freely acting individuals. For this reason we tend to neglect social and cultural dynamics at the macro-social or collective level, for this is a seemingly abstract realm that lies beyond direct experience. Yet historical studies can sensitize us to institutional changes that occur behind our backs, showing us some of the ways in which work structures have left a deep and abiding mark on human societies. Such effects can be momentous, as when large-scale changes in the institutional structure of work lead to dramatic shifts in the social order writ large. As systems of production change, so too does the surrounding society.

This point is made abundantly clear in studies of the transition to industrial capitalism within Western Europe (a topic discussed more fully in Chapter 4). As peasant labor, home-based production, and artisanal forms of work gave way to the factory system, thousands of workers began to be concentrated together in urban areas spatially removed from their homes, set-ting in motion institutional changes that redrew the social landscape throughout European soci-eties. The recruitment of wage laborers (includ-ing men, women, and children) disrupted customary patterns of gender and family life. As women began to earn a wage—they were, it should be emphasized, among the earliest fac-tory workers—male control over women's lives became highly problematic. Women's and chil-dren's labor began to be used against men's in ways that threatened the well-being of all work-ers. And as worker mobility increased, family life more generally was strained as intergenerational ties grew more problematic. Though it had long existed in European countries, the nuclear family (as opposed to the extended, cross-generational family structure) gained greater centrality as the factory system took root.

The rise of industrial production processes also reconfigured the class structure of the European societies, giving rise to a growing commercial class of entrepreneurs who eventu-ally became elite members of a new dominant class. The growth of a large manual working class, whose members could no longer expect to become autonomous craftsmen and who were denied political rights, provided the basis for the great social and political movements that defined the nineteenth and early twentieth centuries and that won many rights now taken for granted (such as universal education, voting rights, fair labor standards, and universal access to public education).

Industrial capitalism, and with it the machine-based rhythms of daily life, also led to subtle yet significant shifts in the nature of Western culture. Discipline, punctuality, reg-ularity, and compliance with organizational

demands all became norms that were imposed on populations only with the greatest difficulty, in ways that often disrupted deeply established customs and traditional ways of life (Thompson 1964). Interestingly, most historians view the rise of the prison as a mechanism of social control as itself an outgrowth of the factory system, as it borrowed much of the factory's harsh and coer-cive logic. Indeed, the function of incarceration in early prisons was precisely to inculcate the norms of work discipline, imposing harsh ritu-als on unruly masses as a form of penance, while also providing an object lesson about the norms that industrial capitalism now demanded of its members.

As capitalism developed, it left its mark on education as an institution as well. Schooling of course had traditionally been restricted to the children of elites, the aristocracy, or the clergy. As the need for office and administrative labor grew, and as the demand for literacy expanded, schooling on a more generalized basis arose, but again in ways that often adopted the logic of industrial production. Educational reformers in the United States frequently looked to industrial management as a model for the organization of schooling, often viewing students as "raw materi-als" that needed to be shaped in accordance with "customer specifications" (that is, the demands of employers), using industrial methods of con-trol as the model for the structure of schooling (Bowles and Gintis 1974).

Perhaps one of the most momentous of all shifts that the rise of industrial capitalism produced was its redefinition of "human nature." This is a complex issue but an important one. Most histo-rians and anthropologists have now agreed that Adam Smith was quite wrong to view the ten-dency to "truck and barter" as a characteristic of human nature. Increasingly, scholars have shown that for the greater part of human history, economic transactions have been governed by social codes of conduct that established powerful limits and constraints on commercial activity. Indeed, traditional societies did not have "an economy" as a separate and distinct institution, for economic activity was woven into and guided by the fabric of social and moral life. It was only when the market became the dominant mechanism for the distribution of wealth—especially during the early nineteenth century (see Chapter 4)—that economic transactions began to break free of moral constraints, reshaping social institutions and cultural norms so extensively that people came to redefine the past in the light of the market relations that only recently gained the upper hand (Polanyi 1944; Block 1990). This is a dangerous and deceptive redefinition of history, in that it projects backward onto all of human experience social norms that have only recently prevailed.

If, as just argued, shifts in the structure of work that occurred during the rise of industrial capitalism had massive effects on the institutional landscape, the question quickly emerges: How have changes in the structure of work affected us in the present era? Will the transition to a *post-industrial* capitalism transform the institutional fabric (and with it, conceptions of human personality) in which we currently live? We address these questions at various points in this book, but especially so in Chapter 15, where we discuss the future of work. For now, it seems important to observe that many scholars have begun to point to the numerous difficulties that result from major shifts in the institution of work. For example, W. J. Wilson's influential book, *When Work Disappears* (1996), empirically connects increasing rates of crime, drug use, and violence within the inner city to the suburbanization of employment, the decline of mass production industries, and the shift toward postindustrial sectors of the economy. Wilson's argument is that work provides the institutional supports that are needed to maintain a community's social and cultural strengths; in the absence of these structural supports, communities begin to suffer strains and tensions that are beyond their capacity to control. Debates about work, then, reach deep into many wider debates and issues our society must confront.

The Sociology of Work: Core Principles

Given the primacy of production within social life, the question naturally arises as to how work might be approached sociologically. Immediately following this chapter we discuss the various theoretical traditions and approaches that have arisen within this field and provoked heated debate. At this point, however, it will be helpful to provide a set of fundamental principles that are shared among most sociologists of work regardless of their theoretical orientation. Some of these are implied in the foregoing discussion, but it will be important to spell them out nonetheless.

Individuals Are Embedded within Larger Units of Analysis
We tend to view human behavior as a reflection of individual attributes. But sociological studies have repeatedly pointed out that work organizations are more than the sum of their component parts and that groups, organizations, and economic institutions tend to develop characteristic features that operate in accordance with their own logic, quite apart from the individuals

that make them up. For this reason, sociological analysis of work organizations proceeds by emphasizing the relations that emerge among the elements involved, rather than viewing them as atomized or unconnected entities. Another way of saying this is that *the nature of work is not reducible to the characteristics of individuals, but is instead the product of social, organizational, and cultural influences far beyond personality or individual choice.*

This point first began to emerge quite by surprise, in an early and widely famous piece of industrial sociology that has come to be known as the Hawthorne studies (see Roethlisberger and Dickson 1939; see also Chapter 5). Conducted by Elton Mayo and his associates, these studies were conducted at the Hawthorne, Illinois, plant owned by Western Electric, then the manufacturing arm of AT&T, the Bell Telephone monopoly. The researchers began by exploring ways in which individual productivity could be increased. Following the conventional wisdom of the time, they manipulated various aspects of the work situation, introducing such things as bonus pay systems that rewarded higher individual productivity. What the researchers were eventually led to conclude, however, was that the emphasis on individual rewards of work was completely misguided. In fact, workers did not behave merely as individuals responding to material rewards; rather, workers consistently declined to pursue higher pay, owing to their sense of obligation to the norms they and their fellow workers had developed. A key point the Hawthorne researchers drew was that workers did not behave as isolated individuals, but were deeply embedded in groups, whose informal codes of behavior exerted a powerful gravitational "pull" on workers' actions and affiliations. Indeed, management's utter failure to understand the norms

and culture of the company's own employees lay at the root of many of this plant's problems, for it led workers to seek out their own sources of respect and recognition, often *in opposition to* the firm's production goals. The Hawthorne studies can be said to have discovered the importance of the work group as an influence on industrial attitudes and behavior, which is discussed at multiple points throughout this book.

The importance of social and organizational influences also appears in many other studies that likewise point to the limitations of a purely individually focused approach toward workplace life. A good example is Rosabeth Kanter's widely read study *Men and Women of the Corporation* (1977a). An internationally recognized organizational theorist, Kanter studied patterns of interaction among employees at the corporate headquarters of a large multinational corporation producing industrial supplies and machines. She found that executives and managers were often frustrated by the low levels of job involvement and commitment they encountered among subordinate-level office workers employed as secretaries and clerical staff. Since the employees in these jobs were overwhelmingly women, managers tended to view their behavior as reflecting stereotypically female traits—a greater interest in family life and correspondingly low career aspirations. But Kanter was able to show that managers had in fact misunderstood the origins of the behavior they found so frustrating. In fact, it was not the gender of these workers that was at issue, but the structure of the organization—especially the company's failure to provide opportunities for advancement for employees located at the bottom of the organizational pyramid. These workers were simply behaving in the manner of workers of whatever gender who face blocked career opportunities. The point of Kanter's analysis is that appearances can be terribly misleading. We often "misread" worker behavior as reflecting the characteristics of the workers, when in truth it is the structure of their work situations—in this case, the structure of opportunity—that accounts for the behaviors we observe. In accounting for how people think, feel, and act at work, much more is at play than individual attributes (Epstein 1988).

Technology and Markets Are Themselves Shaped by Social Forces

Especially in a highly competitive era in which technology seems to reign supreme, the tendency is to regard the workplace as shaped by the demands of technologies and/or the marketplace. Yet a wealth of data has accumulated that invites us to question these assumptions, suggesting that cultural norms and institutional influences actively shape the manner in which technologies are used, often in ways that have little to do with the pursuit of efficiency. Put more formally, we can say that *the structure of work is seldom a reflection of either technological or economic imperatives. Rather, social and institutional influences intervene, often accounting for the way work is organized, assigned, and perceived.*

This point is illustrated in a highly useful study by Gallie (1978), who explored the effects of automation on the structure of manufacturing work. Gallie's study began as an effort to address an important debate about whether the introduction of new workplace technologies tends to allow workers greater autonomy and control over their jobs (as many theorists contend), or instead enables companies to regulate workplace life more tightly than before. What was missing from this debate, he realized, was any attention to social structural influences quite apart from

technology as such. To address this gap in our knowledge, he designed a study that systematically compared the effects of automation at four industrial plants located in two different countries: France and Great Britain. All of the plants were petrochemical refineries that used much the same technology. All produced very similar products. And all were owned by the same multinational corporation. Yet despite these similarities, Gallie found sharp and enduring differences in three aspects of these work structures: their management systems, their workers' attitudes toward management, and the workers' conceptions about the proper role that labor unions should play. These differences persisted (and seemed likely to persist for some time) quite apart from the introduction of new technologies.

Gallie's findings are worth discussing in some detail (see Table 1.1). First, in the French mills, he found that managers—who were often educated in elite educational institutions—enjoyed "paternalistic" decision-making powers that were largely unchecked by any organizational constraints. The French managers even reserved the right to determine the wage levels of individual workers more or less as they pleased. Second, the French workers held defiant and often quite militant attitudes toward their employer and challenged management's right to control the production process. Third, union leaders in the French plants saw their role as one of mobilizing workers to challenge managerial authority.

The situation in the British plants was dramatically different on each of these points. In the British plants, managers had developed a "quasi-constitutional" form of authority that provided for procedural checks and balances. Workers accepted management's authority; indeed, when they were critical, they accused their bosses of

TABLE 1.1 Enduring Differences in the Structure of French and British Oil Refineries

DIMENSION	FRANCE	ENGLAND
Management systems	Paternalistic system of control over each individual's pay and job evaluations	"Quasi-constitutional" system of control, with due process and checks and balances
Workers' attitudes toward management	Oppositional—an "exploitative" view of the firm predominates Management control over work viewed as illegitimate "Relational" critiques of supervisors common	Semi-deferential outlook Management control viewed as legitimate "Technical" critiques of supervisors common
Function of labor unions	Mobilization	Representation

Source: Adapted from Duncan Gallie, *In Search of the New Working Class* (New York Cambridge University Press, 1978).

not being managerial enough. Finally, in the British plants, union leaders saw their role as one of representing, not mobilizing the membership. The pattern that Gallie found, in short, involved systematically different patterns of work organization on opposite sides of the English Channel, even among plants that used identical technologies and were subject to the same market influences. These differences, which showed little sign of declining even as automation proceeded, provide a good example of what is sometimes called the "societal effect"—here, the effect that the national context had on work structures—which seemed to overwhelm any technological or efficiency imperative.

Other studies have also found that how workplace technologies are used varies markedly across national boundaries. For example, Hartman and his colleagues (1983) selected machine tool plants in Germany and England that were carefully matched for the size, age, and technology of the establishments. In the German plants, the work of programming computer-based machines was

often assigned to blue-collar workers, but in British plants these functions were exclusively reserved for white-collar staff. Apparently, the strong German tradition of craft apprenticeships and technical education enabled manual workers to gain control over programming, while Britain's sharp status boundaries favored white-collar engineering groups. Much as in Gallie's study, deeply rooted traditions reached into and shape the work that people did, defining certain arrangements as more "natural" or "normal" than others (see Kelley 1990). Again, social norms and institutional arrangements served to define how work ought to be arranged, quite independent of technology or market influences.

It is important to point out that while corporate organizations are indeed driven by the pursuit of profit, this is only one among several imperatives they must obey. It is sometimes the case that when managers, professionals, and other occupational groups make reference to the importance of organizational efficiency, they do so in ways that really aim to justify claims or proposals that are driven by very different concerns. This was precisely the conclusion that emerged from Thomas's (1994) important multi-industry study of technological change. Studying manufacturing firms in four different industries—aircraft production, computer manufacturing, aluminum smelting, and automobile assembly—Thomas found that managers and engineers commonly justified new proposals for technological change by pointing to the huge improvements in rates of return that their projects would make possible. But Thomas found that the proposals were *actually* made with the interests of one or another occupational group, and not the firm's profitability, as the primary concern. Thomas summarized this pattern by writing that "the rules of the [corporate] game required that all participants present themselves as rational, calculating utility maximizers, but beneath the official rules an entirely different game was being played" (1994: 64–65). What Thomas meant was that different groups of professionals and managers often competed to advance the status, power, and autonomy their occupational group enjoyed. Often their proposals were motivated by the effort to enhance their group's position within the firm. Put differently, projects involving technological change often served as vehicles for occupational self-aggrandizement. Ironically, Thomas found that the implementers of such projects often did enhance their work situations within the firm, but seldom delivered the profitability improvements they had projected in their proposals. Revealingly, the firms seldom held them to their promised rates of return.

The limits of efficiency-oriented theories of work have also emerged in research focused on the relation between firms and their wider social and political environments. As organizational theory has stressed, if firms are to maintain or expand their operations, they must be concerned with not only the efficiency of their operations but also the legitimacy of the firm in the eyes of the public, including such constituencies as customers, investors, governmental regulators, and prospective employees (Fligstein 1987, 1990; Edelman 1990; Sutton et al. 1994). This concern for organizational legitimacy has in fact been found to account for many of the new practices that corporations have adopted in the past. Thus, after the civil rights movement of the 1960s and 1970s, firms often needed to indicate that they were committed to the norm of equal opportunity. They therefore embraced new personnel systems that helped to express their commitment to the socially valued ideal of equal opportunity. Likewise, firms often seek to represent themselves as innovative and forward-looking organizations, and thus adopt structural arrangements such as best practices, team systems, or new work and family programs—again, not because these are more efficient, but because they portray the firm in a favorable public light. Ironically, such innovations may have beneficial effects on the firm—not because of their technical or efficiency advantages, but simply because of the enhanced legitimacy that such arrangements often provide. Indeed, some literature suggests that the innovations which firms adopt (such as high-technology systems for inventory control) can sometimes hinder the firm's operations, but still improve the firm's revenues, for example by delivering new contracts with other businesses, increased attention from investors, an improved ability to recruit the most desirable employees and customers the firm would not otherwise have wooed (Meyer and Rowan 1977). This is perhaps one reason why managerial fads are so influential within the corporate world—they are important means through which firms seek to enhance their reputational position in the public eye. Again, the logic of efficiency is only part of a larger and more complex set of influences that are brought to bear on work organizations.

Informal Relations at Work Often Stand at Odds with Formal Expectations

In the advanced capitalist societies, we are often led to expect that formal rules and practices govern organizational life. Most large corporations have formidable employee handbooks, which carry the implied force of a legal contract. Elaborate job descriptions spell out what workers are expected to do, how managers will evaluate their performance, and how any infractions will be handled. It therefore bears emphasizing that the formal aspects of workplace life often constitute only the surface of workers' behavior. The point here is that *beneath the formal rules and procedures can often be found a second, informal web of rules that stands at odds with the formal trappings, exerting a powerful influence over what actually occurs at work.* Ironically, it is this very discrepancy between formal and informal behavior that often enables organizations to achieve their goals. Indeed, good managers and administrators intuitively understand this point. They know that the informal ties and affiliations that develop within organizations (the relationships that clerical personnel or secretaries establish among their own ranks, for example, or the hidden conduits along which strategic information flows) can constitute enormously useful resources—or powerful impediments to success.

The power of informal social relations is well illustrated in Gresham Sykes's *Society of Captives* (1958), a classic study of the social organization of prison life. Sykes began his study expecting that

prisons would be especially likely to elicit the compliance of their subordinate employees, the corrections officers. Prisons are, after all, highly coercive institutions. Yet he was surprised to find that when prisons succeed in securing control over their inmates, the reason often lies in the guards' willingness to *violate* formal rules and procedures. Sykes found a pattern of informal negotiation or subtle bargaining between the officers and the inmates—especially those inmates who controlled the flow of contraband within the prison walls. Because they needed to maintain control over the prison population, corrections officers often cultivated an alliance with inmate leaders, enforcing prison rules selectively or even breaking the rules entirely (as when officers provided an inmate with advance warning that his cell was about to be searched, or when officers agreed to look the other way when drug transactions were taking place). In return for these favors, inmate leaders helped the guards keep the prison population in check. Such informal understandings or alliances obviously violated prison statutes and were often blatantly illegal, yet they continued because they helped the authorities achieve their goal of maintaining custody over prison populations. In fact, Sykes found that prison riots were most likely to occur when a new warden or administrator arrived, for the new administrators tended to emphasize formal rules and regulations in ways that disrupted the hidden understandings that officers and inmates had reached. What Sykes's study suggests, then, is not only that a sharp discrepancy can exist between the formal and the informal realm of behavior, but also that caution is needed in assuming that formal procedures have any privileged connection to the achievement of organizational goals.

Especially well developed in research on manual workers employed in manufacturing settings (Halle 1984), as will be discussed in Chapter 5. Here we observe that such informal patterns also shape the behavior of white-collar and service employees in various settings. Thus, restaurant work (with its kitchens defined as "backstage" areas) is notorious for the ability of employees to flout formal conventions and even the expectations of common decency (Fine 1996). Indeed, the quality of the food that customers eat often depends on subtle bargaining that unfolds among food servers, cooks, and chefs. Perhaps more surprising is the study conducted by anthropologist Julian Orr (1996), who unearthed a rich and highly textured occupational community among photocopy machine technicians. Although we commonly think of these workers as isolated employees, Orr found that they are in fact embedded in a rich occupational community whose members frequently meet outside of work to share not only a drink or a meal, but also (and more importantly) a wealth of informal knowledge about the technical challenges they have encountered on their jobs. By talking about the particular models of machines they have repaired, and by sharing various tricks and "war stories" in their occupational experience, these workers sustain a rich "community of practice" and body of knowledge about the characteristics and idiosyncrasies of various models of machines. This knowledge could never be codified in any written documentation or repair manuals. It was, however, essential to the ability of these technicians to perform their jobs. In fact, because of the knowledge and social bonds they developed among their own ranks, these workers were able to limit their employer's efforts to standardize their troubleshooting methods. As Orr's study reveals, there is often a communal aspect to even the most seemingly mundane of occupational worlds, and such social ties can have a crucial significance for the maintenance of workers' skills.

Organizational Elites Often Benefit from a "Hierarchy of Credibility"

As members of advanced Western societies, we are often deeply immersed in a culture that invites us to regard elite-defined judgments as more credible, legitimate, or authoritative than the homespun wisdom of subordinate groups. Yet this can often introduce bias into our analyses, leading the analyst astray and often distracting him or her from the most sociologically pertinent line of analysis. This is why sociologist Howard Becker (1967) coined the term "hierarchy of credibility," a concept he used to refer to the subtle biases that often incline people (including social scientists!) to lend greater weight to the views of powerful or official sources rather than those of the unschooled or unauthorized employees they oversee. The point here—one that is important to keep in mind throughout this book—is that the sociological investigation of work organizations often requires that we turn a critical eye toward established accounts about work, for these often reflect the preferences of those in positions of power. Put differently, *studying work sociologically often requires that we "break" with common-sense assumptions and beliefs, asking questions that challenge "what everyone knows" to be the case.*

Pursuing sociological questions about work often requires that one ask questions that may seem unreasonable or impertinent to powerful groups. For example, while developing his classic study of machine tool workers, *Manufacturing Consent,* Burawoy (1979) noted that conventional theorists in the study of work had previously asked why workers so often resist managerial directives. The question from this common-sense perspective is simply: "Why don't workers produce as much as they might?" This was precisely the question the Hawthorne studies posed, as we discussed above. But as Burawoy pointed out, such an approach is implicitly biased toward the managerial point of view, in that it naïvely assumes that all groups within the firm—both managers and workers alike—stand to benefit from the well-being of the firm. In fact, the sociologically interesting approach (which Burawoy chose to pursue) was to turn the question on its head and to ask why workers produce as much for management as they typically do. In other words, what social and cultural mechanisms exist that induce workers to cooperate with management as often as they do? Posing the question in this way, Burawoy was able to develop in-depth studies of how power has been exercised over workers in various social and historical contexts, from the English textile mills of the nineteenth century to Eastern European factories under Communist rule (Burawoy 1985). Burawoy's perspective is controversial, but it opens up a provocative line of analysis that breaks with conventional approaches toward work organizations and encourages us to ask difficult questions about how power and authority are exercised by elite groups within work organizations (see Chapter 5).

Conclusion

In this chapter we have provided an overview of the conceptual foundations on which the sociology of work has developed. We have seen that,

despite arguments about the growth of leisure and consumer pursuits, work continues to exert an extraordinary influence over human life, shaping the experience and well-being of individuals and the contours of social structure writ large. As systems of production change, so too does the web of institutions within which we live out our lives. The jobs we hold, moreover, shape us as individuals, affecting our health, well-being, and intimate relations—even influencing the length of our lives and our personality attributes. These findings suggest that it is quite possible to be *unconcerned* with the nature of our jobs; it is far less possible, it seems, to be *unaffected* by our jobs.

We further outlined certain basic postulates that have informed the sociological study of work, and which set the sociological approach apart from those adopted by other disciplines. Surely what is key to the sociology of work is its emphasis on the structure of groups, organizations, and institutions, as these have taken shape within particular societies. Equally important, as we have seen, are the cultural norms and values that define how work is viewed and how workers define their obligations to one another and to their employers. This informal fabric of social life is nowhere to be found in an organization chart or an employee handbook, and yet it can make a life-or-death difference in what happens on the job (as any airline pilot, police officer, or nuclear power plant operator can attest). Understanding the structural and cultural factors that impinge on work behaviors is an important and rapidly developing task within the sociology of work—one that is further discussed in many of the following chapters.

Chapter 2

Theoretical Traditions in the Sociology of Work

The principles that inform the sociology of work (as discussed in Chapter 1) are widely embraced by researchers in the field. Yet precisely *how* those principles are put to work—that is, the specific theoretical outlooks that researchers find most useful—has been the object of sharp and often spirited debate. In this respect, the sociology of work is no different from other fields, from psychology to physics. Because these debates reach deep into the very questions that researchers pose—and because they also affect the way we think about work, how we explain its course, and the choices we might consider as a society—it is important to grasp the competing perspectives that advocates have advanced within the field.

In this chapter we will compare and contrast the perspectives that have emerged to make sense of work, organizations, and economic institutions. Our discussion is organized chronologically. We begin by discussing the classical theoretical perspectives that arose in the middle and late nineteenth century within Western Europe, then wracked by the large-scale transformations that accompanied the transition to industrial capitalism. We next consider more contemporary schools of thought that arose in the United States, largely after World War II. In many respects, our society faces widespread structural changes not unlike those that the classical theorists addressed. Like them, we too must struggle to understand the emergence of new technologies, new economic arrangements, and new social norms governing how work ought to be performed. All the more reason to explore the ways in which sociologists have sought to explain the nature and operations of work organizations and the behavior of the people they employ.

Classical Perspectives on Work and Society

The study of work and, more broadly, the division of labor has been at the center of sociological thinking from the very inception of the discipline. Most obviously, Karl Marx based his theories on the premise that human labor was the foundation of all social institutions and social consciousness. Max Weber disputed this argument, but also saw organized systems of domination—especially, bureaucratic ones—as key features of the modern world. Emile Durkheim also devoted much attention to the increasing division of labor within advanced societies, arguing that occupational associations would provide a key nexus for human solidarity. Contemporary theorists have built on these classical approaches, developing new perspectives as a result. But it is difficult to understand contemporary schools of thought without a brief discussion of these classical thinkers.

Karl Marx's Contribution

Although the collapse of most Communist regimes has discredited Marx's writings in the eyes of many, his work remains a source of insight and inspiration for analysts who are concerned with the human consequences of commodity production for workers themselves. Because his work devoted so much attention to questions of labor, it warrants especially close attention.

Marx was born and educated in Germany, taking his doctorate in philosophy. Rather than follow a conventional academic career, Marx took a job as the editor of a German periodical that covered important issues of the day. He soon realized how little he knew about economic questions and spent the rest of his life struggling to understand the "laws of motion" of the capitalist economy.

Marx's earliest writings focused on the problem of alienation from work. In 1844, in a series of fragmentary essays he never intended for publication, Marx sketched out a critical analysis of the impact that capitalist production had on the organization and the experience of work. Marx argued that with the rise of the factory system, workers lost the artisanal (or craft-like) connection to their products and tools they had previously enjoyed. As merchants and capitalists gradually took control of the production process, workers became estranged, or alienated, from their labor in four distinct but interrelated ways:

First, since workers no longer owned the goods they produced, which now belonged to the capitalist, what workers produced was a matter of complete indifference to them. They therefore grew alienated from the *product* of their labor. Second, since work was increasingly just a means to the end of survival, workers came to view their own labor as devoid of any intrinsic meaning. They therefore became alienated from their own labor activity, or from the *process* of their labor. Third, owing to the cut-throat competition that the labor market imposed, Marx contended that workers were forced to fight tooth and nail for their mere subsistence. They therefore grew increasingly alienated from their *fellow workers*, with whom they were forced to compete. Fourth, although humans possess characteristics (language, consciousness, the capacity to plan) that are qualitatively distinct from those of most animals, under capitalism these characteristics became all but irrelevant. Used like beasts of burden, workers began to seek out only the most animal-like satisfactions, such as food, drink, or sexual gratification. Marx therefore concluded that workers were increasingly alienated from their own *"species-began"*—that is, from their own specifically human abilities.

Marx's writings on alienation were driven by a humanistic passion that many sociologists have found unscientific. Likewise, some contend that Marx's writings have lost their relevance, arguing that the advanced capitalist societies have overcome the worst features of the factory system. Other theorists vehemently disagree and argue that Marx's observations have particular relevance in an era of global capitalism, when workers in less developed countries are compelled to produce objects for export to wealthy consumers on distant shores (see Chapter 16).

Even within the advanced societies, some theorists have pointed to instances in which entirely new forms of alienation have begun to emerge in ways that resonate with Marx's thinking. Thus, Arlie Hochschild (1983) points out that many occupations serving the public now formally oblige workers to perform "emotional labor," thus placing their facial expressions and emotional sensibilities under the control of the corporations that employ them. Building on this observation, Robin Leidner's (1993) study of fast food workers and insurance salesmen explores the ways in which corporations seek to routinize the interactions that occur between service workers and customers—a task that compels corporations to train workers how and when to smile, how to sound upbeat and enthusiastic, and how to incorporate standardized scripts into their interactions with customers. These sorts of developments can be viewed as signs that Marx's theory of alienation has retained a certain relevance to this day. We discuss emotional labor and alienation at greater length in Chapter 10.

Marx's contribution to the sociology of work is not limited to his theory of alienation. In his later economic writings—most notably in *Capital*, a multivolume historical critique of capitalist development (Marx 1977 [1867]), he sketched out an argument about industrial capitalism that has proven highly influential for contemporary theorists and political movements. Marx argued that during the transition to capitalism, the organization of the production process revolutionized traditional forms of work. In place of the craft-like arrangements that characterized traditional workshops and early factories (which placed the instruments of production under the control of skilled workers), capitalism overturned any such organic relationship between the workers and

their tools. "Every capitalist process of production has this in common," Marx wrote, "that it is not the workers who use the instruments of production, but the instruments of production that use the workman" (1977 [1867], p. 548). Marx meant that machinery, as a form of capital, had become a power over the workers, controlling their actions in ways that helped factory owners to extract profits from the workers they employed. It was not technology that did this, Marx stressed, but the system of commodity production on which capitalism relied.

It is important to stress that Marx was not uniformly critical of capitalism. In many ways, Marx acknowledged the historical contribution that capitalism made to the evolution of humanity. Capitalism civilized human societies. It fostered the spread of universal literacy. It also reduced the degree to which humans lived at the mercy of their natural environment. Marx's sternest critiques, however, were reserved for the ways in which capitalism subjected workers to the private will of the factory owners, whose wealth grew at the expense of the workers they employed. Marx believed that the competitive pressures of the capitalist marketplace compelled factory owners to impose an increasingly authoritarian form on the production process, first by lengthening the working day and then by intensifying the labor process, especially with the aid of machines.

Marx felt that these changes were likely to generate a feeling of resignation and powerlessness among workers, who often had little alternative but to comply with their overseers. But these changes in the nature of work also generated a growing sense of exploitation and resentment among the workers, which in turn led them to form organizations for their own defense, generating ever-sharper forms of industrial conflict. Eventually, Marx felt that workers would come to see the folly of bargaining over the particular wage they might receive and see the problem they confronted as the wage system itself—that is, the system of capitalism which defined their working time as a commodity to be bought and sold. Indeed, Marx believed that the problems within capitalism could only be overcome with the transition to socialism, for only then might workers come to exercise collective, democratic control over the production process. For Marx, socialism was identical to the notion of worker control, which he saw as a necessary condition for the rise of a truly democratic society. From this perspective, Soviet-style socialism arguably had little in common with Marx's conception of socialism.

Many have argued that Marx's worldview is inescapably utopian. Others have held that although Marx was right that class conflict would sharpen as capitalism advanced, the most authoritarian aspects of work under capitalism have now largely been reduced, whether through union representation, government regulations, or (more recently) participatory forms of work organization. Still others take a different perspective and insist that many of the realities that Marx observed have persisted to this day and that Marx's theories have retained much of their relevance. Especially in a period when corporations can almost "drag and drop" production facilities with the click of a mouse button, and when even highly profitable corporations engage in downsizing campaigns aimed at increasing their rates of profit that much more, workers become increasingly vulnerable to their employers' decisions. Stressing precisely these points, Marxist views of work (often known as the "labor process school")

have developed a vibrant approach toward work, technology, and social inequality, as discussed later in this chapter.

Max Weber and the Sociology of Economic Organization

Max Weber was a German intellectual who was broadly trained in economics, history, and the law. Born four decades after Marx, much of Weber's work has come to be viewed as a "debate with the ghost of Marx," in the sense that Weber sought to refute many of the arguments that Marx had advanced. Still, like Marx, Weber placed work at the very center of his analyses, although he did so in very different ways.

Two themes within Weber's work are especially relevant to us here. One is his effort to demonstrate a link between economic institutions and broader social and especially religious institutions. The question that Weber posed was deceptively simple: Why did modern capitalism first arise in the West, rather than elsewhere in the world? In posing this question, Weber meant to identify the social and cultural preconditions that account for the rise of modern capitalism (a theme discussed further in Chapter 4).

In developing his answer, Weber began by noting a curious correlation between social class and religious affiliation: The members of the wealthier classes in Germany tended to be Protestants, while the working classes were largely composed of Catholics. Weber took this point as suggesting a causal link between a society's religious beliefs and its economic institutions. He developed this theme both in his book *The Protestant Ethic and the Spirit of Capitalism* (1996 [1904–1905]), a famous work which introduced the term "work ethic" into everyday discourse, and in his major work *Economy and Society* (1968 [1914]).

In the most general terms, Weber's argument was that the religions of the West, most notably Protestant denominations such as Calvinism and Lutheranism, proved to be uniquely favorable to the disciplined, acquisitive behaviors that capitalism required. The reason was that Protestantism defined work as an expression of one's devotion to God. Working hard in one's calling (and, better still, prospering in it) provided worshippers with a sign of their salvation in the next life. At the same time, Protestantism involved a deeply ascetic view—that is, it required the worshipper to renounce frivolous or idle pursuits of pleasure. This combination of factors—a divinely ordained obligation to work hard, but never to consume the fruits of one's labor—provided a uniquely favorable set of conditions for the accumulation of capital within Western Europe. Eastern religions such as Hinduism or Buddhism shared the West's ascetic values and often encouraged the worshipper to renounce the pursuit of worldly pleasures. But in so doing, they gave rise to what Weber called "other-worldly" asceticism: That is, they defined the material world as a distraction from the real path to the divine state of grace. In so doing, the Eastern religions tended to impede the development of capitalism.

Weber's argument is important for an understanding of economic institutions, for he argues powerfully that economies do not develop in a vacuum. Rather, the course of economic development is deeply affected by the norms, values, and cultural ideas that exist within a given territory. In a word, the argument powerfully demonstrates the point that ideas matter. More recent studies, such as Saxenian's (1994) study of Silicon Valley and the Route 128 region in Massachusetts, have reiterated this point, suggesting that the cultural traditions that exist within economic regions or nation-states have an important bearing on the economic activities they are likely to develop.

A second theme that emerges from Weber's work has been even more influential. Although much of his analysis was aimed at refuting arguments made by Marx and Engels, Weber did agree with Marxism in certain respects. He was well aware of social inequalities, for example, and of the power that elites exercised over subordinate groups. Indeed, in *Economy and Society*, Weber surveys the history of slavery, serfdom, and colonial domination and concludes that in general, "every highly privileged group develops the myth of its natural superiority" (1968 [1922]: 953). As this quote suggests, Weber was aware of elite domination, and of the need for powerful groups and classes to define their power as legitimate. Weber therefore inquired into the mechanisms which dominant or elite groups used to accomplish this end (Bendix 1956).

Weber identifies three distinct types of such legitimate domination or authority: traditional, charismatic, and rational-legal (or bureaucratic). *Traditional* authority refers to inherited or divinely ordained privilege, as used by noblemen, kings, or leaders of established religions. Historically, slaves or peasants under the sway of traditional authority were expected to labor for the benefit of their rulers because these arrangements were part of the natural order of the universe, in which the position of one or another group was divinely ordained and thus not subject to change. *Charismatic* authority, which is volatile and difficult to establish for long periods of time, refers to domination that is rooted in the powers of inspiration that flow from a leader's personal abilities and characteristics. Here, followers comply with a leader's commands out of a sense of personal obligation to the leader, who is viewed as possessing extraordinary characteristics. Leaders of religious or political movements often wield charismatic authority and use it to push their followers to make sacrifices that can seem remarkable to outside observers (think of Jim Jones and the Jonestown cult).

It is the third type of legitimate domination that Weber felt was most common to our time. Indeed, to capture the operations of rational-legal or *bureaucratic* domination, Weber develops a rich characterization of the pure ("ideal") type of bureaucratic organization. Simply put, Weber defines bureaucracy as marked by at least six key features: the specialization of functions; the codification of norms within written rules and regulations; the emergence of an elaborate hierarchy of authority, often stretching upward across many layers of supervision; hiring on the basis of certified expertise; the establishment of a sharp separation between official duties and personal relationships; and—perhaps most important—decisions based on the rational calculation of the most efficient means to attain a given organizational end. Weber's point was that bureaucratic domination enveloped workers in so elaborate a system of rules and procedures as to place powerful constraints on the behavior of employees at all levels of the organization. Weber was no fan of bureaucracy—quite the contrary—but he predicted that bureaucratic authority would spread relentlessly throughout the industrializing world. He viewed the bureaucratization of work as part of a larger process of "rationalization," in which rational or scientific calculation took the place once held by sentiment, myth, and religious belief. This process greatly expanded the role of scientific and technical staff, professional experts, and managerial officials, whose very positions rested on their technical expertise.

From Weber's standpoint, bureaucracy operates much like an engine whose movements compel each part—workers, work groups, departments, divisions—to perform its expected function.

Weber's argument is in many respects diametrically opposed to the popular view of bureaucracy as inefficient or unproductive (the meaning of "red tape"). Indeed, the reason why Weber saw bureaucracy as destined to spread across the globe was precisely because it provided a more effective system of social control than human society had previously devised. Ironically, Weber believed that even social movements aimed at furthering the cause of democracy would be compelled to establish highly centralized bureaucratic organizations in order to achieve their goals (Michels 1962 [1915]). Implied here are two important points. First, in Weber's view, bureaucratic structures left precious little room for democratic debate: The essence of bureaucracy is rule on the basis of technical expertise. This is a pessimistic view of how work might be organized. Second, we begin to see why Weber rejected most of the solutions that Marxists had proposed. Not only did he see the expansion of bureaucratic authority as inevitable; in addition, he thought that socialism would only concentrate power in fewer and fewer hands, thereby actually deepening bureaucracy's grip on human life.

The Weberian theory of bureaucracy has been challenged on many grounds. Often, critics have suggested that Weber overestimated the control that elites can wield over their subordinates. In this connection it is useful to recall the discussion in Chapter 1 of informal patterns of behavior, which often enable lower-level manual employees to defy the formal expectations of their superiors. The point is that because Weber's analysis is written at a macro-social level of analysis, it often neglects the hidden under-side of organizational life (see Kanter 1977a). Moreover, some recent theorists have suggested that Weber's analysis may be historically obsolete. In an era when large corporations are seeking to institute leaner, flatter, and more decentralized structures, "rule by command" may give way to "rule by commitment"—that is, to participative forms of authority that Weber could not have foreseen. This question is subject to debate and is discussed at length in Chapter 15.

The Contribution of Durkheim's Sociology

The last of the classical theorists to be discussed here is Emile Durkheim, a French sociologist who was born in the mid-late nineteenth century. Like both Marx and Weber, Durkheim was concerned with the social consequences that stemmed from the increasing division of labor within modern societies. Again, like his German counterparts, Durkheim also paid great attention to the economic theories of his time. He ultimately developed a perspective that was sharply different from that developed by the other two classical figures.

In his first major work, Durkheim (1933 [1893]) responded to the growing fear among many theorists and philosophers, who were concerned that modern societies had taken the division of labor to such an extreme as to jeopardize any notion of a broadly educated, socially conscious public. Although many thinkers of the time called for efforts to return to a simpler time in which social unity was more easily maintained, Durkheim rejected such an approach.

Drawing on the anthropological evidence of his day, Durkheim developed an evolutionary conception of social change, in which the development of human societies was characterized by increasing differentiation: Societies evolved from simple units (in which all members shared the same values, and in which little individualism existed) to much more complex, internally differentiated societies. This evolutionary process led to far-reaching changes in social organization that were as irreversible as they were significant. It was true that members of the advanced societies no longer enjoyed a sense of unity or shared purpose, as did simpler societies. But this did not mean that advanced societies were destined to break down. Rather, they were increasingly held together by structural interdependence—the division of labor that developed among their various parts. This had two results. On the one hand, it opened up a capacity for individual reflection and self-expression that humans had never previously enjoyed. On the other hand, if taken too far, the growth of individualism threatened the social order itself, leaving societies vulnerable to a weakened cultural condition that Durkheim called *anomie* (or normlessness). The danger here was that the division of labor might, if left unaddressed, weaken the society's norms and values and undermine its ability to find a common cause.

While concerned with this tendency, Durkheim concluded that it was futile to hope for a return to a simpler era in which much the same values would be held by an entire society. Rather, new sources of moral unity were needed that could bind individuals together within groups that fostered a sense of shared purpose and belonging. Interestingly, what Durkheim suggested involved the creation of occupational associations, which he believed might overcome the problem of *anomie*. His idea was that occupational associations would link people together on the basis of their work, providing people in similar crafts, industries, professions of various sorts with the very sense of social and moral integration that the advanced societies no longer produced.

Durkheim's work is noteworthy in several respects. First, it represents an effort to cope with the macro-structural problems to which advanced industrial societies are prone. Second, it provided an alternative perspective on social and economic organization to that developed by either Marx or Weber. The latter figures, who viewed societies in terms of exploitation and domination, are often called "conflict theorists," for they see societies as constituted by groups whose interests are fundamentally at odds. By contrast, Durkheim approached societies (and by implication, the organizations they contain) as organic wholes that must maintain a sense of moral unity and shared purpose if they are to survive. Durkheim's perspective, later called "functionalism" or "order" theory, has been influential among theorists seeking to strengthen the normative bonds that unite the members of a given organization or society, regardless of class or rank—an ideal that has been attractive to those seeking to overcome the tensions and struggles that have often characterized industrial capitalism.

Durkheim's work is relevant in one further respect. In confronting the social theorists of his day (many of whom stressed the overarching influence of social contracts as a medium of exchange), Durkheim responded by pointing to the *non*contractual bases on which all economic transactions rest. It was impossible to write contracts that addressed all conceivable contingencies. Nor was it possible to eliminate the element of trust from economic transactions. Durkheim's point, which has been important for generations of economic sociologists, was that economic transactions and

contractual ties always presuppose shared cultural understandings of some sort. In this respect, he agreed with a point that was evident in Weber's sociology of religion: Economic ties are always grounded in social relationships. Economic activity ought not to be viewed as existing apart from the norms and values in which it takes shape. Chapter 9, in which we discuss the professions, highlights the connection between economic activities and values and norms.

At this point in our discussion we can make several observations concerning classical approaches toward work. First, all these theorists placed the nature of work at the very center of their efforts to understand the transition to modern society. Thus all these thinkers saw the organization of production as holding vital significance for the social order as a whole. Yet these theorists approached the organization of work in very different ways. For Marx, the capitalist mode of production was a system of exploitation that was inherently coercive. As such, it forced employers to devise systems of control that contained worker resistance and ensured a sufficient quantity of profit. For Weber, the organization of production was increasingly a field of formal, bureaucratic domination through which elites established a subtle yet powerful system of authority relations that was increasingly immune to dissent. For Durkheim, what was most important was the increasing division of labor within society—a trend that had undermined traditional forms of allegiance and solidarity, but which might (with the support of sociological thinking) nonetheless be replaced by newer forms of association.

More recent theorists have been profoundly influenced by these thinkers. But they have also drawn on them selectively, often challenging them in various ways, with the goal of producing a theoretical account that helps us understand the structural upheavals that we presently confront as we lurch toward an increasingly postindustrial and postmodern world. It is to contemporary formulations that we next turn.

Contemporary Perspectives on Work and Society

Viewed retrospectively, it is possible to observe three distinct generations of thinking in the post–World War II sociology of work, with each emerging in response to the major events of its time. The first tradition we discuss took the form of a theory of "industrial society," which owed much to Durkheim and the functionalist tradition and which arose during the early days of the Cold War. The second perspective, which reflected a resurgence of industrial conflict in the advanced capitalist world, was a theory of the labor process that rested on assumptions gleaned from Marx and, to some extent, from Weber. The third tradition was a theory of postindustrial society that saw the workplace as giving rise to new organizational forms that were dramatically different from previously established institutions, with massive effects on the economic structures that surround us, now and in the decades to come.

The Theory of Industrial Society

The period following World War II was in many respects marked by the restoration of order and prosperity. The turbulent decade of the 1930s, which witnessed the rise of a vibrant workers' movement in the United States, gave rise to large-scale union organizations that provided a voice for many workers, who for the first time were able to exert some influence over the terms

and conditions under which they were employed (see Chapter 10). During and immediately after World War II, the influence of the workers' movement continued to grow—work stoppages rose to historic peaks, and some managers feared losing control of their own plants (Lichtenstein 1987)—but by the mid-1950s, labor's influence was clearly on the wane. An era of stabilization and labor peace took shape, which analysts variously attributed to the spread of affluence among many industrial workers, to McCarthy-era attacks and divisions that weakened the workers' movement, or to the incorporation of labor organizations and their leaders into the established political order.

As the United States took its place as the dominant capitalist country, many scholars came to formulate a theory of industrial society, using the U.S. experience as indicative of a broader trend affecting the economies and organizations of the world's societies. The notion here was that a new type of society was emerging, characterized by a logic that was sharply distinct from what had gone before. Although societies might seek to reject or resist this trend, few were likely to succeed. Understanding the "logic of industrialism," the occupational structures it promoted, and the different paths down which industrialization might lead became a major concern for the theorists of industrial society.

Perhaps the most comprehensive statement of this theory was the influential book by Kerr et al. (1960), *Industrialism and Industrial Man*. This volume made a number of important points. First, the authors argued that Marx had misunderstood the nature and course of modern societies. Endemic conflict was not, they reasoned, an enduring characteristic of modern society (as Marx had held), but a temporary condition that accompanied the transition from traditional to industrial society. That is, once societies successfully adopt industrial systems, large-scale protest and industrial conflict thereafter tend to decline. Second, although there were obvious variations among different societies, there was a single logic of industrialism that all modern societies would need to adopt (a claim known as the "convergence thesis"). Thus, despite local customs and traditions, industrial societies everywhere would need to recruit an increasingly skilled and educated workforce, hired and rewarded on the basis of ability rather than through such traditional mechanisms as kinship ties or religious affiliation. Third, Kerr and his colleagues argued that workers themselves were a less influential force than had previously been believed. Far more weighty in the industrialization process were the strategies pursued by industrializing elites. The authors therefore developed a complex model that recognized several distinct types of industrial elite, including dynastic, middle-class, revolutionary, and nationalist types. Although each strategy affected the particular path, or form, that industrial societies took (thus creating differences among Japanese, Russian, and U.S. industrial organizations, for example), the general trend would inevitably lead to a common set of occupational and organizational structures around the globe.

Another example of this theory of industrial society was reached in an equally influential analysis, Robert Blauner's *Alienation and Freedom* (1964). Blauner was partly inspired by studies of Marx's arguments concerning the spread of worker alienation, and partly by studies of workers on the assembly line (Walker and Guest 1952), which showed the harsh conditions workers on the line were compelled to endure in the pursuit of decent pay. The question Blauner posed was essentially this: How does the advance of industrial technology affect the meaning of work?

To answer this question, Blauner distinguished four distinct stages in the development of industrial society. In order of their appearance, these were craft, machine-tending, assembly-line, and automated work processes. Using survey data on workers' attitudes toward their jobs, he concluded that the relation between technology and alienation from work was a curvilinear one. That is, prior to the onset of industrialization (where work was still organized as a craft), levels of alienation tended to be low. But as work grew increasingly machine-paced, alienation tended to rise, until it reached its peak under assembly line conditions. However, once work evolved still further and became fully automated, Blauner concluded, alienation would eventually decline to its preindustrial, craft-like levels. The reason he gave for this trend was that machines would assume the most routine of chores, freeing workers from the rigors of machine-paced work and returning to them a sense of control over their own movements. Like Kerr and his colleagues, then, Blauner argued that the transition to industrial society was difficult and painful, but that once it was established, industrial society tended to achieve a state of equilibrium, with alienation and industrial conflict falling into decline the social order, thus achieving social peace.

Blauner's study was much criticized, but it remained an influential expression of the theory of industrial society. As the latter approach gained force, it generated several distinct lines of analysis. One such strand of research sought to trace the effects of industrial society on institutional patterns in multiple societies, conducting comparative studies of work and occupations within different national contexts. An example here is William Form's (1976) study of auto workers in the United States, Italy, Argentina, and India, which concluded that exposure to modern industrial technology generated increasingly similar attitudinal patterns across widely different settings. In a similar vein, other sociologists explored occupational prestige rankings in such societies as the United States, Great Britain, Japan, New Zealand, and the former USSR (Inkeles and Rossi 1956). The most common conclusion was that once societies had industrialized, their members tended to adopt very similar conceptions of occupational prestige, regardless of previous cultural differences. The notion here is that the industrial system everywhere generates similar forms of hierarchy reflecting the emphasis on education, achievement and merit that all modern societies must address.

The theory of industrial society was not without its critics. C. Wright Mills, author of such books as *The New Men of Power* and *White Collar* (1948, 1951), noted the darker side of industrial society. Essentially, Mills argued that the presumptive peace and stability that industrial society achieved were not as benign as they seemed. Rather, industrial corporations had simply established powerful systems of domination that confined unrest among both office and manual workers within manageable bounds. In a more cultural vein, W. H. Whyte (1956) argued that large-scale firms might generate affluence, but in fact required employees to engage in an unthinking form of conformity that had begun to reach into the employee's very soul. Such dissenting views at these tended to constitute a relatively marginal influence until the 1960s, however, when social movements and new forms

of industrial conflict arose that the theory of industrial society seemed unable to explain.

The Labor Process Approach and the Study of Social Inequality

The decade of the 1960s is often remembered for the rise of a student-led counterculture, yet other currents of rebellion occurred at much the same time. Most notably here was the rising tide of worker discontent that emerged and provoked significant concern on the part of corporate and governmental leaders alike. Such discontent— widely referred to as the "blue-collar blues" and the "white-collar woes"—had many sources. One was the rapidly growing economy, which gave workers increased leverage on the job and enabled them to raise criticisms they could not previously voice (Aronowitz 1973). A second stemmed from the spread of rank-and-file movements among union members in the mining, steel, electrical, automobile, trucking, and longshoring industries, who mobilized widespread efforts to ensure that their union structures represented the members' concerns. A third influence was the declining legitimacy of authority more generally, which left corporate elites more vulnerable to dissent and critique. An influential blue-ribbon commission, studying these phenomena, concluded that rising rates of absenteeism, work stoppages, and wildcat strikes were in fact indicative of growing strains within the workplace (U.S. Department of Health, Education, and Welfare 1973). The problem, this commission concluded, was not that the structure of work had changed: to the contrary, the problem was that work structures had *not* changed. Still based on nineteenth-century forms of authority, even though the workforce was increasingly well educated, the commission concluded that a radical disjunction had developed between the workplace as an institution and the culturally based expectations that workers increasingly brought with them into their jobs.

Inspired by the spread of industrial conflict and discontent, a number of scholars began to question the received wisdom about work and society more generally, giving rise to approaches that drew on Marx and, to a lesser extent, Weber. These perspectives viewed work organizations and economic institutions not as the inevitable constructs of modernity, but instead as structures that had been largely imposed by dominant classes and groups. Rather than taking for granted the exercise of elite power, labor process theorists began to formulate more critical analyses based on the notions of domination and subordination, which have continued to receive substantial attention and debate.

One of the most powerful examples of this school emerged in *Labor and Monopoly Capital* (1974), an influential work by Harry Braverman. A former metal worker turned labor journalist, Braverman developed a Marxist analysis of the ways in which capitalism and technology had combined to shape the production process during the twentieth century. Braverman challenged much of the conventional wisdom about work, including a key assumption built into the theory of industrial society: the notion that modern societies required ever higher levels of worker skill and education. Braverman argued instead that corporations were continuing a long, historical tendency that sought to break down skilled work into ever smaller and more simplified parts (see also Marglin 1974; Montgomery 1979). Braverman suggested that this "deskilling" had spread from manual work to office jobs and even to professional occupations.

The reasons for these trends, Braverman argued, were twofold. One was economic. By replacing skilled work with labor requiring little (if any) knowledge or training, employers found it possible to reduce their labor costs and to achieve higher levels of productivity. A second reason involved organizational control. By utilizing unskilled labor, managers were able to reduce their reliance on subordinate-level employees, since workers who lacked skill and production expertise were often unable to exercise independent control over the methods or pace of their work. The long-term result, Braverman concluded, was an historical "degradation of labor," in which more and more jobs were cheapened, emptied of their former skill, and increasingly controlled from above.

While it was influential for a time, Braverman's formulation was criticized on several grounds. Many critics suggested that, like Max Weber, Braverman had neglected the ability of workers to challenge or resist the managerial thrust for control (Stark 1980; Littler and Salaman 1982). By emphasizing a unilinear growth in managerial control, Braverman had in fact distorted the complexities that have historically developed within the contemporary capitalist firm. In light of such shortcomings, a number of more nuanced and sophisticated versions of labor process theory began to appear.

One example is Edwards's (1979) analysis of the internal structure of a dozen large U.S. corporations. He concluded that three types of managerial control systems had developed over time: simple, technical and bureaucratic. Under *simple* control (characteristic of the early corporation), companies relied on either the entrepreneur or his surrogate, the foreman, who used the force of personal supervision to motivate, control, and discipline employees. Yet especially as firms grew in size, such personal forms of control became susceptible to managerial abuse and often produced rising levels of resentment and discontent. Under *technical* control, the task of enforcing the method and pace of work shed its reliance on particular individuals, and came increasingly to be built into the machinery itself (as under assembly line work). But if technical control enabled firms to expand in size, it also raised the stakes: Because it increased the interdependency of plants located in different parts of the country, workers soon learned that strategic work stoppages could bring the system to a halt. Once workers developed the capacity to use such powers of disruption (as the wave of strikes in the 1930s amply displayed), technical control too began to reveal its limits.

Edwards argued that over time, *bureaucratic* control emerged, in which managerial control came to be built into the social structure of the firm. Here Edwards developed an argument not unlike Weber's notion of bureaucracy: By establishing formal rules and procedures that govern workers' performance, companies succeeded in fashioning a new and more powerful system of control, at first within settings that employed office workers and professional employees, but eventually reaching workers in many manual occupations as well. Key here is the fact that by offering employees stable job security, decent pay, and job ladders that provide for upward mobility, bureaucratic control invites workers to identify more with the *firm* rather than with their own social *class*. The result provided management with a formidable means of ensuring worker compliance—all the more so, since the continued co-existence of these three systems of managerial control at any given time results in a workforce

that is continually divided into strata that confront sharply different work situations.

Additional examples of the labor process school are discussed in Chapter 5. Here it is important to point to a number of developments that this school has inspired. One has involved a series of studies that have explored the ways in which team systems have transformed the exercise of managerial authority (V. Smith 1997; Vallas 2003a, 2006). Some researchers have found instances in which team systems have, contrary to widespread claims, in fact worked to extend corporate control over employees' working lives (Grenier 1988; Graham 1995). Others challenge this claim, pointing to workers' awareness of management's goals and intentions and their ongoing ability to shape the ways that team systems are actually deployed (Vallas 2003a, 2003b). This topic is important, in that it raises questions that are important for the labor process school as well as for Weberian theories of bureaucracy. These studies are discussed more fully in Chapter 15.

Another by-product of the labor process school has been a growing body of research on the rise of "nonstandard" employment—usually temporary jobs that offer no security and few if any benefits. Theorists here have interpreted this development as reflecting a managerial effort to reduce the firm's legal, financial, and administrative obligations to employees. (Using temporary employees, for example, one can terminate employees simply by picking up the phone and informing the temporary help firm—now the legal employer of the workers—that the temps will no longer be needed [Pfeffer and Baron 1988; Gonos 1997].) However interpreted, the growth of nonstandard employment has unearthed a troubling development that often opens up sharp disparities in the positions held by distinct groups of employees (Krasas Rogers, 2000; Kalleberg, Reskin, and Hudson 2000; V. Smith 2001a), while potentially undermining the sort of employment stability that workers have traditionally come to expect (Sennett 1999). Nonstandard employment, too, is discussed in Chapter 15.

As the labor process school has grown, it has increasingly adopted a broader focus than was initially the case. Its initial emphasis on the often conflictual relation between management and workers has begun to give way to an increasing recognition of many other sources of conflict and division within the firm—especially differences and inequalities rooted in the gender and racial group to which workers belong. Inspired by feminist theories and concepts, researchers have identified important linkages between gender inequality and the structure of work organizations—linkages that have often operated, however implicitly, to the disadvantage of women employees (Reskin and Padavic 1994). Theoretical approaches here vary widely, but some theorists have advanced a "dual-systems" theory of inequality at work (e.g., Hartmann 1975–1976; Cockburn 1983; Milkman 1987). Such theorists contend that under industrial capitalism, *two* systems of inequality—one based on class, and a second based on sex/gender divisions—have historically coincided. The result has at times inclined male workers to form common cause with managers, pressing demands that reinforce their own position as men and even excluding women from their labor organizations. At such times, gender interests triumph over class. Regardless of the particular theory these researchers employ, they have generated a growing awareness of the ways in which class

and gender empirically combine, often limiting women's access to managerial and professional positions, reinforcing women's "place" within traditionally sex-typed occupations, in turn reducing the job rewards that women workers can expect to receive (Reskin and Padavic 1994; Tomaskovic-Devey, 1993). Chapter 11 focuses on gender inequality in the workplace.

Despite the diversity found among researchers within the labor process school, a number of points are commonly held by most studies in this genre. First, the notion here is that neither the structure nor the distribution of opportunity can be taken for granted as inevitable or necessary features of modern society. Rather, work is viewed as an arbitrary social construct that owes more to the power of particular groups and classes than to any imperatives of industrial society. In this sense, then, the labor process school can be viewed as drawing on the contributions of both Marx and Weber—in so doing posing a direct challenge to the theory of industrial society.

Second, the labor process school views the firm as a complex arena in which struggles for power are constantly being waged. Increasingly, theorists have acknowledged the existence of multiple groups in addition to the early emphasis on "management" (itself a diverse construct) and "workers" (internally stratified as well). Now the roles played by professional employees, technicians, consultants, and customers are all gaining recognition, as is the impact of broad social movements (such as the civil rights, feminist, and environmental movements) on workplace operations as well. Finally, analysts of the labor process and social inequality have increasingly emphasized the importance of workplace culture as a subtle yet significant factor that affects the distribution of opportunity among different groups. Thus, even seemingly minor aspects of social interaction at work—rules governing particular hairstyles or norms concerning the dress and demeanor of different groups—may constitute important symbols concerning which groups are welcome and which are uninvited guests.

Theories of the labor process have exercised great influence within the field and continue to provide important inspiration. Yet a number of recent developments have begun to erode the influence of these critical approaches. One is the declining fortunes of both the workers' and women's movements. A second is the increasing appeal enjoyed by managerial thinking. A third is the widening belief, fueled by the explosive growth of new information and communications technologies, that a new, "postindustrial" or "knowledge economy" has begun to emerge that cannot easily be captured using the language of labor process theory. We turn now to discussion of this third and most recent school of thought.

Theories of Postindustrial Society

For decades, analysts have charted shifts in the structure of the labor force, studying changes in the proportion of workers who are involved in one of three broad sectors of the economy: the *primary* or extractive sector (fishing, mining, lumbering, agriculture), the *secondary* or transformative sector (manufacturing, construction), and the *tertiary* sector (personal or business services, education, health care, etc.). It has long been known that the proportion of the labor force employed within the primary sector has been consistently declining, largely owing to the mechanization of agriculture, mining, and other industries. Until the latter decades of the twentieth century, however, this decline had benefited employment within

the secondary sector, which had expanded its share of the workforce as manufacturing grew in size. Beginning during the latter third of the twentieth century, the share of workers located in the secondary sector of the economy began to decline, even shrinking in absolute size. Now it is the tertiary sector that has outstripped the others, signaling what some theorists have concluded is a dramatic change in the very nature of the economic system in which people are employed.

These trends, and the conclusions they might imply, were first stressed by Bell (1973) and Touraine (1971), who developed the outlines of postindustrial theory. In more recent years, the theory of postindustrialism has enjoyed increased impetus—not surprising, given the dramatic expansion that has occurred in science-intensive or knowledge industries, such as information technology, communications, biotechnology, materials science, nanotechnology, and the like (Block 1990; Castells 1996; Brint 2001). Although this debate reaches far beyond work organizations, the theory of postindustrialism has found important expression among a number of sociologists concerned with the structure of work, many of whom have developed an argument that has far-reaching implications. Although this third perspective in the sociology of work shares certain elements with its forerunner, the theory of industrial society, in other ways it is unique.

Postindustrial theory makes a number of bold assertions. First, it likens the changes currently remaking our economic systems to the transformations that first gripped England during the Industrial Revolution. Then, the transformations led from an artisanal, preindustrial era to the modern, industrial period. Now, a new and equally momentous revolution is underway that promises to lead far beyond the industrial period and the organizational structures that it fostered (Piore and Sabel 1984). Thus, some theorists contend that the industrial era gave rise to rigid, centralized bureaucratic structures that were well adapted to the mechanical, fixed-motion technologies then in use. But with the rise of more flexible, software-controlled production systems, entirely new forms of work organization are required that no longer establish sharp divisions by organizational rank. Now, it is thought, organizations must emphasize continuous learning, innovation, and collaboration among all groups of employees. This is why Zuboff (1988) speaks of the rise of the "post-hierarchical workplace," in which team systems displace centralized bureaucracies, providing flatter structures that are more conducive to creativity and innovation.

A second point concerns the nature of the employment relationship. Where previous generations of employees took for granted an element of stability in their careers, forming an enduring social contract to a single employer, postindustrial theorists argue that workers no longer invest themselves in the *firm*, but instead form their major attachment to their *occupation* (Powell 2001). Workers increasingly define themselves as independent consultants, contractors, or self-employed professionals who see advantages to be gained through interfirm mobility. For this reason, postindustrial theorists have begun to speak of "boundaryless careers" (Arthur and Rousseau 2001), in which the workers' attachment transcends any single firm or employer. A common analogy now likens workers to artists, who move about from project to project, only forming contingent or temporary ties to a single client or employer. Note that postindustrial theory

interprets the rise of unstable employment patterns in a very different (and far more benign) manner than does the labor process school.

Third, as the pace of scientific and technological change has increased, firms increasingly realize that they cannot provide a sufficient knowledge base by themselves; firms that try to do so (for example, by gambling on a handful of new technologies or lines of research) soon find themselves saddled with obsolete expertise. For this reason, firms begin to avoid vertical integration (in which the company purchases its own supply of a strategic resource). Instead, they begin to favor strategic alliances and networks that provide members with access to the latest knowledge, while at the same time retaining the flexibility they need to survive (Piore and Sabel 1984; Powell 1990). Some theorists argue that the more dynamic and information-intensive the industry, the more likely firms are to rely on such interfirm networks. Thus, in a study of the biotechnology industry, Powell and his colleagues (1996) found that the position of the firm within such networks was a critical predictor of subsequent growth: The more central the firm's position, the greater its expansion within ensuing years. Uzzi (1996, 1997) found much the same trend within the fashion-driven apparel industry.

An excellent example of postindustrial theory is the previously mentioned study by Saxenian (1994), who compared two high-tech economic regions: the Route 128 corridor in Massachusetts and the Silicon Valley region in California. Both regions derived important strengths from prestigious universities adjacent to them (MIT and Stanford). Both gained prominent positions as the computer revolutions of the 1980s gained ground. Although both regions encountered difficulties in the late 1980s, as Japanese competition in the semi-conductor industry arose and as mini-computers were phased out, only Silicon Valley recovered its dominant position and realized its potential. The Route 128 corridor stumbled, never quite regaining its place. The reason, Saxenian argues, lies in the organizational structures and local traditions that characterized the two regions. The Route 128 region relied on a deeply hierarchical set of organizational structures, coupled with traditions that inhibited interaction among local engineers. By contrast, Silicon Valley's firms were more flexible and egalitarian, linked to networks that encouraged innovation, and were supported by local traditions that encouraged interaction among engineers. Saxenian views Silicon Valley as providing an example of precisely the sort of economic institutions that postindustrial society demands.

The theory of postindustrialism remains highly controversial. Its critics suggest that it often celebrates a set of changes that may well operate to the detriment of many groups and classes of workers—especially those who are poorly positioned to benefit from or even survive the very developments these theorists advocate. Indeed, postindustrial theorists have generally neglected the inequalities engendered by work organizations, which have in fact grown dramatically during the recent shifts in the structure of work, with the most affluent groups and classes expanding their advantages in relation to the rest of the population. At minimum, carefully considered policies will be needed to blunt the impact of economic restructuring, if indeed postindustrial theorists are right. Such criticisms aside, the theory has real virtues. It serves to remind us that much of what we have taken for granted—stable economic systems with the

firm as the basic unit of analysis—may in fact be changing rapidly. New concepts and interpretive models may be required if we are to understand, let alone direct, the shifting structure of work organizations.

Perspectives on Work: Present Realities and Future Perspectives

The two major contemporary schools of thought—the labor process and postindustrial approaches—have largely developed in parallel, with little cross-fertilization between the two schools. There are obvious differences between them that are in some ways irreconcilable. Thus labor process theorists rely heavily on Marxist and Weberian theories of domination, for example, and on feminist theories of gender inequality (discussed in Chapters 7, 8, and 11). Postindustrial theorists draw more fully on Durkheim, viewing firms, occupations, and the larger socio-economic system as organic entities. These differences notwithstanding, it may not be too much to ask for greater intellectual exchange and reciprocal influence across these two schools of thought. As noted, postindustrial theorists have been more attentive to the dramatic changes that have occurred in organizational structures and the employment relationship than have theorists in the labor process school. This is ironic, inasmuch as Marx himself was highly attuned to far-reaching historical and economic change. Perhaps advocates of labor process theory have clung to their inherited concepts too conservatively.

For their part, postindustrial theorists have neglected precisely those elements of work—material and symbolic inequalities—that labor process theorists have stressed. In their enthusiasm for the newly emerging structures, and in their eagerness to gain favor among influential decision makers, they have often failed to note the potentially adverse effects the new work structures may have on large proportions of the labor force. This too is ironic, especially in the light of the sharp polarization (for example, in income levels) that has emerged in many advanced economies, but especially in the United States, and which postindustrial theories often neglect.

It remains an open question whether new perspectives can emerge that fuse elements of these approaches and that can grasp the novel forms of work organization currently taking shape without losing sight of the role that power and inequality continue to play even within the new economy. Some efforts along these lines can in fact be seen. Thus, Richard Sennett (1999) takes seriously the notion of "fast capitalism" and has sought to explore the ways in which team systems, temporary work, and the new economy all combine to alter the forms of solidarity and identity that contemporary work supports. Sennett's fear is that a more superficial form of solidarity has begun to emerge that places a premium on the value of newness, on quick and easy decision making, and on forms of employment that make it difficult for workers to sustain a stable and meaningful sense of self. These themes have also been developed by Hochschild (1983) and Leidner (1993), who draw attention to the ways in which the expanding service sector tends to standardize forms of interaction that had previously been left within the personal domain. Again, the result of such new forms of social organization may hold important implications for our very identities. Finally, Kathryn Dudley (1994) has shown how different classes within contemporary society can hold sharply distinct views of the coming of postindustrialism, with some eagerly advocating its emergence and others resisting its rise. Studying a Wisconsin community faced with a massive plant shutdown, Dudley found that many middle-class employees actually favored the shutdown of a local plant and provided support for the building of an elite recreational center—a yacht club, fittingly enough—on the old factory site. Manual workers of course deeply resented such views and saw them as destructive of their entire way of life. Dudley's study is unusual in that she found evidence in an especially compressed form of the polarization that has often arisen in contemporary social and economic institutions. Lines of analysis such as these recognize the conflicts that underlie the new forms of social organization and in so doing open up new and important areas for research. We pursue these approaches at various points throughout the following chapters.

Chapter 3

Studying Workers and Work: Research Methods in the Field

In 1974 Michael Burawoy went to work as a machine operator at the Allied Corporation on Chicago's east side. He said it was the hardest job he ever had. Burawoy did more at Allied than operate machines, however; he also spent his time observing and interacting with his co-workers. As a sociologist, his goal was to answer one simple question: "Why do workers work as hard as they do?" (1979: 35). Burawoy follows a long tradition of sociologists who study work and workers using the method of participant observation.

Shelley Correll began her research on gender differences in scientific careers on the campus of Stanford University, where she recruited undergraduate students to be subjects in an experiment. Correll conducted an experiment designed to test the effects of cultural beliefs about gender on women's and men's career aspirations. The results of this study showed that aspirations are shaped by people's perceptions of their competence at particular tasks and that these perceptions are heavily biased along gender lines (Correll 2004).

In the mid-1990s, a team of researchers led by Philip Moss and Chris Tilly set out to better understand racial discrimination in urban labor markets. These researchers were particularly interested in employers; in particular, they wanted to know more about how employers recruit, screen, and evaluate prospective job candidates and how they perceive different racial and ethnic groups. Moss and Tilly's methodology combined face-to-face interviews with a sample of employers in four large U.S. cities with a larger telephone survey of this population. We will be discussing the findings from their book, *Stories Employers Tell* (2001), later in this chapter.

Cotter and his colleagues used a different type of methodology to study gender and racial disparities in earnings (Cotter, Hermsen, and Vanneman 1999). Instead of collecting their own data through participant observation, an experiment, or via surveys and interviews, these researchers analyzed data collected by the U.S. government. Relying on these data enabled Cotter et al. to trace the patterns of gender- and race-based wage inequality over time and across metropolitan areas. Their sample contained almost three million workers; this included white, African-American, Asian, and Hispanic women and men between the ages of 25 and 54 who worked full-time, year-round for pay in a metropolitan area.

This chapter takes a systematic look at the ways sociologists—like those profiled above—have studied workers and the workplace; that is, we explore their research methodologies. Babbie defines methodology as "the science of finding out" (2004: 6). Our interest here is in understanding the tools sociologists of work employ to "find out" answers to their research questions. The examples mentioned above represent some of the most commonly used methodologies.

As these examples illustrate, the methodologies used to study work and workers are as diverse as those applied to the study of any other area of social life. This diversity in part reflects the discipline of sociology and the ways sociologists historically have gone about collecting data and answering research questions. Methodological diversity in the area of work also stems from the subject matter. Work settings and their inhabitants are diverse, and the questions sociologists ask are wide-ranging.

For instance, some sociologists of work are interested in social-psychological questions relating to people's experiences of work or sense of themselves as workers. Others are interested in the larger contexts within which work unfolds. They may want to understand how people interact at work or examine other social processes that occur on the job. Still others explore the broader structural, cultural, or historical features of work. In general, the types of questions sociologists ask and the perspective they bring to bear on their subject matter shape the methodology they are likely to use in their research.

We will encounter these areas of research and many more in the following chapters. The important point for now, however, is that data collection and analysis are important parts of sociological work, just as they are for most

scientific (and social scientific) disciplines. In order to understand the world, it is necessary to study it systematically. But there are many ways to do this. The particular methodology one uses depends largely on the nature of the research question, as we have mentioned. Each methodology has its own strengths and weaknesses as a technique for gathering data and providing information.

This chapter focuses on four methodologies—official statistics, surveys and interviews, ethnographies, and experiments—giving examples of how they have been used and evaluating their strengths and weaknesses as methods of data collection. The chapter concludes with a broader look at the value of sociological research on work.

Methods for Studying Work and Workers: Official Statistics

One of the most important sources of sociological data on workers and work is the United States government and its departments. These agencies employ sociologists who use their methodological skills to collect data. These data are considered "official" statistics; that is, they are collected by employees of government agencies, overseen by Congress, and used for official purposes. The research by Cotter et al. (1999) on gender and racial wage disparities (described at the beginning of this chapter) provides one example of how sociologists have put official statistics to use in the study of work.

While many government agencies are involved in the collection, analysis, and dissemination of data, sociologists of work rely most heavily on data collected by the United States Census Bureau and the Bureau of Labor

Statistics. These agencies' involvement in data collection extends back many years: The first census was conducted in 1790 and was prescribed by the U.S. Constitution. Congress established the Census Bureau as a permanent agency of the U.S. government in 1902, and it now employs over 12,000 people (http://www.census.gov/acsd/www/history.html). The Bureau of Labor Statistics was created by an act of Congress in 1913 as part of the Department of Labor.

The census was created for the specific purpose of apportioning seats in the U.S. House of Representatives, and census data are still used in this way. These data are also used for many other official purposes, such as distributing federal funds and planning by federal, state, and local governments. The monthly unemployment rate is just one of many important official statistics derived from data collected by the Bureau of Labor Statistics (see Box 3.1 and Figure 3.1).

Definitions That Matter

Although concepts such as "labor force" seem self-explanatory, when U.S. government agencies collect, analyze, and disseminate information that contains these words, they have a precise meaning. Making sense of official statistics thus requires us to define these important terms. This is necessary to ensure a common framework of understanding as we begin our examination of sociological methodologies used to study workers and work.

Consider first the words "occupation" and "job." These words are often used interchangeably in everyday conversation as people communicate about the kind of work they do. The "everyday" meanings of these words evolved over the course of the Industrial Revolution as work became physically and temporally separate from other activities. "Occupation" and "job" came gradually to refer to specific activities linked to a larger division of labor, as well as signifying a person's social standing and role.

Government agencies involved in the collection of data about workers and work rely on somewhat more precise definitions of these words. An "occupation" is "a set of activities or tasks that employees are paid to perform" (http://www.bls.gov/bls/glossary); people who perform essentially the same tasks are members of the same occupation, regardless of the industry or setting where they work. Occupation thus is a fairly general term. In contrast, a "job" is a more detailed description of a person's work, providing information about where and for whom the work is being performed.

The details provided by knowledge of a person's job stem in part from the fact that descriptions of jobs often come with clues about the establishment or industry where a person is employed. An "establishment" is defined as "a single physical location where business is conducted or where services or industrial operations are performed" (http://help.econ.census.gov/econhelp/glossary). A company may have several different establishments in different locations. For example, consider Starbucks or Target. Though each is a single company, they have establishments all over the United States (and the world). "Industry" refers to "a group of establishments that provide similar products or provide similar services" (http://www.bls.gov/bls/glossary). Some occupations, such as insurance adjuster, are industry-specific. Many others, however, can be performed in several industries. People employed in the occupation of research forester, for example, can work in the public sector for agencies like the U.S. Forest Service, or they can work for private timber companies, among other possibilities.

BOX 3.1 *The Bureau of Labor Statistics: Measuring Unemployment*

Why does the government collect statistics on the unemployed?

To know about the extent and nature of unemployment. How many people are unemployed? How did they become unemployed? How long have they been unemployed? Are their numbers growing or declining? Are they men or women? Are they young or old? Are they white or black or of Hispanic origin? Are they skilled or unskilled? Are they the sole support of their families, or do other family members have jobs? Are they more concentrated in one area of the country than another? After these statistics are obtained, they have to be interpreted properly so they can be used—together with other economic data—by policymakers in making decisions as to whether measures should be taken to influence the future course of the economy or to aid those affected by joblessness.

Where do the statistics come from?

Because unemployment insurance records, which many people think are the source of total unemployment data, relate only to persons who have applied for such benefits, and since it is impractical to actually count every unemployed person each month, the government conducts a monthly sample survey called the Current Population Survey (CPS) to measure the extent of unemployment in the country. The CPS has been conducted in the United States every month since 1940 when it began as a Work Projects Administration project. It has been expanded and modified several times since then. As explained later, the CPS estimates, beginning in 1994, reflect the results of a major redesign of the survey.

What are the basic concepts of employment and unemployment?

The basic concepts involved in identifying the employed and unemployed are quite simple:

- People with jobs are employed.
- People who are jobless, looking for jobs, and available for work are unemployed.
- People who are neither employed nor unemployed are not in the labor force.

Who is counted as employed?

Not all of the wide range of job situations in the American economy fit neatly into a given category. For example, people are considered employed if they did any work at all for pay or profit during the survey week. This includes all part-time and temporary work, as well as regular full-time year-round employment. Persons also are counted as employed if they have a job at which they did not work during the survey week because they were:

- On vacation;
- Ill;
- Experiencing child-care problems;
- Taking care of some other family or personal obligation;
- On maternity or paternity leave;
- Involved in an industrial dispute; or
- Prevented from working by bad weather.

Who is counted as unemployed?

Persons are classified as unemployed if they do not have jobs, have actively looked for work in the prior four weeks, and are currently available for work.

Who is not in the labor force?

All members of the civilian noninstitutional population are eligible for inclusion in the labor force,

BOX **3.1** *continued*

and those 16 and over who have a job or are actively looking for one are so classified. All others—those who have no job and are not looking for one—are counted as "not in the labor force." Many who do not participate in the labor force are going to school or are retired. Family responsibilities keep others out of the labor force. Still others have a physical or mental disability which prevents them from participating in labor force activities.

What about cases of overlap?

When the population is classified according to who is employed, unemployed, and not in the labor force on the basis of their activities during a given calendar week, situations are often encountered where individuals have engaged in more than one activity. Since persons are counted only once, it must be decided which activity will determine their status. Therefore, a system of priorities is used:

- Labor force activities take precedence over non–labor force activities.
- Working or having a job takes precedence over looking for work.

Employed persons consist of:

- All persons who did any work for pay or profit during the survey reference week;
- All persons who did at least 15 hours of unpaid work in a family-operated enterprise; and
- All persons who were temporarily absent from their regular jobs because of illness, vacation, bad weather, industrial dispute, or various personal reasons.

Unemployed persons are:

- All persons who were not classified as employed during the survey reference week,

made specific active efforts to find a job during the prior four weeks, and were available for work; and

- All persons who were not working and were waiting to be called back to a job from which they had been temporarily laid off.

Persons not in the labor force are those who not classified as employed or unemployed during the survey reference week.

How large is the labor force?

The labor force, then, is not a fixed number of people. It increases with the long-term growth of the population, it responds to economic forces and social trends, and its size changes with the seasons. On average in 2000, there were roughly 135 million employed and 6 million unemployed making up a labor force of 141 million persons. There were about 69 million persons not in the labor force.

How are seasonal fluctuations taken into account?

As suggested in the previous section, the number of employed and unemployed persons fluctuates during the year in a pattern that tends to repeat itself year after year and which reflects holidays, vacations, harvest time, seasonal shifts in industry production schedules, and similar occurrences. Because of such patterns, it is often difficult to tell whether developments between any two months reflect changing economic conditions or merely normal seasonal fluctuations. To deal with such problems, a statistical technique called seasonal adjustment is used.

SOURCE: U.S. Department of Labor, Bureau of Labor Statistics, "Frequently Asked Questions," (http://www.bls.gov/dolfaq/blsfaqtoc.htm).

FIGURE 3.1 **Annual average unemployment rate for civilian labor force 16 years and older (percent).**

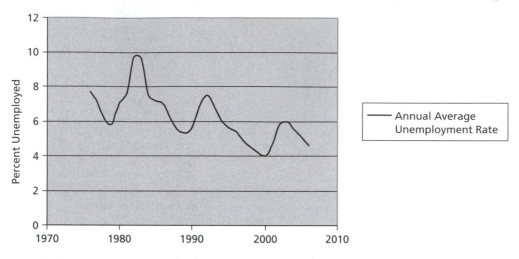

Source: Bureau of Labor Statistics. Annual average unemployment rate, civilian labor force 16 years and over (percent) (http://www.bls.gov/cps/cpsaat2.pdf).

These are among the most frequently used concepts in the sociology of work, as they are the primary ways in which people's work is described. As we will see, these concepts organize virtually all of the information about work that is collected, analyzed, and disseminated by government agencies, and they represent key variables in sociological analyses as well.

Data Sources and Methods of Data Collection

Most work-related data collected by the U.S. government is collected through surveys or interviews. Surveys are typically distributed through the mail or via the computer, while interviews are conducted in person or over the telephone. The participants in both surveys and interviews can be individuals, households, or establishments.

All data collection efforts—large or small—must address issues of sampling. Sampling refers

to "the process of selecting observations" (Babbie 2004: 180). Once researchers have decided *how* to collect their data (e.g., through surveys, interviews, ethnographies), they must decide on a strategy for choosing from whom or where to collect information. This is an extremely important task. Even the most well-designed survey will yield little useful information if there are problems with the sampling techniques.

Sampling starts with identification of the population. This is the "universe" or the theoretical target of the research. A population could refer to a group of individuals (e.g., currently employed women), households (e.g., households containing young children), or other units, such as occupations, establishments, etc. Samples are selected from the population identified for a particular research project.

There are many types of sampling. For our purposes, the most important distinction is between probability and nonprobability sampling techniques. Probability sampling is a method designed to ensure that the sample selected reflects the variations that exist in the population as a whole. For example, because the U.S. labor force is approximately 46 percent female and 54 percent male, a probability sample of employed workers should yield approximately similar percentages of women and men. To the extent that this has been achieved, we say that the sample is "representative" of the population to which it refers.

Probability sampling is not always feasible or desirable. It is not feasible when the population from which the sample is to be drawn cannot be easily identified. For example, Gowan (2002) studied homeless men's work in the recycling industry in San Francisco. The very nature of homelessness inhibited her ability to identify the members and characteristics of this population, thus making probability sampling an inappropriate way to select research subjects. Probability sampling may also be undesirable, not suited to exploring a particular research question. In these instances, researchers may use a convenience sample, relying on available and accessible subjects, or they may use the strategies of "purposive" or "snowball" sampling. To select a purposive sample, the researcher uses his or her judgment about the best subjects to study, given the aims of the research. Snowball sampling is a technique whereby each person surveyed or interviewed suggests additional respondents. Gowan relied on both strategies in her study of homeless men. Nonprobability sampling can yield important insights and information, but its drawback is that results derived in this fashion cannot be considered representative of a population or generalizable beyond the particular group studied.

Probability Sampling and Official Statistics

Virtually all official statistics are derived from some type of probability sampling and thus are representative of the relevant population. The decennial Census is a study of the U.S. population conducted every ten years. Most adults have filled out a census form at one time or another; the "short form" is, in principle, to be completed by every individual in the United States. Because the short form is theoretically given to everyone in the United States—the entire population—there is no sampling required. Probability sampling is used by the U.S. Census to identify which households should receive the "long form." One in every six households receives this version. Sociologists of work are particularly interested in these results, since the long form contains questions on people's employment status, occupations, employers, and income, among other things.

Sociologists of work also analyze data collected by the Bureau of Labor Statistics (BLS) (http://www.bls.gov), a federal agency that is part of the Department of Labor. The BLS collects data on many topics of interest to sociologists of work. Sociologists studying patterns of wage inequality, for instance, would likely turn to the BLS for the most up-to-date data on the average wages paid to workers in over 700 of the largest occupations. Researchers exploring trends in workplace injuries or deaths might rely on the BLS's annual survey of workplace injuries, illnesses, and fatalities.

One of the BLS data sources most frequently used by sociologists of work is the Current Population Survey (CPS). The CPS is a monthly survey of a representative sample of approximately 60,000 U.S. households. Administered through personal or telephone interviews, this survey includes questions relating to household members' employment status, such as their occupation, industry, hours of work, and earnings, among other factors. As described in Box 3.1, the CPS also collects data on the unemployed, including the duration of and reason for unemployment. In addition to information on their employment situation, respondents are asked to provide detailed demographic data (e.g., sex, race, ethnic origin, marital status, family relationship, or Vietnam-era veteran status). CPS data are useful for sociologists interested in understanding broad patterns and trends affecting the labor force and for comparing the employment situations of different demographic groups.

Sociologists of work are also interested in issues that pertain to businesses and employers. The Economic Census is useful for this purpose. It presents a profile of the U.S. economy at the national, state, and local levels. Unlike the Decennial Census, which surveys individuals or households, the Economic Census collects information from "establishments."

The Economic Census takes place every five years. For the most recent survey, conducted in 2007, the Census Bureau sent forms to over 5 million of the largest U.S. companies and a sample of smaller firms. The Bureau created over 650 versions of the survey, each tailored to a particular industry or sector. Businesses were asked to provide information about their size, receipts, payroll, etc. Collecting data at the establishment level is useful for sociologists studying organizational structures and processes.

Coding, Classifying, and Describing Occupations and Industries

The Census Bureau and the Bureau of Labor Statistics have devoted much attention to the coding and classification of occupations and industries. These coding and classification schemes are used to organize information collected not only by these agencies, but by other federal agencies as well. They are also used in other large-scale surveys, such as the National Organizations Survey (NOS) and the National Survey of the Changing Workforce (NSCW), and in many other research projects. In all cases, their primary function is to provide a common framework for describing the types of work people do.

Efforts to classify occupations have resulted in the creation of the Standard Occupational Classification (SOC) System, an elaborate index of major occupations in the United States. The SOC has been revised several times over the years, most recently in 2000, to account for changes in the occupational structure over time and reflect as accurately as possible the nature of the work people perform. To better grasp the challenge of this task, consider that the 2000 census counted 129.7 million employed civilians (over age 16). Every person's occupation was coded according to SOC guidelines into one of 509 detailed occupational categories, which were then categorized into 22 major occupational groups. The 22 groups are further classified into one of six broad categories. To see all these categories, and to learn more about individual occupations, go to the Bureau of Labor Statistics' website: http://www.bls.gov/soc/.

Figure 3.2 shows how workers were distributed across the 22 major occupational groups in 2006. As these data reveal, office and administrative support positions employed the largest number of workers in 2006, followed by sales and related occupations. By contrast, farming, fishing, and forestry occupations employed the fewest number of workers, with less than half a million

FIGURE 3.2 **Total employment by major occupational group, 2006.**

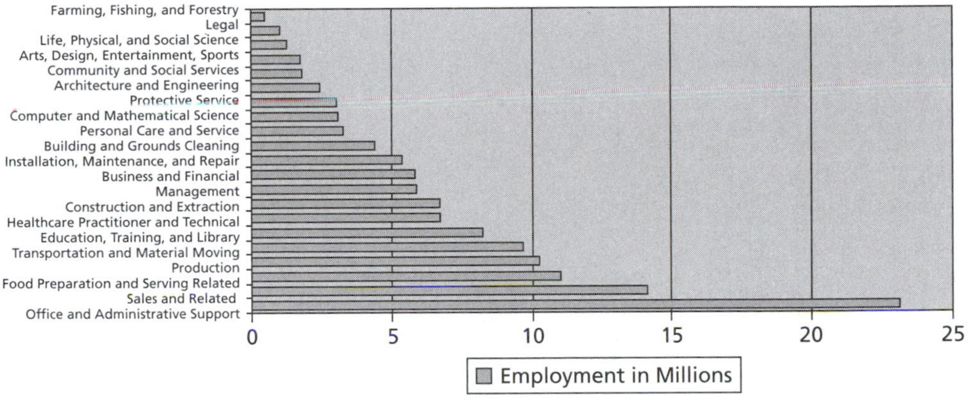

Source: Bureau of Labor Statistics. *Occupational Employment and Wages, 2006.* From Table 1: National employment and wage data from the Occupational Employment Statistics survey by occupation, May 2006.

people working in these jobs. The differences between occupational groups listed in this figure do not coincide with what may be more familiar distinctions between "blue-collar" and "white-collar" work or "mental" and "manual" labor. While a once-useful shorthand for capturing "a status structure in which social standing rested on whether people's hands were clean or dirty at the end of the day," these distinctions have less and less relevance in today's global service economy (Barley and Kunda 2001: 82–83).

Occupational data from the census can also be cross-classified with other variables to provide an informative snapshot of the U.S. labor force. For example, Figure 3.3 shows how each gender and racial-ethnic group is distributed across five broad occupational categories.

Recall that the decennial census has been conducted every decade since 1790. Because each census contains some information about people's employment, there exists an extensive historical record of the occupational distribution of the U.S. labor force. These data have been

extensively analyzed by sociologists and others interested in exploring changes in the occupational structure over time. Comparing occupations over time is not an easy task, however.

As Pilot explains, "[c]oming up with a list of occupations that can be construed as comparable over [50 years] is tricky at best and hazardous at worst, because of changes in occupational classification, definition, coverage, and skills" (1999: 11). The occupation of "desktop-publishing specialist," for example, did not exist in the early or even mid-1900s, while "typewriter servicemen"—an occupation that was recognized in the occupational coding schemes of the mid-1900s—was gone by the end of the twentieth century (Pilot 1999). These examples help remind us that tracking changes in a society's occupational distribution is not simply a technical exercise in coding and classification. Instead, identifying these changes helps us gain insight into much broader social patterns and trends. Both the rise of the desktop-publishing specialist and the demise of the typewriter serviceman, for example, reflect the technological

FIGURE 3.3 Percent distribution of women and men by major occupational category, race, and Hispanic ethnicity, 2006.

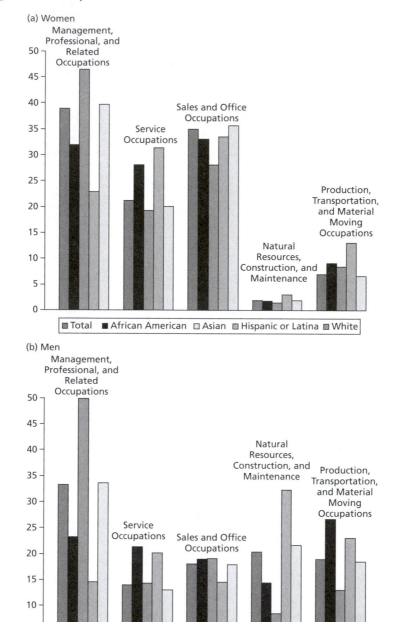

Source: U.S. Bureau of Labor Statistics. Employment and Earnings, January 2007. Table 10: Employed persons by occupation, race Hispanic or Latino ethnicity, and sex.

revolution spawned by the development and widespread use of computer technology.

Other Descriptions of Occupations

Two other sources of occupational information are the *Dictionary of Occupational Titles* (DOT) and the *Occupational Outlook Handbook* (OOH). Both were initially created to aid job seekers, career counselors, and others directly involved in matching people with jobs. The first edition of the DOT was published in 1939, with the OOH following ten years later. Both have been revised regularly over time and are now fully available online. The DOT lists close to 30,000 job titles and contains detailed information about tasks performed, educational requirements, and skills for over 12,000 job types (http://www.occupationalinfo.org). The OOH also contains information about occupations, including a description of the work performed, working conditions, qualifications, earnings, and the employment outlook for the job (http://www.bls.gov/oco/home.htm).

One interesting component of the OOH is its projections of occupational and industrial growth and decline. Approximately every two years, analysts at the Bureau of Labor Statistics attempt to anticipate occupational and industrial trends for the next decade. In order to make these estimates, analysts must factor in a number of variables, such as the demographic characteristics of the population and expected changes in the economy as a whole.

Tables 3.1 to 3.3 report the most recent published occupational projections (Dohm and Shniper 2007). Each of these lists offers a glimpse into the future of American society. In that respect, they tell us much more than whether a particular occupation is growing or declining. Rather, they tell a story about some of the factors

expected to shape American society over the next ten years and the ways those factors will influence the kinds of work people do. For example, American society, as we know, is rapidly "graying" as the Baby Boomers move into retirement. This will affect the workplace in many ways. Most important, as Tables 3.1 and 3.2 show, is the projected growth in health-related occupations, particularly those in health-care support positions. Expansion in health care "reflects an aging population that requires more healthcare, a wealthier population that can afford better healthcare, and advances in medical technology that permit more health problems to be treated aggressively" (Hecker 2004: 101).

Another story contained in these projections concerns the ongoing impact of computer technology on every area of work and life. The fastest growing occupation overall, for instance, is network systems and data communications analysts, and several other occupations on the list are computer-related (e.g., computer systems analysts, computer software engineers, database administrators). Developments in computer technology do not only fuel occupational growth, however. Technological change may also help to explain occupational decline (see Table 3.3). Among the most rapidly declining occupations, for example, are word processors and typists and data entry keyers. Innovations in information technology have automated many clerical tasks and reduced demand for workers in these areas. Telemarketing is also projected to decline as systems for blocking such calls gain in sophistication and use.

Industry Classification Systems

Similar systems were devised to code and classify industries. Until recently, government agencies and everyone who used their data relied on the

TABLE 3.1 Fastest Growing Occupations, 2006–2016

Network systems and data communications analysts

Personal and home care aides

Home health aides

Computer software engineers, applications

Veterinary technologists and technicians

Personal financial advisors

Make-up artists, theatrical and performance

Medical assistants

Veterinarians

Substance abuse and behavioral disorder counselors

Skin care specialists

Financial analysts

Social and human service assistants

Gaming surveillance officers and gaming investigators

Physical therapy assistants

Pharmacy technicians

Forensic science technicians

Dental hygienists

Mental health counselors

Mental health and substance abuse social workers

Marriage and family therapists

Dental assistants

Computer systems analysts

Database administrators

Computer software engineers, systems software

Gaming and sports book writers and runners

Environmental science and protection technicians, including health

Manicurists and pedicurists

Physical therapists

Physician assistants

Source: Dohm and Shniper 2007.

TABLE 3.2 **Occupations with the Largest Absolute Job**
Growth, 2006–2016 (Projected)

Registered nurses

Retail salespersons

Customer service representatives

Combined food preparation and serving workers, including fast food

Office clerks, general

Personal and home care aides

Postsecondary teachers

Janitors and cleaners, except maids and housekeeping cleaners

Nursing aides, orderlies, and attendants

Bookkeeping, accounting, and auditing clerks

Waiters and waitresses

Child care workers

Executive secretaries and administrative assistants

Computer software engineers, applications

Accountants and auditors

Landscaping and groundskeeping workers

Elementary school teachers, except special
education

Receptionists and information clerks

Truck drivers, heavy and tractor trailer

Maids and housekeeping cleaners

Security guards

Carpenters

Management analysts

Medical assistants

Computer systems analysts

Maintenance and repair workers, general

Network systems and data communication
analysts

Food preparation workers

Teacher assistants

Source: Dohm and Shniper 2007.

TABLE 3.3 Occupations with the Largest Absolute Job Declines, 2006–2016 (Projected)

Stock clerks and order fillers
Cashiers, except gaming
Packers and packagers, hand
File clerks
Farmers and ranchers
Order clerks
Sewing machine operators
Electrical and electronic equipment assemblers
Cutting, punching, and press machine setters, operators, and tenders, metal and plastic
Telemarketers
Inspectors, testers, sorters, samplers, and weighers
First-line supervisors/managers of production and operating workers
Computer operators
Photographic processing machine operators
Driver/sales workers
Machine feeders and offbearers
Packaging and filling machine operators and tenders
Word processors and typists
Paper goods machine setters, operators, and tenders
Farmworkers and laborers, crop, nursery, and greenhouse
Molding, coremaking, and casting machine setters, operators and tenders, metal and plastic
Computer programmers
Mail clerks and mail machine operators, except postal service
Postal service mail sorters, processors, and processing machine operators
Grinding, lapping, polishing, and buffing machine tool setters, operators, and tenders, metal and plastic
Lathe and turning machine tool setters, operators, and tenders, metal and plastic
Prepress technicians and workers
Switchboard operators, including answering service
Data entry keyers
Bindery workers

Source: Dohm and Shniper 2007.

TABLE 3.4 Employment in Industry Supersectors, 2006

	Total Employed (in thousands)
Goods-producing industries	
Natural resources and mining	687
Construction	11,749
Manufacturing	16,377
Service-producing industries	
Trade, transportation, and utilities	28,783
Information	3,573
Financial activities	10,490
Professional and business services	14,868
Education and health services	29,938
Leisure and hospitality	12,145
Other services	7,088

Source: U.S. Bureau of Labor Statistics. Employment and Earnings, January 2007. Table 16: Employed persons in nonagricultural industries by sex and class of worker.

Standard Industrial Classification (SIC) system, devised in the 1930s as a way to classify the industries where people worked. The SIC coded just over 1,000 industries using a four-digit code. A new system, called the North American Industry Classification System (NAICS), is gradually replacing the SIC, however (http://www.census.gov/epcd/www/naics.html). The NACIS codes 1,170 detailed industries into ten "supersectors," as shown in Table 3.4.

NAICS was developed primarily to reflect two changes in the U.S. economy. The first is the rise of the service sector and other industries that were not well represented in the SIC. A second change involves the breaking down of economic borders, especially between the United States and its closest neighbors—Canada and Mexico. The NAICS was developed in collaboration with both countries, underscoring

the close economic ties between them and the United States.

Strengths and Weaknesses of Official Statistics

Despite their "official" status, it is important to understand that these data are not perfect and, like all data, have their own distinct strengths and weaknesses. The primary strengths of official statistics derive from their quality, availability, and cost. As discussed earlier, official statistics, such as CPS data, are drawn from nationally representative samples or can be statistically adjusted to reflect the U.S. population as a whole or a particular segment of it, such as a state or region or demographic group. These sampling techniques thus greatly enhance the quality of these data. When researchers analyze official statistics, they can be reasonably confident that their results are generalizable to a larger population and are not purely idiosyncratic.

Because the BLS and the U.S. Census Bureau are agencies of the U.S. government with a congressional mandate to collect certain kinds of information, their employees typically have the financial and technical resources they need to do their work. More important, the products of these efforts belong to the public and can be accessed by researchers with minimal cost. High quality, availability, and low cost together make official statistics a useful tool for answering many kinds of sociological questions about workers and the workplace.

Like other data collected in national sample surveys, however, official statistics are limited in certain respects. Although CPS surveys occasionally do contain specially designed modules that ask about a particular issue or trend affecting workers, these surveys are designed to collect information from large cross-sections of the U.S. population. This broad coverage requires that the survey contain only straightforward, fairly objective questions. Sociologists who want to survey workers or employers about more complex issues or who are interested in a topic that requires focused attention on one narrowly drawn segment of the workforce will not find official statistics of much use. Instead, as we will see later, these sociologists are likely to design and distribute their own surveys.

It is also important to remember that the data-gathering efforts that produce official statistics are funded by Congress; their contents thus are subject to political scrutiny. Sociologists interested in politically sensitive or controversial issues are unlikely to find data on these topics in official statistics. Hence, while official statistics can be useful for some purposes, this methodology is not well suited to the study of many topics of interest to sociologists of work.

Methods for Studying Work and Workers: Surveys and Interviews

Surveys are considered to be the most frequently used method of data collection in the social sciences (Babbie 2004). At one time or another, all of us have responded to a survey of one sort or another; most of us have probably responded to many different kinds of surveys, designed for many different purposes. College courses, for example, are typically evaluated by surveying the students about their experiences in the class and their views of the instructor. Public opinion polls, such as those conducted by The Gallup Organization, represent another type of survey. Gallup has been surveying samples of the U.S. population on a wide variety of matters since the mid-1930s (www.gallup.com). As we saw in the preceding section, census data are also collected via surveys of individuals, households, or establishments.

Surveys can be administered in different ways. The four most common means are by mail, by telephone, face-to-face, or via the Internet. Each has its own set of advantages and disadvantages; there is a large literature devoted to the design and implementation of each form of data collection (Dillman 2007). When properly used, all of these ways of collecting survey data can yield high-quality results. Which method is most appropriate depends on the research question and sample, as well as practical matters, such as the research budget.

Although surveys can be administered in several different ways, virtually all of them rely on some kind of relatively standardized questionnaire; that is, all survey respondents are asked the same questions in the same order and format. Standardization is important because it enables researchers to aggregate responses for the purpose of describing a particular segment of people (e.g., students in a course). In addition, survey researchers attempt to explain variations in responses to particular questions by linking them to other characteristics of respondents.

Many sociologists of work analyze survey or interview data that they have designed and collected themselves. For instance, Moss and Tilly (2001), whose research is described at the beginning of this chapter, used surveys to understand how urban employers in four cities viewed the labor market, workers, and race. Members of their research team administered some of these surveys over the telephone, while others were administered face-to-face.

Secondary Analysis of Survey Data: Large-Scale Surveys of Work and Workers

It is not always necessary or desirable for a researcher to design and administer his or her own survey. Instead, many researchers analyze survey data that were collected by someone else. As we have seen, the U.S. government is a primary source of survey data on workers and work, and many sociologists rely on these data to answer their research questions. There are other large-scale surveys accessible to researchers, however. These are typically funded by U.S. government agencies or private foundations and often reflect their authors' interest in collecting in-depth data on a particular topic (e.g., work–family relations).

For example, The National Survey of the Changing Workforce (NSCW), conducted every five years by the Families and Work Institute, is an ongoing survey of a nationally representative sample of employed workers, focusing on both job conditions and respondents' family and personal lives (http://www.familiesandwork. org). The most recent wave of this survey was completed in 2002. Jacobs and Gerson's (2004) analyses of these data form the basis for their book on work and family, which we discuss in Chapter 15.

The National Organizations Survey (NOS), conducted in 1991 and again in 1996–1997 and in 2002 is another large-scale survey frequently analyzed by sociologists of work. The NOS contains data collected from a representative sample of U.S. establishments, with a focus on human resource policies and practices. The survey also includes data on many other characteristics of establishments, such as their organizational structures, workforce, performance, and locations (see Kalleberg et al. [1994] for examples of research analyzing 1991 NOS data).

The Science (and Art) of Asking Questions

Extensive research has been devoted to the wording of survey questions and possible responses. This research draws from many areas, including cognitive psychology, conversational analysis, and other studies of information processing (Schaeffer and Presser 2003). Studies address issues such as where and with what frequency a survey question should mention a reference period (last week, within the last six months, etc.), the most suitable response categories for particular questions, and whether and how to define behaviors and events for respondents. These efforts are directed toward one primary goal: to improve the validity and reliability of

---

BOX 3.2 *From an Actual "Think Aloud" Interview to Determine Time Spent Working*

"So, for last week, how many hours did you actually work in your main job?"

"I just figured this out for my time card. So, not including that one hour off and the nine hours off I think I worked like, 41 and a half, including that time off. So, minus 9, is 32. I think I worked 32 and a half—something like that. OK. Oh, God, and for XXX, oh my God. My schedule goes from Thursday to Wednesday, I need to fall back on. Let me do it backwards. Did I work Saturday? Yes, I worked Saturday? Sunday to Saturday or Saturday to Sunday? Sunday to Saturday. Saturday I worked from—6 to 10, and I worked Friday—no, Thursday—yes, I worked 12–4:30. Wednesday—yes, I worked—When did I work? I worked 5 to 11. And Tuesday, did I work? Nnnooo. Monday, did I work? Na, I volunteer worked that night. No, I didn't work. Sunday, did I work? Oh gosh, Sunday night, November—What day was that? November 24th. Gosh, did I work that day? I think I may have worked that day—What did I do? I watched the football game with XXX. We stayed over there until about—I don't think I did any work that day. So that's 4, 4 and a half, and 6, 10 and a half—I'll say 14 and a half hours."

SOURCE: Robinson and Godbey 1997: 82.

---

survey data. *Validity* refers to whether a measure accurately reflects the concept it is designed to measure; *reliability* refers to whether the same measure used again and again in the same population will yield the same responses.

As in all areas of sociology, some concepts of interest to sociologists of work can be more easily measured through surveys than others. There are challenges in validity and reliability associated with measuring even the most straightforward concepts, however. For example, consider the issue of how many hours a person works. Knowing the answer to this question has drawn increasing interest from researchers, but is also a subject of great debate (Schor 1991; Robinson and Godbey 1997). U.S. government surveys regularly contain questions about work hours, and these data extend back to at least the 1940s (Robinson and Godbey 1997). In its Basic Monthly Survey, the CPS asks people to estimate how many hours they *actually worked* at their main job in the previous week. Other surveys contain a similar question, usually asking people to think about their average, regular, or normal work hours or their hours worked in the preceding week.

This seems like a simple task. However, as Robinson and Godbey note, "[p]eople think they know how many hours they work—that is, until they actually try to figure it out" (1997: 81) (see Box 3.2). Response error occurs for several reasons: Respondents may not understand the time frame of the question; they may not know what counts as "work;" they may not remember accurately or be unable to sum up hours worked over multiple days; or they may over- or underestimate their hours work in order to present

---

BOX 3.3 *Measuring Job Satisfaction*

Here is an example of a global measure of job satisfaction. These questions are designed to tap people's overall assessment of their jobs. The items are highly general and thus could apply to almost any type of work. Developed by Quinn and Shepard (1974) and modified by Pond and Geyer (1991) and Rice et al. (1991), this measure includes six items, with the original wording in parentheses.

1. (Knowing what you know now), If you had to decide all over again whether to take the job you now have, what would you decide? (Responses range from 1 = definitely not take the job to 5 = definitely take the job.)
2. If a (good) friend asked if s/he should apply for a job like yours with your employer, what would you recommend? (Responses range from 1 = not recommend at all to 5 = recommend strongly.)

3. How does this job compare with your ideal job (job you would most like to have)? (Responses range from 1 = very far from ideal to 5 = very close to ideal.)
4. (In general) how does your job measure up to the sort of job you wanted when you took it? (Responses range from 1 = not at all like I wanted to 5 = just like I wanted.)
5. All (in all) things considered, how satisfied are you with your current job? (Responses range from 1 = not at all satisfied to 5 = completely satisfied.)
6. In general, how much do you like your job? (Responses range from 1 = not at all to 5 = a great deal.)

SOURCE: Fields 2002: 13.

---

themselves in a particular way to the researcher (Robinson and Godbey 1997: 85). In light of these problems of both validity and reliability, Robinson and Godbey argue that estimates of working hours derived from government surveys are generally inflated relative to what is found when other methods are used to collect work hour data.

If a seemingly simple issue like the number of hours a person works is difficult to ask about on a survey, consider a slightly more complicated concept: job satisfaction. Every day thousands of workers are asked to report their level of job satisfaction. Most of the time they do so in response to internal surveys distributed at their workplace. Employers—and the human resource departments

that operate on their behalf—spend many hours attempting to gauge their workers' feelings about their jobs and companies. This research is conducted with the belief that satisfied workers are more productive employees, though studies show only a small positive relationship between these variables (George and Jones 1997).

Job satisfaction can be defined simply as "how people feel about their jobs and different aspects of their jobs" (Spector 1997: 2). It can represent a person's overall assessment of his or her job or a set of feelings about a job's different facets, such as pay, co-workers, supervisor, etc. Much effort has been devoted to creating valid and reliable measures of this concept. Box 3.3 describes one commonly used way to assess job satisfaction.

Job satisfaction is a useful concept for sociologists, in part because it is defined in such general terms, it is a question or set of questions that can be asked of virtually everyone who is employed, and it can be asked the same way from one decade to the next. This has enabled researchers to compare levels of job satisfaction across occupations and across time, thus yielding a systematic portrait of workers' feelings about their work and the ways these feelings are linked to other aspects of the job.

Job satisfaction is an attitudinal variable; that is, it taps workers' feelings about what they do. Surveys of workers also attempt to measure more objective characteristics of jobs. These include qualities such as the degree to which the work is routinized; how much control a worker has over his or her working conditions; the complexity of the job; and the nature of supervision. Concepts like these are typically measured by several survey items, which are later combined into a single scale. Although the items composing each scale may seem straightforward, each is the product of extensive testing and analysis, designed to maximize the measure's validity and reliability.

Sociologists have written survey questions attempting to measure countless other concepts relating to work and workers. In general, the more complex the concept, the more difficult it is to create valid and reliable measures. These difficulties lead some researchers to choose a different method for collecting their data, such as in-depth interviews or an ethnography. Alternatively, some combine surveys with one of these other methods. In fact, it has become increasingly common for researchers to use more than one methodology when studying a particular issue. This strategy enables them to offset the limits of one methodology with the strengths of another.

Methods for Studying Work and Workers: Ethnographies

Michael Burawoy's research in the Chicago machine shop, described at the beginning of this chapter, is an example of an ethnographic approach to the study of work. As the preceding discussion showed, U. S. government agencies have been collecting, analyzing, and disseminating quantitative data about the workplace for many decades. Ethnographers have also been studying work and workers for a long time; most trace the beginnings of ethnographic studies of work to the Hawthorne Studies of the 1930s (Burawoy et al. 2000; Hodson 2001).

Ethnographic approaches "are grounded in a commitment to firsthand experience and exploration of a particular social or cultural setting on the basis of (though not exclusively by) participant observation. Observation and participation (according to circumstance and the analytic purpose at hand) remain the characteristic features of the ethnographic approach" (Atkinson et al. 2001: 4–5). In contrast to survey data, which tend to focus on individuals or organizations as independent or self-contained entities, ethnographic data focus on individual or group behavior in context. Characteristics of the settings and situations where people interact and go about their daily life thus receive much more attention than in survey research.

In addition to focusing on the contexts where behavior occurs, ethnographic methods have other qualities that make them a valuable source of data on workers and the workplace. While survey researchers aim for large, representative samples and generalizability, ethnographers are far more interested in obtaining a close-up, detailed portrait of a very limited number of work settings—perhaps as few as one. Ethnographers may spend weeks, months, or even years in a particular setting, which brings depth, nuance, and richness to their observations. Because ethnographers observe people in their natural environment, they are able to present their subjects' views in their own terms.

Hodson (2001) argues that this makes ethnographic approaches especially well suited to understanding workers' perspectives and opinions. Survey research is less useful for this purpose, because surveys are designed to collect information deemed important by researchers, not workers themselves. Smith (2001b) suggests that the value of ethnographic studies of work stems from their ability to shed light on important features of work, including "how routine jobs are complex; how complex jobs are routine; and how power, control, and inequality are sustained." Because ethnography involves direct observation, it is useful for understanding exactly how work is performed. As Barley and Kunda note, "most work practices are so contextualized that people often cannot articulate how they do what they do, unless they are in the practice of doing it" (2001; 81).

Ethnographers, as Smith notes, "cannot be accused of being armchair academics who examine the world at arm's length....By becoming paid workers, they have capitalized on an avenue into the research field—getting a job, learning by laboring—not readily available to researchers in other domains" (2001b: 220). Organizational or workplace ethnographies, in which researchers "observ[e] workers at their places of employment or even work...directly alongside them," have been conducted in many types of work settings over many years (Hodson 2001: 50). These ethnographies have provided sociologists with some of their most significant insights into workers and the workplace.

Workplace Ethnographies Then and Now: From "Cow Sociology" to Making a Tip

The late 1920s and 1930s was the era of The Great Depression in the United States. The now famous Hawthorne experiments also took place during this time period. These experiments, relying as they did on detailed observations of workers on the job, are generally seen to mark the beginning of organizational ethnography as a tool for understanding the workplace.

The Hawthorne studies, to be discussed more fully in Chapter 5, represent a series of experiments performed at the Western Electric Works in Hawthorne, Illinois, by researchers associated with the Harvard Business School (Mayo 1933; Roethlisberger and Dickson 1939). The researchers' initial aims were to identify ways in which the design of work could be improved so as to reduce workers' levels of fatigue, monotony, and discomfort (Mayo 1933). Over the course of the experiments, however, researchers' interests shifted from job design to broader questions about workers' feelings about themselves and their work. Hence, what began as a study of environmental design and engineering became a study of social relationships—among workers and between workers and supervisors.

What is important to note here is that the Hawthorne studies were the first of many ethnographic studies of workers and their workplaces and that they shaped social research on these issues for years to come. These studies are noteworthy today for two primary reasons. First, the research inadvertently uncovered a phenomenon that has come to be known as the "Hawthorne effect." The Hawthorne effect refers to the possibility that researchers' presence in a setting where a study is being conducted may influence the responses of research subjects. Workers in the Hawthorne plant responded positively to the researchers' presence; Mayo and his colleagues attributed their rising productivity to this attention from researchers (but see Whyte 1987 for an alternative perspective). Ethnographic researchers, whose methods of data collection and observation require them to interact with the subjects of their research, continue to face the challenge of avoiding the Hawthorne effect.

A second legacy of the Hawthorne studies concerns their approach to workers and the workplace. By focusing on workers as they engaged with one another on the job, these studies revealed the important role social relationships play in the workplace. This insight not only affirmed the value and necessity of ethnographic research, it also helped to shape sociological and managerial views of work for decades (Barley and Kunda 2001). Among sociologists, research on work groups and workplace cultures flourished throughout the 1940s and 1950s. A central thrust of these studies was the ways in which work group processes and norms shaped their members' attitudes and behavior. Researchers were especially interested in the informal systems of organizing that emerged on the job alongside of, and sometimes in opposition to, the formal structures of the workplace.

The influence of the Hawthorne studies extended beyond sociologists and social scientists, however. From these studies developed a view of good leadership as being as much concerned with "human relations" as with the technical or bureaucratic aspects of the task (see Chapter 5). Managers thus saw a very practical application

of the Hawthorne effect: People worked harder and more productively when they believed that their supervisors and employers were concerned about them. While these views about leadership, morale, and productivity have proven to be far too simplistic, the "human relations" approach—at least initially—had an important impact on managers' conceptions of their roles in industry (Perrow 1986).

This application of the Hawthorne studies was criticized by some sociologists at the time. These critics referred disparagingly to the Hawthorne researchers as "cow sociologists": "Moo, moo, moo say the cow sociologists" wrote Bell (1947: 88), alluding to a popular advertising campaign at the time in which a brand of condensed milk was sold as being especially tasty because it was produced by "contented cows." As Simpson explains, this research was also "sometimes denounced as managerial sociology—that is, as sociology done to help management" (1989: 567). Instead, some believed that the aims of social science should be to improve the quality of work life for workers. Needless to say, these issues—about the purpose and politics of social research—continue to be debated and raise important ethical issues concerning the uses (and possible abuses) of sociological research.

As the United States moved out of the depression and into World War II, ethnography continued to be the methodology of choice for sociologists studying the workplace. Although many of these studies focused on male workers in blue-collar factory jobs, these were not the only settings of interest to sociologists (Gubrium 2007). Other occupations studied included Donovan's (1929, 1938) studies of "salesladies" and schoolteachers, Gold's (1952) research on apartment janitors, Whyte's (1948) classic study

BOX 3.4 *The Use of Deception in Research*

(a) Sociologists do not use deceptive techniques (1) unless they have determined that their use will not be harmful to research participants; is justified by the study's prospective scientific, educational, or applied value; and that equally effective alternative procedures that do not use deception are not feasible, and (2) unless they have obtained the approval of institutional review boards or, in the absence of such boards, with another authoritative body with expertise on the ethics of research.

(b) Sociologists never deceive research participants about significant aspects of the research that would affect their willingness to participate, such as physical risks, discomfort, or unpleasant emotional experiences.

(c) When deception is an integral feature of the design and conduct of research, sociologists attempt to correct any misconception that research participants may have no later than at the conclusion of the research.

(d) On rare occasions, sociologists may need to conceal their identity in order to undertake research that could not practically be carried out were they to be known as researchers. Under such circumstances, sociologists undertake the research if it involves no more than minimal risk for the research participants and if they have obtained approval to proceed in this manner from an institutional review board or, in the absence of such boards, from another authoritative body with expertise on the ethics of research. Under such circumstances, confidentiality must be maintained unless otherwise set forth in [previous sections of this Code].

SOURCE: Code of Ethics, American Sociological Association, Washington, DC, 1999, Section 12.05, p. 14.

of the restaurant industry, and research on the military (e.g., Stouffer et al. 1949).

In general, the focus of ethnographic research has shifted over time in ways that parallel changes in the occupational structure. While many ethnographic studies have continued to focus on blue-collar jobs in factories (e.g., Burawoy 1979; Juravich 1985; Vallas 2003c), researchers have also turned their attention to the service sector (e.g., Paules 1991; Leidner 1993), the world of high-tech (e.g., Kunda 1991), and the ranks of professionals, managers, and other knowledge

workers (e.g., Pierce 1995). We will discuss many of these studies in forthcoming chapters.

Dilemmas of Ethnography: Access and Ethics

Survey researchers must grapple with wording questions in ways most likely to yield a valid response. Ethnographers do not face this challenge—because they interact extensively with their research subjects, these researchers have opportunities to learn how best to approach a particular topic. They can clarify their questions and ask respondents to do the same with their answers. More important, because ethnographers can observe firsthand what goes on in the workplace, they do not have to rely so heavily on what other people say is occurring. The challenges faced by ethnographers are of a different sort and primarily involve the difficulties associated with gaining entry to work settings.

As Vicki Smith explains, "[g]aining access to American corporations to conduct research on work and employment relations has become a tricky enterprise" (2001b: 15). Organizational gatekeepers are often reluctant to open their doors to researchers because of worries about confidentiality or legal liability or a general fear about how the data are likely to be used. Given this, workplace ethnographers often spend considerable amounts of time and energy and endure multiple frustrating and self-esteem–deflating rejections as they attempt to gain permission to enter a worksite.

For instance, when Pierce approached law firms seeking permission to observe lawyers and their staffs on the job, this permission was denied: "My promise of confidentiality and my stated intent to be as unobtrusive as possible did little to assuage their fears. After several rejections, I realized that overt fieldwork was simply not possible" (1995: 18). Instead, she conducted her study as a "covert fieldworker." She worked as a paralegal in the litigation departments of two law firms and recorded her observations.

Researchers who observe covertly must abide by the American Sociological Association's Code of Ethics regarding deception in research (see Box 3.4). Deception of research subjects is considered ethical only under limited conditions. Most workplace ethnographers do not collect their data covertly (V. Smith 2001b).

Strengths and Limitations of Ethnographic Research

One of the most important messages of this chapter is that no single methodology is best for understanding workers and work. Every methodology brings with it advantages and disadvantages; most methodologies are better at answering some research questions than others. Ethnographies are no different in this regard. As noted above, ethnographic approaches can provide rich, detailed portraits of workers and workplaces. They are especially useful for capturing the social settings and situations of work as they exist naturally. By studying workers within the context of their jobs and workplace, ethnographers can provide information that is not accessible to researchers relying on large-scale surveys or official statistics.

Another strength of ethnographies is the insight they provide into lower-level workers who may lack authority or power within the formal structures of the workplace. Decades of ethnographic research have shown how these workers engage one another on the job and actively participate in shaping their working conditions and lives.

The strengths of ethnographic research are counterbalanced by the limitations of this methodology. Ethnography is a time-consuming, labor-intensive, and exhausting method of data collection and analysis. These qualities deter some researchers. Because the collection of ethnographic data depends upon the researcher having direct access to settings and informants, this methodology may be less successful as a strategy for uncovering the activities, motivations, and actions of dominant groups, who may have the means and motives to shield themselves from researchers. In addition, as the examples discussed in this chapter show, many ethnographic studies of work are case studies, meaning that they focus exclusively on one work setting. As a result, the results of ethnographic research are of limited generalizability. Ethnographies thus are most often used to generate concepts and hypotheses, rather than as a means to systematically test alternatives or discriminate among competing views (Hodson 2001).

In recent years, Hodson and his colleagues (http://www.sociology.ohio-state.edu/people/rdh/Workplace-Ethnography-Project.html) have begun to treat the extensive ethnographic record on the workplace as a data source in its own right. These data are then analyzed quantitatively in ways designed to systematically test hypotheses about workers and their jobs. These efforts reveal the value of using multiple methodologies to advance understanding of workers and the workplace. As Hodson observes: "The study of the workplace is an intellectually vital field in part because it builds on many research traditions and methods of data collection" (2001: 272). Through rigorous use of existing methodologies and creative application of new approaches, researchers have been able to ask and answer many important questions about the workplace.

Methods for Studying Work and Workers: Experiments

Correll's (2004) research described at the beginning of the chapter provides an example of the experimental method applied to the study of work. Recall that her research examines the ways in which cultural beliefs about gender differences in task performance shape women's and men's occupational goals and achievement expectations. Experiments, in Babbie's words, involve

researchers "select[ing] a group of subjects, do[ing] something to them, and observ[ing] the effect of what was done" (2004: 221). Correll's experiments were conducted in a laboratory. Her subjects were male and female college students; they were given information about a (fictitious) task ability and then filled out questionnaires designed to assess the effects of exposure to this information. The questionnaires asked subjects to provide a self-assessment of their task ability, an ability standard for judging themselves to have high ability, and their emerging aspirations related to the task ability.

Another feature of the experimental method exhibited by Correll's study is the use of experimental and control groups. The experimental group is the group of subjects who receive the stimulus; in Correll's research, the stimulus was information about the fictitious ability that linked it with gender. In particular, some of her male and female subjects were told that males, on average, perform better on the test than females. Experiments must also have a control group—that is, a group that does not receive the stimulus. In Correll's study, the control group was represented by the subjects who were told that there was no gender difference in the fictitious ability. With the exception of the information that either linked the task ability with males or explicitly disassociated it with gender, all other information given to the control and experimental groups was exactly the same. This includes other information about the task as well as each subject's (fictitious) score on a test designed to assess task ability.

Because the experimental group is the only one receiving the stimulus, they should respond differently to the items contained in the questionnaire, compared to the control group.

Determining whether this is the case is the way in which researchers assess the effect of the stimulus. In principle, the only difference between the experimental and control groups is the former group's exposure to the stimulus. Hence, when the groups' results differ significantly, researchers conclude that the stimulus had an effect.

Correll (2004) found strong support for her hypotheses. When women and men believed that men, on average, performed better than women on tasks requiring the fictitious ability, men rated their own abilities higher than women and reported more interest in careers requiring this ability. By contrast, among the control group— where women and men were told that there were no gender differences in the fictitious ability— Correll found that women and men did not differ in either their assessments of their performance or their aspirations. In this way, Correll's experiment demonstrated that when tasks or abilities are linked to cultural beliefs about gender differences, these beliefs shape women's and men's assessments of their abilities and their career aspirations. She expects that these processes also operate outside the laboratory in real-world situations as women and men make educational and occupational choices.

Because experimental designs aim to identify one particular effect, while holding constant all other factors, experiments are often conducted in laboratory settings. The benefits of this approach stem from the researcher's ability to control many aspects of the research. Correll (2004), for example, precisely controlled the information her subjects were exposed to, thereby insuring that all subjects received the same information about the fictitious ability and its links to gender. While it is impossible to account for the effects of all extraneous influences, laboratory conditions typically facilitate this goal better than natural settings.

Laboratory settings also have some drawbacks, however. No matter how carefully the experiment is designed, a laboratory setting is always artificial (Babbie 2004). Whether subjects would respond the same way outside the laboratory as inside is always a question. Undergraduate students may be better subjects for experimental research on some kinds of topics rather than others. For example, undergraduates might not be the most suitable subjects for experiments that simulate the hiring process for high-level jobs. Here, students' lack of direct exposure to these kinds of jobs and work situations is likely to limit the external validity of the results. Although laboratory experiments are a valuable methodology, they are not well suited to many of the research questions of interest to sociologists of work.

Another type of experiment is one done "in the field"—outside the laboratory. Field experiments avoid the artificiality of those performed in the laboratory using undergraduate research subjects. In the social sciences, field experiments have played an especially valuable role in uncovering racial (and, to a lesser extent, gender) discrimination in housing, treatment of customers, and employment (Guion 1966; Boggs, Sellers, and Bendick 1993; List 2004; Bertrand and Mullainathan 2004). The results from these studies not only have had intellectual value, but have been used by the courts in discrimination cases.

Discrimination is an extremely difficult concept to measure. Not only are those who practice discrimination unlikely to admit it if asked on a survey or in an interview, but people who themselves have been discriminated against may not know that this has occurred. Applicants for a job almost never know who all of their competitors are, nor do they know how their qualifications have been assessed relative to others. Field experiments (sometimes called "audits"), where job applicants and their qualifications are manipulated by researchers, are ideal for investigating these practices.

An interesting example of a field experiment is Bertrand and Mullainathan's (2004) study of racial discrimination in employment. These researchers (economists) submitted fictitious resumes in response to job ads placed by employers in Boston and Chicago. The resumes were randomly assigned African American—(e.g., Lakisha or Jamal) and white—(e.g., Emily and Greg) sounding names. Resumes with white-sounding names attached received 50 percent more callbacks than those with African American–sounding names. These differences were found regardless of the occupation, industry, and size of the employer. In light of these findings, Betrtrand and Mullainathan (2004) argue that better training programs for African Americans may not do much to reduce racial disparities in employment.

Other field experiments dealing with this topic have sent pairs of "testers" (also referred to as "auditors") into the field to apply for jobs (Bendick, Jackson, and Reinso 1994). Testers are carefully trained beforehand and are matched on all job-relevant criteria (e.g., education, experience), differing only in race or ethnicity (or gender). Examining how far each tester progresses in the job-application process allows researchers to not only identify the extent of employment discrimination, but also better understand how it is expressed. These studies thus reveal an important role for experiments in the sociology of work.

Of all the methodologies discussed in this chapter, experiments are used least often by contemporary sociologists of work. There are at least two reasons for this. First, laboratory experiments are most useful for exploring psychological or social-psychological questions. While some sociologists of work are interested in these issues, they account for only a small part of what sociologists of work find most compelling. Not surprisingly, experimental designs appear much more frequently in the psychological literature on work, reflecting the different emphases of these two disciplines. A second reason was mentioned earlier: The value of laboratory experiments as a means of data collection for sociologists of work is limited when undergraduate students are the only available research subjects.

Summary and Conclusion

This chapter examined the methodologies sociologists use to study workers and the workplace. As we have seen, these methodologies are as diverse as those applied to the study of any other area of social life. We focused particular attention on four methodologies: official statistics, surveys, ethnographies, and experiments. Each has its own set of advantages and disadvantages as a tool for studying workers and the workplace. The choice of methodology depends in part on the research question, but it also depends on other more practical considerations, such as the research budget and time frame.

It is important to understand that these are not methodologies used only by sociologists interested in workers and work. For example, Max Weber, one of the earliest sociologists of work—and an important sociological theorist more generally—relied on comparative historical methods to understand the ascendance of capitalism in the West (Weber 1949 [1905]). Today, comparative historical sociologists interested in work continue to explore these issues and those relating to the development of a global world economy (Mahoney 2004). At the "micro" end of the methodological spectrum, some sociologists of work are beginning to use "experience sampling" as a methodology for understanding how people feel about and respond to particular moments in daily life, from hour to hour during the day, at work and at home. Just as changes in the world of work create new topics and issues for researchers to explore, sociologists are always looking for new ways to answer the research questions that inspire their work.

PART II

THE HISTORICAL DEVELOPMENT
OF WORK

Chapter 4

❧

The Industrial Revolution and Beyond: Culture, Work, and Social Change

Work, in one form or another, is a primordial feature of human life. As part of any culture's survival strategies, humans create not only tools, but also institutional and cultural arrangements that envelop such tools: norms governing who should perform given types of work; customs or laws that define what can be exchanged, when, and under what terms; and notions of honor (and, by implication, shame) that accompany the performance of various types of work. Although each culture tends to define its own work arrangements as "natural," anthropological and historical research indicates just how variable work arrangements are. To take but one example, while our own society often holds medical doctors and surgeons in especially high esteem, the culture of medieval Europe lumped surgeons in with butchers and executioners, affixing to them a "blood taboo" that defined these three trades as unclean (Le Goff 1980). If "work" is a universal feature of human life, the institutional and cultural forms that accompany it can take many forms.

Those who live in the advanced industrial world are most familiar with work in terms of paid employment—that is, labor performed in exchange for a wage. Yet this arrangement is itself a relatively recent invention; it was relatively uncommon even into the eighteenth and nineteenth centuries. Even into the late 1800s, American farmers and workers often regarded wage labor as a morally suspect way of eking out one's living. (Labor unionists often used the term "wage slavery" as a critique of the factory system.) The triumph of wage labor in fact owes much to the Industrial Revolution, which first gripped Great Britain in the late 1700s and eventually launched Western Europe into a position of global dominance. In so doing, the Industrial Revolution set in motion unprecedented shifts in work and economic institutions that have engulfed not only Western Europe and North America, but eventually the entire world. Therefore, to understand work in its peculiarly modern guise requires that we begin our investigation by exploring the massive changes that took hold of work at this historical juncture.

We begin by exploring the cultural meanings that work held prior to industrialization. These meanings, as we will see, were not static, but evolved in ways that actually set the stage for the Industrial Revolution and the coming of the factory system, which in turn have exerted massive effects on virtually all aspects of modern life. An important part of this story involves the sharp separation that arose between home and work, for this division had important effects on gender and intimate life: It positioned men within the public realm of paid employment while confining women workers to unpaid work within the home. This division was fateful, for it gave rise to the traditional notion of the male as breadwinner, which persisted until relatively recent times.

Understanding the Industrial Revolution

It is difficult for us today to grasp the enormity of the institutional and cultural changes that the Industrial Revolution brought in its wake. There had been periods of great expansion and economic growth in previous epochs of history. Some historians point to the importance of such technological developments as the invention of the horse-drawn plow, or water- and wind-driven milling machines, as part and parcel of economic expansions that happened during the preindustrial period of European history. Nor were economic expansions limited to the West. The Qing (pronounced "Ching") dynasty, for example, ruled China for two centuries after the middle 1600s and demonstrated impressive economic growth in the 1700s: Its population doubled in size and enjoyed a standard of living that outstripped the conditions that English and Dutch societies then enjoyed (Goldstone 2002: 348–353). Thus economic growth was hardly new. What *was* unprecedented was the explosive, self-sustaining nature of the industrial expansion that began during the late 1780s.

According to the historian Eric Hobsbawm, what was decisive about the Industrial Revolution

was that "for the first time in human history, the shackles were taken off the productive power of human societies, which henceforth became capable of the constant, rapid, and up to the present limitless multiplication of men, goods and services" (1962: 45). From Hobsbawm's perspective, the Industrial Revolution cannot be conceived as a distinct episode or period in economic and social history. Rather, it involved a "restless, self-sustaining expansion, involving as it does the creation of a mechanized 'factory system' which in turn produces such vast quantities and at such rapidly diminishing cost as to be no longer dependent on existing demand, but to create its own market" (1962: 50). In a sense, the Industrial Revolution inaugurated an era of ongoing expansion—a kind of permanent revolution, to borrow a phrase—that has yet to come to come to a close.

The Meaning of Work in Preindustrial Societies

The triumph of the factory system and of the Industrial Revolution more broadly would have been unimaginable without the unfolding of a centuries-long process that led from classical Greek conceptions of work and leisure, through Judeo-Christian themes of work as moral deliverance, to the Protestant notion of the calling (see Chapter 2). By tracing this cultural evolution we can learn three things. First, we can see just how dramatic were the cultural changes the Industrial Revolution demanded of the laboring masses. Second, we can appreciate how these cultural changes, once spread throughout Western societies, helped advance industrial capitalism, eventually ushering in what one scholar has called "the work society" (de Grazia 1994).

Third, we can begin to see some of the ways in which our contemporary views of work have inherited certain features from societies embedded in the distant past.

One of the earliest conceptions of work that left an imprint on Western society was that of the ancient Greeks. A slave society, ancient Greece was characterized by two key social institutions: the *polis*, or the political realm of government, and the *oikos*, the household (the word *oikos* is in fact the basis for our modern term "economy"). In the Greek worldview, the only honorable forms of work were those that equipped one to participate in the *polis*. Autonomous work within one's *oikos*, such as the cultivation of one's land, met this moral test. But farming was the only manual activity that the ancient Greeks found admirable. Mere toil, undertaken out of economic necessity, was viewed as a degrading activity that ill equipped one to participate in the *polis*; such work was deemed worthy only of a slave. Physical toil was thus viewed with great disdain and as a debilitating involvement that prevented the individual from acquiring the virtues required of all proper citizens.

These themes are evident in the writings of the most important Greek and many Roman philosophers. Thus Plato complained of too many unqualified men being allowed to participate in the *polis* and referred to them as "men with imperfect natures—just as their bodies are mutilated by the arts and crafts, so too are their souls doubled up and spoiled as a result of being in mechanical occupations" (Applebaum 1992: 61; see de Grazia 1994; Gamst 1995). Likewise, Aristotle held that "none of the occupations followed by a populace which consists of mechanics, shop-keepers, and day labourers, leaves any room for excellence" (Applebaum 1992: 65). From the

Greek point of view, those who were forced to toil out of sheer need were thereby unfit to rule, for their souls would be "doubled up and spoiled." Only those who were free from such necessity, and who could enjoy the contemplation that unlimited leisure made possible, could cultivate the habits needed to rule in a wise and effective manner.

With the rise of the Judeo-Christian era, this conception of "work as degradation" underwent a significant change. In the Old Testament, for example, Genesis gives us a distinctively different and more contradictory conception of work. Here, after all, we encounter "a God who *works*, who creates the universe, and must rest; who creates humans in his image, placing them in Eden to 'dress and keep it'..." (Le Goff 1980: 78). At the same time, however, when humans engage in sin and are cast out of Eden, God curses them with the ever-present need to toil (as in God's edict that only "[i]n the sweat of thy brow shalt thou eat bread"). In this biblical account, the notion of work has grown more complex: The world (including humanity itself) is viewed as the product of God's own work—a shift that "blesses the idea of labor" (Ovitt 1986: 487). Yet work also acquires a punitive element, as befits those who engaged in sin.

Christianity continued this twofold conception of work, in which labor appeared as both an ennobling activity and a form of atonement. In the writings of the early apostles, we even begin to encounter a conception of work as a means of spiritual fulfillment and moral purification. Indeed, what the Greeks had most valued—a life of leisure and contemplation and of distance from manual toil—had, by the early medieval period, been redefined as a sinful tendency that was repugnant in the eyes of God. Christian theologians such as Saint Augustine warned against idleness, arguing that "only those who labor and produce an excess of goods can be in a position to practice charity rather than to receive it" (Ovitt 1986: 492).

This moral precept to work on behalf of God was not simply a free-floating doctrine. Rather, beginning in the sixth century, it was put into practice within Christian monasteries spread throughout Western Europe. Monastic orders, especially the one led by Saint Benedict, engaged in a rigid regimen of daily tasks that served to purify their members' souls. The first duty of a monk was one of prayer and worship, but the virtuous effect of manual labor was stressed, partly because it provided training in the practice of self-denial and partly because the products of such labor were materially useful in spreading the word of God. In fact, monasticism helped to fuel economic expansion throughout much of Europe, as its infusion of moral virtue into economic activity inspired such new technologies as wind- and water-driven milling implements, canals, and irrigation methods, whose appearance owed much to the discipline and moral regulation the laboring monks provided.

The broader effects of the monastic orders made themselves felt by the twelfth century, as the "spectacle of the monk at labor impressed his contemporaries in its favor," prompting a broader cultural shift that "raised labor in general esteem" (Le Goff 1980: 80–81). As this new ethos of labor spread to artisans, merchants, and craftsmen generally, the notion of labor as imparting a form of dignity took hold. Summarizing this shift, Le Goff writes that "with the beginning of the 13th century, the working saint was losing ground, giving way to the saintly worker" (1980:115; see also Ovitt 1986; Applebaum 1992; de Grazia 1994).

The Protestant Reformation signaled a massive break with the Roman Catholic Church, but in many ways the doctrines of Protestant theologians like Martin Luther and John Calvin only reaffirmed core themes concerning labor that had long gestated within the Christian fold. Thus, Lutheran criticisms of the Catholic Church rested on the Vatican's tendency to luxuriate in illicit wealth and pleasure, which Luther and his followers condemned. By articulating a doctrine that emphasized the purifying nature of hard work, the Protestant Reformation continued the historical trend that invested work with spiritual significance. To pursue idle pleasures, or to languish in wasteful activities, was to commit sinful affronts to God's will. "In the things of this life," concluded one sixteenth-century theologian, "the laborer is most like to God" (Rodgers 1974: 8).

This spiritualization of labor, once established across the Western European landscape, eventually went so far as to define work as the cardinal virtue through which one defined one's identity, quite apart from any theological significance. The point is evident in the writings of later moralists such as Thomas Carlyle, who in 1843 wrote these words, effusively exclaiming the virtues of the productive life:

> Whatsoever of morality and of intelligence, what of patience, perseverance, faithfulness; of method, insight, ingenuity, energy; in a word, whatsoever of Strength the man had in mind will lie written in the Work he does…Produce! Produce! Were it but the pitifullest, most infinitesimal fraction of a product, produce it, in God's name! (Rodgers 1974: xiv)

Thus was born an ethos that sanctified work—a cultural construct that was well adapted to the moral compulsions needed by "the work society" (de Grazia 1994).

Several broad observations can be made on the basis of this brief historical discussion. First, the Christian conception of work served to turn Greek ideals on their head. Leisure and contemplation, which for the Greeks constituted the highest virtues, were recast by Christianity as sinful indulgences. In the Christian view, it was only through productive toil that deliverance might be found. Second, however, certain elements of the Greek conception of toil did persist, not least its tendency to affix a stigma on forms of work that were held to be degrading. The Protestant Reformation sought to sanctify all forms of work—both the humblest artisan and the most prosperous merchant—yet the broader tendency in Western conceptions of work has been to regard toil in a twofold manner: not only as an ennobling activity, but also as a curse born of human frailty and sin. Interestingly, the French and English word for work—travail— conveys this very double meaning, referring both to arduous toil and excruciating pain. The word descends from the Latin *tripalium,* which referred to a three-pronged instrument of torture that was used to inflict pain on nonbelievers.

The Rise of the Factory System

Yet, if Christianity defined viewed work as a spiritual activity through which one could draw closer to God, many of its worshippers would have been appalled at the world their beliefs helped bring into being. For, much as Max Weber argued (see Chapter 2), by sanctifying work, Christianity (and especially Protestantism) helped open up a path that led to the Satanic mills, which were rife with cruelty and harsh

exploitation. This point can be seen through a brief discussion of the origins of the factory system in Western Europe.

Commercial manufacturing had established a presence throughout England and other Western European nations well before the Industrial Revolution was even conceivable. In Britain especially, agriculture itself had undergone widespread commercialization, since land that had traditionally been used by peasants and tenant farmers was forcibly converted to more profitable use (for example, the grazing of sheep) in conjunction with the woolen trades, giving rise to weaving and textile workshops within many villages in the English countryside. Such enterprises (sometimes called "proto-industrial" settings) were marked by two important features. First, virtually all were of relatively modest scale and were largely dependent on methods and practices employed within artisanal workshops of the medieval period. Second, even into the seventeenth and early eighteenth centuries, the scope of commercial activity was governed by social and cultural norms that established powerful limits on economic exchange. Thus deeply established rules stemming from medieval guilds and trades defined how commerce was to proceed. Indeed, economic historians and anthropologists have agreed that it was only with the momentous changes of the nineteenth century that the unconstrained pursuit of gain through the marketplace managed to break through such traditional constraints (Polanyi 1944).

The process happened gradually at first. As towns grew in size and trade expanded its reach, merchants adopted small-scale production methods as best they could. One such method was the "putting out" system, in which merchants distributed unfinished goods (yarn, cloth, dye) to artisans and farmers in towns scattered throughout the countryside. In such cottage industries, workers earned piece rates that were paid upon the completion of finished goods for the merchant, who then brought them to market. Under this system, merchants had few means of controlling either the pace or the method of production, as workers were located well beyond their supervision. Understandably, merchants began to concentrate work together under the same roof, thus combining artisans who had previously labored in isolation, either in their own shops or else on farmland. In this case (which Marx called "simple cooperation"), the work process retained its artisanal character even though production was driven more closely by commercial goals. As Piore and Sabel (1984; Sabel and Zeitlin 1997) have pointed out, in many European cities such proto-industrial workshops thrived for a time, supporting local commercial activity even after the Industrial Revolution had begun, especially in trades producing high-quality silks, cutlery, and other fine goods.

Pressed by the spur of market competition, merchants operating outside such luxury niches sought out ways of increasing the productivity that could be secured from their workforce. One important way of doing this was to develop a more specialized division of labor within the workshop. It was this system of finely specialized tasks that Adam Smith memorialized in his account of a pin factory, in *The Wealth of Nations* (1991 [1776]), and which Marx later called termed "manufacturing"—literally, production by hand. The notion here was that even using the same hand-powered tools, laborers could produce far more in a given period, and at lower wages, if the workshop adopted a sharp subdivision of labor that assigned to each worker a highly specialized

task (for discussion of the assembly line, see Chapter 5). Because of the dexterity each worker could develop in relation to a detailed task and the efficiency gains that stem from the coordination of tasks, early factories using such manufacturing systems surpassed artisanal methods even though they inherited the same hand-powered instruments of production.

Building on these shifts in the organization of factory labor, the Industrial Revolution in turn dramatically transformed the source of power or energy on which the tools and productive instruments relied. This was a profoundly important change, for it revolutionized the character of the work process and along with it the relation between the worker and the tool.

Prior to the Industrial Revolution, the productive power of a farm, workshop, or mill was dependent on sources of energy that were driven by wind, water, and animals (including human). As noted by the historical sociologist Jack Goldstone (2002), such reliance on existing local resources placed major constraints on the scale and pace of economic activity: Productive power was limited to whatever sources were ready to hand, and these were inevitably scattered about the countryside: a river here, a water mill there. With the chain of scientific discoveries and technical inventions that gathered force in seventeenth- and eighteenth-century England, and which eventually led to James Watt's steam engine in the late 1780s, these constraints were suddenly thrown aside. The advent of steam-powered engines made it possible for manufacturers to exploit the power of fossil fuels—especially coal—which could then be used with much greater force than ever before.

One result was a huge multiplication of the nation's productive powers as steam engines were harnessed to cotton spinning (thus supplying the burgeoning textile industry), iron smelting and molding (to forge rails for transport), grain milling (for the mass production of baked goods and animal feed), brick making (to build yet more factories, offices, and homes), and machines for transport (locomotives and sea-faring vessels). The first to industrialize in this manner, Great Britain quickly became the "workshop of the world," exporting the lion's share of the world's cotton, iron, and steel and accounting for a massively disproportionate share of the world's energy consumption.

A second result was an equally significant transformation in the class structure of English society. As merchants, commercial landowners, financiers, and craftsmen engaged in production for the marketplace, wealth began to accumulate in the hands of the commercial classes that grew rapidly in the industrial towns and cities. A measure of such shifts can be found in the emergence of new terms to capture the new realities. Arguing that "words are witnesses" to historic shifts, Hobsbawm provides a brief catalog of terms that may be familiar to us now, but which were either "invented, or gained their modern meanings" only following the beginning of the Industrial Revolution. On this list he includes the following terms: industrialist, aristocracy, middle class, working class, scientist, engineer, journalism, liberal and conservative [as political terms], ideology, strike, and pauperism. "To imagine the modern world without these words," he concludes, "is to measure the profundity of the revolution which broke out between 1789 and 1848 and forms the greatest transformation in human history" since humans invented agriculture and metal working (1962: 17).

Part and parcel of these shifts was the emergence of a new class of wage laborers. No longer embedded in the customs of artisanal production, and with no hope of attaining the status of either master craftsman (which implied the ownership of one's own shop) or even journeyman (which did not), factory workers grew in number—and, many argued, shame and degradation. For as industrialization proceeded, so too did there occur a deterioration in the working conditions of many workers, a lengthening of the working day, and a growing reliance on child labor; at times, whole families were compelled to work side by side, earning wages that barely enabled them to survive. It was in response to these conditions that Friedrich Engels, colleague and collaborator with Marx, wrote his classic analysis, *The Condition of the Working Class in England* (1993 [1845]), which chronicled the squalid conditions under which industrial workers often lived.

Historians have long engaged in debate over the consequences of the Industrial Revolution for the workers of the nineteenth century. Some analysts advocate a simple thesis of *absolute* "emiseration" (impoverishment), in which workers experienced an actual decline in living standards and conditions of existence as economic competition led employers to lengthen the working day and drive down workers' wages. Others argue that emiseration did occur, but only in a *relative* sense, in that although living conditions may have improved for workers, their improvements nonetheless failed even remotely to keep pace with the growing affluence enjoyed by the more privileged or propertied classes within British society. Still others argue that what is especially critical, and what cannot be decided by even the most careful analysis of wage levels and caloric intake, was the culturally defined *experience* of the new factory system, which forcibly disrupted or destroyed whole ways of life and forms of community that had been established in British cities and towns for centuries.

A brilliant example of this last approach can be found in the classic work by E. P. Thompson, *The Making of the English Working Class* (1964). In a profound and moving analysis, Thompson shows how common it was for members of proud trades in the textile and woolen industries to be wholly and suddenly ruined as mechanization took control of their crafts, compelling them to work ever-longer hours, often alongside their spouses and children, for wages that often fell below subsistence (forcing many onto poor relief). Thompson contends that the impact of industrial capitalism involved much more than simply wages, hours, and living conditions. What needs to be stressed was the *perception* of catastrophic change among factory workers of all strata. Thompson shows how the imposition of a harsh and foreign work discipline on industrial workers, together with the shattering of their customary rounds of social and family life, imbued industrialization with an element of misery that cannot be deduced from their material conditions alone.

Thompson's analysis is instructive in a further way, in that it seeks to show that the effects of the Industrial Revolution in Great Britain did not unfold in a vacuum, but rather were powerfully shaped by the social and political context in which they occurred. Most important, Thompson observes, was that the rise of Britain's factory system occurred in the shadow of the French Revolution of 1789, when artisans and peasants violently overturned the French nobility and aristocracy, seeking to establish a democratic republic but eventually unleashing a reign of terror that provoked widespread fear in the British aristocracy and rising middle

classes. The result was that the British elite adamantly resisted every call for the extension of political rights to the English working classes, whose members were denied the rights to vote, to exercise free speech, and to assemble or to organize on their own behalf. England's Industrial Revolution thus tended to erect powerful boundaries that excluded the nation's working class from the mainstream of society, making workers feel like outcasts in their own society (Thompson 1964).

This point is important to any understanding of how English workers responded to their plight. As they encountered a lengthening of their working day, the exploitation of child labor, and chronically insufficient wages, workers had virtually no legitimate means of redressing their situation. When desperate petitions and appeals to Parliament went unheeded, many workers resorted to underground methods of collective mobilization and resistance, the most interesting expression of which was the phenomenon that came to be known as Luddism. Although this phenomenon has come to be viewed in an entirely negative light—the term now widely conjures up images of an irrational opposition to new technology and to progress itself—more recent scholarship suggests that Luddism was a far more complicated and interesting phenomenon than has so often been assumed. As such it warrants a brief consideration in its own right.

Luddism Revisited

Luddism was an explosive and at times a quasi-insurrectionary movement that began to appear in the English Midlands in the first decade of the nineteenth century. The earliest reports begin to appear in 1802, increasing in frequency during the ensuing decade. The movement took its name from its imaginary leader, General Ned Ludd, whose identity served to unify the members of mill villages throughout much of the English Midlands. The context in which these rebellions arose was one of war-induced hardship (England had been at war against France's Napoleon, with devastating effects on English exports). More than this, employers were fervently uprooting those customary craft arrangements that had secured the livelihood of skilled tradesmen in the woolen and cloth trades. Many of these arrangements were codified in law but were forcibly rescinded by manufacturers eager to increase their profits. To do so, many relied on new mechanical implements (especially wide weaving frames, for example) that undercut the need for skilled tradesmen and sometimes cheapened the value of both the final goods and the workmen's situation.

In response to these challenges to their traditional position, and lacking any rights of assembly, workmen often petitioned Parliament for redress, testifying about the violations of the law that had occurred and about the fraudulent practices they witnessed (in which cheapened goods were sold as first quality). Rather than respond, members of Parliament often accused the workmen of conspiratorial acts. Finding no redress, and faced with the extinction of their way of life, workmen resorted to an underground movement that directly challenged the factory owners' practices. Where owners refused to operate in conformity with traditional practices, Luddites engaged in energetic and highly targeted bouts of machine breaking or—where owners were especially defiant—arson aimed at whole workshops. Here is an example of a letter, written on April 12, 1812, to the owner of a cloth dressing factory that had installed dressing machines which the Luddites regarded as an unacceptable effort to destroy their very livelihood (the spelling and emphasis are in the original document):

> In justice to humanity We think it our Bound Duty to give you this Notice that if you do Not Cause those Dressing Machines to be Remov'd Within the Bounds of Seven Days…your factory and all that it Contains Will and Shall Surely Be Set on fire.…it is Not our Desire to do you the Least Injury But we are fully Determin'd to Destroy Both Dressing Machines and Steam Looms, Let *Who Will* be the Owners. (Thompson 1964: 567)

No violence against persons was committed, and no destruction was aimed at machines that conformed to what the Luddites viewed as honorable practices. What the Luddites were doing was protesting against a new social and economic order that seemed sure to destroy not only their trades, but also the very fabric of their lives (See Box 4.1).

References to the Luddites have in the past portrayed them as members of an irrational and spontaneous mob that was driven by a simple-minded view of a market economy. In this view, the Luddites sought merely to turn back the tide of social change and to obstruct the course of industrial development or progress (a peculiarly value-laden word). Yet more recent scholarship has suggested that such characterizations often took police reports at their word and often sympathized with the middle classes' fear of the dangerous classes generally (a good example of the concept of the "hierarchy of credibility," as discussed in Chapter 1). As Thompson emphasizes,

---

BOX 4.1 *Learning from the Luddites*

We can gain a sense of the Luddites' outlook from the following song, "General Ludd's Triumph," which reveals both the specific target of their protest and the values that underlay their movement as a whole.

The guilty may fear but no vengeance he aims
At the honest man's life or estate,
His wrath is entirely confined to wide frames
And to those that old prices abate.
These Engines of mischief were sentenced to die
By unanimous vote of the Trade
And Ludd who can all opposition defy
Was the Grand executioner made.

★ ★ ★

He may censure great Ludd's disrespect for
    the Laws
Who ne'er for a moment reflects
That *foul imposition* alone was the cause
Which produced these unhappy effects.
Let the haughty no longer the humble oppress
Then shall Ludd sheath his conquering sword,
His grievances instantly meet with redress,
Then peace will be quickly restored.
Let the wise and the great lend their aid
    and advice
Nor e'er the assistance withdraw
Till full fashioned work at the old fashioned price
Is established by Custom and Law.

Then the Trace when this arduous context is o'er
Shall raise in full splendour its head,
And colting and cutting and squaring no more
Shall deprive honest workmen of bread. (From Thompson 1964: 534)

What can we see from this song? First, that the Luddites were careful to insist that no one need fear their actions except those who have violated the industrial behavior that has been established in "Custom and Law." Only where questionable practices had been used—the "engines of mischief" the workers rejected, involving "wide frames," "colting, cutting, and squaring"— would the workers take aim. Second, the Luddites saw themselves as asserting their right to freedom from industrial despotism, in which "the haughty . . . the humble oppress." Finally, and in opposition to what they viewed as "foul imposition," the Luddites were insisting on their right to an economic system that respected their position as honest, dignified working men. Although many have objected to their tactics and portrayed them as irrationally opposed to technological change, scholars have increasingly viewed Luddism as harboring an interesting demand from which we might conceivably learn: their insistence that the structure of work correspond to the needs and wishes of the workers themselves.

---

the Luddites were by no means undiscriminating in their thinking, nor simply backward or reactionary in their outlook:

Their opposition to new machinery does not appear to have been unthinking or absolute; proposals were in the air for the gradual introduction of the machinery, with alternative employment found for displaced men, or for a tax of 6*d* per yard upon cloth dressed by machinery, to be used as a fund for the unemployed seeking work. (Thompson 1964: 526)

Far from representing simply a blind or reactionary lashing out against modernity, Luddism was often a sophisticated movement, requiring widespread organization, discipline, knowledge of markets, and community support. Moreover, it was motivated not only by a backward-looking effort to restore communal economic traditions, but also by a forward-looking effort to institute a collective order that respected the workmen's dignity. The nature of the movement was not narrowly framed in terms of craft privilege, then, but rather comprised a broad attack against the *laissez faire* political economy and the factory system it sought to impose (Calhoun 1982).

Although many analysts have objected to the Luddites' tactics (indeed, some would label them terrorists), some scholars have suggested that their actions hold certain positive lessons for us even today. First, theirs was a spirited, humanistic critique of the factory system that sought to affirm a principle that might well warrant consideration even today: the notion that work ought to conform to the workers' own preferences, rather than to the unbridled demands of the marketplace or wealthy factory owners. Second, their actions provide a revealing contrast with the course of industrialization in the United States. Thus, the United States lacks any significant history of machine breaking and had no underground rebellion against the rising factory system. The question naturally emerges as to why. Although some have explained this contrast on cultural grounds (for example, pointing to the greater influence of entrepreneurial values in the United States), we believe that a stronger explanation follows Thompson's lead and points to the timing of economic and political change. The Luddites resorted to industrial violence because they lacked any legitimate means of dissent: When the Industrial Revolution occurred in Great Britain, workers had no voting rights, no rights of assembly, and no real powers of citizenship. Indeed, these rights were not truly won in England until after the beginning of the twentieth century. By contrast, in the United States, industrialization occurred in a context where working men had *already* secured certain elementary political rights: The ballot had already been won by white working men, who also enjoyed the right to free speech. The argument here is that the existence of the ballot box helped to incorporate American working men into the emerging industrial order, providing a heightened sense of citizenship and social incorporation even as economic institutions evolved. In the famous phrase of historian Alan Dawley (1980), in the United States, the "ballot box was the coffin of [oppositional] class consciousness." A fuller discussion of the rise of mass production in the United States, and American workers' response to it, is provided in Chapter 5.

Gender, Family, and the Factory System: The Rise of the Male Breadwinner Norm

The consequences of the Industrial Revolution were by no means limited to the sphere of production. In fact, the very distinctions that took shape between production and consumption, work and home, or public and private life were themselves largely products of the Industrial Revolution. Precisely how these distinctions congealed seems especially significant today, at a time when traditional conceptions of work, gender, and family life have begun to shift in far-reaching ways. For in truth, many of the apparently timeless or "natural" distinctions we have inherited from the past (such as the tradition of the "male breadwinner" norm) first came into being in response to the rise of industrial capitalism and are thus less than a century and a half old.

Prior to the Industrial Revolution, two interrelated features characterized the laboring household. One was that throughout most of preindustrial Europe households were structured in terms of *patriarchy*, a system that was deeply engrained within political and religious institutions and that compelled wives and daughters to submit to control by men (Hartmann 1975–76; Rose 1992). In practice, the father and the husband represented the household within the community, had control over the family's property, and supervised the family's economic activities. More was involved than sheer economics, however, for patriarchy implied a powerful system of gender symbolism that defined widely held conceptions of masculinity and femininity. Within artisan households for example, the prevailing notions of masculinity were closely bound up with the possession of skill, the independence this provided, and the ability to pass on one's trade to one's son.

The second feature of most laboring households existed alongside such patriarchal norms: the fact that it was the household itself that was the core productive unit. Whether performed in rural settings or in household-based workshops within the towns, work was generally conducted within the home and by members of the family laboring as a joint production unit. A sharp division typically existed between men's and women's tasks, as "men worked at what were considered more skilled tasks, the women processing the raw materials or finishing the end product" (Hartmann 1975–76: 150). Yet even in households affected by the rise of commercial activity, goods were produced within the family, reflecting "a deeply ingrained sense of family

members as contributors to a joint production unit" (Seccombe 1986: 63, 65).

With the rise of the Industrial Revolution, both of these characteristics rapidly began to unravel at one and the same time. As the growth of centralized factory employment grew more pronounced, rural laborers and artisans were drawn out of the system of household production, generating a sharp separation between home and work. Although early factories often employed whole families alongside one another (Burawoy 1985), the general tendency was for family members to be employed as individual wage laborers, employed wherever work could be found. This development posed major challenges to family life, not least because the rhythms of factory production imposed great hardships on the care of infant children. But the movement of work from the household into the factory also began to undermine the patriarchal norms that served to define the proper "place" that men and women held within society.

With the growth of factory employment, fathers often lost control over their children, for they could no longer transmit land or skilled trades to their offspring. Moreover, children began to leave home and work independently, rather than being "sent" out to work. Even more important, out of necessity women began to seek out employment, not as members of a family but as individuals beyond direct control of their fathers or their husbands. A double challenge developed that threatened to undercut patriarchal institutions. In economic terms, since women were almost universally paid substantially lower wages than their male counterparts, the specter arose in many towns and industries of labor competition along gender lines, with men being pitted against lower-paid female rivals. Especially in labor-intensive fields throughout the textile industries, factory owners often sought to hire women workers in place of men, both to reap labor savings and to exert fuller control over their workforce (since women were widely deemed to provide a more pliable workforce). The cultural dislocations that resulted are well described by Seccombe (1986: 67, emphasis added; see also Hartmann 1975–76; Rose 1992):

> Increasingly, factory employment took women away from the protection of their fathers and husbands, fostering extra-familial sex-mixing in anonymous urban settings. Many were offended by the dress and cheeky demeanour of proletarian women, not only at work but getting to and from work, and in their leisure-time as well. What would become of factory girls who used their wages to live away from home in rented accommodation of their own choosing, cohabiting with one another in rough neighborhoods and commercial districts in rooming houses that were not adequately supervised? *Who could say where all this might lead?*

Responding to this twofold (economic and cultural) threat, working class men struggled to maintain some semblance of their traditional privileges, with effects that persisted for more than a century.

Especially in the skilled trades, working class organizations mobilized a far-reaching effort to confront the economic and cultural challenges they faced. Their efforts, which began to gather force in the 1830s and 1840s, generally took three forms. First, petitioning Parliament and their employers, working men sought to define women workers as in need of protective legislation that sharply limited the hours during which

they could be employed and required special safety and health regulations. Second, by defining trade union membership as a necessary condition of employment, yet by refusing to admit women to the trade, union leaders either directly or indirectly barred the employment of women in the same occupations as men. Third, to justify these actions, working men invoked a moral conception that borrowed from the cultural constructs of the Victorian middle class family, which had defined women as having no proper place within the labor market. What working men essentially argued was that they, too, deserved a "family wage"—that is, income levels that were high enough so that men could protect their women against the rigors of the labor market. Third, many working men's organizations publicly decried the emasculation which the employment of women imposed on them. Labor historian Sonya Rose (1992) recounts instances in which men walked picket lines while pushing baby carriages, in this way publicizing the symbolic threat they perceived from factories that hired women in their place. The logic that working men often used found culmination in this statement, made by the leader of the British Trades Union Congress in 1875:

> [The goal of the labour movement must be to] bring about a condition…where wives and daughters would be in their proper sphere at home, instead of being dragged into competition for livelihood with the great and strong men of the world. (Seccombe 1986: 55)

The results were generally highly effective. Faced with the disruption of patriarchal structures, both economically and culturally, working class men led a broad historical effort that reaffirmed their labor market positions, encouraged the seg-regation of women into sex-segregated jobs, or else denied women access to all but the lowest paid positions in the labor market, thus "sharp-ening the distinction between the breadwin-ning capacities of men and the domestic duties of women" (Creighton 1996: 323).

Social scientists, feminist historians, and other scholars have continued to debate the spe-cific features of these developments. Some schol-ars have questioned whether the working class men had any alternative but to exclude women workers from their trades. From this point of view, efforts to include women within trade unions, and to establish equal wages, were most often doomed to fail, since employers generally responded to these strategies by simply refusing to hire women at such elevated wages. For this rea-son, many women workers were actually suspi-cious of "equal pay" policies when union leaders advanced them. Other scholars have argued that the establishment of a "family wage," in which the man serves as breadwinner and the woman as the homemaker, was in fact a triumph not just for men but for working class people generally (Humphries 1977; Horrell and Humphries 1995). The reasoning here is that the family wage actually served the interests of *all* workers—men, women and children—by protecting the most vulnerable groups of workers against market-based exploita-tion. From this point of view, the family wage began to put working class families—or at least, the more affluent among their ranks—on a more equal footing with the middle class.

Such debates should not obscure the out-come of these historical developments, which had massive consequences for the nature of industrial capitalism, gender relations, and the structure of family life for generations to come.

What this broad historical process did was to reaffirm traditional patriarchal notions concern-ing men's centrality within productive activity. Thus reaffirmed, the male breadwinner norm "detached women from the hub of productive life and relegated them to the rump of economic activities that remained domestic: primarily the administration of consumption and the manage-ment of reproduction" (Horrell and Humphries 1995: 89). Although women continued to work, and did so in large numbers, for a century or more their labor market activities were defined as peripheral in importance, as discretionary (even when their earnings were vital to the family's subsistence), or even as signaling a moral failure on the part of the man, who was judged to be an inadequate breadwinner.

The rise of the breadwinner norm had effects that reach from the Industrial Revolution into our own time. As Reskin and Padavic observed (1994: 23), because this norm

> assigned men to the labor force and women to the home, [it] encouraged employers to structure jobs on the assumptions that all permanent work-ers were men and that all men had stay-at-home wives. These assumptions freed workers (that is, male workers) from domestic responsibilities so they could work 12- to 14-hour days. These assumptions also bolstered the belief that domes-tic work was women's responsibility, even for women who were employed outside the home.

Formed in the wake of the male breadwinner norm, the structure of work came to be based on what Williams has called a "system of domestic-ity" that has only recently been challenged (2000, p. 20). This system embodies three elements that hold great significance for the structure of work generally: first, that employers are entitled to demand an ideal (male) worker who is insulated from domestic demands; second, that it is the right—indeed, even the duty—of male employees to conform to this ideal; and third, that the lives of mothers should be oriented around nurturance rather than paid employment. Women and men will of course debate the choices that seem appropriate in their own lives, but that is indeed the point: What the emergence of the male breadwinner norm did—once it was established as a key part of industrial capitalism—was precisely to narrow the choices that women might be able to make.

Conclusion

The coming of the Industrial Revolution had massive effects on Western societies. It built on cultural developments, to be sure. But in turn, it also reshaped them in far-reaching ways. First and at the broadest level, the Industrial Revolution solidified the West's position of global dominance, setting the stage for the extension of Western colonial and neo-colonial power throughout Africa, Asia, and Latin America. Building on the cultural developments that preceded it, the Industrial Revolution literally fueled the growth of a type of society that celebrated work, originally in religious terms, but eventually in terms that became ends in themselves.

A key point that historians have debated is whether the Industrial Revolution and the era of mass production was in fact inevitable (Piore and Sabel 1984). It is of course tempting to see the past as prelude—that is, to see previous developments as necessarily leading toward the familiar world of mass production, massive corporations, and the dominance of a market economy. But we need to be wary of such deterministic views. Did the era of mass production triumph because of its superior efficiency? Or were there other influences involved, with the course of Western development implicitly shaped by social, cultural, political, and even military institutions quite apart from economic efficiency? Are there in fact multiple paths that led (and, arguably, still lead) toward modernity and beyond? Although such debates are not easily resolved, they do serve the useful function of reminding us that industrialization is at its heart not only an economic but also a human or moral accomplishment—one that is shaped by existing conceptions of virtue and sin, discipline and leisure, masculinity and femininity.

A final point that emerges here concerns the possible "end" point of the Industrial Revolution. As we have seen, industrial capitalism has instituted an era of restless, ongoing expansion via the mass production of goods and services. Initially, it took root in Western societies. But in recent decades it has broadened its reach, bringing the developing world much more directly into its grasp, not only as a supplier of raw materials and labor, but now as a center of industrial activity and heavy manufacturing. As the entire world embraces the Industrial Revolution, questions about its fundamental nature and logic, or about alternative forms of economic organization, will cease to seem like academic abstractions, for the environmental consequences of endlessly expanded mass production must inevitably be faced. Precisely how industrialization can accommodate environmental concerns and what forms of governance at the global level will be needed to foster such accommodations are likely to become increasingly pressing concerns as modern industry spreads into every corner of the globe.

Chapter 5

The Second Industrial Revolution: Mass Production and Labor Management

We live in a world in which we take for granted the mass production of goods, whether these are computers, cars, DVD players, or processed chickens. We also know that these products are made on assembly lines (although few of us have ever seen an assembly line, let alone worked on one). We can gain an appreciation of the distinctive characteristics of assembly-line production, and the demands it makes on workers, by considering the following description of the mass production of Dell computers at the company's factory in Austin, Texas:

> Inside Dell, the world's largest computer maker, executives study the assembly process with the intensity of Alfred Kinsey and his researchers. They wheel in video equipment to examine a work team's every movement, looking for any extraneous bends or wasted twists. Designers give one another high-fives for eliminating a single screw from a product, because that represents a savings of roughly four seconds per machine built—the time they've calculated it takes an employee, on average, to use the pneumatic screwdriver dangling above his or head.
>
> Computer software clocks the assembly-line performance of workers, whether they're putting together PC's or the servers and storage equipment that Dell sells to large companies. The most able are declared "master builders," and then videotaped so that others may watch and learn. The weak are told that it takes a special set of talents to cut it on the Dell factory floor—and shown the door. (Rivlin 2004:)

The features of assembly-line production that this article describes—the focus on saving seconds and eliminating unnecessary motions, the monitoring of workers, and the dismissal of those who cannot maintain the required pace—have scarcely changed in the nearly 100 years since Henry Ford's workers began assembling cars on a moving conveyer belt. The big change has been in workers' acceptance of assembly-line routine. At the beginning of the twentieth century this form of work and this way of working were radically different from all other forms of industrial production. Even for those workers accustomed to the routines of factory production, the assembly line signaled a qualitative shift in their daily activities because it now required them to work at a pace dictated by a moving belt.

In this chapter we consider two main questions that build on the previous discussion of the Industrial Revolution. First, how did mass production—most prominently represented by the assembly line—come about in the United States? In other words, how and why was the assembly line invented? Second, how did workers get used to working on the line, given that its work rhythms were so different from other kinds of factory work? In other words, how did employers persuade workers to tolerate working at a pace that was not of their own choosing and over which they had no control?

In answering the first question, we will emphasize the impact of Frederick Winslow Taylor, the founder of scientific management, and of Henry Ford, the pioneer of the automobile assembly line. Taylor showed how the work of skilled craftsmen could be transformed into unskilled and semi-skilled jobs. Ford demonstrated that goods made up of complicated parts and machinery could be mass produced on an assembly line. In answering the second question, we will show that workers did not accept assembly-line jobs easily or willingly. Workers in the mass-production industries fought to improve their conditions of work and of employment for more than two decades following the introduction of the assembly line. In particular, they sought to organize themselves into labor unions to represent their interests. Employers, in turn, experimented with new philosophies of personnel management, including welfare capitalism and the human relations approach, in an attempt to gain the cooperation of their workers. It was not until employers agreed to recognize their employees' labor unions—a topic that we turn to in Chapter 10—that the two sides reached a kind of truce that enabled them to settle their differences through negotiation and bargaining rather than battling it out in the factories and on

the streets. What we see, then, is that the rise of mass production in the United States was a deeply conflicted and often coercive process to which workers did not readily consent.

The Rise of Mass Production

The Craftsmen's Reign

Before factories were introduced in the United States at the end of the eighteenth century, people made most of the commodities they needed to consume at home. For specialized or hard-to-make products, they turned to skilled craftsmen in their workshops. The earliest factories were the textile mills established in New England in the 1790s. Over the course of the next seventy years, the factory system was extended to the manufacture of a variety of products, including steel, shoes, firearms, sewing machines, carriages and wagons, watches, and agricultural tools. Many of these early factories represented a kind of compromise between the old methods of craft production in workshops and the new system of factory production. Foremen were given responsibility for production decisions, but their authority was limited by their need to gain the cooperation of skilled craftsmen, who followed their own well-established work rules and practices (Jacoby 1985).

Skilled craftsmen in the nineteenth century generally enjoyed considerable power and autonomy in the workplace. The reason for this was their knowledge of the product and the manufacturing process; without their cooperation there was no production. Craftsmen demonstrated their independence through a self-enforced code of conduct—a "moral code," as Montgomery (1979) described it. One part of the code specified that every craftsman should keep his output within a fixed limit or quota so as to avoid competition among themselves or any expectation from employers of higher productivity. Another aspect of the moral code was the understanding that a worker should not work when a boss or foreman was watching; to do so was considered unmanly.

In the period after the Civil War, the craftsmen's power and their moral code proved increasingly unacceptable to a new generation of American industrialists. Owners of steel mills, followed by their counterparts in the automobile, electrical, and chemical industries, were eager to introduce new technologies, even if these meant replacing skilled craftsmen. In the emerging steel industry, men such as Andrew Carnegie, the founder of Carnegie Steel, and William Sellers, the head of Midvale Steel, were quick to adopt the new Bessemer process—a production technique invented by an Englishman, Sir Henry Bessemer—in order to mass produce steel. Their goal was to satisfy the enormous demand for steel from the railroads and other steel users. They had little patience with craftsmen who chose to restrict output or who refused to work when being watched. If necessary, they were willing to use force to end the hold of skilled craftsmen over production.

In 1878, the industrialists gained an invaluable ally in their struggle with the craftsmen for control of steel production when a young apprentice machinist, Frederick Winslow Taylor, took a job as a day laborer at Midvale. Taylor was no ordinary worker. Born into a wealthy Philadelphia family, he had turned down the opportunity for a Harvard education to acquire a very different kind of schooling on the shop floor. Ambitious, energetic, and better educated than his co-workers, Taylor quickly rose up the ranks at Midvale. Within a half-dozen years, he had been promoted from journeyman machinist to gang boss, and then to foreman of the machine shop, master mechanic, and, finally, chief engineer. He eventually became one of the most influential figures in the history of American management.

Taylor's impressive career trajectory was not his enduring legacy, however. Few would have anticipated it, but his tenure at Midvale would transform blue-collar work throughout the industrial world. The impending revolution began with small steps. As Taylor gained authority, he was frustrated by the unwillingness of the workers under his supervision to work as hard as he thought they were capable of. Although they were paid by the piece, which in theory meant that the more they produced the more they would earn, the workers showed no interest in maximizing their output. As he later wrote, he estimated that the average worker was doing no more than one third of a good day's work (1911: 49). He thus began a campaign, which included cutting the wages of some workers and firing others, to get them to raise their productivity. Taylor acknowledged that this campaign quickly turned into a war, which became increasingly bitter; some workers resisted Taylor's efforts to speed up their work by sabotaging their machines. He responded, in turn, by fining workers whose machines broke down.

After three years of conflict, Taylor could claim some successes. He had been promoted, he had earned the confidence of the company's president, William Sellers, and productivity had risen. These successes came at a price, however, for as he later remarked when recounting this campaign, "life which is one continuous struggle with other men is hardly worth living" (1911: 52).

Taylor had also come to the conclusion that the real barrier to raising productivity was that workers knew far more about production processes than did their supervisors—himself included. He said that the knowledge and skill of the workers under his supervision was at least ten times greater than his own. For the next quarter of a century he set about redressing this imbalance of knowledge and skill through what he called the scientific study of work. The result was "scientific management," or Taylorism, which was a radical new way of thinking about work.

Frederick Winslow Taylor and Scientific Management

In explaining the principles of scientific management, Taylor asked his readers to imagine a traditional industrial establishment of 500 to 1,000 workers. These workers, representing twenty to thirty different trades, had acquired their knowledge from their predecessors and perfected their skills on the job before passing on what they had learned to the next generation of workers. Two features of this arrangement were significant, Taylor argued. First, transmission of knowledge was through word of mouth; little or nothing was written down or codified. Second, this mass of traditional knowledge was not in the possession of management, including those foremen and superintendents, such as Taylor, who had come up through the ranks. Since workers had this knowledge and management did not, managers had to persuade workers to use their skills and efforts on behalf of the enterprise. Persuasion could mean shorter hours, higher wages, better working conditions, or a promotion. Taylor described this practice of rewarding workers to gain their goodwill and cooperation as "initiative and incentive" management (1911: 35). He saw it

as an obstacle to greater productivity, and he proposed to replace it with scientific management.

Taylor's "science of management" was based on four principles. First, management should plan and direct all work activities by substituting scientific understanding of production processes for workers' traditional knowledge. Second, jobs and tasks should be broken down into their simplest parts to determine the most efficient and productive way of doing each task. Third, managers should evaluate workers before assigning them to specific jobs and then should carefully train and closely monitor their work. Fourth, a worker who performed his duties exactly as specified should receive a premium over and above his regular wage.

The first two principles were crucial to the development of American manufacturing in the late nineteenth and early twentieth centuries. The idea was that managers and engineers would carefully observe workers, recording every action or step and timing how long it took. This was the famous, or infamous—depending on your perspective—time-and-motion study. Having broken down the job into a series of discrete and identifiable tasks, the manager or engineer would then analyze where time and effort were being wasted and how the job could be reorganized with all superfluous time and effort eliminated. No job, according to Taylor, was so simple that it could not be made more efficient through a time-and-motion study.

Taylor himself conducted thousands of such studies. The best known, because it featured so prominently in his subsequent discussion of scientific management, was conducted at the Bethlehem Steel Company in 1899. Taylor had been hired as a consultant to improve productivity. One of the jobs on which he focused was the loading of 92-pound "pigs" (or slabs) of iron into railcars. Each worker picked up a pig, walked up an inclined plank, and dropped it in the car. The 75 men doing the job averaged 12.5 tons per worker per day. After studying the job and the workers, Taylor came to the conclusion that a "first-class" pig-iron handler should be able to load between 47 and 48 tons a day—nearly four times the average being achieved. To achieve this rate, a worker had to load 1,156 pigs per day, i.e., he had to load a 92-pound pig every thirty seconds for ten hours. Taylor insisted that this rate was feasible. He selected one worker—called "Schmidt" in his book—who was told to follow his supervisor's instructions to the letter. At the end of his day of following orders, Schmidt had loaded 47.5 tons, which Taylor regarded as proof of the validity of scientific management. Taylor later wrote that Schmidt practically never failed to achieve a pace or task that Taylor assigned him during his three years at Bethlehem. In return for this extraordinary output, Schmidt was paid $1.85 a day, 60 percent higher than his pre-Taylor earnings, which were never more than $1.15 a day.

Most of Taylor's examples of how to implement scientific management were drawn from simple laboring jobs such as carrying pigs of iron, shoveling iron ore, and bricklaying, Taylor believed that the workers doing these jobs were incapable of figuring out the most scientific way of working. As he put it, "the man suited to handling pig iron is too stupid properly to train himself" (1911: 63). He even described Schmidt as "mentally sluggish," despite the fact that one of Taylor's reasons for choosing Schmidt for his experiments was that the latter was building a house with his own hands in his spare time. As far as Taylor was concerned, pig-iron handlers

and other laborers were beasts of burden. He wrote: "Now one of the very first requirements for a man who is fit to handle pig iron as a regular occupation is that he shall be so stupid and so phlegmatic that he more nearly resembles in his mental make-up the ox than any other type" (1911: 59). He intended his science of management to encourage managers to select, train, instruct, and supervise workers who would be willing to work like oxen.

Taylor picked unskilled, traditional jobs to illustrate scientific management because he wanted to demonstrate that even the simplest jobs should not be entrusted to workers' discretion and judgment. The ultimate expression of Taylor's ideas, however, was to be found in the organization of work on Henry Ford's automobile assembly lines—the most modern factories of the early twentieth century. Although Ford never acknowledged any debt to Taylor, it is difficult to imagine that he was unaware of the scientific management philosophy or movement. The hallmark of assembly-line production—the unrelenting search for greater efficiency by trimming seconds from tasks and by eliminating the smallest of unnecessary motions—is entirely consistent with Taylorism. Henry Ford may have come up with the most productive and cheapest way of making cars, but it was Frederick Taylor who paved the way for him.

Henry Ford and the Assembly Line

On June 16, 1903, Henry Ford and eleven other stockholders formed the Ford Motor Company. It was an event that neither received nor warranted any publicity at the time. The 39-year-old Ford had been unsuccessful in his previous ventures in automobile production, he was entering an already crowded field (88 other automobile firms had entered the business in 1903 alone), and it was uncertain whether consumers even wanted a gasoline-powered automobile. Over the next decade Ford irreversibly changed how work was done, how workers were rewarded, and how Americans lived. His innovations—the Model T Ford, the assembly line, and the Five Dollar Day—came to define industrial capitalist society of the twentieth century and led to a new term for his methods of organizing work and workers: *Fordism*. The adoption of these innovations by other companies consolidated U.S. status as the greatest manufacturing power in the world (the U.S. share of world production of manufactured goods increased from 25 percent in 1900 to over 40 percent in 1929) and created the first modern mass-consumer society.

The early Ford automobiles gave little indication of an imminent revolution in production. They were expensive cars made by skilled craft workers. For example, the Model B Ford introduced in September 1904 was priced at $2,000—a huge sum at that time. Despite Ford's success in selling large, expensive cars, he believed that the future of the automobile lay in increasing its affordability—in selling lighter and cheaper models that were within the price range of the average American consumer. In 1906 Ford and his engineers began work on what would become the company's most famous product: the Model T Ford. Between 1908 and 1927, more than 15 million Model Ts—Ford's "motor car for the great multitude"—were made and sold (Brinkley 2003).

The Model T was a remarkable car. It was light (1,200 pounds), cheap ($850, although this price did not include the top, the headlights, or the windshield!), sturdy, agile, reliable, easy to drive, and economical to maintain. Ford's biggest

problem, in fact, was to keep up with consumer demand for the new car. In 1910 Ford opened a new factory in Highland Park, Michigan, to produce Model Ts and Model T parts that were then shipped to other Ford assembly plants. It was at the Highland Park factory that Ford developed a famous new technology for producing automobiles—the assembly line. This was the technology that announced the arrival of the era of mass production.

Prior to the assembly line, building an automobile was a stationary process requiring the knowledge and experience of skilled assemblers. In the early days of automobile production, one assembler would build an entire car by himself. Photographs of automobile factories from this era show workers seated alongside wooden sawhorses on which are resting the chasses they are putting together. These workers performed a variety of tasks. A skilled assembler, for example, would add wheels, springs, motor, transmission, and generator to a chassis—tasks that might take him an entire day to finish. If a part didn't fit, he would be expected to file it down until it did.

The opening of the Highland Park factory, however, marked a new chapter in the history of the automobile, one in which Ford engineers shifted their focus from the product itself to how it was made. Their efforts to increase productivity by changing production methods were to culminate in the assembly line and mass production. Ford's initial innovations focused on ensuring that parts were interchangeable and that individual workers performed fewer tasks. Interchangeable parts meant that the company could avoid the delays that occurred when parts had to be filed in order to get them to fit. Fewer tasks meant that the company could hire more unskilled workers, especially if the tasks were fairly simple. It was a foreshadowing of the extreme division of labor and work simplification that was to characterize the assembly line.

It is not absolutely certain where the idea for the automobile assembly line originated, although historians agree that the most likely source was the Swift meatpacking plant in Chicago where Ford employees had observed pig and cow carcasses being disassembled. Whatever its roots, we do know that the first assembly line at Highland Park was introduced in the spring of 1913 and was used to produce magneto flywheels. It was quickly followed by assembly lines to produce motors and then transmissions. By the summer of 1913, the engineers had developed a conveyer belt for the final and most important step in the manufacture of the automobile, the assembly of the chassis. In January 1914, Ford completed his revolution by introducing the automated conveyer belt, which allowed management to control the pace of the lines and, therefore, the pace at which the assemblers worked (Halberstam 1986; Donkin 2001).

The moving assembly line was based on three basic principles. First, workers were stationary, while their jobs came to them. Second, the tasks that had been previously performed by a single skilled worker were now subdivided among different assemblers, each of whom performed a tiny number of standardized and repetitive operations. Third, the speed of the assembly line dictated the pace at which these workers carried out their tasks.

The results of the moving assembly line were astonishing. Stationary assembly of one car took about 13 hours; on the assembly line it took a little over 90 minutes. The task cycle of the average worker—the length of time it took before he repeated an operation—dropped

from 514 minutes to 79 seconds (Womack, Jones, and Roos 1990). As production went up, prices went down, from $850 for a Model T in 1908 to $360 in 1914. During the same period, Ford's share of the U.S. automobile market increased from 9 to 48 percent, as hundreds of thousands of cars poured off his assembly lines each year. Ford Motor Company, once a modest Detroit auto manufacturer making 100 cars a month, had within a decade raised its production to 1,000 cars a day and had become the greatest industrial enterprise in the world (Brinkley 2003). Further, the company had established a method of making goods that transformed manufacturing processes around the world, which, as the example of Dell Computers shows, remains the key to industrial productivity today.

What has changed in the nearly 100 years since Ford introduced the assembly line are the conditions under which the assemblers on these lines work. Although the inherent monotony of assembly-line work has persisted, the emergence of powerful labor unions in automobile manufacturing and other mass-production industries between 1935 and 1945 limited the ability of employers in these industries to increase the speed of the assembly line to get more production out of workers. Union contracts have also provided other benefits, such as good wages, pensions, and health insurance and protection from harsh or arbitrary treatment by supervisors. A union contract, for example, typically requires a supervisor to provide a performance-related justification for firing a worker, which has to be preceded by oral and written warnings. Before the rise of unions, "speed-ups" of the assembly line were common and workers had no rights in the workplace.

The story of mass production is, therefore, really two stories. One is about the invention and implementation of a new system of production. The other is about the fight of the workers who experienced this system to retain their dignity in a difficult and sometimes degrading work environment. In the remainder of this chapter, we discuss why life on the early assembly line was so unpleasant and how workers expressed their displeasure. We also show how employers invented personnel management in an effort to reduce worker dissatisfaction.

How Workers Responded to Mass Production

Absenteeism and Quitting

Workers reacted to the assembly line immediately and unfavorably. They expressed their dissatisfaction by being absent from their jobs and by quitting them altogether. It was at Ford, the symbol of mass production, where these responses were at their most extreme. In the first decade of the twentieth century, many manufacturing companies experienced turnover rates of 10 percent a month and more. Few companies, however, matched the Ford Motor Company's staggering 370 percent annual quit rate that followed its introduction of the assembly line in 1913. By the end of the year, turnover was approaching an annual rate of 1,000 percent. In the same year, an average of one out of every ten Ford workers was absent from his job at some point during the week. So pronounced were the problems of turnover and absenteeism that labor expert John R. Commons suggested that by staying away from the job in such numbers, workers were in effect "conducting a continuous, unorganized strike" (Meyer 1981: 85).

There were many reasons why workers went absent or quit their jobs. Partly it was the

work itself—jobs in the mass-production industries were dirty, hard, dangerous, repetitive, and fast-paced. A 1914 report estimated that 35,000 workers had been killed and 700,000 injured in industrial accidents the previous year (Brinkley 2003). Partly it was the way in which the workers were supervised—it was foremen who decided who would be hired, who would be fired, how much workers would be paid, and how hard they would have to work. In many instances, foremen engaged in what today would be considered outrageously unfair or discriminatory hiring practices, such as relying on ethnic stereotypes to determine what jobs workers were capable of doing. Polish workers, for example, were often chosen for jobs involving heavy physical labor. Jewish workers were regarded as dexterous. In many instances, foremen demanded a bribe— whisky, cigars, or cash—in return for the job (Jacoby 1985). Once hired, workers became part of what has been called the "foreman's empire" (Nelson 1975). Foremen used what was known as the "drive system" to get as much effort as they could out of workers. Their supervisory methods included intimidation and the threat of dismissal to compel workers to produce as much as possible.

Finally, workers went absent or quit because they were so unfamiliar with the rhythms and routines of industrial employment. It is estimated that in 1900 about half of all the unskilled workers in manufacturing were immigrants—the majority from rural or at least preindustrial backgrounds in southern and eastern Europe (Jacoby 1985). Seventy-one percent of Ford's workers in 1914 were foreign-born, with one third of them coming from Poland or Russia (Brinkley 2003). The giant factories echoing to the roar of strange new machines were an alien environment; the relentless pressure to maintain high levels of production made it a hostile one as well.

Craft Unionism

A more threatening expression of worker dissatisfaction with mass production, as far as employers were concerned, was their newfound willingness to join labor unions and to strike. American labor unions had traditionally been associations of skilled craftsmen. There were unions of carpenters, butchers, machinists, cigar makers, bricklayers, stonemasons, coal miners, iron molders, and windowglass makers. The craft unions had three primary goals. One was to restrict performance of the tasks and duties that the union defined as belonging to its members to those who had been licensed or certified by the union. The second was to establish work rules specifying how union members should perform these tasks. The third was to negotiate higher wages for their members. For example, in 1884 a windowglass workers' union included, among its numerous "rules for working," the stipulation that work crews should produce no more than 48 boxes of glass a week and that no work was to be done on Thanksgiving, Christmas, or Washington's birthday. In 1867 the Iron Molders Union, which at that time represented over 80 percent of the iron molders in the country, forbade its members from going to work earlier than 7 A.M. The United Mine Workers had a rule specifying that a bituminous miner could hire only one unskilled helper (Montgomery 1979).

Union activity among skilled craftsmen, including strikes, had been steadily increasing since the late 1890s, as the new managers and efficiency experts eager to modernize their companies' operations began to challenge these longstanding work rules and restrictions. Union

membership rose from 447,000 in 1897 to over 2 million in 1904 (Brody 1980). Between 1896 and 1903 the number of strikes in the United States tripled. But these efforts by skilled craftsmen to preserve their control over production were mostly unsuccessful. Once they no longer needed skilled workers to operate their machines, employers simply replaced them with cheaper unskilled workers.

Craft unions before 1900 seldom included unskilled workers. In fact, one of the purposes of the craft unions was to prevent unskilled workers from doing what they considered to be skilled work. Many of the work rules that the unions were defending were explicitly designed to prevent unskilled workers from encroaching on what union members considered their legitimate prerogatives and privileges. Craft-union exclusiveness had been formally recognized with the formation of the American Federation of Labor (AFL) in 1886. (The AFL had been set up as an umbrella organization to enable individual unions to come together and to speak with a single voice on a variety of issues.) The delegates to the founding convention had decided that only workers who belonged to unions would be permitted to join the new federation. Since unions were organizations of skilled craftsmen, unskilled workers were effectively shut out of the AFL.

The Industrial Workers of the World

The exclusion of unskilled workers from union activities changed in 1905 with the founding of the Industrial Workers of the World (the Wobblies), which was one of the most colorful and defiant of all American labor organizations. Unlike the AFL unions, the Wobblies were a general union—their ultimate goal was to organize all workers, regardless of skill and regardless of the industry or occupation in which they worked, into a single union. Another difference from the AFL was that IWW leaders had a radical set of political goals that included the overthrow of capitalism. Finally, their tactics differed from those of the more cautious AFL. One of their cardinal principles—enshrined in their famous slogan "an injury to one is an injury to all"—was that all workers had an obligation to assist any other group of workers who were engaged in a conflict with their employer.

The Wobblies' brand of aggressive, confrontational unionism led to their involvement in some of the most famous labor conflicts of the World War I era. The IWW organized a strike of the workers in the wool mills of Lawrence, Massachusetts, in 1913 that was successful in preventing mill employers from lowering wages and that triggered a series of strikes among the textile workers of New York and New Jersey. (The Lawrence strike, in which many immigrant women workers in the textile industry demanded both higher wages and better treatment, found its signature slogan when a journalist asked one striker what she wanted above all. She replied "Bread—and Roses!") The IWW also led strikes at Firestone Rubber and Studebaker in 1913, and it attempted to organize workers at Goodyear and Ford in the same year.

More often than not, however, the IWW's efforts to organize workers were unsuccessful because of employer reluctance to negotiate with it. On occasion the setbacks were deadly. One of the most famous and most bloody of the union's defeats was the coal miners' strike against the Colorado Fuel and Iron Company in Ludlow, Colorado, in 1914. The strikers and their families had been evicted from their company houses

and were living in tents. While the men were at a meeting one night, agents of the company set fire to the tents and even used Gatling guns against the strikers as they fled. A total of 18 men, women, and children died in the Ludlow massacre.

Despite its often violent defeats, the IWW developed a loyal following, particularly among the coal miners, lumberjacks, seamen, and migrant farm workers of the American West. The union also produced some of the most famous labor leaders of the day, such as "Big" Bill Haywood, as well as the song that was to become the anthem of the U.S. labor movement, "Solidarity Forever." It was written in January 1915 by Ralph Chaplin, an IWW organizer, who was participating in a strike of West Virginia coal miners in the Kanawha Valley. The lyrics of "Solidarity Forever"—sung to the tune of the "Battle Hymn of the Republic"—convey the sentiment and philosophy of the Wobblies (see Box 5.1).

The IWW's ability to inspire workers was not translated into long-term success, however. It was unable to maintain its foothold among unskilled workers when an employers' backlash against its radical tactics and philosophy developed following the entrance of the United States into World War I. Federal, state, and local authorities harassed, arrested, and jailed IWW organizers, leading to the union's rapid decline.

Even with the virtual elimination of the IWW, the American labor movement appeared to have made significant strides between 1910 and 1920. One of its basic demands, for an eight-hour day or a 48-hour week, had been achieved by nearly half of all workers by 1919. Labor union membership more than doubled between 1910 and 1920, from 2 to 5 million workers. These gains proved short-lived, however. Over the next

BOX 5.1 *Solidarity Forever* by Ralph Chaplin

When the union's inspiration through the workers'
   blood shall run,
There can be no power greater anywhere beneath
   the sun;
Yet what force on earth is weaker than the feeble
   strength of one,
But the union makes us strong.

Chorus:
Solidarity forever,
Solidarity forever,
Solidarity forever,
For the union makes us strong,

Is there aught we hold in common with the greedy
   parasite
Who would lash us into serfdom and would crush
   us with his might?
Is there anything left to us but to organize and fight?
For the union makes us strong.

It is we who plowed the prairies; built the cities
   where they trade;
Dug the mines and built the workshops, endless
   miles of railroad laid;
Now we stand outcast and starving 'midst the
   wonders we have made;
But the union makes us strong.

All the world that's owned by idle drones is ours
   and ours alone.
We have laid the wide foundations; built it skyward
   stone by stone.
It is ours, not to slave in, but to master and to
   own.
While the union makes us strong.

They have taken untold millions that they never
   toiled to earn,
But without our brain and muscle not a single
   wheel can turn.
We can break their haughty power, gain our freedom
   when we learn
That the union makes us strong.

In our hands is placed a power greater than their
   hoarded gold,
Greater than the might of armies, magnified a
   thousand-fold.
We can bring to birth a new world from the ashes
   of the old.
For the union makes us strong.

SOURCE: Industrial Workers of the World 1973: 4–5

---

decade the union movement steadily lost ground, and union membership in the manufacturing industries in particular declined sharply. Union membership as a whole dropped from 5 to 3.4 million between 1920 and 1929 (Jacoby 1985). The movement simply was not strong enough to overcome an economic depression in the early 1920s and an antiunion employer counteroffensive based on personnel management. Union decline was not reversed until the late 1930s, when a new movement emerged following the passage of pro-labor legislation during the

New Deal administration of President Franklin Roosevelt (see Chapter 10).

The Invention of Personnel Management

The Five Dollar Day

Confronted with employees who either quit their jobs or went out on strike, employers responded with a mixture of sticks and carrots. These measures were designed to punish workers who would not cooperate with employers and to reward those who would. They represented the first real effort to bring what we now recognize to be modern methods of personnel management into the American workplace. The result was a significant change in the relationship of employer to employee and in the economic position of blue-collar workers in the society at large. Employers took on the responsibility of providing for the well-being of their employees, which meant paying wages and benefits to unskilled workers that would lift them out of poverty and enable them to afford the goods that they made. It was a philosophy of labor management that, in combination with the assembly line, became known as Fordism because once again the person and company that initiated the change was Henry Ford and the Ford Motor Company.

On January 5, 1914, Ford shocked the business world by announcing that he was cutting the working day for his employees from nine to eight hours and that he was raising their pay to a maximum of $5 a day. Overnight, Ford had effectively doubled the pay of the average autoworker. The company would now be paying its workers nearly three times the wage of the average steelworker. Ford's move was widely criticized by other industrialists, who complained that they would be unable to match it, and unleashed a flood of applicants on the Ford hiring office. Ten thousand job seekers presented themselves at Ford's Highland Park plant on the day after the announcement. On January 12, the day the $5 day officially took effect, the crowd of applicants became so unruly that the city's fire department turned hoses on them. Eager job seekers continued to pour in from all over the United States during the following weeks; many were African Americans from the South for whom a job at Ford's meant an escape from poverty and segregation.

The eight-hour workday and $5-per-day wage was an inspired response to Ford's high absenteeism and turnover rates and to the interest that the IWW was beginning to show in organizing automobile workers. The inspiration was Ford's realization that a single bold innovation could turn workers from opponents of the assembly line into its advocates. He believed that workers who became part of the new consumer society that his low-priced cars had helped to create would be less likely to quit. By giving workers the eight-hour day, Ford had adopted one of the labor movement's long-running demands, which he hoped would undermine the appeal of unions.

The radical premise underlying Fordism was that unskilled workers should be paid enough to buy the products of their labor. Previously, the economic benefits of capitalism had seldom reached further down the company hierarchy than skilled craftsmen; unskilled workers were paid low wages and treated badly. Companies had relied on the waves of immigrants entering the country to provide a constant flow of workers to their factories and to compensate for high turnover. But the steep decline in immigration during World War I, coupled with continued turnover and the enthusiastic response of these workers to labor unions, had caused employers like Ford to rethink their management of their workforces.

It is vital to understand that the Five Dollar Day was not automatically awarded to every Ford employee, however. Only half of the $5 was defined as a wage; the other $2.50 per day was framed in terms of a profit-sharing plan that workers could earn only by allowing the company to regulate their behavior and activities while not at work. This meant submitting to a company investigation in which neighbors and family members were interviewed by Ford's "Sociological Department," which inspected and oversaw the workers' private lives. As the company decreed, "if a man wants to remain a profit sharer, his wife should remain at home and assume the obligations she undertook when she married" (Meyer 1981: 141). Married men had to be living with and taking good care of their families. Single men had to be over the age of 22 and had to have "thrifty habits." Men under the age of 22 had to be the sole breadwinner for their next of kin. Ford did not want workers who drank alcohol, smoked, or fraternized with union members. They were also expected to be regular churchgoers and to save part of their wages (Brinkley 2003). Thus the Five Dollar Day was in fact a deeply paternalistic system that "extended the frontiers of managerial control from the shop and factory in the homes and communities of Ford workers," allowing the company to establish "a wide-ranging and tightly-knit web of social controls over the workforce" (Meyer 1981: 96).

The results of this system were, from Ford's perspective, highly satisfactory. Following its introduction, the average daily absenteeism rate dropped from 10 percent to less than 0.5 percent. Turnover in 1915 was 10 percent. Factory productivity increased 15 to 20 percent (Brinkley 2003). As long as they conformed to Ford's system, workers received a wage that provided them a middle-class standard of living. They had become part of a society of consumers. A survey of 100 Ford families in 1929 found that 32 owned their homes, 47 owned cars, 36 owned radios, and 49 owned washing machines. On the average they spent slightly more than they

earned during the year, financing the difference by buying on credit (Brody 1980). What had not changed for these workers, as we discuss in the next section, were the harsh conditions on the assembly lines.

Welfare Capitalism

The bargain that Henry Ford had struck with his employees—economic rewards in exchange for commitment to the company and a high level of effort—became the model that many large American corporations followed and expanded upon during the 1920s. In addition to higher wages, they offered a variety of other benefits intended to reconcile workers to the rigors of factory life and to impose substantial penalties on employees who quit or who were fired. Their approach to personnel management, initially called "industrial betterment," came to be known as "welfare capitalism."

There were various incentives that companies offered during this period to cement the tie of employee to employer. They included home-ownership plans, in which companies offered financial aid packages to employees who wished to buy their own homes; stock purchase plans, in which companies made it possible for workers to buy the stock of the companies by whom they were employed; accident, health, and life insurance plans; company-sponsored pension programs; and paid vacations. Some companies established employee representation plans—these were known as company unions because they were intended as manager-led alternatives to independent labor unions. Corporate leaders appointed a new breed of manager—the personnel manager—to administer these programs. All of these benefits were contingent, however, on workers' keeping their jobs, maintaining high levels of output, and staying away from independent unions.

The higher wages and welfare programs did not moderate the tough and even brutal treatment of workers in the factories and on the assembly lines. Ford, for example, was notorious during the 1920s for continuing to speed up its assembly lines and for firing workers who could not keep pace. By 1928 Ford had completed the enormous River Rouge plant in Dearborn, Michigan. In what was then the largest and most modern factory in the world, employing nearly 100,000 workers, Ford produced its new Model A automobile—one every nine seconds. "The Rouge" contained its own steel mill, glass factory, and inland docks for the iron ore, coal, and other raw materials. It took just four days for the iron ore that was unloaded at these docks to be turned into a new Model A (Bantich 2001).

Ford achieved this level of output at The Rouge and its automobile plants by maintaining an unforgiving work rate and draconian work rules. Workers could be fired for the most trivial of offenses, including talking and smiling. Workers who displayed any union sympathies were immediately dismissed. There was no lunch break or any other rest periods. No worker was allowed to sit down, even if he got injured on the job. Company doctors treated workers standing up, unless the worker had suffered a leg injury. These rules were enforced by Ford's private police force—the 3,000 stick- and gun-wielding members of the Ford Service Department under the leadership of the notorious Harry Bennett (Brinkley 2003). A Ford worker later described his working conditions at the company: "There were no relief breaks, no lunch periods, nothing to break the terrible speedup. You were really driven. There was no time to talk, to say hello to anybody. You ate lunch with a sandwich in one hand and worked with the other" (Bantich 2001: 9).

The welfare programs and the strong antiunionism that accompanied them had their intended effect, however. Between 1920 and 1929 union membership declined by over 30 percent and strikes by around 70 percent (Jacoby 1985). On the threshold of the Great Depression, American workers may have been better rewarded than their parents and grandparents were, but they had also been cowed into submission by their employers. Their rewards, and the docility that accompanied them, were about to be shattered.

The Great Depression

The stock market crash of October 1929 marked the beginning of the Great Depression. Over the next four years, blue-collar workers experienced prolonged and devastating economic misfortune. They lost their jobs or, if lucky enough to remain employed, they suffered wage cuts. At both General Motors and Ford, employment was cut in half between 1929 and 1932. Ford reduced the minimum daily wage during this period from $7 to $4. By March 1933 one of out every three workers in the U.S. labor force was out of work. There was no federal unemployment assistance and little unemployment compensation from the companies that had laid them off; once unemployed workers had exhausted their meager savings, they and their families were forced to depend on local and private charities for their daily living needs. Blue-collar workers and their families now experienced soup kitchens, hunger marches, and home evictions.

The catastrophe of the Great Depression had two immediate consequences. The first was that it led workers to reconsider their loyalty and commitment to their employers. Welfare capitalism was based on the understanding that workers would receive employment security and good wages in return for avoiding unions, showing up for work regularly, and tolerating assembly-line speed-ups and tyrannical foremen. This effort-for-earnings bargain became meaningless once companies starting cutting employees and wages. To make matters worse, many companies laid off the oldest workers first, even though they had served their employers the longest. The loss of worker goodwill became complete when protests against low wages, hunger, and unemployment were met with corporate indifference or outright violence.

The most notorious incident of company violence took place at Ford's giant River Rouge plant in Dearborn, Michigan. On March 7, 1932, 3,000 protestors, many of them unemployed Ford workers, marched from downtown Detroit to the Rouge factory. Their demands included hiring of laid-off workers, an end to the speed-up of the assembly line, two fifteen-minute rest periods during the working day, abolition of the Service Department, and an end to the foreclosures of the homes of former Ford workers. At the gate of the factory, they faced Dearborn police and the men from Harry Bennett's Service Department. Bennett's men turned fire hoses on the marchers and then opened fire with a submachine gun. Four marchers were killed and nineteen were seriously wounded. Harry Bennett himself was the only policeman or Service Department member to be hurt—he was hit on the head by a rock when he approached the crowd. The hunger march killings completed Henry Ford's transformation from the corporate hero of the Five Dollar Day to corporate villain (Brinkley 2003).

The second consequence was that the federal government, following the victories of the Democrats in the 1932 elections, began to intervene in the employment relationship on the side of workers. The changed mood in Washington was demonstrated by the passage of the National Industrial Recovery Act (NIRA) in 1933. One of its provisions specified that workers "shall have the right to organize and bargain collectively through representatives of their own choosing, and shall be free from the interference, restraint or coercion of employers...." Two years later, Congress passed the National Labor Relations Act (NLRA), also known as The Wagner Act, an even more pro-labor piece of legislation that, among other things, prohibited employers from firing workers who engaged in union activities.

The effect of this legislation guaranteeing workers' right to organize was profound. When combined with workers' anger toward their employers and their newfound determination to stand up for their rights, it revitalized the dormant labor movement and led to one of the great social movements in American history—the rise of industrial labor unionism in the 1930s and 1940s. We consider the labor movement at greater length in Chapter 10.

But it was not just workers' attitudes that were changing during the 1930s. This decade also saw the emergence of a new philosophy of personnel management—human relations. This philosophy, which is most closely identified with the studies conducted at the Hawthorne plant of Western Electric by Elton Mayo and his colleagues, was an enormously important step in the history of American industrial management and has been broached in Chapters 1 and 3. What the human relations approach did was to introduce a new idea about workers that challenged the Taylorist conception of the worker. Taylor regarded workers as *economically* motivated and socially isolated individuals, an idea that Ford and his contemporaries implicitly accepted. The idea behind Taylorism was that employers should find the appropriate economic incentives to motivate workers. Mayo, however, claimed that the workers were motivated by *social* needs, the most important being the need to fit in with the informal social groups they formed in workplaces. Consequently, he argued, employers should reconsider how they conducted personnel management.

The Hawthorne Research: The Discovery of the Work Group

In the mid-1920s, Elton Mayo, an Australian-born researcher affiliated with the Harvard Business School, began a series of experiments at Western Electric's Hawthorne Works factory, just outside Chicago. Western Electric, which was part of the Bell System, manufactured telephone equipment for its parent company, which enjoyed a monopoly over the telephone business. Western Electric had been one of the first companies to adopt scientific management. At the Hawthorne plant, which had been built in 1905, semi-skilled and unskilled workers had replaced skilled workers. Engineers, using time-and-motion studies, now determined how the 20,000 workers in the factory were to do their jobs. The Bell System, like other large corporations, became concerned with worker hostility to scientific management and offered its employees a package of benefits to encourage their loyalty. At Hawthorne, the benefits included a pension plan, sickness and disability benefits, and a sports club. In 1920 the company appointed personnel managers at the plant. The factory, therefore, was in the forefront of the changes that had transformed the American workplace in the early twentieth century, and it proved a receptive setting for researchers eager to test their new ideas about personnel management. The Hawthorne studies began there in 1924 and continued for the next eight years (Gillespie 1991).

The Relay Assembly Test Room Study

Mayo's involvement at Hawthorne began with the relay assembly test room study in 1927. The assembly of telephone relays was a repetitive task that required dexterity and concentration, and the study was designed to measure the effect of fatigue on productivity. Six young female workers—five assembly operators and one layout operator, whose job it was to fetch and distribute parts for the assemblers—were chosen to work in the test room. The experimental protocol consisted of establishing these workers' base rate of production, followed by changing their working environment and then measuring whether their productivity increased or decreased. These changes were introduced over the course of twelve periods, ranging from 2 to 31 weeks in length. The entire experiment lasted five years. In period three, for example, the women were placed on a separate group rate; previously they had been part a department group rate, which meant that their pay was determined in large measure by the performance of the other 95 workers in their department. In the fourth period, the women were given two five-minute rest breaks. In the next period, these breaks became ten minutes in length. Period seven saw a lengthening of the morning rest break to fifteen minutes, and the workers were provided refreshments—coffee or soup and a sandwich—during this period.

Over the next few periods, the experimenters maintained the conditions of period seven, while shortening the length of the working day and working week. As each change was made, the productivity of the five workers rose. Finally, in period twelve, seventeen months into the experiment, the researchers returned working conditions to their period three state. Contrary to their expectations, however, the women's productivity did not decline. For the three months of this period it was in fact 19 percent higher than it had been in period three. The subsequent reintroduction of some of the earlier benefits resulted in further increases in productivity—as the experiment progressed it became apparent to the researchers that the women were more productive in the later periods than in the earlier ones, although in many cases their working conditions were identical (periods three and twelve, for example).

The Hawthorne researchers concluded that there was no evidence to support their initial hypothesis that workers' fatigue reduced their productivity. The steadily rising productivity in the relay assembly test room had demolished that theory, but it left the question of how to explain what had happened. The researchers pointed instead to the social changes that had occurred in the test room. First, the attitude of the women had improved because they were supervised less strictly (they were allowed to talk while they worked, for example) and they were given more control over their work pace. The women were happier and, therefore, more productive (Mayo 1933). The reason for the loosening of supervision was that the investigators needed to gain the cooperation of the workers in order for the experiment to succeed. The result, two of the original researchers,

F. J. Roethlisberger and William J.Dickson, later remarked in their classic study of the Hawthorne studies, was that "the investigators inadvertently altered the total social situation of the group.... In the process of setting the conditions for the test, they had completely altered the social situation of the operators and their customary attitudes and interpersonal relations" (1939: 182–183).

Second, over time the women in the relay assembly test room formed a group or informal organization, linked initially by their common work and their separation from the other factory workers and later by a sense of participation in an important project. It was a group that had been allowed to develop autonomously and spontaneously, yet did not exist in opposition to management. On the contrary, their group ties reinforced the idea that the experiment and their work mattered, which encouraged them to work harder. Roethlisberger and Dickson observed that this group was "an organization which not only satisfied the wishes of its members but also worked in harmony with the aims of management" (1939: 560).

In the years since the Hawthorne studies were conducted, sociologists have debated whether the increased productivity was really due to relaxed supervision; some have questioned whether supervision was in fact more relaxed. We will not pursue this debate here. What is widely accepted is the idea that workers act in solidarity with others in their work group, not as isolated individuals. The important role that groups play in determining workers' productivity was confirmed by another Hawthorne study, the Bank Wiring Observation Room study, which was conducted from November 1931 to May 1932.

The Bank Wiring Room
Observation Study

The bank wiring room contained a group of fourteen workers, consisting of nine wiremen, three soldermen, and two inspectors. The researchers decided to focus their attention on group dynamics. Unlike the relay assembly room study, there were to be no experimental manipulations of the daily working environment. The workers were simply to be observed working under standard shop conditions. Other than placing these workers in a separate room, the researchers wanted to disrupt the men's work as little as possible; they received no special treatment or favors, and they were to be monitored by a single observer, who was instructed to remain unobtrusive throughout the course of the study.

Observation of the workers generated some remarkable findings. First, although the workers were on a group piece rate, which presumably gave them an incentive to produce as much as possible, every worker was restricting his output. Restriction of output meant that the workers had decided on their own not to exceed an upper limit and to ensure that their weekly output rates remained relatively constant. Second, workers had sanctions ranging from ostracism and ridicule to "binging" (punching one's co-worker as hard as one could on his shoulder) for workers who exceeded the output quota. Third, there were noticeable differences in the weekly output rates of the workers—some workers produced well below the quota and one worker regularly exceeded it—that could not be attributed to differences in soldering ability and dexterity or intelligence because test scores did not correspond to output. For example, the worker with the lowest output among the nine wiremen ranked highest on the intelligence test and third highest on

the soldering and dexterity test. The worker who scored highest on soldering and dexterity ranked seventh in output (Roethlisberger and Dickson 1939: 409–446).

Restriction of output by workers and sanctions to enforce compliance with a quota were not, by themselves, a big surprise. Frederick Taylor had commented on this behavior in his writings on scientific management, as we see in Chapter 6. The variations in output, however, were more startling. The researchers ultimately explained these by pointing to the emergence of two distinct subgroups or cliques within the bank wiring room. One was based among the workers in the front of the room (clique A), the other among the workers in the back (clique B). Although the group as a whole was unified on certain issues, such as the need for a quota, in other respects the workers were quite divided. Further, there was a difference in status: clique A was the dominant group. Productivity differences corresponded to group membership and status. The highest producer was a worker who was a loner, who chose not to associate with the members of clique A, even though he was located in their section of the room. He apparently did not care that he was ostracized for exceeding the quota or "ratebusting." The lowest producers were the three members of clique B, who were criticized by some of the other workers for goofing off too much and not contributing their fair share of total output (this was called "chiseling") (Roethlisberger and Dickson 1939: 508–522).

The relay assembly test room and the bank wiring observation room studies had both demonstrated that workers formed groups or informal organizations in the workplace. The difference between the groups in the two settings, the researchers later concluded, lay in the extent to which they promoted cooperation with or resistance to the company's management. The group of women in the relay assembly test room encouraged these workers to develop a sense of themselves as being special and to take pride in their work; the group of men in the bank wiring room encouraged these workers to maintain their established patterns of working and to oppose any changes that their supervisors wanted to make.

The Human Relations Philosophy of Personnel Management

Elton Mayo and his fellow Hawthorne researchers used this dichotomy between cooperation in the relay assembly room and resistance in the bank wiring room to promote a new philosophy of personnel management: human relations. The basic assumption underlying human relations was that workers' group loyalties could be either an asset or an obstacle to company management. To make them an asset, however, managers had to know what workers' sentiments and feelings were. This meant studying workers both differently and more intensively than was customary. The researchers proposed a new therapeutic approach to managing workers, which they named "personnel counseling." The personnel counselor, who would not hold any formal authority in the organization, was to be an expert in handling human problems. The intervention of the counselor marked a different approach to factory discipline. If a worker was unproductive or unhappy, the counselor would take that worker aside and probe the reasons— personal or job-related—for her discontent. Together they would identify the causes and the counselor would then help the worker to identify some possible solutions. Once the worker

understood the reasons for her dissatisfaction, human relations advocates claimed, she would work more effectively with her co-workers, would be more cooperative with management, and would be more productive.

The strength of the Hawthorne research lay in two important discoveries. First, the researchers had found that workers formed alliances with one another to defend their mutual interests rather than acting as isolated, self-interested individuals. Second, they had found that productivity depended on whether managers could get workers to cooperate with them. These two discoveries went hand in hand. Managers could not assure themselves of workers' cooperation by providing economic incentives but had to accept that workers would act primarily out of loyalty to their work group. The weakness of the philosophy of labor management—human relations—that arose from these discoveries was that the solution to the problem of how best to handle workers remained firmly individualistic. Despite showing that workers could only be understood in the context of the groups to which they belonged, the researchers' practical recommendations emphasized individual counseling and therapy. They believed that workers who resisted management, such as those in the bank wiring room, had personal problems that needed to be brought to the surface through a one-on-one open-ended interview with a personnel counselor. They did not consider whether output restriction might be a form of collective worker resistance to managerial control. They did not consider whether workers might be justified in resisting managers.

The shortcomings in the human relations approach were exposed in the next decade as workers in industry after industry organized themselves into labor unions (see Chapter 10). The rise of the labor movement was fueled by the resentment that workers felt toward their employers for ignoring their grievances. Given the intense conflict between workers and managers in the 1930s, it is hardly surprising that personnel counseling was not widely adopted. The enduring legacy of human relations is not its specific techniques of personnel practice, however. Its lasting contribution was that it changed how managers thought about and talked about their organizations. First, human relations elevated the status of personnel management as a discipline by placing it on a base of scientific knowledge. Second, it highlighted a new managerial talent—the exercise of social or emotional skills. A good manager was now one who understood what made others—colleagues, subordinates, and superiors—tick. Third, it encouraged managers to experiment with ways of increasing worker participation and promoting teamwork. More than seventy years later, companies continue to strive for participation and teamwork in the workplace (Bendix 1956; Gillespie 1991).

Summary

In order to mass-produce manufactured goods, American employers replaced skilled craftsmen with semi-skilled and unskilled workers. Mass production meant that employers had to acquire the knowledge of the craftsmen, reorganize their work, and reallocate it among workers who were to operate machines and to work on assembly lines. Frederick Taylor's philosophy of scientific management gave employers a strategy for understanding workers' skills and replacing them with their own work arrangements. The most important of these arrangements was the assembly line, which was first introduced in Henry Ford's automobile factories. The result was fast-paced, repetitive, and highly productive work.

Workers disliked assembly lines and other forms of mass-production work because of the relentless pace of the line in combination with pressure from foremen to maintain high levels of output. They responded by going absent, quitting their jobs, and joining unions, one of the most prominent of which in the first decades of the twentieth century was the Industrial Workers of the World. Employers responded by introducing personnel management—the creation of incentives for employee cooperation—to combat resistance to factory discipline and to extend their ability to control the workforce they employed. These incentives included Henry Ford's famous Five Dollar Day and various incentives, such as home- and stock-ownership plans and company pensions and health insurance plans, which were known as "welfare capitalism." Welfare capitalism came to an end with the Great Depression, which destroyed the bargain between employer and employee on which it was based.

In the years following the Depression employers began to rethink their view of workers, largely in response to a series of studies conducted by a group of researchers, led by Elton Mayo at the Hawthorne plant of Western Electric. The results of two of these studies—one conducted in the relay assembly test room and the other in the bank wiring observation room—challenged the notion, implicit in both scientific management and welfare capitalism, that workers were isolated individuals who responded to economic incentives. The Hawthorne researchers showed that workers formed groups and that the code of the group determined whether they cooperated with management in achieving high production or resisted management in restricting output. Mayo and his colleagues promoted a new approach to personnel management, known as human relations. Although the techniques of the new approach, such as personnel counseling, were not widely adopted, the influence of the philosophy of human relations can be seen in contemporary practices such as team building and encouraging employee participation.

PART III

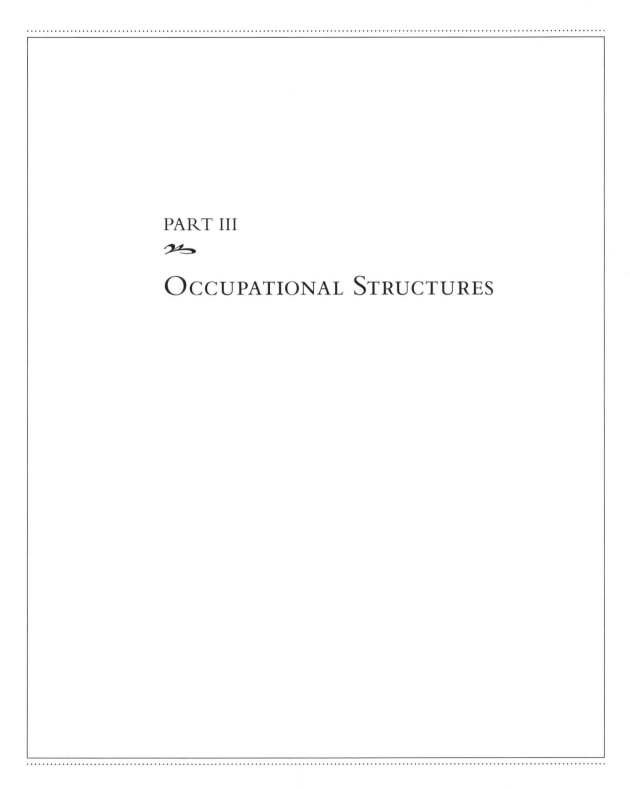

OCCUPATIONAL STRUCTURES

Chapter 6

~

Blue-Collar Workers and the Hidden World of Work

In 1977 Ben Hamper took an assembly-line job at the General Motors Truck & Bus Division in Flint, Michigan. He was assigned to the Cab Department, where he operated an air gun that installed splash shields and pencil rods in the cabs of Chevrolet Blazers and Suburbans. Once he had completed his job, the next worker on the line, Bud, operated a spot-welder that welded together the truck bed and wheel well. After a week on the job, Bud encouraged Hamper to "double-up" jobs with him. This meant that while one of them performed both jobs, the other would relax. Hamper initially had some doubts about taking on Bud's job in addition to his own. He questioned his ability to perform both jobs, and he was concerned as to whether their supervisor would permit a rookie to double-up. Bud convinced him that his concerns were groundless. Hamper struggled with the spot-welder at first, but figured it out after practicing for two or three days. Doubling-up, he found, was the perfect antidote to the fixed pace and tedium of the line and he quickly became a convert:

> Bud had certainly been right. Doubling-up jobs, whenever and wherever possible, made the utmost sense. This arrangement totally destroyed

the monotony of waiting for that next cab to arrive. When it was my turn to handle the two jobs, I'd be so busy with my work that I wouldn't have time to agonize over the crawl of the clock. I patterned myself a brisk routine and the minute hand whirled by.

> When it was Bud's turn at the grind, I would hop the line and read paperbacks next to Roy at the workers' picnic bench. It was like being paid to attend the library....The more shortcuts I learned, the more Bud and I would lengthen our tour of duty. We went from doubling-up for an hour at a time to two hours. The longer the layover between times up at work, the more time we had to sprawl out and investigate methods of passing time. I read two newspapers, a magazine and a good chunk of a novel every evening. (Hamper 1986: 39–40)

Hamper's depiction of doubling up is one indication of how the norms of work in the mass-production industries changed in the wake of the collective bargaining agreements that U.S. companies and powerful labor unions negotiated in the years immediately following the end of World War II. Although doubling up was not typical of blue-collar jobs, it became quite common to find production workers enjoying considerable autonomy and loose supervision on the job. To understand why these changes occurred, we have to consider the nature of the social contract that had been established in both unionized and nonunionized workplaces after the war.

Production workers in the period after World War II were far better off than their prewar predecessors. Over one third of the nonagricultural workforce now belonged to unions, including almost every worker in the mass-production sector that had made so significant a contribution to the Allied war effort. The unions representing these workers had successfully negotiated for a variety of benefits, including good wages, generous fringe benefits, job security, and protection from arbitrary supervision. Workers who were covered by collective bargaining agreements had little fear of the line speed-ups and summary firings that they had so often experienced before the war, especially during the 1920s and early 1930s. Even companies whose workers were not covered by a union contract often felt compelled to offer a similar array of benefits, if only to keep unions out. The result was that coercion, i.e., intimidation by supervisors backed up by the threat of dismissal, had become an ineffective form of labor management. Instead, employers had to gain workers' consent to get them to work hard. All employment relationships contain a mixture of sticks and carrots, but in the postwar era employers were compelled either to offer more carrots or to face employee resistance and hostility. In this chapter, we examine how employers have gone about obtaining the cooperation of their blue-collar employees.

To understand and to appreciate the different forms that cooperation has taken, we will delve into the private or hidden world of work. Unions and collective bargaining belong to the public or visible side of blue-collar employment. They provide the framework within which employers and employees meet on a daily basis to determine how work will be done and how their different and sometimes conflicting needs will be met. Employers want conscientious workers and high production at low cost. Workers want good wages; they also want to minimize boredom, to have some variety in their workday, to control their work pace, to regulate their work effort, and to perform tasks that are interesting and even challenging. Wages and labor costs are negotiated off the job. It is on the job—in the hidden world of work—that employers and workers determine who sets the work pace and how interesting the work will be. This means that the workplace is a place of unofficial agreements among workers and between workers and employers. One outcome of this bargaining is doubling-up.

This chapter explores three issues. First, we consider the skills of blue-collar workers. We show that these workers frequently exercise greater skill than they are presumed to possess. Second, we examine the informal arrangements that workers and their supervisors have developed to get the work done, showing how both sides have often been willing to violate official rules and procedures to achieve their objectives (higher productivity for employers, control of their work for workers). Third, we consider the reasons why some workers have been willing to work extraordinarily hard without receiving any tangible benefits in return.

The Skills of Blue-Collar Workers

In the early nineteenth century, as we saw in Chapters 4 and 5, production work was dominated by skilled craftsmen. They had accumulated their knowledge painstakingly, often beginning as lowly apprentices and then honing their skills through years of practice. The appearance of factories signaled the beginning of the end of the craftsmen's dominance, with the exception of the metal-working industries, where craftsmen remained in control until, in some cases, early in the twentieth century. By the beginning of World War I in 1914, however, the combination of new technologies and the new ideas of Frederick Taylor and Henry Ford had pushed the skilled craftsmen to the margins of production. Mass production was symbolized by the work of the semi-skilled machine tender, whose duties apparently provided little opportunity for creativity or autonomy and whose work pace was set by the moving assembly line. Skilled craftsmen have not completely vanished, it should be noted. The craftsmen of today maintain and repair machinery of all kinds and are also prominent in the construction industry, where they work in occupations such as carpenters, stonemasons, electricians, and plumbers. But they play little part in the manufacturing of goods, which is the focus of this chapter.

The Assembly Line

To many observers, the automobile assembly line has long epitomized the lack of skills of workers in modern industrial societies. Even though a relatively small percentage of all jobs are on assembly lines, they have become a symbol of monotony in the workplace. This is not surprising. Engineers designed assembly-line work to be repetitive and specialized, with very short "task cycles". That is, these workers were expected to repeat the same few activities hundreds of times a

day in a precise and unvarying sequence at a pace set by a moving conveyer belt.

Studies of the assembly line have confirmed that machine pacing and repetitive tasks have significantly reduced workers' skill and creativity. Charles Walker and Robert Guest (1952) conducted one of the first of these studies, an examination of the experiences of 180 automobile workers in a factory in New Haven, Connecticut. Nearly two thirds of these workers had assembly-line jobs. One of their main conclusions was that skill had been replaced by dexterity and an ability to work quickly. Assembly-line jobs required practice and concentration but did not call upon workers to draw upon experience, judgment, or knowledge. Walker and Guest wrote: "Quite often, however, they do call for a great deal of concentrated practice to assure easy and accurate performance. 'Practice' and 'knack' appear to be the appropriate words, then, rather than 'skill'" (1952: 41).

Walker and Guest also asked workers how they felt about their jobs. The results were further confirmation that the assembly line provided little scope for worker initiative or ingenuity. A substantial majority of workers strongly disliked working on the moving assembly line because they could not set their own work pace. They claimed that the pressure to keep up with the pace of the line jeopardized the quality of their output, as the following comments from workers indicate:

> The bad thing about assembly lines is that the line keeps moving. If you have a little trouble with a job, you can't take the time to do it right.
>
> On the line you're geared to the line. You don't dare stop. If you get behind, you have a hard time catching up.

It's not the monotony. It's the rush, rush, rush.

You cannot get quality and quantity. That's my big worry about the place. I don't like it. I always liked to be proud of my work.

But I can't be on this job very much. Everyone is working on too much pressure for speed and "get it out."

I try to do quality work, but I'm too rushed. This keeps me from getting pleasure from the work. They say, "haste makes waste," and they're getting plenty of both. (Walker and Guest 1952: 51–60)

The second most disliked feature of assembly-line work was the repetition. Over 60 percent of the workers whose jobs involved five or fewer operations reported that their work was not interesting. What the assembly-line workers in Walker and Guest's study really wanted was to get off the line and into another job in the plant. They wanted to be utility men (workers who were trained to perform a variety of jobs so that they could fill in for an absentee on the line), inspectors (who checked the cars as they came on the line), repairmen, and foremen.

Three years after Walker and Guest's book, Eli Chinoy published *Automobile Workers and the American Dream*, a study of General Motors workers at an Oldsmobile plant in Lansing, Michigan. Chinoy confirmed that workers strongly disliked the machine pacing of assembly-line jobs. He reported that workers regarded the assembly line as "work to be avoided if possible and to escape from if necessary" (1955 [1992]: 70). Escape meant getting off the line and, ideally, out of production work entirely. Workers valued nonproduction jobs, such as inspecting, repair, material handling, and truck driving, because

these were subject to neither the fixed pace of the conveyer belt nor the constant urgings of foremen to maintain production.

Chinoy reported that workers unable to escape into nonproduction jobs had developed a variety of strategies to cope with the pacing and monotony of the assembly line. Some had established a steady rhythm of work in which there was no wasted effort or motion; in effect, their movements and the motion of the assembly line had become synchronized. Others tried to perform their jobs a little more quickly than the time allotted, so that they gained a few seconds to rest before the next chassis or motor reached them. Still other workers daydreamed while doing their jobs, allowing their minds to roam over topics and places unconnected to the assembly line. Playing practical jokes on one another was another common diversion from the boredom of the line. Finally, some workers engaged in "doubling-up," a practice in which two workers would take turns performing both their jobs, each working very intensively while the other took a break.

The Deskilling Question: Braverman Versus Blauner

A question that sociologists have argued over for many years is whether the assembly line represents just another step downward in a steady decline in workers' skills since the days of craft production or whether it represents a kind of technological low point from which skills have actually started to rise. The first interpretation, known as the deskilling or degradation-of-skill thesis, is vigorously stated in Harry Braverman's famous book, *Labor and Monopoly Capital* (1974). The second interpretation, the skill-upgrading thesis, is well expressed in Robert Blauner's equally renowned book, *Alienation and Freedom* (1964). We introduced some of Braverman's and Blauner's main ideas in Chapter 2.

According to Braverman's deskilling argument, scientific management (see Chapter 5) was the defining moment in the separation of workers from their skills. It encouraged managers to separate the activity of thinking at work from that of doing or making things. The effect of Frederick Taylor's philosophy was to turn workers (the doers) into the uncomprehending executors of simple tasks that managers and engineers (the thinkers) had planned and organized. Workers' skills were replaced with dexterity, which Braverman derided as a "limited and repetitious operation" that required neither knowledge nor talent (1974: 443–444). The shift to automated production, in which machines that correct themselves are monitored by workers who do not have direct contact with raw materials or products, had further reduced the control workers exercise over their daily activities on the job. Finally, Braverman argued that even office work had become increasingly factory-like, as employers simplified white-collar jobs in order to make these workers more productive.

Blauner, in contrast, asserted that automated production had created a new kind of skill: the exercise of responsibility. Under traditional craft methods of production, workers had to be able to operate directly on the product, employing a variety of techniques, using simple tools, and drawing on their accumulated knowledge. The assembly line eliminated these physical and mental skills and replaced them with tasks that were repetitive, were based on predetermined tools and techniques, and required workers to exercise surface mental attention only. Automated production, represented by the continuous-process

techniques used in oil refining and chemical plants, called upon workers to monitor dials, inspect machinery, adjust valves, and record data. According to Blauner, these tasks required workers to be able to exercise responsibility. He wrote: "In place of the *able workman*, required when the worker's role in the productive process is to provide skills, *a reliable employee*, capable of accepting a considerable load of responsibility, is now needed in the automated industries" (emphasis in original, 1964: 167). In short, skills have evolved rather than declined.

Blauner regarded the shift from skill to *Alienation* responsibility as a positive development because it reduced workers' sense of alienation. He measured alienation along four dimensions: (1) powerlessness (a lack of control over work methods and work pace), (2) meaninglessness (a sense that work serves little organizational purpose), (3) self-estrangement (a sense that work provides little personal fulfillment), and (4) isolation (a lack of community or sense of belonging in the workplace). On all four dimensions, continuous-process workers were better off than assembly-line workers. The continuous-process workers carried out their tasks in an order and at a pace they chose, they were assigned responsibility for the smooth functioning of the plant (a responsibility that became particularly important if production was disrupted or there was any other kind of crisis), they had opportunities for learning and personal development, and they worked in crews or groups.

Consequently, Blauner concluded, alienation in the workplace has traced the shape of an inverted U-curve. It was at its lowest in the craft industries in which workers enjoyed considerable freedom and scored low on all dimensions of alienation. It rose to its peak in the assembly-line industries, which intensified all aspects of alienation, and the curve began to slope downward in the continuous-process or automated industries, with workers gaining dignity through the exercise of responsibility.

Tacit Skills

More recent studies of the workplace, however, have faulted both Braverman and Blauner. These studies have argued that workers are not the helpless victims of managerial control, as Braverman claimed, but neither is modern technology as liberating and satisfying as Blauner asserted. By using ethnographic methods of sociological data collection, modern researchers have shown that although blue-collar work is seldom inherently challenging or interesting, workers themselves have devised a variety of techniques to make the hours pass more quickly, to gain more free time on the job, to display their prowess in their work, and to exercise greater control of the conditions under which they work. These techniques, although not always acknowledged by management and seldom apparent at first glance to the casual observer, are crucial to understanding how manual work is performed. They are the foundation of efficient production. We refer to them as "tacit" skills.

Consider, for example, David Halle's (1984) study of the blue-collar workers in a New Jersey chemical plant. This plant was a highly automated facility, and the operators were expected to assume considerable responsibility. An error on an operator's part would not only jeopardize production but could potentially threaten the lives of his co-workers. Escaping chemicals were both a fire and a poison hazard. Despite their responsibilities, however, these workers found their jobs to be dull and repetitive. Workers obtained satisfaction instead from their secrets: their special knowledge of the production process that enabled them to perform their jobs on their terms rather than according to the official instructions.

Halle found that there were three kinds of secret. First, there was knowledge of individual differences in the functioning of the various pieces of machinery. A particular valve, for instance, might tend to stick. Second, workers knew how far they could push the machinery beyond its normal operating condition before they risked a severe accident. They had discovered they could operate the machinery at higher temperatures and at greater pressures than the manuals recommended, but they also had to know what its true limits were. Third, workers had learned the shortcuts that made the job easier and quicker. One such shortcut was knowing that they did not always have to cool a product for the recommended length of time; cooling it down in half the time had no effect on its quality and allowed the workers to relax when they were supposed to be monitoring the cooling.

For another example of tacit skills, take Tom Juravich's (1985) description of a shortcut devised by a worker at "National Wire and Cable Company," a manufacturer of wire and wire assemblies. The worker's job required her to attach spade terminals to each end of a sixteen-inch-long cut and stripped piece of wire. The difficulty lay in ensuring that the terminals at each end were parallel to each other. One worker, however, had solved this problem:

> I had seen other women struggle with this job, placing a terminal on one end, turning the wire around, lining it up and applying the other terminal. Betty, however, had found another way

to do it. As I was checking the machine, I saw her pick up a handful of wires and bounce them in her hand. When I asked what she was doing, she said she was finding the "bend" in the wire. This "bend" she referred to was due to the fact that the wire had originally been coiled on a spool. Although the machine that stripped and cut the wire included a mechanical device called a straightener, it was impossible to remove the bend entirely, and when lined up in a tray, the wires bent one way or the other.

Once Betty had bounced the wires and they lined up the same way (with the ends bending down as she held them); still holding them as a bunch, she put a terminal on one end of all of them. She then turned the bundle around and put terminals on the other end. Because she let the memory of the wire keep the ends turned the same way, the terminals were easily applied in the proper parallel fashion. (Juravich 1985: 51)

William Kornblum's account of work in a South Chicago steel mill attests to the value to employers of workers' knowledge of both equipment and product, even though mill hands are not considered to be skilled employees:

Nominally all jobs on the mill are considered unskilled or semiskilled when compared with craft occupations....While the mill hand may have no generalizable skills, he is intimately familiar with the idiosyncrasies of a particular mill. This is a familiarity which may take years to acquire, depending on the range of sizes and shapes of steel rolled and on the age of the mill. Old installations such as No. 3 Mill are said to be held together with "baling wire and spit." The machinery seems to have a personality of its own and the men who coax steel through it know

they cannot easily be replaced with new men. (Kornblum 1974: 56–57)

For a final illustration of tacit skills, consider the various "tricks of the trade" that Gary Fine reveals in his study of restaurant cooks. One such trick was to toss sticks of butter wrapped in paper into a hot frying pan—it was quicker and easier to remove the paper once the butter had started to melt. Another was to wash parsley in dishwashing detergent—it revived the wilting vegetable. Many of the cooks' tricks were ways of coping with mistakes, such as sealing eggs when the yolk was accidentally broken and began to run (Fine 1996: 30–31).

Tacit skills serve four purposes. First, they are a source of satisfaction to workers because they mean that they have figured out how to carry out a task more efficiently or more quickly than they are supposed to. Knowing more than their supervisors enhances workers' sense of dignity and pride. Second, tacit skills allow workers to assert their power. Supervisors who do not know these production secrets have to depend on the cooperation and goodwill of workers. If workers choose not to use their tacit skills, production may be slowed and their supervisors will be made to look bad. Consequently, supervisors have an incentive to treat workers well. Third, tacit skills give workers greater free time and autonomy at work. Production secrets that enable workers to get the job done more quickly also create more down time at work. Workers increase their efficiency with the understanding that the time they have saved belongs to them and they are entitled to spend it relaxing, socializing, or goofing around. Fourth, tacit skills enable production to proceed smoothly. Because machines and equipment seldom operate exactly as they are supposed to, the knowledge of those who have to use them every day becomes indispensable to maintaining an interrupted flow of production. Employers need workers to develop their tacit skills and to be decision makers at their jobs.

How Work Gets Done: Informal Work Practices

The existence of tacit skills means that blue-collar jobs are often more complex than outsiders may realize. These jobs may not be particularly enjoyable or satisfying, but they are seldom as easy to perform as people who have not tried them may think. Tacit skills are not the only way in which the reality of the workplace refutes preconceived ideas about how it is supposed to function. Equally striking are the various activities and behaviors in which blue-collar workers engage while at work that are not part of their formal job descriptions or duties. These activities and behaviors, which we term "informal work practices," may even be explicitly prohibited by company managers or collective bargaining agreements, yet are commonplace.

There are three kinds of informal work practice. The first are "games," which consist of workers turning their tasks into a challenge or contest with their co-workers to see who can do it the best. Games are a way of demonstrating proficiency and competence and earning the respect of others. The second are "times," which consist of workers entertaining themselves and others at work with various jokes and pranks. Times enable workers to cope with boring jobs because they are a diversion from the task at hand. The third are "deals," which are arrangements with other workers and with supervisors about carrying out their tasks in a different way

from that specified by company officials. Deals allow workers to acquire control over their work time and their work pace.

Games: How Workers Display Competence

In 1903 Frederick Taylor denounced workers for loafing or, to use the terminology of the era, "soldiering." Soldiering came in two guises, he suggested. First, there was natural soldiering, which he described as a natural tendency for workers to want to take it easy rather than to work hard. Taylor reserved his greater contempt, however, for the second type of soldiering, systematic soldiering, which he described as workers' deliberate and calculated effort to conceal from their employers how fast they could work. He was indignant that the older and more experienced employees explicitly instructed new employees to soldier, i.e., to work at a pace that the workers themselves had decided was reasonable. He went on to say that when workers were on piece rates, i.e., when they were paid according to their output (by the piece) instead of by the hour, systematic soldiering was most pronounced. The reason for this was simple: "after a workman has had the price per piece of the work he is doing lowered two or three times as a result of his having worked harder and increased his output, he is likely entirely to lose sight of his employer's side of the case and become imbued with a grim determination to have no more cuts if soldiering can prevent it" (Taylor 1911: 23).

Taylor's solution to systematic soldiering was scientific management. If managers took knowledge of the production process from workers, they could control how work was done as well as its pace. In the years since Taylor put forward his ideas, companies have adopted many of scientific management's practices, including time-and-motion studies. Nevertheless, systematic soldiering or the restriction of output remains common, especially when workers are on piece rates. We will use Michael Burawoy's (1979) analysis of piece-rate production to explain why workers continue to restrict output and why their supervisors allow them to do so.

Burawoy began work as a miscellaneous machine operator in the small-parts department of an engine division of a company he calls Allied Corporation in July 1974. He quickly discovered that workers were restricting their output (as they had been doing thirty years earlier when the same factory was studied by another sociologist, Donald Roy, who had taken a job there).

Burawoy's interpretation of output restriction was the complete opposite of Taylor's, however. He argued that it did not mean that workers were loafing or soldiering. On the contrary, he was struck by how hard they were working. The company had specified base rates for the different piece-rate jobs that workers performed; the objective of every worker was to produce above the rate but to remain below an agreed-upon (by the workers) upper limit or quota. This was the "making-out" game. It meant producing between 100 and 140 percent of the base output rate for a particular task or job. The machine operators regarded the 100 and 140 percent as real limits. If a job was particularly difficult and a worker had to struggle to get to 100 percent, he would simply not bother to try to make the rate, knowing that he was guaranteed the base rate regardless of his actual production. This was known as "goldbricking." If a job was relatively easy, a worker might produce more than 140 percent, but he would not turn in more than that—the surplus would be banked or kept as a "kitty" for time

when he was working on a job where making out was hard. A skilled operator might build up a kitty of a week's worth of work. Workers did not turn in more than 140 percent because they believed that the rates would be raised if company management realized that the workers were capable of producing well in excess of them.

Burawoy was initially contemptuous of his co-workers' efforts to make out—despite the increase in pay that it provided—because he felt it was mostly a way of increasing the company profits at their employees' expense. His attitude soon changed, however: "It wasn't long before I too was breaking my back to make out, to make the quota, to discover a new angle, and to run two jobs at once—risking life and limb for that extra piece" (1979: xi). Workers, including Burawoy, wanted to make out because it demonstrated prowess and conferred status. Workers evaluated one another in terms of their success at making out, and a worker who was unable to make out would be scorned and derided. In addition to displaying competence, making out made the time at work pass more quickly. As with many games, the challenge of playing it well took concentration and energy and made the task at hand seem less burdensome.

One of the more striking aspects of making out was the role of supervisors, especially foremen, in assisting the workers to make out. They showed operators various shortcuts, encouraged them to build a kitty, and tolerated goldbricking. Upper management may not have approved of these practices, but the lower-level managers who had direct responsibility for production were willing players in the game. By supporting and facilitating making out, foremen were gaining the cooperation of workers and ensuring steady levels of high output.

Times: How Workers Cope with Boredom

Donald Roy was something of a legend among sociologists of the workplace for his extraordinarily wide range of blue-collar work experiences. He later estimated that he had worked in 24 different entry-level jobs in 20 different industries, including the factory that Allied Corporation later bought and in which Burawoy observed output restriction. None of his previous jobs, however, prepared him for work as a clicking-machine operator in a factory in Chicago. The job itself was extraordinarily simple. It consisted of placing steel dies of varying sizes over leather or plastic sheets and then punching a clicker that would cut the sheets. The job was so simple that it required what Roy described as "an all-time minimum of job training" (1959: 159).

It took Roy very little time to realize that the job's simplicity was its biggest problem for him. It offered no challenge, no interest, and few opportunities for game playing, despite his best efforts to invent games for himself to make the time pass more quickly. The work was the most boring he had ever experienced: "I had struggled through many dreary rounds with the minutes and hours during the various phases of my industrial experience, but never had I been confronted with such a dismal combination of working conditions as the extra-long workday, the infinitesimal cerebral excitation, and the extreme limitation of physical movement" (1959: 160). It was not until he began to pay closer attention to the activities and talk of his three co-workers that he found a different source of job satisfaction. He discovered that these workers—George, Ike, and Sammy—had developed a pattern of informal interaction that, although at first glance appearing to consist of nothing more than silly, meaningless, and juvenile pranks, actually had subtlety and significance.

The interaction among the three workers consisted of interruptions to the workday that Roy categorized as "times" and "themes." Times occurred regularly each day on the hour and usually involved the consumption of food and/or drink. There was coffee time, peach time, banana time, fish time, coke time, and lunch time. These times were far more than pauses for refreshment, however. Each of the breaks triggered a round of bantering that reflected the operators' status in the work group, with George at the top and Sammy at the bottom. For example, peach time took place at mid-morning. Sammy would announce "peach time" and would then take two peaches from his lunch box, which he shared with his three colleagues. Ike invariably disparaged the quality of the peaches. An hour later banana time followed peach time. Again Sammy supplied the food, but this time he did not eat any of it. Instead it was Ike who took the banana from Sammy's lunch box and, after shouting "banana time," ate it all himself. Every day this pattern was repeated: Sammy always brought a banana and Ike always ate it. Almost as remarkable as the behavior of the two men was the change in Roy's attitude toward it. The behavior that he had previously dismissed as childish and scarcely worth his attention now began to engross him: "At first this daily theft startled and amazed me. Then I grew to look forward to the daily seizure and interaction that followed" (1959: 162).

Themes were standardized conversations among the men that ranged from the jocular to the serious. Joking themes included Sammy's being a henpecked husband, Roy's sexual prowess, and his alleged ownership of a farm (in reality, two acres of land). Serious themes included

Ike's wife's chronic ill health and the marriage of George's daughter to a professor who taught in one of the local colleges. Like the times, the themes were highly repetitive and reflected each operator's status in the group; this meant that Sammy and Roy were on the receiving end of the jokes. Unlike the times, they followed no particular sequence, and a serious theme could easily degenerate into a kidding one.

The combination of times and themes made the long twelve-hour workday pass quickly. As Roy noted, "it reduced the monotony of simple, repetitive operations to the point where a regular schedule of long work days became livable" (1959: 166).

Deals: How Workers Control Time and Effort

A common finding in studies of workers is that they strongly dislike jobs in which they have no control over their work pace. This is the most common complaint about the assembly line and the reason why many workers on the line are so eager to take nonassembly jobs. Even the most tedious and repetitive of operations become slightly more bearable if workers can decide for themselves when to speed up and when to slacken their production.

Workers will go to considerable lengths to gain even a small measure of control over the pace of production. Walker and Guest (1952) reported that some of the automobile workers in their study had been able to establish a degree of control over their work pace by "working up the line" a distance of four or five cars or units. They could then take a break until the line caught up with them. Many workers, however, could not control their work pace by in this fashion. A worker whose tools or equipment were stationary

had to remain immobile. A worker whose task could not start until the one performed by the worker ahead of him had been completed was also constrained in his ability to earn an extra few seconds of rest time.

A more effective way of earning free time on the job than working up the line is "doubling-up." Doubling-up is when a worker does both his own job and that of the worker next to him on the assembly line. It rests on the ability of each worker to master both jobs and to perform them flawlessly. In return, workers may spend up to half the shift doing no work. Ben Hamper, whose description of doubling-up opened this chapter, experienced the full benefits of doubling-up—absenting oneself from the workplace for half the shift—when he acquired a new partner, Dale, after Bud quit:

> Dale and I clicked well together. He was much more experimental than Bud had been. Dale shared the same commitment that I had to tryin' anything that would budge that minute hand in our favor. We quickly scrapped the hour on, hour off arrangement and went straight for the summit of the double-up system—a half day on, a half day off. This meant you could actually spend as little as four or five hours in the plant, get paid for the full time, and escape out of the chaos by sunset. What a setup. (Hamper 1986: 61)

One of the more striking aspects of Hamper's portrayal of doubling-up is that his supervisors made no direct effort to stop it. Their supervisors did add an additional task to their workload—the attachment of air-conditioning clamps—but when that did not stop their doubling-up, their supervisors allowed them to continue. Hamper attributes the tolerance of doubling-up to the fact that he and his partner were good produc-ers: "As exasperated as they probably felt, they knew there was nothing they could really do to stop us. We showed up for work each and every day. We ran nothing but 100 percent defect-free quality.... GM was very big on the bottom line and the bottom line as it pertained to Dale and me was that we were exemplary shoprats" (1986: 64).

Doubling-up in the GM factory, accord-ing to Hamper, was far from widespread. Many workers either chose not to do it or were unable to accomplish the challenge of doing two jobs successfully. Not all supervisors accepted it. Much of his account stresses how difficult it was to pull this off and how much it depended on the determination and skill of an equally commit-ted co-worker as well as the acquiescence of the foreman. Even when foremen did not prohibit doubling-up, they did not encourage or assist workers who were doing it.

To see what a workplace looks like when doubling-up is widespread, we turn to a very different industry: the loading and unloading of ships by longshore workers (also known as dock workers) in the ports along the West Coast. These ports were the environment in which a version of doubling-up, known as working "on and off," or "working the deal," became a pervasive fea-ture of the work culture on the docks in the years after World War II. This practice was actively promoted by foremen and readily accepted by the companies that employed longshore workers. An explanation of how the longshore deal works and why it has been so popular is provided in William Finlay's (1988) study of the industry.

The context to the longshore deal lies in two of the industry's most distinctive characteristics. First, the loading and unloading of cargoes from ships differs from the other kinds of jobs we have been discussing in this chapter. Cargo handling requires a short-term intensive work effort to unload and load the vessel and to get it back out to sea. Ships earn money when they are on the ocean, not when they are sitting in port. Unlike chemical companies and auto companies, which expect their employees to provide a regular work effort for the full length of the workday because the job is never really finished, steamship com-panies want their employees to increase their efforts if it means saving hours or even minutes of the time it will take to get the ship out of port. Finishing early in the cargo-handling indus-try is more valuable to companies than keeping employees working until the end of their shifts.

Second, the employment relationship in the industry, i.e., how employers hire employees, is an unconventional one. Its origins lie in the resolution of the famous 1934 strike of the West Coast longshoremen (see Chapter 10). The set-tlement, handed down by an outside arbitration board, established a single dispatch or hiring hall in each port on the coast that would funnel work-ers to jobs on the waterfront. Workers would have to be registered at the hiring hall before they could be hired. Registration of workers and the hiring hall itself were to be jointly adminis-tered by a powerful union that now represented longshore workers (the International Longshore and Warehouse Union) and the employers' asso-ciation in the port. The dispatcher in each hiring hall, however, was selected by the union alone, which gave it effective control over how these halls operated. The union used its power—over employer objections—to end permanent employment. All longshoremen were dispatched from the hiring hall for the duration of the job only—the loading and unloading of a single ship. At the end of the job, they returned to the hall and awaited dispatch to their next job, in all likelihood with a different company. The union permitted longshoremen to choose their employers, using a system known as "low-man-out" dispatching. Under this system, the first choice of available jobs would go to the worker with the fewest accumulated hours worked. The result was that longshoremen got to decide if, when, and for whom they worked on a job-to-job basis.

In short, the longshore workplace was one in which employers lacked the customary pre-rogatives of evaluating and selecting workers but needed to obtain a high level of production from workers. Further, these workers belonged to a vigilant and effective union. This combina-tion of factors presented a supervisory challenge that foremen confronted on an almost daily basis. The solution was the on-and-off deal.

Finlay found that the deal operated very similarly to doubling up on the assembly line, except that all workers participated instead of just a handful. When workers reported to a ship, they were organized into gangs of six or eight workers—each gang worked one hatch of the ship—and then the gang divided itself into two. One half worked the first four hours of the shift and the other half worked the second four hours. The longshore contract explicitly prohib-ited "four-on four-off," yet it was widespread. A foreman would disallow it for those workers under his supervision only if they were unable to maintain the necessary level of production or if they were uncooperative.

All sides favored the deal. Longshore workers liked it because it turned 50 percent of the work-day into free time. They had traded the leisure during the time they were off for intense effort during the time they were on—the members of the gang who were working had to be able to maintain the same level of production that would have been achieved by the entire gang. Foremen liked it because it made the workers far easier to supervise—they had a strong incentive to work hard and uncomplainingly. Company managers liked it because the workers were productive and because they were likely to overlook any safety violations on the operation—the industry had a very strict safety code, and it was legitimate for the workers to stop working until violations of the code had been corrected. Finlay writes: "[on and off] is openly accepted by managers and supervi-sors.... The deal is an informal and permanent work arrangement of a quasi-contractual stand-ing that shores up the tenuous relations among workers, supervisors, and managers, and imposes a set of reciprocal obligations" (1988: 97).

The prevalence of games, times, and deals among blue-collar workers has led to a vigor-ous sociological debate over the meaning and interpretation of these practices. Some soci-ologists, among whom Michael Burawoy is the most prominent, see them as a trap for workers: workers may think they are getting away with something but they are in fact being lured into working harder on behalf of their employers. By playing the game or making the deal, workers are unwittingly consenting to their own exploi-tation because their efforts lead them to generate profits for others. Other sociologists, e.g., Vallas (1993), have questioned this interpretation, sug-gesting that informal practices should not be taken as an indicator of consent. Workers may play games and still feel that their interests are not aligned with those of their bosses. We are more persuaded by this second view. More specifically, we regard these practices as an indicator of power in the workplace. Workers pursue them because they gain something—more money, free time, or entertainment—that the job itself does not formally offer. Employers allow these practices when the cost of stopping them—in terms of lost production, lack of cooperation, and increased supervision—is too high.

Good Citizenship in the Workplace

Deals and games are a kind of conditional work effort. Workers are highly productive, but only if they receive the right incentives. There are some work settings, however, where hard work is unconditional. Workers voluntarily provide extra effort, a practice that Hodson (2001) calls "citizenship." The restaurant cooks in Fine's study provide one example of this. Fine comments on the high level of cooperation he observed, which was "most dramatically evident in the surprising reality that cooks regularly work unpaid overtime to help peers" (1996: 38). They arrived early and stayed late to ease the load for others.

UPS drivers are also good citizens. This is the conclusion that the journalist Alex Frankel draws after his two-year undercover stint working at six different companies, including, in addition to UPS, Starbucks, Gap, and the Apple store. Frankel worked alongside UPS drivers during one Christmas season and came away with respect for them and an appreciation of their work ethic and organizational commitment. He writes of his own transformation from wary and slightly cynical temporary worker to true UPS believer:

> There I had been, just three weeks before, sitting at my desk distracted by email and reading books and magazine articles about branding and corporate culture. Then, sporting brown from head to toe, I physically moved packages to the people of San Francisco. With no great effort on its part, UPS had inculcated me. I had delivered several thousand UPS packages and I had felt what it was like to represent UPS, to *be* UPS. I went in thinking that I'd be working at another soulless company, but I was wrong. I thought it would be a cold, sterile environment, yet it was vibrant. People were not automatons; they were living in the moment.... As an employee I got a chance to see what my career trajectory might look like. I went from thinking it would be a fun experiment to maybe wanting to stay longer. Wearing a uniform and learning the on-the-job lingo pulled me in and made me feel like part of the group. Then the hard physical work drained me and I wanted to flee. Then I got interested in staying and doing a good job. Other drivers welcomed me and shared with me their own ways in. I went in neutral and came out a believer. I went in as an anybody, and I came out a somebody. (Frankel 2007: 207)

Although employers benefit when workers are good citizens, citizenship is often found, as in Frankel's case, when employers have neither solicited this behavior nor rewarded it. Why, then, are workers good citizens? An answer to this question is suggested by Lawrence Ouellet's (1994) study of California truck drivers.

Ouellet observed truck drivers from three different firms. In two of the firms, the drivers were on piece rates, which meant they had a powerful incentive to drive fast, minimize their rest breaks, and put in long hours. Drivers for the third firm (PetroHaul), however, were paid by the hour, which guaranteed them a fixed wage regardless of how much work they actually completed. Drivers had quotas that they were supposed to meet over the course of their fifteen-hour work shifts—fuel-tanker drivers, for example, were supposed to be able to make five local gasoline deliveries during a single shift—but if they failed to meet this quota, which was quite common, they were not penalized or even reprimanded by PetroHaul's management. Finally, supervision of the drivers was minimal. The company had technology that allowed it to monitor the drivers (the tachograph, which records a truck's speed and mileage), but did not use it to determine why a quota had not been met.

Given this combination of a guaranteed wage, loose monitoring, and low supervision, the PetroHaul drivers might have been expected to loaf while at work. They did not. Ouellet explains how hard they worked:

> PetroHaul drivers worked fast, rarely took more than an hour for breaks per fifteen-hour shift, and typically thirty minutes or less, and attempted to meet the quotas. Drivers bragged about how fast they could complete a trip, how long they could work without a break, and the speed with which they could unload (1994: 69).

Drivers did not hesitate to exceed the speed limit to save time, even though they risked citations, which could result in their licenses being suspended, and dangerous accidents, because the truck-and-trailer tankers that they drove were notoriously top-heavy. Their focus on meeting their quotas became all the more apparent when one of the firm's largest customers switched from gasoline to gasohol. This required the driver to make an additional stop at an alcohol plant, where

the gasoline would be converted into gasohol. It became difficult for the drivers to meet the five-delivery quota if they were trucking gasohol, as is clear from Ouellet's conversation with a fellow driver:

> For example, Donnie asked me how many gasohol loads I usually managed to haul per shift; when I told him three to four, he said, "Oh, good, I was beginning to wonder if I was some sort of fuck-up or what, because I've been averaging only three or four loads." It is important to remember that drivers were not punished for failing to meet the quota (1994: 69).

Ouellet goes on to say that these conversations were never intended to establish how little a driver could get away with and still appear to be working hard. Instead, he writes, "the consensus sought seemed to be based on a calculus quite favorable to the owner: in effect, drivers asked, 'How much can be accomplished by a competent driver who works very hard?'" (1994: 69).

Why were the PetroHaul drivers so concerned about working quickly and meeting their quotas in the absence of incentives such as securing more free time or earning more money? Ouellet argues that they did this because of an intrinsic reward: the self-esteem of being recognized as a skilled driver. Drivers used productivity scores, such as how long it took them to complete a single job or how many deliveries they could complete in a single shift, as indicators of their skill. Drivers had few opportunities to observe one another's driving, so these scores were the next best way of assessing skill. Skill, in turn, mattered because it was a measure of a driver's worth and upheld the ethos of masculinity that the trucker embraced—his sense of being someone special, a king of the road, the last American cowboy.

One of the themes running through Ouellet's analysis is the importance that workers attach to not being closely supervised. The notion that a worker who is under a foreman's scrutiny has been emasculated is an old one in the American workplace. David Montgomery portrays nineteenth-century craftsmen as favoring a moral code that "demanded a 'manly' bearing toward the boss." He continues: "The worker who merited it refused to cower before the foreman's glares—in fact, often would not work at all when a boss was watching" (1979: 13). The flip side of this code was working hard when a boss was not watching. The introduction of mass production made this kind of attitude difficult to sustain in many workplaces, especially for workers on assembly lines. The exceptions were those settings where workers were physically separated from their supervisors, such as truck driving. For truck drivers, therefore, working hard was honorable because it was what they had chosen to do rather than being made to do.

Alvin Gouldner's (1954) classic study of a gypsum plant that operated an underground mine and a factory above it is another illustration of how the physical distance between workers and supervisors influences workers' behavior. The factory workers on the surface, who were closely monitored by supervisors, followed instructions, seldom performed tasks that exceeded their job descriptions, and were deferential toward their supervisors. In contrast, the miners, who spent most of their day out of contact with any supervisor, decided for themselves how to do their jobs, paid little attention to official job descriptions or work schedules, and showed little respect for their supervisors. In Gouldner's words, "miners

looked upon them in much the manner that the stars of the show look upon the stagehands" (1954: 108).

Gouldner goes to some lengths to emphasize that the miners were not lazy or unproductive. It was the quite the opposite, in fact. The consensus among supervisors, surface workers, and mine workers was that the miners worked far harder than their surface counterparts. Some miners even complained about the lack of effort by the surface workers and said that they would not be able to work up there because of the slow pace. Supervisors declared that they had to watch the workers on the surface carefully to make sure they did not loaf, whereas those in the mine could be trusted to produce without supervision.

Another organization that gives its employees—or at least its drivers—considerable latitude is UPS. Frankel comments on the autonomy that UPS drivers enjoy and notes that the company allowed its drivers to make minute-to-minute decisions. He suggests that this was a deliberate management strategy: "If the most prized workers were spending 90 percent of the workday on their own in the field, UPS had to train them to think and act for themselves or the system would quickly fall apart" (2007: 33).

These studies of UPS drivers, truck drivers, and miners remind us of Studs Terkel's observation, over thirty years ago, that work is "a search, too, for daily meaning as well as daily bread" (1974: p. xiii). Blue-collar workers, like other workers, want their jobs to be more than just a paycheck; they want them to provide dignity, satisfaction, and self-worth. Their willingness to perform their jobs well, even in the absence of material rewards, attests to their determination to find meaning and value in what they do for a living.

Summary

The rise of mass production eliminated many of the skills that craftsmen had developed when they determined the method and pace of production. Assembly-line jobs, in particular, are repetitive and monotonous and offer little scope for creativity. Studies of assembly-line workers have found that they focus on trying to distract themselves from the boredom of their jobs. A major debate in industrial sociology concerns whether work is going to be increasingly deskilled or whether automated production offers the opportunity for a new kind of skill, the exercise of responsibility. This debate overlooks two common features of blue-collar work. First, many workers have accumulated secret or "tacit" skills. These skills are inside knowledge of shortcuts and machinery quirks that enable them to do their jobs more easily and more quickly and that they hide from managers. Second, workers have invented informal work practices—games, times, and deals—that they pursue with varying degrees of support from their supervisors. These practices give workers greater control over their work pace, make their jobs more interesting, and make the time pass more quickly. Workers embrace tacit skills and informal work practices because they increase their power in the workplace. Employers accept them, even if they do not approve of them, because they make production smoother and more efficient. In some cases, however, workers are highly productive without these incentives—a practice known as good citizenship. Workers are most likely to be good citizens if high productivity brings recognition from their peers and if they are loosely supervised.

Chapter 7

Managers: Careers at Work

Alfred P. Sloan Jr., the legendary chief executive officer of General Motors from 1923 until 1946, began his memoir of his years at the company with a statement drawing attention to the coincidence of two events in 1908 that decisively shaped the future of U.S. automobile production: "Two events occurred in 1908 that were to be of lasting significance in the progress of the automobile industry: William C. Durant, working from his base in the Buick Motor Company, formed the General Motors Company—predecessor of the present General Motors Corporation—and Henry Ford announced the Model T" (1963: 3).

Today most people know far more about Henry Ford and the Model T Ford than they do about William Durant. This is not surprising. The invention of a car, particularly one that reached such heights of popularity, is an achievement that is easier to appreciate than is the invention of a company. Further, Ford's name lives on in the company he founded and its products. Nevertheless, it was General Motors, not the Ford Motor Company, which was to become the symbol of American industrial capitalism and American management.

Sloan's memoir explains why it was GM rather than Ford that became the world's dominant corporation. He pointed out that although Ford and Durant were great entrepreneurs and innovators, whose ideas transformed not just businesses but entire societies, neither was up to task of running the huge company he had created. Ford was reluctant to share authority—to delegate responsibility to others in the corporation. Durant was a remarkable organization builder but failed to figure out how to control the many different enterprises that made up his sprawling GM empire. On two separate occasions this failure brought GM to the brink of financial ruin, and on two separate occasions he was forced to give up control of the company he had created; his second ouster, in November 1920, was permanent and led directly to Sloan's accession to the leadership of the company and to GM's subsequent emergence as the dominant industrial corporation in the world.

Ford and Durant, despite their differences, suffered from the same problem, according to Sloan. Their management style was too subjective and "personal": "They were of a generation of what I might call personal types of industrialists;

that is, they injected their personalities, their 'genius,' so to speak, as a subjective factor into their operations without the discipline of management by method and objective facts." Durant, according to Sloan, was "a great man with a great weakness—he could create but not administer" (1963: 4). He contrasted Durant and Ford with himself; he was first and foremost a manager. As he stated in the book's introduction, "I have also considered myself as one of the breed that we now call the 'executive.' Management has been my specialization" (1963: xiii).

What exactly does managing or administering mean, and why did it pose such a challenge for William Durant and Henry Ford? This chapter takes up these questions through an examination of the work of managers. We begin with an explanation of the emergence of the manager as a distinct occupation, followed by an analysis of the nature of managerial work and a discussion of their careers. We then consider gender and racial differences in access to this occupation, especially at the highest levels. Finally, we discuss the future of management.

The Managerial Occupation

Managers supervise workers, including other managers. This means they hire these workers, assign and coordinate their tasks, evaluate and reward them, and fire them. About 6 million workers (about 4.5 percent of the workforce) are classified as belonging to "management occupations," according to the Bureau of Labor Statistics (see Table 3.2). This category includes some familiar managerial occupations, such as chief executives, marketing and sales managers, and human resources managers, as well as other

occupations that we might not normally associate with management positions. For instance, legislators, farmers and ranchers, funeral directors, preschool administrators, and postmasters are all classified as management occupations. The category of manager, therefore, is a very broad one.

Our attention in this chapter will be on the managers who direct activities within the large corporations that dominate the U.S. economy. The typical manager is what is known as a "middle manager," i.e., he or she reports to one manager and supervises other managers. The growth of management as an occupation was largely due to the rise of the corporation in the mid to late nineteenth century. The corporation created a need for a new category of employee who would assess and coordinate the activities of the multiple units that were now housed within a single enterprise, generate the data that were critical to evaluating the performance of these units, and supervise the workers within them. All of these factors combined to produce the modern corporate manager.

Managers, especially middle managers, hardly existed before the middle of the nineteenth century. Up to that time businesses were run by individual proprietors, who needed no more than a couple of assistants—often other family members—to handle all aspects of their enterprise, which included purchasing raw materials, supervising and paying workers, and selling the finished products. The owners of these businesses carried out whatever administrative tasks were needed.

It was the railroads—the booming American business of the 1850s—that invented organization charts and were the first to employ salaried managers to run these organizations. The railroads, as the business historian Alfred Chandler has noted, were "the nation's first big business" (1980: 37). Managerial hierarchies were created to solve a fundamental organizational problem: how to operate fast-moving trains safely over long distances. At first railroads had few managers. The typical railroad headquarters or central office included little more than a president, who took care of the financial side of the business, and a superintendent, who oversaw the movement of the trains. But as railroads added more and more miles of track, it became increasingly difficult for an individual superintendent to supervise this far-flung network of rail lines. This difficulty was, in some cases, a matter of life and death because the trains traveled on a single track; accidents, occasionally with fatalities, became a significant concern.

The solution was to divide the railroads into divisions or operating units of 50 to 100 miles of track. Each division had its own superintendent, who reported to the general superintendent at the central office and was responsible for the movement of trains within his unit. Other managers in the divisions were responsible for the flow of passengers and freight traffic and supervised the maintenance of the trains. The lower-level managers in the divisions reported to middle managers at the central office, who in turn reported to the superintendent and the president (Chandler 1980: 37). Once the problem of management had been solved, railroads were able to continue expanding—and to continue adding managers. By the end of the nineteenth century a typical railroad company employed hundreds of managers and operated thousands of miles of track.

This solution for operating a railroad safely may seem to us today to be so simple as to be almost obvious. In that era, however, it was a remarkable innovation. It was widely imitated in other industries, most notably by firms in the wholesale and retail trade, which were the next generation of big businesses. Companies such as Sears, Roebuck and Macy's used the railroads to ship their goods all over the country and copied the railroads' organizational model when establishing their own administrative structures (Micklethwait and Wooldridge 2003).

At the same time that big businesses were beginning to dominate the economic landscape in the late nineteenth century, the ideas of Frederick W. Taylor had started to change the way in which manufacturing companies organized the work of their production workers (see Chapter 5). We have already examined the lengths to which Taylor went to eliminate skill, discretion, and judgment from workers' jobs. Taylor believed that knowledge of production methods should be learned by managers in a business school rather than passed down from worker to worker on the shop floor. Inspired by Taylor's ideas, Harvard opened its business school in 1908—the first graduate school in the country to offer a master's degree in business. Its first-year curriculum was based on Taylor's theory of scientific management (Stewart 2006).

The combination of big business and scientific management transformed American manufacturing at the beginning of the twentieth century. Organizational hierarchies and assembly lines in the mass-production industries such as meatpacking, electrical products, and automobiles led to an enormous expansion of the managerial occupation and to American economic domination of the world economy. Factories and offices in corporations like General Motors, General Electric, DuPont, IBM, Coca-Cola, and Procter & Gamble were run by managers sometimes described as "company men"—salaried employees who devoted their entire working lives to a single organization in return for the financial security of a career. In the next two sections we take a closer look at the work and careers of the men (and later women) who manage the modern corporation.

What Do Managers Do?

The job of managers is to manage, but what exactly does this mean? How do managers spend their time? A number of studies have sought to answer this question over the years (e.g., Sayles 1964; Stewart 1967; Mintzberg 1973; Kotter 1982), and we now have a fairly comprehensive picture of managerial work. Drawing on these studies, Hales (1986) constructed a list of nine tasks that defined the managerial role: acting as a figurehead, liaising, gathering and disseminating information, negotiating for resources, allocating resources, handling conflicts, innovating, planning, and directing subordinates. Let's consider each of these in more detail.

As a *figurehead*, the manager's job is to represent the unit that she leads. For example, when a dissatisfied customer asks to speak to the manager, this action is taken under the assumption that the manager symbolizes authority within the organization and, therefore, is an appropriate person to whom to make the complaint. In many cases, however, the manager will simply take note of the complaint before returning it to a subordinate for resolution. As a *liaison*, the manager maintains links with those outside her unit. These are people not directly above or below the manager in the line of authority, whose cooperation is needed for achievement of the unit's goals. For example, a manager may

cultivate good relations with her company's human resources office because she wants that office to be prompt in responding to her staffing needs. *Gathering and disseminating information* reflects the manager's role in receiving information from those above him and collecting it from those below him. Much of a manager's power lies in his access to information, which ranges from salary and productivity data to information about corporate objectives and goals. His position at the intersection of these streams of data or information means that others are dependent on him if they want to know either what or how the unit is doing.

The next three tasks involve the management of resources: money, time, material, and personnel. *Negotiating* refers to a manager's ability to gain resources for her unit. She must compete with her counterparts to gain resources for her unit from her supervisor. *Allocating resources* enables a manager to make clear what her priorities are by rewarding those whose performance she values and by promoting projects that she favors. *Conflict handling* describes how a manager resolves competition among her subordinates, who want his support for their ideas and projects that often are incompatible. Her decisions will please some and displease others; her task is to maintain the loyalty and commitment of those whose projects she has turned down.

As an example of how all three of the above tasks go together, consider the manager of a group of hardware engineers who work in small teams on a variety of projects. Assume that this manager submits a proposal to his boss for the additional hiring of two engineers who will work on some of the projects that his group is developing. The manager is requesting time (a meeting to discuss the proposal) and money (for hiring the new employees). If both requests are met, the manager will assign the newly hired engineers to whatever projects he deems most likely to succeed (and that will make him look good). His engineers will of course compete with one another to gain the additional staffing support, with each team claiming that with just a little bit of extra assistance it could bring its project to fruition. But only two teams (at most) will gain new engineers. The manager will have to assure the other teams that he regards their projects as meritorious and would have gladly supported them, if only he hadn't been limited to hiring just two engineers.

The final three tasks—*innovating*, *planning*, and *directing subordinates*—require the manager to make an assessment of opportunities that are available and to respond to them. Innovating requires her to determine if the time is right for a new project or initiative that will, for example, enable her unit to satisfy what she perceives as a growing market demand for a certain product. Planning refers to the process by which she evaluates the projects under her overall supervision and decides which ones merit additional resources and which ones should be scaled back. Directing subordinates refers to how she allocates the employees that she directs to different projects and tasks.

The range of tasks that managers perform helps to explain why their working day is characterized by what Mintzberg (1973) has called "brevity, variety, and fragmentation." They quickly move from one task—or problem—to another, with little time to analyze issues in depth. Mintzberg reported that half of the observed activities of the managers he studied were completed in less than 10 minutes, and only one tenth took more than an hour. It was

only meetings that occupied significant blocks of time. Their work was fragmented because they were so frequently interrupted, with managers seldom able to get more than 20 or 30 minutes of uninterrupted time. Remember that this was in an era long before email, PDAs, and multitasking, which have added to managers' interruptions and have made it even more difficult to focus on one activity for any length of time.

One of Mintzberg's most striking findings was that managers actually welcomed brevity, variety, and fragmentation. Routine duties and chores bored them; they responded most enthusiastically to unforeseen difficulties and unscheduled meetings, and they welcomed instant communication and the latest information (before email this was often over the telephone or in person). They preferred to make decisions quickly and in response to an immediate concern rather than to ponder an issue from all sides.

Other studies (e.g., Kanter 1977a; Jackall 1988) have emphasized how much time managers spend talking, which they value more highly as a means of exchanging information than written documents. They have quick, informal conversations in their own or others' offices, they give instructions to their assistants, they hold meetings, and they talk on the phone. Rosabeth Kanter (1977a), in her classic analysis of corporate life, *Men and Women of the Corporation*, estimated that the managers in the corporation she studied spent between one third and one half of their time in meetings alone. A reasonable estimate is that between 70 and 80 percent of a manager's time is spent talking. Communicating defines the job, as Mintzberg pointed out:

> Unlike other workers, the manager does not leave the telephone or the meeting to get back to

work. Rather, these contacts *are* his work. The ordinary work of the organization—producing a product, undertaking research, even conducting a study or writing a report—is seldom undertaken by its manager. The manager's productive output can be measured primarily in terms of verbally transmitted information. (1973: 44)

This information was not always reliable or accurate—much of what they exchanged with one another was gossip, speculation, and hearsay. Today, email and text messages have augmented the traditional forms of instantaneous verbal communication that Mintzberg described. Their immediacy and informality make them well suited to meet managers' need for obtaining and sharing the latest information as soon as possible.

Most of this communication is with subordinates, followed by contact with peers and those outside the organization. Managers spend comparatively little time talking to their superiors. Managers submit formal reports and memos to their superiors and make a variety of requests of them (particularly if the superior is required to authorize something a manager needs), but do not maintain frequent contact with them as they do with their subordinates.

Being a manager is in many respects a political job, which is why communication matters so much to them. Managers gain and exercise power by cultivating relationships with others, resolving conflicts, sifting through the various forms of information that are spread by the corporate rumor mill, anticipating changes in corporate priorities, and allocating resources. Their ability to do all of these effectively determines how successful their units will be and how far they will rise in the organization. In the next section we turn our attention to their careers.

Managers' Careers

Take a business-school graduate who is newly hired by a major corporation. He will spend the early years of his career serving a kind of corporate apprenticeship. If he is in a line or operations position, he will be moved from one supervisory position in one of the company's plants or factories to another (perhaps in a different plant) in fairly short succession, often spending no more than six months in any one job. If he does well, he may eventually be promoted to manage one of the company's plants and then to group manager, with other plant managers under his supervision. By this point, he will probably have spent ten years with the organization. He will have successfully negotiated the transition from lower to middle management and will be poised to enter the highest tiers of the corporation's managers. If he is selected for upper management, he will be made a vice president, with the possibility of working his way up to senior vice president, executive vice president, senior executive vice president, and finally to president and chief executive officer. A similar progression up the corporate ladder may occur for a new graduate who takes an entry-level management position in any of the company's other areas, such as marketing, finance, engineering, or legal affairs.

The process that we have just described is of course better known as a career. It is the primary reward that corporations offer their managers—as a manager advances in her career by moving up the hierarchy, she gains income, power, and status. It is a competitive process: how far a manager rises depends on how well she compares to her peers in the organization. Corporate hierarchies have the shape of pyramid; the closer to the top one gets, the fewer opportunities there are.

There are fewer positions in upper management than in middle management, and there is only one CEO in any organization.

The hierarchy of positions is the basis for decision making and the exercise of authority in the corporation. The mechanism through which it operates is the reporting system. Every manager reports to a boss, who in turn reports to someone above him. At the very top of the reporting hierarchy is the CEO, who reports to the company's board of directors. Reporting is the cornerstone of the "management by objectives" approach to running a business—a staple of business administration for more than fifty years. Management by objectives means that a manager identifies the goals of her unit—profit targets or sales revenues, for example—and then makes a commitment to her boss about achieving these goals within a specified time frame. He takes her commitment and those of the other managers he supervises and makes a similar commitment to his boss about achieving his goals. In this fashion a chain of commitments from the CEO down to the lowest-level manager in the corporation is established.

The Difficulty of Evaluating Managers

In theory, at least, this reporting system and management by objectives should make it easy to evaluate managers. A manager's boss would examine whether he had actual met the specified objectives and would evaluate him accordingly. In practice, however, two factors limit the extent to which evaluations occur in this fashion. The first is that managers go to considerable lengths only to make commitments that they know are achievable. There is no incentive for them to set ambitious targets that they might not make and that could lead to a poor evaluation.

The second factor is more fundamental and stems from the nature of managerial work itself. The job is inherently difficult to evaluate because of the uncertain connection between managers' efforts and the objectives they have set. Unlike other workers, they do not make or sell products, although they often supervise those who do. Unlike professionals, they do not deal directly with patients or clients. Managers' work involves hard-to-measure skills, such as the ability to communicate, to lead, to anticipate problems, and to respond to them effectively. The assessment of these skills is inevitably imprecise and subjective. A manager's ability to meet the commitments he has made to his boss does not indicate whether he has these skills and is, therefore, a good manager. It instead reflects the quality of the work of those below him in the hierarchy. Kanter quotes a sales manager who states: "It's hard as a manager to know when you're doing well. You can't *really* take credit for improvements in sales" (1977a: 60). The higher in the hierarchy the manager rises, the more difficult it becomes to determine how much of the credit he deserves for the work of those many levels below him.

Supervisors of lower-level managers may make an attempt to evaluate managers using management-by-objectives targets, but formal evaluation criteria appear to play little part in the evaluation of more senior executives. Consider, for example, how a senior vice president in a large American financial institution described his annual evaluation to Calvin Morrill, a sociologist who studied corporate life among 305 managers and their staffs in thirteen private corporations:

> He [the executive vice president to whom the senior vice president reports] calls the meeting. It lasts about twenty minutes max. He goes over

what he understands my department accomplished during the year; nothing too specific, just sticking with the generalities. He talks about what he wants out of the division the coming year and what he wants out of the company the coming year and that's really it. I don't really say much. Oh, I might clarify something if it's unclear, but I don't say much. You're in and out in twenty minutes. (Morrill 1995: 97)

The executives in Morrill's study were unable even to identify the formal criteria used for performance evaluations. When questioned about these criteria they responded that they were "not well spelled out," were based on unspecified "contributions to the bottom line," or were "hazy" (1995: 98).

Other studies have confirmed that corporations have difficulty specifying their criteria for evaluating managers. Kanter found that when an executive personnel committee in the corporation she studied attempted to come up with a list of characteristics that would make a manager "officer material" (i.e., a candidate for the top ranks of the organization), the traits that the committee recommended "were so vague as to be almost meaningless." They included characteristics such as empathy, integrity, ambition, risk-taking, being a good delegator, and being a good communicator (1977a: 61). Robert Jackall, who analyzed managers' careers at three private corporations, reported that once managers have reached the "breaking point" in the hierarchy—the point of transition from middle to senior management—"managerial competence as such is taken for granted and assumed not to differ greatly from one manager to the next" (1988: 42).

The difficulty of evaluating managerial work results in senior managers using informal criteria when they review their subordinates. One of the most important of these criteria is social similarity—there is considerable evidence that managers favor, often unwittingly, those who are socially similar to them. This has implications for diversity and discrimination in the workplace. Let's take a closer look at these informal criteria and how they are used.

Informal Evaluation and Promotion Criteria

In contrast to the vagueness and uncertainty surrounding the formal criteria that will be used to evaluate them, managers seem to be well aware of the crucial informal criteria that they will have to meet if they are to be promoted. First, and perhaps most important, a manager must *support the boss*. Support has a number of different connotations. It means a manager must not allow his boss to be caught by surprise or to make a mistake, particularly if he is making a presentation to his boss. A manager who allows this is to happen is either incompetent or deliberately wants his boss to look bad. The latter does sometimes happen—Morrill (1995) describes a case in one of the corporations he studied in which a disliked and incompetent senior vice president, nicknamed "the pig," was deliberately set up to fail by a subordinate at a meeting with his boss, the executive vice president. The subordinate appeared to give "the pig" a thorough briefing before the meeting, but left out some crucial questions that he knew would be asked. As expected, the executive vice prresident became angry when these questions were not answered, and he subsequently shifted the senior vice president to a different part of the division, where he enjoyed neither responsibility nor respect (Morrill 1995: 3–4). The strategy of making one's boss look bad succeeded in this case, but it also carries many risks, the most likely being that the boss will take his subordinates down with him.

Support also means that a manager should not contradict her boss, at least not in public. It means that a manager should be aware of her boss's plans and pet projects and be able to talk about them in a knowledgeable way. Morrill quotes an executive vice president on the importance of his subordinates' familiarity with his ideas and schemes:

> An important part of performance that is graded around here is whether your people are in the mix. By being in the mix, I really mean knowing what I'm up to, what I'm planning. One of my senior vice presidents is really out of the mix on most of the stuff that I'm doing. I can't ever run an idea by him on something that we're engaged in. That kind of stuff comes up in an evaluation. It's core. (1995: 98)

The importance of support means that personal loyalty plays a huge part in determining who gets promoted. It explains why managers go to such lengths to please their bosses, especially the CEO. It also explains why managers rise in the organization as their bosses do—a newly appointed CEO, for example, will want to place his trusted and loyal subordinates in key positions in the company because he knows he can count on them.

Second, a manager must be perceived as a *team player*. A team player is someone who accepts her role, fits in, and gets along well with others. She makes others, whether peers or customers, feel comfortable being around her. She puts in long hours at the office, where she makes sure that others notice that she is around. She has a positive, enthusiastic attitude toward her work and the company (Jackall 1988: 49–56).

Third, a manager must have the right *style*. This means he must look and dress the part, i.e., follow his organization's informal rules for how a manager should present himself. He must be able to control his emotions—he should not be perceived as emotionally unstable or volatile. He must be able to express himself well—he must be articulate, quick on his feet, and able to present his ideas clearly and forcefully. He must be able to persuade others of his own credibility. A middle manager in Jackall's study explained the importance of style for being promoted:

> Persons who can present themselves well, who can sell themselves the best are the kind of people who get ahead. It's an image type thing. Not just doing the job right but being able to capitalize on it in certain ways. Some people are gifted at doing that. They handle themselves very well. They may not be take-charge people but they give you the impression they are. They dress properly and dress is very important. And how they handle themselves at a meeting is extremely important. This is especially true at pressure-cooker-type meetings which is what divisional meetings are. People get up and review their numbers. It's a stagelike atmosphere. People have to justify their numbers. And everybody knows why things fall apart sometimes, but some people are able to explain things better and highlight the good points in ways that impress other people. It's having a certain grace, charm, adroitness, and humor. (1988: 57)

It is easier for a manager to convince his boss that he is supportive, is a team player, and has the right style if he is *socially similar* to his boss.

Social similarity refers to a wide range of common ties among people. It includes whether people share common class backgrounds, whether they are from the same ethnic group or religion, and whether they are of the same gender. It refers to whether they have common educational backgrounds, interests, or hobbies. It can also mean whether people talk, act, and dress in ways that are alike. The reason that social similarity matters is that people are comfortable with and trust others who are similar to them (Kanter 1977a; Jackall 1988). A person whose boss is comfortable with him or trusts him is more likely to get an important assignment or a promotion. This is one reason why managers sometimes seem to be clones of one another, as Morrill's description of the top executives at a firm he calls "Old Financial" illustrates:

> Most executives are of northern European stock, male, and in their fifties. Male and female executives tend to be tall, the men near or over six feet and the women near or over five foot eight. Whether male or female, all executives wear dark suits, dark shoes, and white shirts or blouses....Consistent with their conservative dress, Old Financial executives display studied, almost stiff control of their bodily movements or as one executive noted, a "buttoned-down" style. Old Financial executives never hurry or saunter as they walk to and from their offices on E2 and E1. They stride in an even, measured pace. This style carries over to executive speech as well. In conversation, executives speak in measured sentences with confident assurance of what they are saying. (1995: 94)

Gender and race are the two most obvious and controversial dimensions of social similarity.

Kanter's study, conducted more than thirty years ago, was one of the first to point out that when managers selected others because they could be trusted, the result was the exclusion of women and others with "discrepant social characteristics" from the senior levels of the organization. We take up this issue in the next section.

Gender and Racial Differences in Access to Power and Authority

Sociologists have long viewed a worker's ability to exercise authority on the job—by supervising others or making decisions about organizational resources—as a critical factor in understanding the distribution of other work rewards, such as income and occupational status. Studies that have looked broadly at gender and racial differences in the distribution of job authority are unequivocal in finding that women have less authority than men at work, and minorities have less than whites. Moreover, Smith (2002: 535) concludes that: "Despite important social, economic, political, and legislative achievements in the last 20 years, these results remain robust and consistent in regional, national, and cross-national studies at single points in time and cross-temporally."

Gender and racial differences in authority can be seen most clearly at the highest level of the organization. At the top of the managerial hierarchy is the chief executive officer. In 2006, among the largest and most prominent companies ("The Fortune 500"), women ran just ten corporations. That number increases to 20 if we include the top 1000 corporations listed by *Fortune* magazine (see Table 7.1). The number of minorities in these top positions is worse. The first black CEO of a Fortune 500 company was

TABLE 7.1 Women CEOs for Fortune 1000 Companies, 2006

NAME	COMPANY	RANK
Claire Babrowski	RadioShack	423
Brenda C. Barnes	Sara Lee	111
Dorrit J. Bern	Charming Shoppes	641
Mary E. Burton	Zale	715
Patricia Gallup	PC Connection	992
Susan M. Ivey	Reynolds American	280
Andrea Jung	Avon Products	281
Kay Krill	AnnTaylor Stores	786
Linda A. Lang	Jack in the Box	692
Kathleen A. Ligocki	Tower Automotive	551
Anne Mulcahy	Xerox	142
Janet L. Robinson	New York Times	557
Paula G. Rosput Reynolds	Safeco	339
Patricia F. Russo	Lucent Technologies	255
Mary F. Sammons	Rite Aid	129
Marion O. Sandler	Golden West Financial	326
Stephanie A. Streeter	Banta	940
Margaret C. Whitman	eBay	458
Mary Agnes Wilderotter	Citizens Communications	768
Dona Davis Young	Phoenix	666

Since publication, Patricia A. Woertz was named CEO of *Archer Daniels Midland* (rank: 56) effective April 28, 2006, and Claire Babrowski, who was the interim CEO of *RadioShack* (rank: 423), was replaced by Julian Day effective July 7, 2006. The total of FORTUNE 500 women CEOs remains 10, and FORTUNE 1000 women CEOs 20.
Source: http://money.cnn.com/magazines/fortune/fortune500/womenceos/

not appointed until 1998, when Franklin Raines became chairman and CEO of Fannie Mae.

Publicly held corporations are led not only by CEOs but also by boards of directors. Boards are powerful entities in corporate America. They hire and fire CEOs and make other consequential decisions for companies. A 2005 report from the Alliance for Board Diversity found that of the 1,195 seats on Fortune 100 public corporation boards, only about 29 percent were held by women or minorities. Women of color held only 3.1 percent of these seats. Because it is possible to serve on more than one board at a time, this study also looked at the average number of seats a person held. The report identified a pattern of what it called a "recycling" of minorities, meaning that the same few individuals were serving on more than one board. This was especially true for African American men, who held an average of 1.5 seats per person (as compared to white men who averaged 1.18 seats). These results show how rare it still is for a woman or person of color to reach the top levels of corporate America.

Things improve somewhat if we consider the share of *all* managerial jobs held by women and minorities. The percentage of women employed as managers in the private sector has been steadily increasing since 1990. By 2006 women held approximately 37 percent of these jobs. Roughly 17 percent of managerial jobs were held by minorities, a slight increase from the previous decade. Overall, these numbers suggest that while women and minorities have made inroads into the ranks of managers, they have found it much more difficult to penetrate the top echelons of the corporation.

The Glass Ceiling

A 1986 *Wall Street Journal* article introduced the term "glass ceiling" to describe the invisible barriers that women and people of color confront as they move closer to the top of the managerial hierarchy. This term was later adopted by the U.S. Department of Labor when it created the Glass Ceiling Commission, charged with studying and recommending ways to eliminate "those artificial barriers based on attitudinal or organizational bias that prevent qualified individuals from advancing upward in their organization into management-level positions" (U.S. Department of Labor 1991). The term "glass ceiling" continues to resonate with the public as a way to understand women's and minorities' relative lack of access to the highest levels of the corporate world.

Behind the metaphor of the glass ceiling is an assertion that as women and minorities move up the corporate ladder, their chances of continuing to do so gradually decrease. In other words, there are presumed to be more obstacles to upward mobility at the top than at the bottom of the managerial hierarchy. Many sociological studies have tested these claims, with somewhat inconsistent results (Cohen, Broschak, and Haveman 1998; Baxter and Wright 2000; Petersen and Saporta 2004). What recent research does seem to suggest, however, is that gender and racial biases operate at *all* levels of an organization. These processes are intensified at the top, however, by two sets of factors: one involves the particular features of high-level managerial work, while the second concerns the cumulative effects of decisions at lower levels and their consequences for the "supply" of women and minorities at the top (Gorman and Kmec 2007). We consider each of these factors below.

Homosocial Reproduction, Social Networks, and Stereotypes

Delegating decision-making authority to others is risky, and this is especially true when a lot is at stake. This is part of the reason why trust matters in managerial circles and why it matters more the closer one gets to the top of the managerial hierarchy. Henry Ford is an example of a leader so reluctant to delegate that he almost destroyed his company. A reluctance to trust outsiders is part of the reason why leaders sometimes turn first to family members to fill high-level positions. It also explains what Kanter (following Melville Dalton) referred to as "homosocial reproduction," or the tendency for managers to seek out and surround themselves with others like themselves (a phenomenon sometimes known as "homophily," or the preference for members of one's own group). To the extent that people are selected for managerial jobs partly on the basis of their perceived ability to "fit in" or their similarities to those already in these positions, outsiders will find it difficult to break in and crack the glass ceiling.

There are many bases of similarity and dissimilarity, but ascriptive characteristics like gender and race are especially powerful (see Chapters 11 and 12). Because gender and race are visible markers of difference, women and people of color must work extra hard to be perceived as similar to co-workers from another gender or racial category. Hence, while all top managers may face pressures to fit in with their peers, these pressures are intensified for women and minorities, whose gender and race make them highly visible "outsiders" in settings that have been traditionally dominated by white men.

Because of their outsider status, studies suggest that women and minorities have less access than their peers to the informal networks that are so essential to advancement in managerial careers (Ibarra 1993, 1995). Sociologists consider network ties as social resources, or "social capital." Like other forms of capital, social capital represents a valuable asset: those we interact with on the job can provide us with information, expertise, and career advice, and they can also offer social support and friendship. While access to this social capital is always desirable, it is especially so for managers. As we saw earlier, managerial positions are intensely political. Informal interaction with others is necessary to forge the close bonds of trust and loyalty that are expected in managerial circles, and being connected—especially to the "right" people—is important to managerial success. Managers looking to get ahead need to cultivate relationships with people

who are powerful, trustworthy, and upwardly mobile themselves.

Women and minorities in top jobs must be politically savvy and strategic in order to overcome these obstacles and be successful. They must constantly work to fit in and be accepted by members of the dominant group, but they also need social support and mentorship from others like themselves. In her study of white and African American managers' social networks, Ibarra (1995) illustrated the importance of both strategies to managerial success. Specifically, she found that African American managers rated as having the highest potential for advancement developed "instrumental relationships" with whites who could provide important career advice, but did not interact with them exclusively. In fact, "high-potential" managers had more racially diverse informal networks than other African American managers, whose informal networks were dominated by whites. And the "high-potential" managers were more likely than other managers to seek social support from other minorities outside their departments and organizations. Hence, being different is a liability for women and minorities in top managerial jobs, yet as this research shows, assimilation has its own drawbacks.

To understand the glass ceiling and the experiences of women and minorities in management, we must also consider the effects of stereotypes and status on perceptions and performance of managers. Stereotypes are both descriptive and prescriptive (Heilman 2001). They are used to describe presumed differences between groups, but they also prescriptively denote how group members should behave or what activities are appropriate.

Much has been written about gender stereotypes and their role in limiting or enhancing opportunities for women and men in management. Leadership is one important quality expected of managers. It is therefore useful to look at studies of leadership behavior and specifically at stereotypes regarding men's and women's leadership qualities. Studies of leadership behavior suggest that male and female leaders behave about the same: when found, differences are small, and women and men in leadership positions are rated as equally effective (Powell and Graves 1999; Heilman 2001). Despite these findings, research on people's perceptions of leadership qualities find that most (especially men) view leadership positions as requiring more stereotypically male than female qualities.

Whether people would rather work for a man or a woman is one of the more commonly asked questions in popular surveys. One recent survey of over 60,000 people conducted by *Elle* magazine and MSNBC.com reported that three quarters of women would rather work for a man if given the choice. Powell and Graves (1999) report that when Gallup asked a similar question of people in over 22 countries, they found that the preference for a male boss was held worldwide. Although the preference for a male boss seems to have decreased over time, roughly 60 percent of each gender would rather work for a man.

These preferences are interesting in light of the fact that many behaviors now considered essential to being an effective leader may be more strongly associated with feminine stereotypes than masculine ones. In a recent study, the research nonprofit organization Catalyst (2005) surveyed more than 200 corporate leaders, just over a third of whom were CEOs, and asked them to rate women's and men's leadership effectiveness. The study's authors first identified ten

essential leadership behaviors, then classified each according to whether it was more stereotypically feminine or masculine (see Table 7.2). Both men and women agreed that men were more effective than women at delegating and influencing upward, while respondents from both genders judged women more effective than men at supporting and rewarding. These responses are consistent with a long tradition of research on gender stereotypes (Schneider 2005).

The women and men surveyed by Catalyst did disagree in several areas, the most notable being problem-solving behaviors. Male respondents judged women as least effective in this area, while women rated women as more effective problem solvers than men. Given the importance of problem solving to leadership, this disagreement seems to signal that women and men in leadership roles may have somewhat different views about women's and men's relative suitability for leadership positions. This is consistent with other research, as Powell and Graves (1999: 136) explain:

> No matter what the comparison, male managers still associate men more than women with the managerial role. They also feel that women managers, when compared to men managers and successful middle managers, are more bitter, quarrelsome, jealous, and obsessed with the need for power and achievement.

Further, according to these researchers, men *and women* in Great Britain, Germany, France, and China share these views, and only U.S. women associate the managerial role with both genders. One consequence of these deeply held stereotypes is that "women who aspire to management in most societies contend with common

TABLE 7.2 How Leader Behaviors Connect to Feminine and Masculine Stereotypes

FEMININE BEHAVIORS—"TAKING CARE"	MASCULINE BEHAVIORS—"TAKING CHARGE"
Supporting	**Problem-Solving**
Encouraging, assisting, and providing resources for others	Identifying, analyzing, and acting decisively to remove impediments to work performance
Rewarding	**Influencing Upward**
Providing praise, recognition, and financial renumeration when appropriate	Affecting others in positions of higher rank
Mentoring	**Delegating**
Facilitating the skill development and career advancement of subordinates	Authorizing others to have substantial responsibility and discretion
Networking	
Developing and maintaining relationships with others who may provide information or support resources	
Consulting	
Checking with others before making plans or decisions that affect them	
Team-Building	
Encouraging positive identification with the organization unit, cooperation, and constructive conflict resolution	
Inspiring	
Motivating others toward greater enthusiasm for, and commitment to, work objects by appealing to emotion, value, or personal example	

Source: "Women 'Take Care,' Men 'Take Charge': Stereotyping of U.S. Business Leaders Exposed." *Catalyst* 2005.

stereotypes of their being unfit for the role" (Powell 1999: 335).

These stereotypes may be intensified at the top of the management hierarchy. More so than middle management, the very top jobs in an organization are likely to be filled by men who believe that masculine qualities are required for success in the role. If women as a group are believed not to possess these qualities, women will have a difficult time being selected for top-level positions and, if selected, will likely face negative performance expectations. A female brokerage manager who sued and won a large award for having been discriminated against by a large Wall Street firm said of her employer:

"They really don't believe they are discriminating....If you come in and you look like they want you to look—probably a white male profile—they'll project success on you. They have a specific view of what a successful broker or manager will look like, and it is not usually a woman or a black or Hispanic." (McGeehan 2004)

When people are judged to be a poor fit for a role, they are not expected to succeed; when fit is presumed to be good, success is expected (Heilman 2001). Performance expectations—whether positive or negative—affect how work is evaluated. Regardless of their competence or accomplishments, those not expected to succeed may find their performance devalued relative to their peers. These issues are further compounded by the features of top management positions described earlier, especially the lack of clear and objective criteria for evaluating managers' performance. When there is uncertainty about how people should be evaluated, evaluators may fall back on gender stereotypes.

To see role stereotypes in action, consider the experiences of Carol Bartz, former CEO of the international software company Autodesk. Ms. Bartz has a reputation as a competent and savvy businesswoman. Nevertheless, when attending meetings with other business and political leaders, she is often ignored by men who assume she is an office assistant: "Happens all of the time.... Sometimes I stand up. Sometimes I just ignore it," she said in a *New York Times* interview (Creswell 2006). Ms. Bartz's experience of not being recognized as a peer, despite a record of success, is not atypical for a woman in a high-level job. Now consider her possible responses to this treatment: By saying nothing, she implicitly helps to perpetuate the stereotype that a woman in a room of high-powered executives must be someone's assistant. By "standing up" and asserting herself, however, she puts her "likability"

at risk and possibly perpetuates biases against women as bossy or authoritarian when given authority over others. Women who try to behave too much "like men" face disapproval, especially in predominantly male settings. Because success in a high-level managerial job not only requires competence, but also acceptance by one's peers, women who challenge gender stereotypes may be at as much of a disadvantage as those who allow them to go unchallenged.

Most working women and men are not CEOs of major corporations, and many of the same factors that limit women's access to these top-level positions limit men's access as well. Further, despite the stereotypical treatment she may face because of her gender, Ms. Bartz is highly successful and very well paid. The point of the above example, however, is to demonstrate that even women who reach the highest levels of a corporation are not immune to deeply entrenched gender stereotypes regarding women's ability to exercise authority. These stereotypes are among the factors that make it difficult for women in any type of managerial position to be as successful as their male counterparts.

Although this discussion focuses on gender, the way in which stereotypes (and their violation) shape perceptions and evaluations of performance is applicable to other ascriptive characteristics as well. Because views about what type of person is best suited to a role are influenced by the characteristics of those who have traditionally held the position, minorities are also likely to be seen as a poor fit for top management jobs. This perception of a lack of fit sets into motion the same potential for biased evaluation processes as occurs for women, and the consequences of violating stereotypes are similar.

The Managerial Pipeline

We turn now to the "supply side" of the issue. Perhaps the small numbers of women and minorities in high-level managerial jobs result less from barriers encountered at the top than from these groups' relative lack of qualifications for or interest in top positions. If there are not enough women and minorities in the pipeline who are qualified to fill top jobs, their representation in higher-level positions will necessarily remain low. Researchers have identified a number of factors that might affect the numbers of women and minorities qualified for top jobs.

Gorman and Kmec (2009) suggest that selection decisions at lower levels of the managerial hierarchy may have a cumulative effect on the qualifications of women (and minorities) for positions at the highest levels. As they explain:

> Through promotions, transfers, and specific task assignments, organizations provide (or deny) opportunities to build skills. Employees who are repeatedly assigned to the same tasks will not develop as extensive a set of skills as those who are given varied and challenging assignments. In addition, senior employees serve as mentors for some junior employees, providing advice and coaching to protégés. Over time, differences in the allocation of assignments and mentoring are likely to generate a substantial skill gap between men and women who began their careers at the same time and with similar responsibilities. (Gorman and Kmec 2009)

Another way in which selection processes operating at lower levels can affect the availability of minorities for higher level jobs involves what Smith and Elliott (2002) call "the sticky floor." Instead of a "glass ceiling" limiting access to the very top of the managerial hierarchy, the "sticky floor" may prevent minorities from leaving entry-level jobs. Because employers tend to hire supervisors of the same ethnicity as those whom they supervise, minorities' opportunities for exercising authority at work are dependent upon their ethnic group's relative position within the organization: "If one's ethnic group dominates only entry-level jobs within an organization, then one's authority chances will be restricted largely to supervising entry-level workers. If one's ethnic group dominates higher-level positions, then one's authority chances will increase accordingly" (Smith and Elliott 2002: 274). The "sticky floor" thus is created at the level in the organization where members of one's ethnic group are most likely to predominate.

Frequent or repeated experiences with bias on the job may take their toll on people by reducing their confidence and enthusiasm for the job. Moreover, as many have noted, getting to the top of the managerial hierarchy is a career path that does not appeal to everyone. Managers and executives in high-level positions work long hours, often travel extensively, and have little, if any, time for personal or family life. Success requires a single-minded focus on work and an overarching commitment to the job. Blair-Loy (2003) refers to this mindset as a cultural schema of "work devotion." Not surprisingly, work devotion is very difficult to combine with family commitments and childcare responsibilities. Hence, some argue that the undersupply of women in executive positions reflects an inability or unwillingness to make the kind of career commitments demanded by high-level jobs.

For a more precise account of exactly how work time and gender combine to shape career decisions, we turn to the case of Wall Street financial professionals. Our discussion here is a summary of Louise Roth's research on the Wall Street securities industry (2006). One of the advantages of focusing on this industry is that its members, unlike doctors, change their specialties, so we can determine whether women shift into less demanding specialties when they have children or take on other domestic responsibilities.

Professional jobs on Wall Street are similar to large law firms in their career patterns and demands. Securities firms—firms that manage the flow of capital between corporations and investors—hire MBA graduates from the top business schools and place them in jobs where they work 80-hour weeks in a highly competitive environment. Securities professionals work either directly with clients, in corporate finance or in sales and trading, or behind the scenes in equity research or support roles. There is a high level of attrition during the first four years of employment. Those who survive this grueling apprenticeship are promoted to vice president, the first step on the career fast track that will culminate, if they are successful, in being named a managing director.

In 1998 and 1999 Roth interviewed 76 randomly selected MBA graduates (44 women and 32 men) who had begun their careers in one of nine major Wall Street securities firms in the early 1990s. The median annual earnings of her interviewees in 1997 was $410,000. But there were significant differences by gender and position. Women earned just over 60 percent of what men earned: $325,000 compared to $525,000. Those in corporate finance earned nearly $540,000, whereas those in equity research and support positions earned slightly over $300,000. Women earned less than men in part because they were much more likely to be in research

and support. More than 36 percent of the women in her sample were in these areas, compared to 16 percent of the men. Conversely, 52 percent of the men were in corporate finance, compared to just under 30 percent of the women.

One of the most striking findings in Roth's research is the shift of women out of corporate finance over the course of their young careers. Over half of the 44 women (and 60 percent of the men) had begun in corporate finance—the area with the longest hours and greatest amount of travel—but only 13 women remained in it at the time of her interview. In fact, nearly half of the women in her sample had changed work groups and/or firms since starting their careers. Women who moved out of corporate finance into equity research and support functions were intentionally giving up the opportunity to maximize their earnings.

There were two main reasons for these career shifts. First, 11 of the 44 women changed jobs or left the industry because of overt and subtle discrimination. In some cases this meant a hostile work environment—some women reported that they were singled out after becoming pregnant, with their male co-workers and supervisors suggesting that they should not return to work after childbirth. In other cases, women got the feeling that they did not belong—they did not receive informal mentoring from upper-level investment bankers or they did not form the "buddy" relationships with clients that were crucial to success in corporate finance. Second, family responsibilities led 10 women who started in male-dominated specialties to move into lower-paying jobs and caused another four to quit their jobs entirely. This decision highlighted a basic difference between financial professionals who were also fathers and those who were mothers: the men were married, in the vast majority of cases, to full-time homemakers, whereas not one woman had a homemaking husband. It was women, most of whom were married to other professionals in demanding jobs, who had to manage their careers to balance home and work. No man in Roth's study assumed the bulk of caregiving duties in his family.

One of the questions studies like these raise is whether we can say for certain that concerns over work time and childcare are driving women's career decisions. At best the data are suggestive rather than conclusive. We suspect that the long hours required of senior-level managers encourage some women to pursue less demanding managerial or executive roles, even if they are less well rewarded. But most researchers agree that such decisions cannot fully explain the dearth of women (and minorities) at the highest levels of organizations. Instead, as we have shown here, people's career paths are shaped not only by their own decisions and choices, but also by the structure and organization of the occupation and the particular jobs and firms in which they work. The unique aspects of managerial positions—especially at the highest levels—have made this sector of the occupational world more exclusively male (and white) than any other area of economy.

The Future of Management

In the 1950s, managers were sometimes mocked as anonymous bureaucrats who lived in identical suburban homes with their stay-at-home wives and devoted their energies to climbing company career ladders. Book with titles such as "The Organization Man" (Whyte 1956) and "The Man in the Gray Flannel Suit" (Wilson 1955)

suggested that managers had traded their autonomy and individual identities for the rewards of corporate life. These stereotypes underscored the fact that managers climbed the corporate ladder by spending their entire careers within a single organization. This promotion-from-within system (sometimes described as an "internal labor market"; see Chapter 15 for further discussion of this concept) rested on a straightforward bargain: managers provided loyalty and hard work to their employers, and companies rewarded them with job security and career advancement. The result of this system was that the corporation's top executives were men who had spent many years in the organizations for which they worked and who were highly knowledgeable about the products the organization made and the markets in which it competed. Two major factors have undermined the corporate promote-from-within approach. First, competition has become global. Second, institutional investors have acquired a significantly larger ownership share of U.S. companies. We consider each of these factors and their consequences for managers next.

The Impact of Global Competition

In the 1950s, U.S. companies faced little outside competition at home and were able to dominate world markets. By the 1970s, however, not only were companies from other countries challenging U.S. companies abroad, they had also become formidable competitors within the U.S. market itself. For a good illustration of this shift, consider the rise of the Japanese automobile companies—Honda, Nissan, and, especially, Toyota. In the 1950s it was inconceivable that any of these manufacturers could threaten American companies like GM, Ford, and Chrysler. When Toyota exported its first car—the Toyopet Crown—to the United States in 1957, it was described as a brick with a roof on top, and it completely failed to impress U.S. consumers. Toyota decided to pull it from the market in 1960. But Toyota recovered from its initial setback, introducing models such as the Corona and the Corolla, which buyers found attractive for their reliability and, after the oil crisis of the 1970s, for their fuel economy. Since the mid-1970s Toyota has become one of the most successful companies in the world, with nearly 50 factories in 26 countries. It has doubled its share of both the world and the U.S. automobile market during this period, while GM, in contrast, has had its market share cut in half. GM, which has been the world's largest carmaker for over 70 years, is now in a virtual tie with Toyota for the top spot in worldwide auto sales.

The auto industry is just one into which non-U.S. companies have made significant inroads over the past three decades. A result of this international competition was that U.S. corporations began to focus on making themselves more competitive. CEOs now wanted to build "lean and mean" companies. This has meant cutting payrolls—even in companies that are prospering. In the past layoffs were most likely to occur in companies that were struggling to make a profit. In the last two decades, however, it has been common for successful and profitable companies to fire employees, including large numbers of middle managers. One sign of the new lean and mean approach is the official reasons that corporations have given for job cutting. Paul Osterman (1999) has compared the justifications that companies gave for layoffs in 1972 with those that they provided in 1994. In 1972 nearly 70 percent of the firms attributed layoffs

to poor economic performance; in 1994 less than half the firms cited this factor and more than half claimed it was due to "structural adjustments," which is business-speak for making the firm more competitive.

The *New York Times* summarized the impact of the drive to become lean and mean with a series of articles in 1996 entitled "The Downsizing of America." The articles described a new experience for large numbers of middle-aged white men in middle-management positions—losing their jobs. Companies such as AT&T, IBM, Chase Manhattan, and General Electric, long regarded as firms whose employees virtually had jobs for life, began to lay off employees by the tens of thousands in the 1980s and 1990s. IBM, for example, fired more than 120,000 employees between 1990 and 1995. An entirely new set of corporate euphemisms was developed to use instead of the terms "firing" and "layoffs." There was "downsizing," "decruiting," "dehiring," "deselected," "destaffed," "disemployed," "nonretained," "nonrenewed," "degrowing," "refocusing of the skill mix," "resource allocation," "right-sizing," and "workforce imbalance correction" (Uchitelle and Kleinfield 1996).

The stars in this new era of corporate downsizing were CEOs like Jack Welch, who ran General Electric from 1981 to 2001. Within five years of becoming CEO, he had cut one quarter of the GE workforce. "Neutron Jack," as he was nicknamed (the employees were gone but the buildings remained), had a simple strategy for pruning managers: he ranked all of them every year and fired the bottom 10 percent.

After his retirement from GE, Welch went on to write a best-selling memoir, *Jack: Straight from the Gut*, and was hailed as the "Manager of the Century" by *Fortune* magazine in 1999.

The loss of job security and the cutting of management jobs is reflected in the shorter job tenure of employees, middle-aged men in particular. (Job tenure refers to the number of years an employee remains with one employer.) The median number of years of tenure of men between the ages of 45 and 54 (the typical age of middle managers) was 12.8 in 1983. By 2000 it had dropped to 9.5 for men in the same age category. But it would be incorrect to conclude from these data that managers are disappearing. The change is in their job security—they cannot count on remaining with the same company for their entire careers. Career advisors now instruct managers that they have to be as flexible in considering new opportunities with new employers as their companies are in deciding whether to keep them or let them go. The opportunities are particularly attractive for managers at the top of organizations. To understand why CEOs are in such high demand, we turn to the growing institutional ownership of corporate shares.

The Power of Institutional Investors and the Cult of the CEO

We began this chapter with a discussion of the difficulties of William Durant and Henry Ford, the respective founders of General Motors and Ford Motors. Both Durant and Ford were entrepreneurs of great vision, but neither was a particularly adept manager. The successful running of large business organizations depended on the administrative talents of professional managers such as Alfred Sloan. This story is a familiar one in the history of the modern corporation. Time and again the organization's founders have stepped aside—or been pushed aside—and someone from outside the company has been hired as CEO. For a contemporary illustration, consider

the fact that neither Larry Page nor Sergey Brin, the founders of Google, is its CEO. In 2001, Page and Brin, who remain in the organization as co-presidents, recruited Eric Schmidt from the Novell Corporation to be Google's chairman of the board and CEO. The business historian Alfred Chandler has argued that the rise of professional managers to the highest levels of the corporate hierarchy represented a new form of capitalism—"managerial capitalism" (Chandler 1977).

By the 1950s managerial capitalism was firmly established in U.S. companies. Although the CEO, in theory, reported to the board of directors, who were elected by the shareholders, in practice shareholders exercised little real power. The vast majority of them owned too few shares to be able to influence the corporation's directors; in practice, it was the CEO who controlled the board rather than the reverse. This arrangement began to change in the 1970s and 1980s as institutional investors—mutual funds, pension funds, state and local government retirement funds—that had accumulated vast pools of money from individuals now began to invest these funds in the stock market. Institutional investors owned less than 10 percent of all shares on Wall Street in 1950. By 1980 they owned 30 percent, and by 2000 they owned more than 60 percent (Micklethwait and Wooldridge 2003).

The funds available to the institutional investors provided the financial base for what Khurana (2002) has called "investor capitalism." Their substantial stockholdings enabled the new institutional investors to determine who sat on boards of directors and thus gave them real power over the managers in the companies in which they owned shares. The clout of the institutional directors was most dramatically demonstrated in

1992 when one of the largest of them, CalPERS (the California Public Employees Retirement System), forced the GM board of directors to dismiss all the company's seniors managers because of its poor performance. Although the GM case was unusual in that an entire layer of senior management was fired, the dismissal of CEOs because of their companies' performance has become far more common in the era of investor capitalism. Khurana found that for the same level of corporate performance, CEOs hired between 1990 and 1996 were three times more likely to be fired than a CEO hired before 1980 (2002: 59–60). Institutional investors have little patience with poor corporate performance; they expect good results in short order, and they hold the CEOs accountable if these are not achieved.

The assumption that the CEO is directly responsible for the corporation's successes and failures has produced a kind of cult of the CEO. This is reflected in who gets selected as CEO. In the past, the new CEO was generally appointed by the board of directors on the recommendation of the outgoing CEO; he generally nominated one of his top lieutenants. In the 1970s, over 90 percent of CEOs were internal appointments. Today the board of directors will often look outside the organization for a charismatic superstar who, it is hoped, will transform the company. Those who have patiently climbed the corporate ladder are frequently passed over in favor of outsiders who may know comparatively little of the firm they are expected to run or the markets in which it competes. In 2000 more than one third of all CEOs were outside hires (Porter 2007).

The superstar CEOs come with very high expectations and even higher salaries. Take the case of Bob Nardelli. Nardelli, a GE executive, was one of the contenders to succeed Jack Welch.

He was passed over and immediately took the CEO's position at Home Depot, despite having no experience in the retail industry. Although sales and profits increased during his tenure, Home Depot's stock price did not. More important, Nardelli demoralized employees with his autocratic management style, alienated customers by cutting staff at Home Depot stores, and antagonized shareholders by refusing to answer their questions at the company's annual meeting. His outsize salary (nearly $40 million) in 2006 was a further provocation. In January 2007, the board of directors attempted to amend his compensation package; when he refused to make the changes the board wanted, he was forced to resign. He was, however, given a severance package of $210 million. In August 2007, Nardelli was hired as chairman and CEO of the Chrysler Corporation. Box 7.1 has a more detailed account of Bob Nardelli's rise and fall at Home Depot.

One effect of the search for superstar CEOs, as the Nardelli affair illustrates, is that CEO salaries have soared. The average pay of the top executives of the 50 largest companies in the United States (adjusted for inflation) rose from less than $10 million in the early 1990s to over $50 million within less than a decade. Considerable attention has been drawn to the widening gap between the pay of the CEO and that of the average employee in his or her company. Less well known is how wide the gap has become between the CEO and the executives immediately beneath him. In the past the second-ranked or third-ranked person in the organization could expect to earn from 50 percent to 75% of what the boss made; today they are likely to earn one quarter or less of the CEO's salary (Porter 2007).

The cult of the CEO and the inflated salaries that often accompany this position have

BOX 7.1 *Nardelli: Out at Home Depot: Behind the Flameout of Controversial CEO Bob Nardelli*

In the end it came down to the headstrong CEO's refusal to accept even a symbolic reduction in his stock package.

Home Depot Inc.'s board of directors wanted their controversial chief executive, Robert L. Nardelli, to amend his whopping compensation deals for recent years. After he pulled down $38.1 million from his last yearly contract, angry investors were promising an ugly fight at the company's annual meeting in May. Nardelli agreed to give up a guarantee that he would continue to receive a minimum $3 million bonus each year. But that's as far as he would go. When board members asked him to more closely tie his future stock awards to shareholder gains, he refused, according to people familiar with the matter. Nardelli has complained for years that share price is the one measure of company performance that he can't control. After weeks of secret negotiations, things came to a head at a board meeting on Jan. 2, leading to Home Depot's stunning announcement the next day that the company and Nardelli had "mutually agreed" that he would resign.

"The board loved him and hates the way this ended up," says a person familiar with the matter. But in a season of growing antipathy toward extravagantly paid executives, the directors felt they had no choice. On his way out the door, however, Nardelli negotiated another jaw-dropper: a $210 million retirement package that assures that he and his former employer will remain at the center of the swirling debate over CEO compensation. Nardelli declined to comment.

The sudden fall of one of America's best-known CEOs illustrates how perilous times have become for corporate leaders. Pointing to gargantuan pay and widespread manipulation of stock options, institutional shareholders are calling for top executives and board members to be held accountable. At Home Depot there were other points of contention: a sluggish stock price in an otherwise rising market and Nardelli's notoriously imperious manner. Judged solely by certain company financial measures, Nardelli, 58, should have enjoyed acclaim for transforming Home Depot from a faltering retail chain into an earnings juggernaut. Driven by a housing and home improvement boom, sales soared from $46 billion in 2000, the year Nardelli took over, to $81.5 billion in 2005, an average annual growth rate of 12%. Profits more than doubled, to $5.8 billion that year.

During the current housing slowdown, however, the financials have eroded. In the third quarter of 2006, same-store sales at Home Depot's 2,127 retail stores declined 5.1%. And with the stock price recently stuck at just over 40, roughly the same as when Nardelli arrived six years ago, he could no longer rely on other sterile metrics to assuage the quivering anger his arrogance provoked within every one of his key constituencies: employees, customers, and shareholders. Nardelli's "numbers were quite good," says Matthew Fassler, an analyst at Goldman Sachs. But "the fact is that this retail organization never really embraced his leadership style." . . .

Nardelli arrived at Home Depot after losing out in 2000 in a three-way race to succeed GE's legendary Jack Welch. Despite that setback, Nardelli was anointed one of Corporate America's most talented executives, and Home

BOX **7.1** *continued*

Depot seemed to have scored a big victory by snaring him. Almost immediately, he embarked on an aggressive plan to centralize control of the nation's second-largest retailer after Wal-Mart Stores. He invested more than $1 billion in new technology, such as self-checkout aisles and inventory management systems that generated reams of data. He declared that he wanted to measure virtually everything that happened at the company and hold executives strictly accountable for meeting their numbers. All this was new at a relatively laid-back organization known for the independence of its store managers and the folksy, entrepreneurial style of retired co-founders Bernard Marcus and Arthur Blank. One of Nardelli's favorite sayings is: "Facts are friendly." He seemed less concerned about people being friendly. Some saw this as a strength. "This guy is maniacal about goals, objectivity, accomplishments within the boundaries of the values of the company," Kenneth Langone, the third co-founder of Home Depot, a member of its board of directors, and a strong Nardelli ally, said in a 2004 interview.

But among many of Home Depot's 355,000 employees, especially rank-and-file workers in its orange big-box stores, there was little sympathy as Nardelli dug himself into a deeper and deeper hole. They resented the replacement of many thousands of full-time store workers with legions of part-timers, one aspect of a relentless cost-cutting program Nardelli used to drive gross margins from 30% in 2000 to 33.8% in 2005. As the news of his resignation on Jan. 3 shot through Home Depot's white-walled Atlanta headquarters and reached stores, some employees text-messaged each other with happy faces and exclamation points. "I think that it is being received well. Most people believed that Bob was autocratic and stubborn," says an assistant manager in an Atlanta store who asked not to be named.

Possibly more devastating to his chances of a longer reign at Home Depot, Nardelli alienated customers just as thoroughly as he did employees. Staffing cuts led to persistent complaints that there weren't enough workers in Home Depot's cavernous stores to help do-it-yourself customers. That was a marked change from the era when Blank and Marcus, who started the company in 1978, preached that employees should "make love to the customer." In 2005, Home Depot slipped to last among major U.S. retailers in the University of Michigan's annual American Consumer Satisfaction Index. To try to make amends, Nardelli announced a plan in August to add 5.5 million man-hours back to stores and invest $350 million to spruce up aging outlets. "Bob Nardelli is a smart man, but he doesn't need to be in a high-profile business like retail," says a former top Home Depot executive. "He needs to be in manufacturing, a business that does not have such consumer attention."

Indeed, Nardelli's data-driven, in-your-face management style grated on many seasoned executives, resulting in massive turnover in Home Depot's upper ranks. Former chief marketing officer John Costello, a retailing veteran from Sears Holding Corp., quit in late 2005, and Carl Liebert III, the executive vice-president who oversaw store operations, resigned last October. "He would say that you're just not leadership material, you're just not Home Depot material, you're just not the type of person we need," says a former senior executive. Managers who weren't hitting their numbers—"making plan" in Home Depot parlance—were routinely culled, their posts often filled with former executives from GE. That led some bitter insiders to dub the company "Home Gepot." In fact, since 2001, 98% of Home Depot's top 170 executives are new to their positions; 56% of the changes involved bringing new managers in from outside the company...

Corporate America hasn't seen the last of Bob Nardelli, however. According to people familiar with the situation, while store workers were celebrating, the former CEO was already fielding calls from private equity firms interested in his formidable operational talents. The bright side for Nardelli in the world of privately owned corporations, of course, is that he won't have to deal with any annual meetings or shareholder questions.

SOURCE: Grow 2007

---

prompted two concerns. First, it implies that the levels of management beneath the CEO are less valuable—their contribution to the success of the organization is now less important, which is why the pay gap between the top corporate position and everyone else has widened. There is in fact no evidence to support the claim that the CEO has a significantly greater effect on the organization's performance than those below him or her in the organization's hierarchy. In fact, CEOs, especially those brought in from the outside, may hurt the company's performance by undermining employee morale. The history of management, some of which we have covered in this chapter, is that it is a collective enterprise in which individual superstars are less effective than a good team.

Second, the search for superstar CEOs, as Khurana (2002) has documented, tends to produce candidates for CEO positions who are remarkably similar to the people who serve on the boards of directors who appoint the CEOs—white males from economically and socially advantaged backgrounds. The selection of CEO candidates according to vague and undefined criteria such as charisma or stardom very seldom produces female or minority candidates for the top slots. It means that CEOs today are not only much better paid than just about everyone in the society around them, but they are much less representative of that society.

Summary

The occupation of manager is a relatively new one. It did not exist in the United States until the middle of the nineteenth century. Prior to then the administration of a business was a relatively simple task that could be handled by the owner and one or two assistants. The administrative challenge of operating railroads safely and efficiently produced the first organizational charts and created a need for managers to fill the slots on these charts. Being a manager involves a wide range of activities. These include acting as a figurehead, liaising with others, gathering and disseminating information, negotiating for and allocating resources, handling conflicts, and innovating, planning, and directing subordinates.

Organizational hierarchies make it possible for managers to have careers. If they perform well, managers expect to be promoted. Every manager reports to and is evaluated by a manager higher up in the organization. The cornerstone of this reporting and evaluation system is management by objectives: every manager identifies the goals of his or her unit and makes a commitment to achieving these goals within a specified time period. In practice, however, the evaluation of managers is less objective and formal than the management-by-objectives approach suggests. First, it is very difficult to determine how much a manager is really responsible for the performance of those under his or her supervision. Second, as managers move up the organization, informal evaluation and promotion criteria become increasingly important.

Informal promotion criteria, such as trustworthiness, the ability to "fit in" well, or being part of the right network, place women and minorities at a disadvantage because they often do not have the necessary personal connections or are judged as being too different. Stereotypes about female and minority managers also contribute to the barriers they face as they climb the corporate ladder—as they rise, they bump into the "glass ceiling." The lack of women and minorities at the highest levels of the corporation is also due to the fact that they get trapped at the lower levels of the corporation—the "sticky floor" factor. Sticky floors are created by bias and discrimination, by a lack of opportunity, and as a result of women curtailing their careers to raise children.

Managerial careers today are different from those of the past in at least two significant ways. First, job security is considerably lower. Global competition has led to corporate downsizing, as companies have trimmed their managerial (and nonmanagerial) workforces in order to become "lean and mean." Second, institutional investors, such as mutual funds and pension funds, now own more than half of all shares of companies listed on Wall Street. They have used their power to demand a high level of corporate performance, which in turn has led to a search for superstar CEOs who are believed to have the ability to increase a company's profitability very quickly. The rise of superstar CEOs, who are paid extremely high salaries, is a further demonstration of the role of subjective factors—being charismatic and having star quality—at the highest levels of corporate hiring.

Chapter 8

The Professions: Power and Status in the Workplace

It takes a considerable investment of time, energy, and resources to become a physician. Four years of medical school are followed by five years of in-hospital residency training, at which point the new doctor is certified to enter private practice, although many undertake additional years of subspecialty postresidency training before starting their practices. The hours are long and demanding during these nine or more years of training. Since July 1, 2003, however, this burden has been eased somewhat. As of that date, all physicians undergoing training in residency programs in the United States have been limited to 80 hours of work a week. They must also receive one 24-hour day out of every seven that is free of all work duties, they may not work more than one night in three if they are also working days, and they may not remain on duty for more than 30 hours. Prior to July 2003, medical residents—particularly those in time-consuming fields such as surgery—frequently worked more than 100 hours a week, 36-hour shifts were common, and residents often received no more than one day off a month. The restriction on work hours was enacted by the Accreditation Council for Graduate Medical Education (ACGME), a physician-controlled body that regulates and monitors the nearly 8,000 residency programs in the United States, which feared that Congress would enact similar restrictions if it did not.

For most of us the residents' reduced hours are still extraordinarily long. It seems odd to state that they can work "only" 80 hours a week, when this is double the standard of 40 hours (although people in other professional and managerial occupations often also work well over 40 hours a week, as we show in the final section of this chapter). But in the medical community the 80-hour limitation remains controversial. For the past two decades physicians have argued over the extent to which long hours and fatigue impede residents' learning and performance and diminish the quality of care they provide to patients. Opponents of work-hour restrictions have gone so far as to claim that these are a greater threat to training and patient care than fatigue. They also point out that long hours for residents have been a rite of passage for the last 100 years; originally, physicians in training were called residents because they were expected to live in the hospital (and to remain single).

The debate over whether residents' work hours should be limited began in earnest following the death of 18-year-old Libby Zion in New York Hospital in 1984. She died a few hours after being admitted to New York Hospital complaining of an earache and fever. The circumstances of Libby Zion's death were bitterly contested by her family and the hospital. The postmortem attributed her death to bilateral bronchopneumonia compounded by probable cocaine use. Her family claimed it was caused by fatigue due to overwork on the part of the two junior residents who supervised her care; they had spent 18 and 19 straight hours on duty, respectively. The grand jury that investigated the case did not indict either the hospital or its physicians, but did question the hospital's training and supervision of residents. The grand jury's report led to the appointment of a special commission in New York in 1987 that eventually recommended an almost identical set of restrictions on residents' work hours that ACGME imposed nationwide in 2003 (Ludmerer 1999). In the late 1980s, however, New York was the only state to mandate these restrictions. Over the following decade, federal agencies, public advocacy groups, and members of Congress all called for New York's regulations to become national policy. ACGME finally yielded to this pressure in 2003.

Opponents of the work-hour limits usually give two reasons for their stance. First, they cite practical concerns: reduced hours mean less time in training for residents and less time for them to spend on patient care. Second, they suggest that there are also intangible costs: restricted hours mean that residents do not feel the same commitment to the service ideal that many physicians regard as the hallmark of their profession. Consider, for example, the following remarks by a professor of surgery at a leading medical school

in response to a question about the impact of the 80-hour rule:

> There's also a little bit of a concern on our part that it gives the wrong message about what medicine is; and medicine we feel in surgery is not a job, it's a way of life, it's a mission, it's a calling, and there has to be a sense of duty and a sense of selflessness. And I don't want to sound too evangelistic about all this, but when you all of a sudden limit hours, you are going to limit their commitment, and again the message comes out that I as a person and as an individual am more important than the patient I am taking care of. And that's the antithesis of the way medicine and surgery has been run for 2,000 years.

He went to explain his conception of surgery as a calling, whose members had obligations far beyond those of other occupations:

> I mean, you know, I am sitting here thinking gosh, you know, 80 hours that is a ridiculously long week, and so there is part of me that says well, we people in medicine and surgery are just totally abnormal in the way we run our lives and our expectations. But again it's just how you view what you've been called to do. I think of the—and I don't want to get preachy here—but I think about the apostle Paul who when he was talking about doing his evangelical work in the early church, and he never married and he never, you know, he wasn't against marriage obviously but there is a couple of passages that says basically if you cannot marry that is really a good thing because that frees you up to be totally devoted to spreading the gospel. Well, I am married and I have two wonderful children, and so I don't advocate anybody going into

surgery being a celibate individual for the rest of their life, but there are people that do feel a little bit that taking care of sick people is somewhat analogous to that situation I describe with the apostle Paul. And again it just gets back to the whole issue of that sense of duty as it relates to patient care. (Interview conducted by William Finlay)

Although it may seem farfetched to compare a surgeon to an apostle, early sociological studies of the professions emphasized that they differed from other occupations in that practitioners were required to conform to moral norms. These norms specified not only that practitioners had to perform their tasks to the best of their abilities, but that they should also adopt a service ideal that required them to place their clients' interests ahead of personal or commercial gain (e.g., Wilensky 1964). Seen in this light, we can appreciate why the established members of a profession would be dismayed when new practitioners work on the clock rather than until the job is done. Medicine, they insist, is not just a job, and physicians should not be shift-workers or clock-watchers.

We can also understand why professions acquired the reputation of being inhospitable to people who had family obligations in addition to their work responsibilities. Implicit in the surgery professor's comments is the assumption that a partner or spouse will handle any household and childrearing chores—how else could he follow his calling and work unlimited hours? We know that women are far less likely than men to have a stay-at-home partner who is willing to perform these chores, so the service ethic and the long working hours with which it is associated make it difficult for women with families to

pursue professional careers. We will take up the issue of work time and gender at the end of the chapter. For now let us note that the professions developed as male-dominated occupations and that professional norms continue to reflect a view of the world in which men are the breadwinners and women are the homemakers.

The service ethic or altruism is in fact one of four historical characteristics that we argue separate the professions from other occupations. The other three characteristics are that a profession has a set of techniques and skills based on abstract knowledge; it is autonomous, i.e., it has exclusive jurisdiction over the work performed by its members; and it has authority over the clients it serves (Abbott 1988; Freidson 1994). These characteristics are the reason professions are more powerful and of higher status than other occupations. Let's review the four characteristics in greater detail.

Characteristics of the Professions

Abstract Knowledge

Many occupations have specific techniques or skills that their practitioners must master. Consider, for example, the work of plumbers, electricians, bricklayers, butchers, bakers, and auto mechanics. Every one of these occupations takes considerable training, and yet none is considered a profession in the sense that sociologists use the term. (In everyday speech, of course, just about any kind of paid employment may be called a profession, but the sociological usage is far more precise.) So why aren't plumbers considered professionals in the way that surgeons are? It's not because professional work is always more difficult or complicated than that of a craftsperson, many of whose tasks may require both diagnostic skill and manual dexterity. Much of the work that professionals do, including that of surgeons, is routine. In fact, surgeons become good by making their work routine, as Katrina Firlik, a neurosurgeon, explains in her memoir: "...in surgery, you should strive for routine and a consistent focus.... The ideal surgeon would be one who doesn't mind doing the same cases, over and over again, the same way, with the same instruments, year after year, continually enhancing safety and efficiency while building case volume" (2006: 101).

Another argument is that medicine and surgery are professions because of the length of time it takes to become fully trained—an undergraduate degree, medical school, and a residency are all mandatory before someone is authorized to practice as a physician or surgeon in the United States. But this too does not stand up under scrutiny. A lengthy training period of twelve or more years is not really needed to conduct the majority of medical procedures and surgeries. A surgeon's skills can be acquired in far less time, as Atul Gawande, himself a surgeon, makes clear in his recent memoir (2002). He points to the work of the surgeons at the Shouldice Hospital, a medical center outside of Toronto. They perform hernia operations only—about 600 to 800 a year each (which is more than most surgeons perform in a lifetime). These surgeons perform this surgery more quickly, more cheaply, and with a lower hernia recurrence rate than at any other hospital in North America. Gawande was struck by the flawless performance of three of the surgeons he observed. He remarked that none of the three would have been permitted to practice this operation in the United States because none had completed general surgery training, which makes him wonder if this

lengthy training is always necessary: "Yet after apprenticing for a year or so they were the best hernia surgeons in the world. If you're going to do nothing but fix hernias or perform colonoscopies, do you really need the complete specialists' training (four years of medical school, five or more years of residency) in order to excel?" (Gawande 2002: 41).

In fact, the length of the training period is significant to becoming a professional, even if the work itself does not require more skills than are found in other occupations and even if these skills can be developed in less time than the length of the training program. A long training program matters because it means that the skills and techniques of practitioners can be tied to abstract knowledge. Abstract knowledge is produced and taught by other practitioners. It is the acquisition of this knowledge in medical schools and residency programs that defines a surgeon, not skill in handling a scalpel or manual dexterity. The possession of abstract knowledge is what has allowed the traditional professions—medicine, law, and university teaching—to maintain their monopolies over treating patients, arguing in court, and lecturing to students and to impose lengthy training programs on those who wish to enter the profession. These professions have successfully insisted that mastery of their professions' cognitive foundations is necessary to practice (Abbott 1988). For example, a sociology department in a research university that hires a faculty member to teach courses in the sociology of work will expect that person to have, at the very least, a Ph.D. in sociology. A candidate who lacks this credential but has an extensive firsthand knowledge of the workplace and is a fine public speaker will almost certainly *not* be considered for the position.

Autonomy

Autonomy means that the members of the profession alone decide *who* is qualified to perform their work and *how* this work should be performed. The members of the profession determine how aspiring members should be trained, certify or license them when they regard their training as sufficient, hire them, evaluate them, and discipline them if their work falls short of expected standards. The professions, in other words, have secured the right to regulate themselves and to govern themselves.

Autonomy is reflected in a number of distinctive features of professional work. First, professionals are expected to be able to think and act autonomously: they are required to use their judgment, knowledge, and skill in order to address whatever problem is presented to them. The fact that most professionals work for organizations rather than being self-employed has not loosened professional control over work in the way that nineteenth-century craftsmen were stripped of their right to set the work pace and to determine work procedures when Taylorism swept through manufacturing (see Chapter 5). Take the legal profession, for example. Although lawyers—especially those who work for large law firms—have become highly specialized, they are expected from the outset of their careers to expand their skills. As Eve Spangler has put it, "in the law firm, the transformation of a promising law student into an accomplished attorney is secured by emphasizing skill development rather than work simplification" (1986: 44). Similarly, the teaching faculty who supervise medical and surgical residents do so with the intent of making these residents proficient and independent practitioners of their craft who will eventually take their place alongside the faculty as skilled equals, not less skilled subordinates.

A second feature of exclusive jurisdiction is that evaluations of professional work performance often take the form of peer review. In academic departments, for example, faculty vote on hiring and tenure decisions, which are usually conducted completely independently of the university's human resources office. (On the other hand, if an academic department wishes to hire an administrative assistant, it is very likely that the human-resources staff will screen all applications and will prepare a short list of suitable candidates.) Another example of peer review is the morbidity and mortality (M&M) conference that hospital physicians convene to discuss cases where there have been complications or death. These are occasions for physicians to review mistakes that have been made, to assign responsibility for those mistakes, and to decide what action to take to ensure that the mistakes are not repeated. Box 8.1 provides an illustration of a case at an M&M conference.

A third feature of exclusive jurisdiction is that employed professionals are normally supervised by other members of their profession. In the case of universities, for example, this means positions such as department chair, dean, and provost are filled by other Ph.D.-holding academics rather than by managers with business degrees. It is only at the very top of the organization—the university's president—that nonacademics are considered for a role in the academic hierarchy. One reason for this is that presidents are assumed to be mostly engaged in working with external constituents, such as state legislators, major donors, and alumni, and to have a limited involvement only in the teaching and research side of the enterprise.

BOX 8.1 *Morbidity and Mortality Conference: The Case of the Botched Tracheostomy*

One of the patients on whom Atul Gawande worked during his surgical residency was a woman who had been brought unconscious to the hospital's emergency room after being ejected from her car in a rollover. The patient began to experience severe breathing difficulties and Gawande was required to perform an emergency tracheostomy, which meant cutting a hole in the cricothyroid membrane below the patient's throat in order to insert a breathing tube into her trachea. The procedure is also known as a cricothyroidotomy. Gawande, however, was unable to locate the membrane in the woman's neck—she was overweight and the light in the emergency room was poor. As a result, the patient was deprived of oxygen for approximately three minutes, until an experienced anesthesiologist arrived and managed to thread an endotracheal tube through her vocal cords. The patient survived and, in fact, made a complete recovery. The incident, however, was extremely serious. Loss of oxygen for three minutes could have resulted in permanent brain damage or even death. Here is Gawande's vivid description of the subsequent discussion at the M&M conference:

At my hospital, we convene every Tuesday at five o'clock in a steep, plush amphitheater lined with oil portraits of the great doctors whose achievements we're meant to live up to. All surgeons are expected to attend, from the interns to the chairman of surgery; we're also joined by medical students doing their surgery "rotation." An M&M can include almost a hundred people. We file in, pick up a photocopied list of cases to be discussed, and take our seats. The front row is occupied by the most senior surgeons....

For each case, the chief resident from the relevant service—cardiac, vascular, trauma, and so on—gathers the information, takes the podium, and tells the story....Ms. Williams's case, my failed tracheostomy, was just one case on a list like this. David Hernandez, the chief trauma resident, had subsequently reviewed the records and spoken to me and others involved. When the time came, it was he who stood up front and described what had happened...

These presentations can be awkward. The chief residents, not the attendings [the staff surgeons who have formal responsibility for the cases], determine which cases to report. That keeps the attendings honest—no one can cover up mistakes—but it puts the chief residents who are, after all, underlings, in a delicate position. The successful M&M presentation invariably involves a certain elision of detail and a lot of passive verbs. No one screws up a cricothyroidotomy. Instead, "a cricothyroidotomy was attempted without success." The message, however, was not lost on anyone....A front-row voice immediately thundered, "What do you mean, 'a cricothyroidotomy was attempted without success'?" I sank into my seat, my face hot.

"This was my case," Dr. Ball [the attending] volunteered from the front row. It is how every attending begins, and that little phrase contains a world of surgical culture....When things go wrong the attending is expected to take full responsibility. It makes no difference whether it was the resident's hand that slipped and lacerated an aorta; it doesn't matter whether the attending was at home in bed when a nurse gave a wrong dose of medication. At the M&M, the burden of responsibility falls on the attending.

BOX 8.1 *continued*

Ball went on to describe the emergency attending's failure to intubate Williams and his own failure to be at her bedside when things got out of control. He described the bad lighting and her extremely thick neck, and was careful to make these things sound not like excuses but merely like complicating factors....

At no point during the M&M did anyone question why I had not called for help sooner or why I had not had the skill and knowledge that Williams needed. This is not to say that my actions were seen as acceptable. Rather, in the hierarchy, addressing my errors was Ball's role. The day after the disaster, Ball had caught me in the hall and taken me aside. His voice was more wounded than angry as he went through my specific failures.

SOURCE: Gawande 2002: 58–61.

Authority over Clients

Professionals expect clients to follow their instructions, even though the client is the one paying for the professional's services. Professionals regard these payments as a request for them to use their judgment and skill to decide what is in the client's best interests.

In some settings the authority of professionals is formally recognized and institutionalized. The student–professor relationship in universities is one example of institutionalized authority. In other settings the professional may have to persuade the client to follow his or her advice. The doctor–patient and lawyer–client relationships fall into this category. Even if the patient or client is formally free to reject his physician's or her lawyer's advice, however, his or her likelihood of doing so is constrained by a lack of knowledge and a lack of other options. If, for example, a client's lawyer tells her to settle in a divorce case on the grounds that she has received the best offer she is likely to get, she will probably have to take the lawyer's word for this. It is only the most affluent and the most powerful clients who will be able to resist the professional's authority by seeking (and paying for) the advice of other professionals. Professionals are aware that clients sometimes seek second opinions; one of the ways they attempt to preserve the authority of the profession as a whole is by refusing to criticize the work of their colleagues to a client. They may be critical of one another in an M&M conference, but in front of laypersons they will remain silent in order to maintain the profession's autonomy (Freidson 1994).

Altruism

As we saw in the discussion of residents' work hours at the start of the chapter, some physicians opposed work-hour restrictions because they felt that they undermined the professional ethic of service to patients. It is professionals' sense of altruism—that they should put their clients' interests ahead of their own—that explains why the public at large entrusts them with exclusive jurisdiction and authority over clients. This is particularly true of medicine, which deals with matters of life and death. Larson explains: "Of all the professions, it [medicine] appears to have the strongest claims to an ideal of service and devotion to human welfare. This view is widespread. It constitutes a massive capital of social credit on which medicine draws" (1977: 39). Working extraordinarily long hours was one way physicians in training demonstrated that they were motivated by altruism rather than by self-interest.

We know also that professionals are high-status and well-paid workers. Table 8.1 confirms this, showing that many professionals earn well over $100,000 a year. Surgeons average close to $300,000 a year. Professionals may claim to represent their clients or the public at large, but they sell their services in the marketplace—often to the highest bidder. They may serve the greater good, but they do not take a vow of poverty. In addition, professional associations defend the economic interests of their members

TABLE 8.1 **Median Annual Earnings in Selected Professions, 2006**

PROFESSION	EARNINGS ($)
Architects	64,150
College and university teachers	56,120
Dentists	136,960
General surgeons	282,504
Lawyers	102,470
Pediatricians	161,331
Pharmacists	94,520
Psychiatrists	180,000
Veterinarians	71,990

Source: U.S. Bureau of Labor Statistics, 2007d.

by controlling professional training and thereby restricting the number of new practitioners who enter the profession. How, then, do professionals reconcile altruism with the economic success that they enjoy? One answer is to require new members of the profession to swear an oath of service to their clients or the community at large. The most famous example of this is the physician's Hippocratic Oath, which dates back to the fourth century B.C. It has been revised and updated since then. One of the contemporary versions is the Declaration of Geneva, first adopted in 1948 in the wake of the Nazi atrocities of World War II, in which some physicians had been complicit. The Declaration of Geneva (Box 8.2) was most recently modified in 2006.

A profession's code of ethics may even require its members to do work for which they are not paid. This is explicitly stated in Rule 6.1 the American Bar Association's Model Rules of Professional Conduct: "Every lawyer has a professional responsibility to provide legal services to those unable to pay. A lawyer should aspire to render at least (50) hours of *pro bono publico* [i.e., legal services for which no fee is charged] per year" (Center for Professional Responsibility 2008).

It is difficult to find out how much pro bono work lawyers actually perform. One source of information is Mather, McEwen, and Maiman's (2001) study of divorce lawyers in Maine and New Hampshire. In these states, as in others, lawyers who are willing to do pro bono work place themselves on a referral list and must accept cases that are sent to them from a central intake and screening agency. Seventy-six percent of the 163 lawyers they interviewed had taken pro bono referrals in divorce cases. A more informal way for lawyers to do pro bono

> ### BOX 8.2 *The Declaration of Geneva*
>
> At the time of being admitted as a member of the medical profession:
>
> - I solemnly pledge to consecrate my life to the service of humanity;
> - I will give to my teachers the respect and gratitude that is their due;
> - I will practice my profession with conscience and dignity;
> - The health of my patient will be my first consideration;
> - I will respect the secrets that are confided in me, even after the patient has died;
> - I will maintain by all the means in my power, the honor and the noble traditions of the medical profession;
>
> - My colleagues will be my sisters and brothers;
> - I will not permit considerations of age, disease or disability, creed, ethnic origin, gender, nationality, political affiliation, race, sexual orientation, social standing or any other factor to intervene between my duty and my patient;
> - I will maintain the utmost respect for human life;
> - I will not use my medical knowledge to violate human rights and civil liberties, even under threat;
> - I make these promises solemnly, freely and upon my honor.

work is to waive or discount fees or to undercount their hours when representing clients of limited means. Seventy-seven percent of the lawyers had assisted clients in one or more of these ways (Mather et al. 2001: 135–137).

For another example of the service ethic in practice, consider the jobs of university professors. It is well known that they are evaluated on and rewarded for their teaching and research. It is less well known that they also spend time on activities for which there are no financial rewards: serving on committees, reviewing manuscripts for journals and grant proposals for foundations, reviewing candidates at other institutions who are being considered for promotion and/or tenure, and mentoring students. The reward systems at universities, particularly research institutions, provide few, if any, benefits

for faculty who engage in these activities, nor do they penalize those who do not perform them; if they were not done, however, universities' teaching and research missions would be conducted far less effectively.

Controlling Professional Work: The Professional Ethic

One of the consequences of these four characteristics is that the work of professionals is subject to different kinds of controls from that experienced by other workers. Workers in most organizations are controlled through rules. Rules establish when a worker should be at his job and when absences are permissible. Rules define a worker's job duties, responsibilities, and authority. Rules specify whose instructions a worker should follow, how tasks should be carried out, and to whom she should report. These are all established principles of bureaucratic organizations (see Chapter 2). But the work of professionals, including those who work in organizations, is far less governed by rules. University professors, for example, may have only eight to ten hours a week in which they are required to be in their classrooms or offices—or less if it is a semester in which they are not teaching. Aside from these hours, they are expected to be able to judge for themselves how best to allocate their time and efforts in order to get their work done.

Some scholars have argued that professionals who work in organizations that are run by managers are being "deprofessionalized" (e.g., Ritzer and Walczak 1988). This argument is based on a belief that the ethic of service is being replaced by a drive to achieve efficiency and accountability, which is undermining professional independence. Although it is true that the doctor who is a salaried employee of a for-profit hospital is less autonomous than the doctor in private practice, who sees only fee-paying patients, the difference between the two is more in how resources are allocated than in how medicine is practiced. The private practitioner will get to decide where and how to spend the revenues generated by his or her business, whereas the salaried physician will have to accept hospital administrators' decisions about investments in equipment, facilities, or personnel. There is little evidence, however, that employed professionals are prevented from using their discretion and judgment to make decisions about how to get their jobs done (Freidson 1986). To use the example of university faculty again, administrators control matters such as salaries and which departments will get additional positions but have no say over an individual faculty member's core activities of teaching and research, which remain individual prerogatives.

The primary mechanism for controlling professional work is *socialization* into the values, norms, and standards of the occupation. Another way of stating this is that professionals learn what to do and how to do it through being socialized by fellow practitioners into their profession's ethic. Socialization means that established doctors, lawyers, and scientists teach newcomers how to be a "good" doctor, a "good" lawyer, or a "good" scientist. It is a process that begins with the lengthy and often grueling terms of education that must be completed before the aspiring professional is admitted into the occupation, but it mostly takes place on the job through mentoring from more seasoned professionals. In the next two sections we discuss, first, what it takes to be good in a professional sense (to be a "real professional," as it is sometimes referred to) and, second, how veteran professionals instill this ethic in neophytes.

Being a "Real Professional"

We use two studies to illustrate what it means to be a real professional. The first is Joan Cassell's (1991) book about surgeons, and the second is Mather et al.'s (2001) study of divorce lawyers. Both cases suggest that the members of these professions are largely in agreement as to what constitutes good professional behavior.

Surgery is one of the most intrusive of professions. Its practitioners physically violate the human body and their clients, i.e., the patients, entrust their lives to these men and women. We all have an interest in having only the best surgeons operate on us, although the normal distribution of abilities and skills means that many of us will not get the best. What, in fact, makes a surgeon good? Cassell lists six characteristics that surgeons value in one another. First, there is technical proficiency or "good hands." A technically proficient surgeon makes the work look easy and copes with emergencies swiftly. Second, a good surgeon has knowledge, usually acquired through experience, upon which he or she can draw in deciding how to handle the challenges of a particular case. Third, a good surgeon has judgment—the ability to diagnose whether a particular ailment requires surgery and, if it does, how to carry out that surgery. Fourth, a good surgeon has the right temperament, which means that he or she reaches decisions quickly and acts decisively. Fifth, a good surgeon has the ability to concentrate unwaveringly for long periods and to remain obsessively focused on minor details. Sixth, a good surgeon cares about his or her patients (1991: 10–21).

Divorce lawyers lack the status of surgeons, or of other lawyers for that matter. The legal community has long regarded divorce law as one of the least creditable branches of the law, and divorce lawyers themselves are often singled out for ethical breaches (Heinz and Laumann 1982; Nelson 1988; Sandefur 2001). Nevertheless, Mather et al. show that divorce lawyers too have a strong sense of what it means to be a real professional, which they define as being a "reasonable lawyer." The first characteristic of a reasonable lawyer—and one that mirrors the technical proficiency of the good surgeon—is that he knows divorce law. This means knowing the likely outcome of a divorce case and knowing when it needs to be settled rather than continued. A reasonable lawyer knows which battles are worth fighting and which are not. Second, a reasonable lawyer remains objective and does not adopt her client's emotions. By maintaining control of her

emotions, the lawyer maintains control over her client and gets him to accept the most likely outcome. Third, a reasonable lawyer is honest and trustworthy in his dealings with other lawyers. He keeps his word and does not let disagreements with opposing lawyers become personal (Mather et al. 2001: 48–50).

In both of these professions, being a "real professional" includes the attainment of technical competence or expertise and earning the respect of colleagues. We discuss next how new professionals acquire these characteristics.

Becoming a Professional

Although socialization into a profession's ethic begins in its professional schools, it mostly takes place after hiring. It is in the workplace that the new professionals discover what they know and, more important, what they don't know, that they learn the difference between major and minor errors in their work, and that they find out how they should behave. In short, they learn how to be real professionals. This kind of learning happens in all jobs, but socialization of professionals is more complicated than that of other workers because professionals work independently and with little or no supervision. In some cases, such as universities, the unit's leaders (deans or department heads) may not even understand the research work of the professors under their nominal supervision.

A common mechanism of socialization in the professions is mentoring. A mentor is a senior member of the profession who offers advice and counsel to the junior member. The mentor may or may not be the person's formal supervisor; in either case, the mentor's role is different from a supervisor's. The mentor guides a subordinate's behavior rather than issuing direct instructions. Another difference is that mentoring often occurs informally—in conversations over lunch, for example, or in social gatherings after work. One consequence of this, however, is that it is usually easier for male professionals to find mentors than it is for females because senior professionals are more likely to be male and because mentoring relationships are more likely to be formed between people of the same gender (Kanter 1977a; Padavic and Reskin 2002). The presence of a mentor has been identified as a crucial determinant of professional success, providing one explanation for why female professionals earn less than their male counterparts and are less likely to be promoted to the highest ranks of the profession (e.g., Epstein, Saute, Oglensky, and Gever 1995; Noonan and Corcoran 2004).

Another socialization mechanism is peer review. Peer review is common in the academic world, where it is used to evaluate the merits of manuscripts that have been submitted for publication or of candidates who are being considered for tenure and promotion. In these instances it is an anonymous procedure, with blind reviews for manuscripts (the names of author and reviewer are concealed from one another) and secret ballots for tenure candidates. On occasion, though, there is a public peer review. Gatherings of this kind provide a powerful demonstration of professional norms. We will present two examples. The first is the weekly "muffin meeting" held in the neuroscience laboratory of a major research university, at which scientists presented preliminary research findings. The second is the conference held in hospitals to discuss unexpected success (grand rounds) or unexpected failure (the mortality and morbidity conference) in patient care.

Jason Owen-Smith (2001) explains how the "muffin meeting"—it was named this because it included muffins from a local bakery—was used to monitor, evaluate, and control the work of a group of research scientists in a university neuroscience laboratory. The lab, which he calls the H-lab, consisted of 26 people, 17 of whom were researchers who either had or were pursuing doctorates. The lab's director, Jim, was also its founder. At the time of Owen-Smith's research, which consisted of 11 months of fieldwork, the lab had been in existence for more than a decade. The H-lab was primarily funded through external grants for which Jim was responsible, which meant he had to ensure that the work in his lab was of high quality and was completed on time. His reputation also depended on the quality of the scientists' work because his name was included on every research publication.

All scientific work is difficult to oversee. In part this is because scientists cherish their autonomy and resist efforts to manage their time. In part it is because the complexity of their tasks makes it difficult for supervisors to know what exactly the scientists have been doing. In the case of the H-lab, an additional supervisory complication was the wide range of scientific disciplines participating in the research effort. Although the scientists shared a common general focus—learning how the *Manduca sexta* (the tobacco hornworm moth) distinguishes one smell from another—they approached it from nine different disciplines, ranging from applied mathematics to field ecology. No supervisor could be an expert in all these fields. The muffin meeting was Jim's solution to the problem of controlling his subordinates without understanding, or even knowing, what they were up to.

The muffin meeting, which was held on a Wednesday and which all members of the lab attended, began with Jim inviting the scientists to share any news they might have regarding the progress of their experiments or any other topics that might be of interest to others. This open-ended and seemingly innocuous question was actually the trigger for a peer-review system of control that Owen-Smith calls "scientific skepticism." It occurred when a scientist presented a claim or finding that Jim challenged, often by questioning the method used to obtain that finding. If a scientist defended her method effectively, Jim might concede the point; if not, he would make it clear what he considered the right method to use. Jim's strategy of questioning and suggesting pushed the researchers in the direction he wanted them to go without his having to tell them directly what to do. Other scientists observed and learned from the interactions, as Owen-Smith explains:

> By watching skeptical interactions like these, other group members learn the group's critical norms, the acceptable strategies for defending novel claims and methods, and the premises that guide decisions about scientific work in the lab. Muffin-meeting skepticism provides public rewards or punishments, and, thus, teaches group members the standards of practice acceptable in the lab without ever explicitly stating them. Muffin meetings offer Jim opportunities to signal his approval of claims, methods, and behaviors, further hammering home the priorities he wishes to govern behavior in the lab. (2001: 435)

Claims that survived scientific skepticism were considered ready to be written up as manuscripts for submission to professional journals (at

which point they would be subjected to the skepticism of external peer reviewers of these manuscripts). Consequently, it was important to the scientists' careers that they made it through the in-house review of the muffin meeting.

Another example of public peer review occurs in hospitals when cases result in unexpected success or unexpected failure. Unexpected success is discussed in grand rounds, unexpected failure in the M&M conference. We have already provided one example of the latter (see Box 8.1); we now discuss both in greater detail, drawing on Charles Bosk's (1979) study of surgeons in "Pacific" Hospital. Pacific—not the hospital's real name—is one of the country's elite hospitals, affiliated with a top medical and major research university. In this setting, some of the most distinguished surgeons in the world announced their successes and accounted for their failures.

Grand rounds is a celebration of surgical virtuosity. At Pacific it took the form of a weekly meeting at which a senior or attending surgeon would report how he had operated successfully on a patient who was seemingly beyond hope. The presentation of the case followed a set ritual. A resident would outline the patient's clinical history, explaining the particular complications it posed. The attending surgeon would then take over, outlining what the medical literature had to say about cases of this nature and explaining the novel surgical techniques he had decided to employ. At this point the patient would often be displayed briefly as visible proof of the operation's success. Once the patient had left the room, the surgeon would argue for the superiority of his new technique. Like the muffin meeting, grand rounds is a form of social control of subordinates. Attending surgeons use this setting to show off their surgical skills and to show how much residents still have to learn before than they can be treated as equals. Bosk states: "Such displays of patients dramatize the difference between attendings and housestaff who do not have a ready stock of miraculous cures to parade" (1979: 127).

The M&M conference, although ostensibly an examination of medical failure and a forum in which senior surgeons take criticism and accept blame, actually serves to highlight the skill and status differences between attending surgeons and residents. The M&M conference is a carefully structured presentation, just as grand rounds is. It begins with a resident providing the case history. Once this is concluded, however, the resident remains on stage to answer questions about his or her decisions and actions. Unlike grand rounds, the attending surgeon does not always step forward to answer questions or to provide additional explanations. Particularly if the complications are routine—such as a wound infection following surgery—an attending may well leave all answers and explanations to the resident, who is expected to be able to show that he or she understands the causes of the problem and how they should be prevented in the future. Attending surgeons take charge of the presentations in cases where it was not clear which operational procedures should have been used or where the surgeon deviated from an established procedure. They take the blame (a practice Bosk calls "wearing the hair shirt") by pointing, for example, to the clinical evidence they overlooked or their failure to supervise residents effectively. They fault either their own judgment or the performance of the residents for whom they are responsible.

Bosk argues that admitting error is a humbling experience for a senior surgeon, even when it is a resident's mistakes that are being exposed.

How, then, does it serve the purpose of social control? First, for a surgeon to wear the hair shirt is a mark of status. Only the top surgeons get to confess their errors in public and criticize themselves. Residents receive criticism, but it is not given in a public forum and it is not self-administered. Public confessions are a privilege that has to be earned. Second, surgeons' self-criticism includes a discussion of what they should have done; they use the forum to deliver a lesson on how cases of this nature should be handled. By wearing the hair shirt surgeons display humility and wisdom, thus setting a further standard to which the residents should aspire (Bosk 1979: 128–145).

Mentoring and peer review, whether anonymous or public, are powerful socialization mechanisms. Their impact is not limited to newcomers to the profession, however; particularly when the review is public, it is a reminder to all practitioners of the profession's central norms.

Professional Careers

In the final section of this chapter we turn to the careers of professionals. We begin with two observations. First, professional jobs take a substantial commitment of time and energy, particularly in the early years of the professional's career. If a professional is self-employed, this is the period in which he will be attempting to establish his reputation and to get his business going. If she works for an organization that is run by professionals, such as a large law firm or a research university, pressure comes from the "up-or-out" policies that these organizations follow. An up-or-out policy gives the new associate (in a law firm) or assistant professor (in a university) five to ten years to become a partner or to earn promotion to associate professor with tenure; those who don't make it are fired.

Second, the percentage of women in professional jobs has continued to rise sharply. In 1970, for example, less than 5 percent of all lawyers and doctors in the United States were women; by 2004 nearly 30 percent of each group were women. By 2010 women will become a majority of pharmacists and veterinarians. Women comprise about three quarters of all veterinary students, two thirds of pharmacy students, half of all law students, and nearly half of all medical students. Table 8.2 shows the increased percentage of women in a variety of professions over the last fifteen years.

The rising percentage of women in professional occupations makes it all the more important to consider how professionals have coped with the long hours of their jobs. These time demands are at their greatest during the early stages of professional careers, when professionals are most likely to have young families. Let's examine how men and women have responded

to the challenge of time-demanding jobs and how their responses have affected their professional achievements.

The Work Hours of Professionals

There are plenty of anecdotes about professionals' long hours, but what kind of hard empirical evidence do we have? A good source of data, because of the intense debate surrounding the introduction of the 80-hour-a-week limit in 2003, comes from studies of medical residents. A national study of medical residents found that in the late 1990s their average weekly hours ranged from about 60 for those in psychiatry and dermatology to over 110 for those in neurological surgery (Baldwin, Daugherty, Tsai, and Scotti 2003). Surgeons, whether residents or faculty, appear to put in consistently long hours; a recent study of teaching surgeons in a single academic institution found that they were averaging 74 hours a week (Winslow, Bowman, and Klingensmith 2004). We have some data on work hours in other professions as well. An American Bar Association survey in 1990 found that half of all lawyers worked 200 hours or more a month (Landers, Rebitzer, and Taylor 1996). Finally, Roth's (2004) study of young financial professionals in nine major Wall Street securities firms found they averaged nearly 62 hours of work a week. It seems apparent, therefore, that many professionals are working much more than the standard 40 hours a week.

There are at least three reasons for the long hours of professionals. The first is organizational: the success of some organizations depends on the how much work time they can get out of their professional members. Hospitals are an obvious example. Residents are not particularly well paid and are not paid overtime: they earn between

TABLE 8.2 Female Employment in Selected Professions

Profession	Women's Percentage of Total Employment	
	1988	2004
Architects	14.6	24.0
Postsecondary teachers	38.5	46.0
Dentists	9.3	22.0
Lawyers	19.3	29.4
Pharmacists	31.9	47.0
Physicians and surgeons	20.0	29.4
Veterinarians	23.0 (est.)	39.1

Source: U.S. Bureau of Labor Statistics 2005.

$40,000 and $50,000 a year. The result is that over the years they have become a highly skilled and relatively cheap labor pool for hospitals. The more hours hospitals get out of residents, the fewer ancillary staff, such as nurses and physicians' assistants, they need to hire.

In law firms, where revenues are shared among the partners, every partner directly benefits when other lawyers work long hours and generate high revenues. The more hours that lawyers bill, the more clients pay them. Consequently, a willingness to work long hours has become a key determinant of whether associates get promoted to partner. Landers et al. (1996) asked associates and partners in two large law firms in a Northeastern city to evaluate the importance of twelve different factors in their firm's promotion process. The factors included, in addition to long hours, the quality of the associate's work, his or her demonstrated ability to bring new clients and business to the firm, willingness to pursue the interests of clients aggressively, mastery of an important area of specialization, and mentoring relationships with senior lawyers in the firm. Associates identified the associate's work hours as the most important factor, followed by the quality of the work; partners reversed this order, but had these same factors as their top two (1996: 341).

A second reason professionals work long hours is that they feel an obligation to respond to clients. This explains why surgeons continue to work long hours, even after completing their residencies. It is quite common for surgeons to be paged overnight and to have to return to the hospital to take care of a patient. Winslow et al. (2004) asked surgical faculty to keep track of their work hours for a particular week, including how many times they were paged after hours in a typical week and how many times they returned to the hospital. Ninety-five percent of the surgeons reported at least one page during the week; they averaged fourteen pages over the seven days. Seventy-three percent reported returning to the hospital at least once during the week; they averaged two returns per week.

The third reason for the long hours of professionals is that there is no clear distinction between work and nonwork and no clear indication of when a task is finished. For example, the divorce lawyers in Mather et al.'s study complained about being unable to stop thinking about their work, even when they went home. One said: "The other thing I have trouble with is sort of the obsessiveness of it. It's very hard to get away from it. If you're not at work, you're worried about your work, or worried about the fact that you're not there or something…" (2001: 163). Lawyers realize that there is no real limit to the amount of work they could do on a particular case, so they always have the uncertainty of wondering whether they have done enough.

University professors whose careers depend on the articles and books they publish face a similar dilemma of knowing when a manuscript is ready to be submitted to a journal or publisher for review. More work—whether reviewing the literature, analysis of data, or writing—can always be done, so every scholar has to decide when and where to draw the line. The awareness that every case or every research product is, in this sense, unfinished makes it difficult to stop working. Moreover, much of the work of both lawyers and professors consists of activities such as reading and writing that can easily be done at home, which further contributes to the blurring of the line between work and nonwork and causes work hours to increase.

Career Outcomes for Men and Women

The long work hours of professionals often come at the expense of their personal lives. People who are working 60 to 80 hours a week have limited time for partners, spouses, family, and friends or for leisure pursuits. Men and women have responded to this challenge differently, however. Male professionals, such as doctors, tend to be married—their marriage rates are higher than those of men in general. In 2000, for example, 67 percent of men between the ages of 30 and 50 were married compared to 82 percent of all male physicians in the same age range; 69 percent of all women between 30 and 50 were married, as were 69 percent of all female physicians in this age range (Boulis 2004: 181). In addition to being more likely to be married and to have children than female doctors, male doctors with families average 27 percent more hours of work per week than female doctors with a spouse and children at home; in contrast, female doctors without children work the same numbers of hours as their male counterparts without children (Boulis 2004: 194).

These statistics suggest that female professionals are choosing one of two strategies for coping with the demands of having a career and rearing a family. Some professional women have chosen to remain single and, if they do marry, not to have children, so that they can devote the same amount of time to their careers that their male counterparts—with or without children—are doing. Other female professionals are choosing to have children and to curtail their work hours, even if this decision comes at the price of their professional success. We find evidence of both of these adaptations among female doctors and lawyers. For one example, let's examine the

areas of medicine in which women have chosen to specialize in recent years.

Since 2000 women have made up nearly 50 percent of all medical school students and about 40 percent of medical and surgical residents. But women have not been equally attracted to all residencies. Fifty percent or more of residents in obstetrics and gynecology, pediatrics, dermatology, and pathology are women compared to less than 25 percent in general surgery, orthopedic surgery, and neurosurgery (Blakemore, Hall, Biermann 2003; Darves 2005). Surgery, as we have seen, is the medical field with the longest and most unpredictable work hours—considerably in excess of those in pathology especially, but also those in pediatrics and obstetrics/gynecology. Surgery is also, however, one of the highest-paid medical specialties—the median income of general surgeons in 2006 was more than $282,000. In comparison, the median income of pediatricians in 2006 was about $161,000 (see Table 8.1). Women who therefore choose the more manageable hours of pediatrics over the long days and occasional nights of surgery are also selecting a less lucrative career path.

Women who do become surgeons are less likely than men to have families. A survey of the surgeons who had completed the residency program at the University of California–Davis between 1989 and 2000 found that 86 percent of the men were married at the time of the survey, and 95 percent of them had had children during or after their residency training; 70 percent of the women were married, and 40 percent had had children. Twenty-six percent of the male surgeons had wives who were homemakers, whereas none of the women had a homemaking husband (Mayer, Ho, and Goodnight 2001). Stay-at-home spouses allow men to enjoy the rewards of the highest paid specialty *and* the pleasures of family life; for women it was more likely to be one or the other.

In the case of lawyers we find a similar division between women who have pursued the rewards of career success and those who made career sacrifices to have families. Lawyers in private practice, especially, work long hours at the start of their careers when law firms hire them as associates and they are on the treadmill that will either lead to a promotion to partner, a decision that typically occurs five to eight years after hiring, or to employment elsewhere. Although women now account for half the graduates of law schools, they were just 17 percent of all partners in 2005—a very slight increase from 1995, when 13 percent of all partners were women (Epstein 1993; O'Brien 2006).

A study of the more than 2,000 men and women who graduated from the prestigious University of Michigan Law School between 1972 and 1985, combined with research on Wall Street lawyers, by Cynthia Fuchs Epstein (1993) helps to explain why women are less likely than men to make partner. The Michigan study focused on those who had spent at least one year in private practice, which 87 percent of all male graduates and 82 percent of female graduates did. After their first year, however, women began to leave private practice at a much greater rate than men; the end result was that 59 percent of the male Michigan graduates made partner compared to just 33 percent of the women. The men and women in the study displayed some striking differences in their family and work arrangements. First, men were more likely to be married and to have children than women. Second, those who were fathers almost never worked part-time or took time off to rear children—only 2 percent of the sample did either. In contrast, 62 percent of the mothers worked part-time or took time off. Although women as a whole worked fewer hours than men, those women who had not taken time off or worked part-time averaged almost the same number of work hours as did the men. Once again we see clear evidence of women, but not men, having to choose between a work-first or family-first strategy (Noonan and Corcoran 2004: 135–139). Epstein (1993) found a broadly similar set of dilemmas for women trying to become partners in Wall Street law firms.

We cannot conclude, however, that part-time work or leaving the labor force are the only reasons why female lawyers don't make partner at the same rate as men. Noonan and Corcoran (2004) estimated that these factors accounted for one quarter to one third of the promotion gap between men and women. They found that having a good GPA in law school and having a mentor were equally strong determinants of whether women made partner. But even when all of these factors were taken into account, there was still a gender gap between men and women, which suggests that discrimination or other features of law-firm culture continue to hamper the careers of women. Indeed, the study by Epstein (1993) found that women faced abiding obstacles in their effort to succeed, partly because of structural obstacles (social networks linked men much more strongly to clients, relegating women to less rewarding opportunities) and the occupational culture that persists in legal circles (in which women have no clearly defined way of behaving "appropriately").

The examples of physicians and lawyers suggest that there are various reasons why women in these professions do not achieve the same levels of career success as their male counterparts. Discrimination, organizational cultures, professional norms, mentoring, and even performance in professional school all play a part. It is equally apparent, however, that traditional gender expectations about women's primary responsibility for childrearing encourage women to find slots within these professions where the demands on their time are manageable. The professions rose to power and status at a time when their members were male and their wives took care of their households, a division of responsibilities that encouraged long working days for young professionals, and they have been slow to accommodate the huge influx of women into their ranks. Female professionals have been forced to decide whether to have a family and, if they do, how to balance the needs of their families against the demands of their careers. The consequence is that female professionals will continue to lag behind males until their employers adopt family-friendly policies that do not penalize women (or men) who use them.

Summary

Professions are high-status, well-paid occupations with four main characteristics: a set of techniques and skills based on abstract knowledge, exclusive jurisdiction over the work performed by their members, authority over the clients they serves and a service ethic that requires their members to subordinate their interests to those of their clients. Professionals control the work of professional subordinates by socializing them into the values, norms, and standards of the occupation. Socialization includes defining what it means to be a real professional and showing subordinates—through mentoring and peer review—how to behave like a professional.

Professionals work long work hours, especially at the start of their careers. If they are married and have children, they have to decide how much time to invest in their careers and how much in their families. The growing percentage of women in the professions has made the issue of balancing work and home particularly important. The response of female professionals to this challenge is different from that of males in two ways. First, female professionals are less likely to be married and to have children. Second, if they do have families, female professionals are more likely to seek out specialties within their professions that have less demanding hours. These specialties, however, are usually lower paid than those that involve heavy time commitments, which limit women's earnings. Female professionals make this sacrifice because they have primary responsibility for childcare and, unlike male professionals, almost never have stay-at-home spouses.

Chapter 9

☙

Service Jobs: Close Encounters with Customers

A quick glance through the Yellow Pages of any major city reveals businesses that would have been hard to conceive of a half-century ago. Need a place to drop your dog off while you are at work? Businesses providing "doggie day care," that feed, walk, groom, and entertain your dog, have sprung up all over the country in recent years. Is your garage a mess? Businesses that will help you organize your garage—or any other area of your house, for that matter—have spread like wildfire. Are you sending your child away to camp this summer? Why not hire the services of a business that will purchase and mail her care packages on a weekly basis? All of these businesses provide important services that people—especially those in the middle class—are ready and willing to pay for. And, on the flip side, these businesses provide jobs—for the most part, relatively low-paying ones—for millions of people in the United States and other industrial economies.

Businesses like these make up just a tiny fraction of a giant portion of the economy known as the service sector. This sector includes many more types of businesses, most of which are well established and thoroughly taken for granted by the large segments of the population who rely

on them. Fast food establishments, dry cleaners, barber shops, janitorial services, and day care centers are among them. We could also include doctors' and dentists' offices, tax preparers, and law firms. What do all of these services have in common? Why have they come to dominate the U.S. economy, while other types of businesses have declined or moved to other less industrialized areas of the world?

We will answer these questions in this chapter and consider several others as well. In particular, we will look at the broad array of service jobs, focusing on what they have in common with one another and how they are distinct. We will also look more broadly at what it means to live in a service economy and its implications for services workers and consumers. Before taking up these issues, however, it is important to clarify some important concepts.

Defining Service

In his 1973 book, *The Coming of Post-Industrial Society*, Daniel Bell described work in a preindustrial society as a "game against nature;" in the more mechanized, technologically advanced industrial societies, work was a "game against fabricated nature." Work in a postindustrial economy, he argued, was a "game between persons" (1973: xx). Though rather abstract, Bell's description captures a key feature of service work and an important way in which it differs from the production of manufactured goods.

To better understand these differences, consider the meaning of the term "service." At the broadest level, performing a service means that people are paid for the activities they perform for others. These "others" include individuals and organizations, such as businesses. The activities involved in performing a service are diverse. They include physical activities, such as repairing a computer or preparing a meal; they include intellectual activities, such as teaching or training. Other important categories of service activities involve those in the aesthetic realm—organizing art exhibits or musical and theater performances—and activities that provide recreational experiences for people, such as in theme parks.

Underlying these differences in types of service activities are features that they share and that distinguish the production of services from the production of goods. First, in contrast to goods, like cars or computers, services are *intangible*. That is, they cannot be picked up, unwrapped, or stacked in a warehouse. In addition, unlike goods, which might sit on a shelf awaiting purchase long after they have rolled off the assembly line, services are *produced and consumed within a relatively short time span*. For example, imagine a visit to the dentist or a trip to a fast food outlet. Here, the services provided (a dental check-up or a meal) are produced and consumed almost simultaneously.

Their intangibility and the close connection between production and consumption introduce two other distinctive aspects of services as compared to other types of work. First, services are delivered through people and thus are inseparable from the person who produced them. This means that the production and delivery of services is a social encounter requiring the direct involvement of service producers themselves. A second element of this encounter is the involvement of consumers or customers. Customers are implicated in the production and delivery of services to a greater degree than in other types of production. While all of these characteristics of service work are important, the social relational dimensions of service work perhaps most set these jobs apart from those involving the production of goods.

Service Industries and Service Occupations

Moving from these broad features of service work to a more specific description, we can take a look at what kinds of occupations and industries are officially counted as part of the service sector. First, consider where people work or the types of industries that employ them. Until 1997, the United States relied on the Standard Industrial Classification System (SIC) to categorize types of economic activity. This system allowed for a broad distinction to be made between "goods-producing" and "service-producing" economic sectors. The goods-producing sector included agriculture, forestry, and fishing; mining; manufacturing; and construction. The remaining industries were all designated as service-producing, including: finance, insurance, and real estate; wholesale and retail trade; transportation and public utilities; and services.

Since 1997, a new industrial classification system has been in place. As we saw in Chapter 3, the North American Industry Classification System (NAICS) was designed to classify economic activity in all of North America, not just the United States. Another important feature of this system is an expanded categorization of service industries. Although service-producing industries account for almost 75 percent of the U.S. gross national product, these industries were not fully represented in the previous classification system. The NAICS added over 150 new service industries, such as software publishing, paging, cellular, and other wireless telecommunications, satellite telecommunications, HMO medical centers, diagnostic imaging centers, and casino hotels (www.census.gov/epcd/www/naicssvc.html; retrieved 9/25/06).

Service industries are generally organized according to the nature of their activities (e.g., to provide entertainment or recreation; to provide education), but another way to differentiate them is to consider whether the service is provided primarily to a consumer or to a business. Services provided to consumers are what many people imagine when they consider the term service industry. Health care is the largest consumer-oriented service industry and is the one that has grown most rapidly over the past two decades (Goodman and Steadman 2002). This expansion can be attributed to the aging of the U.S. population.

Business services grew even more rapidly than consumer services from the late 1980s to 2000, but then declined steeply as the economy went into recession (Goodman and Steadman 2002). The two largest categories of business services are in the areas of personnel supply and computer and data processing. As the economy expanded, companies hired temporary staffing agencies to help them keep up with the demands for new products and services. It is not surprising that these agencies would contract rapidly during a recession. Computer and data-processing services, which grew rapidly as the Internet expanded, were also subject to a downturn after 2000.

In certain respects, however, this type of industry-based definition is too narrow. Many companies known primarily as goods-producing also have a strong service component to their business. IBM, for example, is a company that most people probably associate with computers and computer-related equipment. Although IBM is still in the computer business, it now receives over half of its revenue from the services it provides, especially to businesses (Lohr 2006). Service jobs thus can be found in any business or industry where services are provided, although they have historically been most concentrated in the industries comprising the service sector.

From this description it is apparent that services encompass a wide variety of jobs and that these jobs, while plentiful in service-producing industries, can be found throughout the economy. Service jobs include lawyers and stockbrokers, janitors and childcare workers; it includes those who repair your computer, run the rides at Disneyland, and prepare your taxes. This diversity of wages and working conditions make it extremely difficult to generalize about the service sector. This sector encompasses many of what we might consider the "best" jobs in the economy, but it also includes many of those we would view as the "worst" (Meisenheimer 1998).

Despite this diversity, because interaction is a feature of all service jobs, they share some important characteristics. In the next section we will look at these shared features of service occupations. Then we will turn our attention to some of the important differences between those service jobs that are among the "best" in the economy and those that many view as less desirable.

Characteristics of Service Jobs

"Now Hiring Smiling Faces"

In a goods-producing economy, many workers perform jobs that require physical labor, the operation of machinery, or the use of tools. A service economy, by contrast, generates jobs that require what sociologists call "soft skills." Soft skills refer to abilities that "pertain to personality, attitude, and behavior rather than to formal or technical knowledge" (Moss and Tilly 2001: 44). Soft skills thus derive in part from how people present themselves to others; they may include such things as workers' demeanor, physical appearance, style of speech and work attitude. As we have seen, one of the salient features of service jobs is that they involve social interaction between the worker who provides the service and the client or customer to whom it is sold. Because the quality or value of the service provided depends heavily upon the nature of this interaction, employers have a large stake in the soft skills of their workers.

Emotional Labor

In her 1983 classic, *The Managed Heart*, sociologist Arlie Hochschild provided a penetrating look at service jobs and their implications for workers. Hochschild introduced the concept of *emotional labor* to capture what is expected of service workers in the era of "soft skills." One way to understand emotional labor is to consider it in relation to physical or mental labor.

All are forms of work that require people to direct a particular kind of energy toward a goal. What differs is the nature of the energy used to produce the product. Recall that service jobs typically require workers to interact directly with clients or customers. Employers expect these workers to express a particular emotional demeanor during these interactions. Emotional labor refers to the effort involved in displaying these characteristics.

Hochschild argues that we all routinely manage our emotions and emotional expressions for private ends. For example, when we generate a display of enthusiasm that we may not feel on occasions where we feel cheerfulness is expected, we are managing our emotions. Emotion *management*, however, is typically done of our own volition; we decide what kind of emotional demeanor is required in a particular situation and work to create this feeling in ourselves or, at a minimum, to display the appropriate emotion. Emotional *labor,* in contrast, refers to this kind of work when it is performed for pay as a job requirement. For example, fast food workers are expected to be friendly and helpful and can be disciplined if they fail to display these qualities (Leidner 1993). Bill collectors are required to be hostile and confrontational with debtors (Sutton 1991).

Emotional labor on the job generally takes one of two forms. First, many jobs require workers to generate and display emotions that they may not necessarily feel. Flight attendants are expected to be cheerful to passengers, regardless of how they are treated and despite being busy or under stress. The ability to generate and maintain good humor and politeness is a requirement of many customer service jobs. A second broad type of emotional labor involves the suppression or masking of emotion. Workers in these jobs are expected to be emotionally neutral and detached, regardless of the emotions expressed by others and in spite of how they themselves are feeling. Police officers, for example, are supposed to remain calm and unemotional even when dealing with people who may be experiencing strong emotions. Funeral directors, who deal with others' grief and loss, are expected to maintain emotional distance, as are many types of workers in the fields of medicine and mental health, whose jobs require close contact with patients or clients.

Jobs requiring both kinds of emotional labor have increased rapidly as the service economy has grown. Sociologists have studied many of these jobs. Examples of this research include Sutton and Rafaeli's (1988) study of convenience store clerks, Paules's (1991) research on waitresses, Sutton's (1991) research on bill collectors, Leidner's (1993) study of fast food and insurance workers, and Pierce's (1995) study of litigators and paralegals (among others). Emotional labor has also been studied among adventure guides (Sharpe 2005), police officers and detectives (Stenross and Kleinman 1989; Martin 1999), and college professors (Bellas 1999; Harlow 2003).

Gender and Emotional Labor

Women and men do different amounts and types of emotional labor. Hochschild (1983) estimated that over half of all the jobs held by women involved emotional labor, while emotional labor was required in only one quarter of jobs held by men. Later studies are consistent with this general finding. In particular, women report spending more time than men at interacting with others in the course of performing their jobs (Erickson and Ritter 2001).

As important as how much emotional labor one's job requires is the type of emotional labor people are expected to perform. Jobs that require emotional labor ask a worker to be a certain kind of person on the job and to display certain qualities when interacting with others. As a result of these connections between workers' subjectivity and job requirements, jobs that involve emotional labor are likely to be strongly gender-typed. For example, as we have seen, many service jobs require workers to generate and display emotions such as friendliness, sociability, and cheerfulness. Because these qualities are stereotypically feminine, such jobs are likely to be viewed as more appropriate for women than for men (Steinberg and Figart 1999).

By referring to jobs involving "an application of social skills to activities providing a service to customers or clients" as "nurturant" occupations, England (1992: 136) makes clear the gendered character of this type of emotional labor. The interactional work involved in instilling feelings of satisfaction and well-being in others bears obvious similarities to the caretaking activities typically assigned to women in families.

Not all jobs that require emotional labor are gender-typed as female, however. Many professional and managerial jobs, for example, require a self-presentation designed to convey and wield authority. Authority in American society is conveyed through an emotionally inexpressive persona. In fact, studies show that workers equate behaving "professionally" as being in control of one's emotions. As Tannen observes, however, in our society, "[i]mages of authority come drenched in gender...[t]he very notion of authority is associated with maleness" (1994: 166–167). Jobs involving authority, such as law or medicine, thus are often gender-typed as masculine; they are seen as more appropriate for men than women, and men are seen as more qualified to fulfill the job requirements.

Some service jobs combine elements of both forms of emotional expression. Deference and compliance are expected from citizens in encounters with the police, and the public image of policing as "crime-fighting" reinforces the stereotypically masculine characteristics of gaining and maintaining control over others (Martin 1999). Policing also involves other activities, however, such as providing emotional support to crime victims and families. These parts of the job are often unrecognized and undervalued, but are essential for being an effective police officer.

Even when women and men occupy the same job, they may be expected to do different kinds and amounts of emotional labor. For example, in her research among paralegals, Pierce (1995) found that while assisting lawyers was expected of paralegals of both sexes, women and men were rewarded for different kinds of behavior. Women paralegals were expected to be deferential and nurturing to lawyers, sometimes jokingly referred to as their "therapists." Men in these support roles were expected to act more as "political advisors," remaining affectively neutral and polite, rather than emotionally supportive (Pierce 1995).

Consequences of Emotional Labor

These studies have raised several issues that are worth exploring in more detail. Among the most important has been a desire to understand how jobs that require emotional labor affect workers. In *The Managed Heart,* Hochschild (1983) warned of the potential psychological dangers of emotional labor, which she attributed to the loss of control over emotion that occurs when

employers begin to regulate the feelings workers experience and display. Hochschild drew parallels between workers' loss of control over their forms of emotional expression and the sorts of alienation that Marx identified at an earlier stage of capitalist development (see Chapter 2).

Although workers in all types of jobs must comfortably balance the person they are—or are expected to be—at work and their own sense of self, this balance may be trickier for people engaged in emotional labor. In particular, workers may *experience* certain emotions during their interactions with customers and clients, but feel compelled to *display* other emotions. This dissonance between what one feels and what one is expected to display may create problems for some workers if it occurs too much or too often at work. Among the flight attendants Hochschild studied were those who felt estranged from their feelings and their sense of themselves. Workers felt inauthentic, insincere, and cynical about the false self they were expected to present to customers.

Long-term performance of emotional labor has also been associated with burnout. Burnout involves the numbing of the inner signals of emotional feelings, resulting in the inability to create or feel any emotion (Maslach and Jackson 1981). Some also refer to this condition as "contact overload," a situation where workers become "robotic, detached, and unempathetic" (Albrecht and Zemke 1985: 114). In contrast to inauthenticity, which occurs when there is a gap between what people feel and what they are expected to display, burnout results when workers overidentify with the emotional demands of their jobs. Not surprisingly, burnout has been most often uncovered among people in service jobs where it is difficult to fake one's feelings and avoid empathy with others. People holding jobs such as teachers, nurses, counselors, and social workers are especially vulnerable to burnout.

Qualitative researchers have also contributed to our understanding of the consequences of emotional labor for workers' lives off the job. For example, a 1989 study by Smith and Kleinman examined how male and female medical students learned the emotional style of "affective neutrality" required of medical practitioners and other professionals (see Chapter 8). These researchers showed that medical students of both genders developed strategies to suppress and manage the feelings often evoked in their encounters with human bodies. While useful professionally, Smith and Kleinman note that "[f]or some students, medical training creates a problem as new meanings for the body and for body contact go home with them at night" (1989: 65). Emotional labor required on the job thus may conflict with that involved in sustaining intimate relations in private life.

Despite these potential psychological dangers of emotional labor, research suggests that the consequences of emotional labor are strongly contingent upon other characteristics of the job, the organization, or the worker (Wharton 1993). Jobs requiring emotional labor may also have positive aspects, especially when compared to jobs not requiring emotional labor. Opportunities for social interaction at work are generally experienced as satisfying and authenticating for workers. Overall, it is difficult to generalize about the consequences of emotional labor, given the wide variety of jobs that involve this activity and the ways in which emotional labor is performed. For example, a courtroom lawyer and a fast food worker both have jobs that require emotional labor, but these jobs differ in fundamental ways.

This suggests the need to look more carefully at specific types of service jobs and the ways in which their particular features may shape workers' experiences.

Control, Routinization, and Technology in Service Work

One theme underscored in previous chapters is the issue of workers' control over their jobs and working conditions. Routinization and technological change are closely linked to this issue, as both processes affect how much and what kinds of control workers have. Just as in other occupations, control over working conditions plays a critical role in shaping service workers' experiences of their jobs. In addition, understanding employers' efforts to control the work activities of these employees sheds light on the organization of service work.

Routinization serves at least two purposes for employers: by simplifying and standardizing tasks, it lessens the cost of labor. Routinization also helps to create a uniform product. A trend toward routinization can also be seen in the organization of service work. Although routinization and technological change affect all service jobs to some extent, the impact of these forces has been much greater among nonprofessional workers.

In her 1993 study of McDonald's, Leidner identified the dilemma service employers face when attempting to reap the benefits of routinization: because human interaction of some form is integral to the performance of service work, it is impossible to standardize the process without also "standardizing" the worker. But as Leidner notes, "since good service is often equated with 'personal' service, standardization may undercut quality in human interactions" (1993: 25). Given this trade-off, Leidner concludes that employers are likely to routinize service jobs only under three conditions: (1) when the quality of the interaction is essential to the success of the business; (2) when employers believe that workers are unable or unwilling to interact appropriately on their own; and (3) when the service to be produced is amenable to routinization (i.e., it is not too complex or context-dependent).

McDonald's, known worldwide for its highly standardized production of fast food, occupies one end of the continuum. At McDonald's, workers' interactions with customers are tightly regulated and monitored. The standard phrase, "Would you like fries with that?" is a line used so often by fast food workers that it has become synonymous with this service job. Many other service jobs also require workers to adhere to a script in their interactions with customers. Firm adherence to these scripts may be a job requirement in some cases, while other employers may allow workers to improvise when needed. By scripting workers' interactions, employers attempt to control exactly how the job is performed and thereby ensure the quality of the product. Since the "product" in a service encounter emerges through interaction between worker and customer, quality control requires control over the worker's role in this encounter.

Some scripts may be short and simple, such as those for restaurant servers who are expected to introduce themselves to diners before taking an order. Other scripts may be more elaborate, as this description of training for life insurance salespeople describes:

> Trainees were required to memorize long scripts for selling specific products as well as subsidiary scripts for responding to specific customer

objections and interruptions; they were taught that speaking loudly and quickly would boost their confidence; they were told how to stand when waiting for someone to answer the door and given precise movement training for entering the house; they learned exactly when to make eye contact and when to break it in the course of their speeches; how to gesture with a pen to guide prospects' eyes and attention, and how to deliver The Standard Joke. (Leidner 1993: 87)

Technology plays an important role in the processes associated with routinization. It is easy to forget that many personal services that were once provided by people are now performed almost exclusively by machines—specifically, computers. Banking, grocery store and library check-outs, travel arrangements, and other kinds of purchases can be done entirely electronically. Though the vast majority of transactions in these areas can be performed with very little, if any, interaction between the customer and a service provider, personal service remains available for those who can afford to pay a premium.

The experiences of workers employed in highly routinized personal service jobs bear some similarities to those of workers in other types of routine work (see Chapter 5). Highly routinized jobs are often low-paying and monotonous, thus offering few intrinsic or extrinsic rewards for workers. For service workers, however, routinization raises additional issues. By scripting workers' interactions or requiring them to display particular emotions, employers are engaging in a form of personality control that seems far-reaching—especially when compared to the control employers exercise in other types of jobs. As

Leidner explains, "employers' assertion of control over workers' appearance, words, and self-presentation seems intrusive to many workers and observers, and efforts to reshape demeanor, attitudes, and feelings are often seen as attacks on workers' dignity" (1993: 217–218).

Service workers use a variety of strategies to express themselves within the constraints of their job and protect their dignity. Some psychologically disengage from the work role. They protect their identity by drawing a clear line between the person they are at work and their "real" self. These workers operate on "automatic pilot" at work, adhering to standardized scripts but not engaging with customers any more than is necessary. Other service workers may modify the assigned scripts or routines in small ways, thus asserting some control over how they present themselves to others on the job. Some workers deliver their scripts with humor or exaggeration, signifying to their customers that they know they are reciting lines and not interacting as they would in a real conversation. All of these behaviors represent ways that service workers in highly routinized jobs resist intrusions on their dignity and sense of self. Overall, this points to the important role that control over working conditions plays in shaping service workers' experiences of their jobs.

Other personal service jobs are much more difficult to routinize—either because the tasks themselves are inherently too complex or they are highly context-dependent. Consider the work of a childcare provider or a police officer, for example. It would be impossible (and undesirable) to rigidly script these kinds of relationship-intensive activities. The ways that a childcare worker interacts with a child depends on the worker, the child, and the situation. Police officers

are asked to deal with a variety of people and settings and must adjust their demeanor accordingly. Similarly, many professional services, such as legal transactions or medical procedures, are too complex to be easily routinized, though even these areas have experienced some pressures toward routinization.

Doing Deference: Personal Service Work

Many of the examples given at the beginning of this chapter are considered "personal" service jobs because they involve workers performing services directly for consumers. Personal trainers, stylists in hair salons, doormen, childcare workers, and restaurant servers are examples of this type of service work. Also included in this category are jobs that are performed in private households, such as nannies, cooks, or housecleaners. Yet the category also includes many professional positions, such as doctor, lawyers, or college professors.

Professionals generally have much more control over the day-to-day aspects of their jobs than other workers (Chapter 8). The same is true among professionals in service occupations, as compared to other type of service workers. At the other end of the continuum are workers in "frontline" service jobs. Macdonald and Sirianni (1996) refer to these service workers, whose jobs (and emotional labor) are tightly regulated by employers, as "the emotional proletariat." Because professions were the focus of Chapter 8, we concentrate here on these frontline personal service jobs.

Like other forms of service employment, the number of personal service jobs rose steadily over the last half of the twentieth century and continues to increase. This increase can be seen as both consequence and cause of other important societal trends. In particular, the rise of personal services can be attributed in part to the increase in women's labor force participation, which began in the 1960s and has only recently leveled off. As women left home for the labor market, they created a demand for certain kinds of activities. Personal service workers of all kinds thus have increasingly performed jobs that were once done by women in the home. Childcare, cleaning and laundry services, food services, and nursing care for the elderly are merely a few examples of these activities.

Rising numbers of personal service jobs were not simply a consequence of women's labor force participation, however. As these jobs (and the services they provide) proliferated, women's absence from the home became less of an inconvenience for them and their families. It was much easier for women to go to work when they and their families could replace women's unpaid labor with services purchased in the marketplace. Hence, just as industrialization was associated with the move of goods production from home to factory (Chapter 4), so too has "postindustrial" society been associated with the move of services from home to the marketplace.

Other factors have also contributed to the growth of personal service jobs. In particular, rising levels of disposable income and affluence have made personal services increasingly affordable. Real disposable personal income rose 22 percent between the late 1980s and 2000 (Goodman and Steadman 2002). Although the numbers of households employing "domestic servants" has declined dramatically over the course of the twentieth century, many middle- and upper-class families rely on a range of service

providers for a variety of tasks. In this "new servant economy," as it has been called, "servants" are not just for the rich. Higher levels of disposable income also contributed to increases in services oriented toward recreation and amusement and travel-related entertainment.

"The Customer Is Always Right"

Although many aspects of personal service work reflect current trends and patterns, in other respects, personal service work retains many of the characteristics that it has always had. These characteristics are features of all service jobs to some degree, but they are most directly reflected in the organization of personal services. Consider the relationship between the customer and the worker. Customers or clients play a role in all service encounters, but their role in the personal service relationship is somewhat unique in that they direct and supervise the work being performed. The nature of the relations between worker and customer can be seen in the adage—especially strong in the United States and less so in other countries—that "the customer is always right." The expectation here is that the worker will be, at some level, deferential and accommodating to customers. This capacity may also be expressed as "niceness" or the ability to get along.

Hierarchy is a taken-for-granted aspect of work in organizations, but it is normally embedded in formal roles and relationships, such as that of a supervisor or manager with authority over subordinates. By contrast, in face-to-face service encounters, customers' authority over workers is more personal and less structured by formal roles and responsibilities. This makes these relations potentially socially awkward for both parties. This awkwardness stems from the tensions between the patterns of deference and hierarchy involved in personal service work and U.S. ideals of classlessness and egalitarianism. In contrast to these norms, personal service work, as Paules notes, is imbued "with the symbolism of servitude" (1991: xx). This symbolism, as well as the resistance it inspires, has been chronicled in best-selling books and films, such as *Nickel and Dimed* (Ehrenreich 2001), *The Nanny Diaries* (McLaughlin and Kraus 2003), and *The Devil Wears Prada* (Weisberger 2003).

Many aspects of personal service work reinforce the subordinate status of the worker vis-à-vis the customer. For example, in some service establishments, workers and customers have separate entrances. Workers may be required to enter from the back, rather than the front door. This arrangement is perhaps a vestige of a time when separate entrances or living spaces were designated for household servants, who were not to be visible in the main area of the home. Patrons of fine restaurants have learned that being seated next to the kitchen is less desirable and connotes lower status than seating in a more central location. Hence, Paules observes: "Much as domestic servants in the nineteenth century did not dine with or in the presence of masters, so today waitresses are forbidden to take breaks, sit, smoke, eat, or drink in the presence of customers" (1991: 132).

Workers in personal service jobs are required to wear a uniform. The black and white uniforms often worn by restaurant servers are reminiscent of the clothing worn by household servants in previous eras. Uniforms and other strict rules about appearance sharply delineate the worker from the customer in ways that mark the worker as subordinate (Paules 1991). Uniforms have become a social marker of a low-status job, and

anecdotal evidence suggests that workers of all kinds are increasingly resistant to wearing them. In *Nickel and Dimed*, Ehrenreich explained her experience as a housecleaner this way: "True, I don't look so good at the end of the day and probably smell like eau de toilet and sweat, but it's the brilliant green-and-yellow uniform that gives me away, like prison clothes on a fugitive" (2001: 100).

Deference and status distinctions of all kinds are also signaled through other means. Many service workers, for example, are required to wear name tags when on the job. In some cases, these name tags display only the worker's first name. The use of name tags allows customers to refer to workers by name, but does not give workers the same opportunity to refer to customers in this manner. The asymmetrical usage of first names conveys a status distinction between the worker and customer. This is analogous to the way that status norms surrounding age give adults the right to address children by their first names, but may require a child to more formally address an adult.

The symbolism of servitude is also reflected in other aspects of customers' interactions with service workers. Service workers occupy what sociologist Erving Goffman (1959) referred to as "the non-person role." Unlike people in most other roles or settings, nonpersons can be overlooked and ignored. Goffman (1959) used the concept of a "non-person" to refer to the treatment of the elderly, the sick, and the young, but studies of frontline service workers—especially those employed in private households—have drawn on Goffman's ideas to capture service workers' experiences.

For example, in her ethnographic study of domestic work, Rollins described the following experience cleaning the house of a professional couple who had both left for work:

> About a half hour after they left, I noticed the house getting cooler. The temperature continued to drop to, I would guess 50–55 degrees—not comfortable even with my activity. I realized that they had turned the heat down as if there was no one there! I looked for a thermostat but couldn't find it. Worked in that temperature until 5:00 when I left. (1985: 208)

Paules explains:

> That customers embrace the service-as-servitude metaphor is evidenced by the way they speak to and about service workers. Virtually every rule of etiquette is violated by customers in their interaction with the waitress: the waitress can be interrupted; she can be ignored and stared at; and she can be subjected to unrestrained anger. Lacking the status of a person she, like the servant, is refused the most basic considerations of polite interaction. She is, in addition, the subject of chronic criticism. (1991: 138)

The "tip" is another feature of personal service work that reinforces the hierarchical relationship between customer and worker. The tip has both real and symbolic value. In real terms, tips are an important source of income for personal service workers of all kinds and are useful to employers as a way of reducing the costs of supervision. Tipping is also highly symbolic, both for the worker and the customer.

Economists, psychologists, and sociologists have generated an enormous literature on tipping. Many of these studies attempt to identify factors that predict the size of a worker's tips, focusing on such factors as the demographic and personal characteristics of service workers and their customers or factors related to the nature of the service (Lynn, Zinkhan, and Harris 1993). While interesting, this research fails to capture the symbolic aspects of tipping, including but not limited to its role in evaluating the service provided. Because services are bound up with the people who provide them, however, tipping is a means through which customers pass judgments on workers. This helps to explain the symbolic power of the tip.

The symbolism of unequal power conveyed through tipping is reinforced by the tip's "gift-like" status. Like other gifts, tips from customers are expected, but cannot be required or demanded. Unlike most gift exchanges, however, the tip is given unilaterally; customers give tips, but there is no expectation of reciprocity. This lack of reciprocity underscores the unequal power relations between customer and worker. The customer demonstrates his or her superior status by providing a tip; the service worker implicitly acknowledges this status by providing nothing in return.

To summarize these characteristics of personal service jobs, we can compare them with professional services (see Chapter 8). In general, professionals provide services to "clients" or "patients," not "customers." Professional services involve guidance and advice on topics in which professionals are assumed to have more expertise than those to whom this guidance and advice are provided. Professionals thus wield authority over others and expect to be treated with deference and respect by their clients, rather than the other way around. For example, patients are likely to refer to their physician as "Dr." whereas it is socially acceptable for a doctor to refer to a patient by his or her first name. Neither doctors nor lawyers operate strictly on the principle of "the customer is always right." We would never consider tipping our doctors, lawyers, dentists, or professors. (You might experiment with this last group and see what happens.)

From a sociological perspective, one of the features of professions that distinguishes them from other occupations is their capacity to exercise authority over clients and patients. That professionals are viewed as entitled to this authority stems from widespread acceptance of the legitimacy of their expertise. This underscores the fundamental differences between professional service jobs and those of the "emotional proletariat."

Gender, Race, and Personal Service Work

The deference expected of workers in personal service jobs raises important issues of gender and race. Deference—or the capacity to place oneself in a "one down" position vis-à-vis others—is a characteristic demanded of all those in disadvantaged structural positions, including women, racial-ethnic minorities, and others in subordinate statuses. When deference is made a job requirement, members of structurally disadvantaged groups are likely to be overrepresented in such jobs or even be seen as better suited for the work than members of more advantaged groups. Referring to personal service jobs, Macdonald and Sirianni claim that "[i]n no other area of wage labor are the personal characteristics of the workers so strongly associated with the nature of the work" (1996: 15).

Hochschild (1983) argued that women's higher representation in jobs requiring deference—in the form of niceness, sociability, and the like—coupled with their lower overall social status, gave women a weaker "status shield" against others' negative emotions than men. In other words, angry, frustrated, or unhappy customers are more likely to vent these emotions to women service workers than to men. Extending this argument, it implies that workers from all structurally disadvantaged groups—people of color, immigrants, teenagers, the poor—would be more vulnerable to customers' negative emotions than those in more advantaged social categories.

In her book *No Shame in My Game: The Working Poor in the Inner City*, Newman (1999) demonstrates how this process operates for poor youth seeking jobs in fast food. While fast food workers are expected to accommodate customers' demands, minority youth in the inner city have learned that respect is earned by standing up to others, not deferring. This may be especially true for young men. As Newman explains, "...jobs that routinely demand displays of deference force those who hold them to violate 'macho' behavior codes that are central to the definition of teen culture" (1999: 95). Hence, while all workers employed in personal service jobs may have a difficult time maintaining their dignity and engendering respect from customers, such issues may be especially potent for workers from more disadvantaged social groups.

Conclusion: Beyond the Service Economy

There is no dispute that the American economy—along with most of the industrialized world—is dominated by services. As the service-producing sector has grown, it has become increasingly clear that the old ways of understanding work and economic structure are less useful than before. As this chapter has shown, the government agencies that classify, categorize, and track employment and economic activity have begun to transform their way of thinking about service production and service jobs. New systems of industrial and occupational classification reflect this transformation. These changes were inspired not only by the growth of services, but also by their diversity. Along with new classification systems, sociologists have devised new concepts for understanding the distinctiveness of service work as compared to other types of jobs. The concept of emotional labor is an example of these efforts.

Although services are distinct in many important respects, many of the same processes that shape the organization of work in other areas also apply to services. For example, service jobs have been affected by technological change and continue to be a focus of technological innovation as it relates to the workplace. As in other types of work, issues of race, gender, and other forms of status disadvantage also permeate the service sector. It remains to be seen whether service jobs will evolve in radically new ways in the years ahead or continue to demonstrate continuity with the twentieth-century workplace.

PART IV

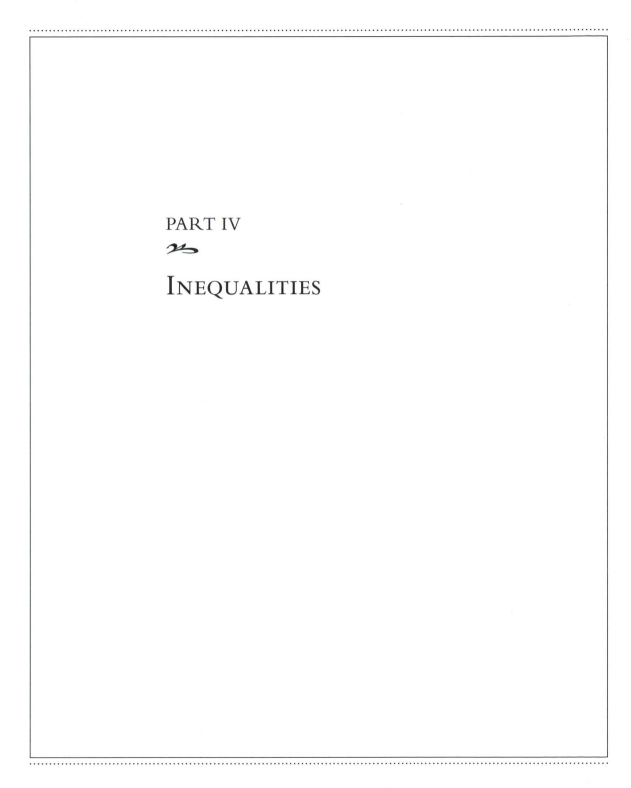

INEQUALITIES

Chapter 10

≈

Unions in America: The Struggles of the Labor Movement

Workers in service occupations—janitors, hotel maids, dishwashers, waiters, waitresses, and bartenders—are among the lowest paid in the labor force. Low wages and, in some cases, lack of opportunity for full-time work combine to keep these workers' earnings at or below the poverty level. Fringe benefits, such as health insurance, are often nonexistent. There is one exception to this trend. Hotel and casino workers in Las Vegas receive wages that are more than double the minimum wage, enjoy a guaranteed forty-hour work week, and have employer-provided health insurance. The difference between the Las Vegas service workers and their counterparts elsewhere in the country is that over 90 percent of Vegas workers belong to a union. In the country as a whole, less than 5 percent of workers are union members.

The Las Vegas casino and hotel workers join Major League baseball players, General Motors automobile workers, Delta Air Lines pilots, Costco clerks, West Coast longshore workers, and Hollywood screenwriters in being loyal members of labor unions. Union members, studies have repeatedly shown, enjoy better wages and fringe benefits than workers who do not have union contracts. In view of the apparent benefits

of union membership, therefore, it may come as a surprise to some that the labor movement is in a fifty-year decline that shows no sign of ending. Less than 8 percent of workers in the private sector belong to unions, a figure so low that some observers have drawn the conclusion that unions are obsolete—that they are simply lingering holdovers from our industrial past. It is true that unions today are seldom noticed unless a union of professional athletes is on strike. Aside from this group of workers, whose industrial conflicts are invariably accompanied by derisive headlines and commentary about multimillionaire strikers, we read, see, and hear little about the labor movement. The rare news tends to be bad news, at least for union advocates: another story about the declining percentage of American workers who belong to labor unions or about Wal-Mart's successful efforts to keep unions out of every single one of its stores.

We do not believe, however, that the lack of a union presence makes unions unimportant or that union decline, at least on the scale that has occurred in the United States, is inevitable. There are specific economic and, more important, political reasons why the union movement has become weaker. Further, unions do matter, otherwise there would be no reason for workers as different as Las Vegas casino workers and Major League ballplayers to want them and for companies like Wal-Mart to oppose them so vehemently.

Stories about the absence of unions or their defeats make it hard to remember that just fifty years ago one of every three nonagricultural workers belonged to a union. Unions were a highly visible presence—in the workplace and during political campaigns. They had achieved their preeminence through the sacrifice, bravery, and commitment of individual workers during the turbulent years between the end of the Great Depression in 1933 and the beginning of World War II. The labor movement gained its place at the bargaining table because its members were willing to confront national guardsmen, state troopers, city police officers, and company security guards in upholding their legal right to form unions.

The contrast between organized labor's past glory and its current weakness raises three questions that we will address in this chapter. First, what caused this movement to rise so rapidly and to spread so widely in the period between 1933 and 1945? Second, why did it fail to sustain its momentum after 1950 and instead enter a long period of decline? Third, what are the consequences for workers of a working environment that is largely union-free, particularly in the private sector where the unionization rate has fallen from 40 percent to 8 percent?

The Glory Years of Industrial Unionism: 1933–1945

In the United States in 2007, 15.7 million workers—just over 12 percent of the nonagricultural workforce (this includes the private and public sectors)—belonged to unions. Union membership is in percentage terms approaching a level not seen since the Great Depression, a time when the union movement was at its lowest ebb. In 1933 fewer than 3 million workers in the United States belonged to unions, around 10 percent of the nonagricultural labor force. Coal mining, construction, and railroads were among the very few industries in which unions had a foothold. In the early 1930s unions were absent from mass-production industries, i.e., from those industries dominated by the largest firms, which used the most advanced technology, and which employed the greatest numbers of unskilled and semi-skilled workers.

One of the puzzling features of the low level of unionism today is that it has developed in a political, economic, and legal environment very different from that of Depression-era America. Unions are now protected by law and are accepted by many companies, particularly in the mass-production industries. They have been an important part of a political coalition that has consistently supported the Democratic Party, beginning with the election of Franklin Delano Roosevelt. Moreover, union decline has developed in the wake of astonishing success: the U.S. union movement was 15 million strong by 1945 (this amounted to over one third of the labor force) and included almost all the mass-production workers, such as those in steel, automobiles, electrical products, and rubber. These unions produced high wages and good benefits for their members in addition to on-the-job safeguards against violations ranging from unsafe working conditions to assembly-line speed-ups. Why, then, has labor fallen from these heights? To explain its fall we need to start with its rise.

Industrial unionism triumphed between 1933 and 1945 because workers and their leaders had legislation on their side and were willing to go to extraordinary lengths to implement this legislation. The two crucial laws, passed in President Franklin Roosevelt's first term, were the National Industrial Recovery Act (NIRA) of 1933 and the National Labor Relations Act (NLRA) of 1935. The NIRA contained the famous statement that workers "shall have the right to organize and bargain collectively through representatives of their own choosing, and shall be free from the interference, restraint or coercion of employers...." The NLRA or Wagner Act was the more important of the two bills because it provided specific legal protections for workers who wanted to form unions. Neither bill would have been effective, however, were it not for the willingness of workers to endure economic hardship and physical danger, sometimes risking their lives, to ensure that their employers recognized their right to union representation and engaged in collective bargaining with them.

From the NIRA to the Wagner Act

Workers quickly put the right-to-organize section of the NIRA to the test by going on strike when employers refused to accept their unions. An outburst of strikes in 1934 included auto parts workers in Toledo, truck drivers in Minneapolis, textile workers in the South, and longshoremen in the West Coast ports. These disputes often erupted into violence, as was the case in the longshore strike.

The West Coast longshoremen's strike began in May 1934 when workers walked off the job to press their demand that employers recognize their union. Over the next three months,

longshoremen battled state troopers and city police, the latter often mounted on horseback, in ports up and down the coast. The dispute reached its bloody climax in San Francisco on July 5, when ship-owners attempted to reopen the port using strikebreakers. The police dispersed the strikers' picket lines by hurling tear-gas bombs into the crowd and then firing on the unarmed strikers. Two longshoremen were killed and thirty-one were injured in the gunfire. ("Bloody Thursday," as the day was known, became part of longshore legend; every year on this date West Coast longshore workers stop work to commemorate those who died fighting for their union rights on July 5.) On July 9, 1934, 15,000 workers marched up Market Street in San Francisco in a two-mile-long funeral procession for the slain workers. Two weeks later there was a general strike in San Francisco supporting the longshoremen and demanding that the police leave the waterfront. President Roosevelt brought an end to the eighty-three-day strike when he submitted the dispute to a national arbitration board to resolve (Kimeldorf 1988).

The inherent shortcoming of the NIRA, as the longshoremen's strike so violently demonstrated, was that it did not provide a means for resolving labor disputes or for determining whether employers were interfering with the right to organize. After the Supreme Court ruled that the NIRA was unconstitutional, Congress quickly moved to remedy its limitations by passing the National Labor Relations Act (NLRA) in July 1935.

The NLRA, also known as the Wagner Act after its sponsor, Senator Robert F. Wagner, a Democrat from New York, contained explicit provisions protecting the rights of workers who wanted to form labor unions. The Act defined any action by an employer "to interfere with, restrain, or coerce employees in the exercise of the right of self-organization" as an "unfair labor practice." It made it illegal to fire workers for union activities; they were to be reinstated with back pay. It mandated secret-ballot elections in workplaces so that the workers could decide by simple majority vote whether they wished to be represented by a union. If a union won the election it became the sole bargaining agent for those employees and the employers were obliged to bargain with it in good faith. Finally, the Act created an agency, the National Labor Relations Board (NLRB), to investigate whether employers were engaging in unfair labor practices, to enforce its provisions and to oversee representation elections. The Act was a powerful statement about workers' rights and an unambiguous declaration that union organizing and collective bargaining now had the endorsement of the federal government.

The Congress of Industrial Organizations (CIO)

The passage of the Wagner Act reinforced the determination of workers to establish unions. The question was how to do this. The American Federation of Labor (AFL) was still the umbrella organization for the union movement as a whole, but as we showed in Chapter 5, the unions that made up the AFL were mostly associations of skilled workers. AFL unions had little experience in organizing the unskilled and semi-skilled workers in the mass-production industries. By 1935 the AFL was also a deeply divided body. Some of its members supported forming a single union for each of the mass-production industries, i.e., one union for all the automobile workers, another for all the rubber

workers, a third for all the steel workers, and so on. This was the philosophy of industrial unionism. Its chief advocate was John L. Lewis, the formidable head of the United Mine Workers. The official AFL position, however, was that the skilled craftsmen in the mass-production industries—the machine-makers and installers, the maintenance workers, the tool- and die-makers—should be allowed to maintain separate craft unions rather than be required to join the industrial unions.

The dispute erupted in a contentious AFL convention in 1935. Tempers were so frayed that John Lewis came to blows with the president of the Carpenters Union, William Hutcheson, a strong believer in craft unionism. Lewis punched Hutcheson, knocking him to the ground. Despite Lewis's pleas, the convention ultimately voted against industrial unionism. Undeterred by this setback, in November 1935 Lewis and seven other union presidents who supported him formed the Committee for Industrial Organization to pursue their vision of industrial unionism. They were subsequently expelled from the AFL and formed the Congress of Industrial Organization (CIO), which thus became a rival federation to the AFL, with Lewis as its first president.

The CIO wasted little time in putting its philosophy of industrial unionism into practice. Lewis had targeted four industries for unionization: automaking, rubber, steel, and electrical products. New industrial unions, such as the United Automobile Workers (UAW), the Steel Workers Organizing Committee (SWOC), and the United Rubber Workers were brought into the CIO alliance; CIO leaders provided funds and organizational assistance with union drives. The first of these unions to achieve a breakthrough was the UAW, in large part due to its successful adoption of a new bargaining tactic—the "sit-down" strike. The sit-down strike evolved almost by accident. In 1935 workers at a Firestone plan in Akron, Ohio, were told that the company had introduced a new system for calculating their wages. Upset by the change and angry that management refused to discuss it with them, the workers refused to leave the factory at the end of their shift. The dispute was settled after a few days, but a new tactic had been born (Brinkley 2003).

Sit-Down Strikes

The sit-down strike was a solution to a problem that had long plagued union organizers: how to have a strike without having strikebreakers or scabs replace them at the factory, mine, mill, or dock. Moreover, confrontations with strikebreakers outside the plant gates were often the prelude to the violent intervention of the police, who would forcibly disperse the picketing strikers to allow the strikebreakers into the workplace. Sit-down strikes, however, meant that workers were occupying the workplaces and thereby keeping out the strikebreakers who would take their jobs. The only question was how long they could hold out.

An answer to this question was provided in January 1937 when the UAW organized a sit-down strike at the GM plant in Flint, Michigan, in an attempt to force the company to recognize the union. For 44 days the strikers refused to leave the factory. They slept on unfinished car seats and ate food passed to them by friends and family members through the factory windows. The strikers persisted despite being tear-gassed, having the heat shut off, and being attacked by the police and company security guards who were trying to retake the plant. Sit-down strikes soon spread to other GM plants, eventually bringing production to a standstill. Finally, on February 11, faced with serious losses and under pressure from the White House to settle, GM agreed to recognize the UAW as the workers' sole bargaining agent and to enter into contract negotiations with it. There was to be no retaliation against the strikers. The sit-down strike was over—in the space of just six weeks the UAW and the workers at GM had forced the biggest automobile company in the world to the bargaining table. It was an event that redefined industrial relations in the United States and that rivaled in importance the Five Dollar a Day wage in establishing the principle of economic security for blue-collar workers.

The UAW's astonishing victory over GM had immediate repercussions. One was a wave of sit-down strikes across the country. Nearly half a million workers were involved in 1937; they included hotel clerks, waiters and waitresses, and even teachers. Another was that some companies decided not to resist union organizing drives. For example, U.S. Steel, America's largest steel producer, renowned for its anti-unionism, caused considerable surprise when on March 2, 1937, it signed a contract with the Steel Workers Organizing Committee (SWOC) in which it formally recognized the union as its employees' bargaining agent.

Although sit-down strikes got the publicity, the less dramatic representation election became the main route to union recognition, once the Supreme Court had upheld the validity of the Wagner Act in 1937. By the middle of 1941, the NLRB had held nearly 6,000 elections in which nearly 2 million workers had voted. In over 80 percent of these votes, workers voted for union representation (Brody 1980).

In a few cases, however, companies continued to resist unionization by refusing to allow representation elections. For these workers, there were still years of conflict, bloodshed, and defeat ahead before they finally achieved company recognition of their unions. For example, when SWOC turned its attention to the smaller steel companies, known collective as "Little Steel"—Bethlehem Steel Corporation, Youngstown Sheet and Tube, National Steel, Inland Steel, American Rolling Mills, and Republic Steel—it met instant and strong resistance. Tom Girdler, the president of Republic Steel and the leading figure in Little Steel's union-fighting campaign, was well known for his implacable anti-union views. They were summarized in his famous remark that he would never sign a contract with a union: "We won't sign a contract. I have a little farm with a few apple trees and before spending the rest of my life dealing with unions I [will] raise apples and potatoes."

On May 26, 1937, SWOC called for a strike at three Little Steel companies: Republic, Youngstown Sheet and Tube Company, and Inland Steel Corporation. Republic's management had anticipated this action and had acquired a considerable arsenal of firearms and ammunition in order to prevent its mills from being occupied by sit-down strikers. It also arranged for police to be permanently stationed inside its mills. On May 30, striking Republic steel workers and their families gathered for a Memorial Day rally near one of the company's mills on the south side of Chicago. At the rally, one of the speakers proposed a march to the mill. The police blocked their path before they could get close to the mill. Arguments and scuffles ensued; some of the strikers threw sticks and stones, at which point the police suddenly opened fire on the marchers. Ten were killed and over sixty were wounded. After another striker was killed in a confrontation with police in Youngstown, Ohio, the state's governor decided to reopen the mills under the protection of the National Guard and to limit union picketing around the mills. His actions broke the strike, as thousands of steelworkers returned to their jobs. SWOC and the CIO had suffered a serious defeat.

Henry Ford was an equally intransigent foe of unions. In April 1937 he declared that "labor unions are the worst things that ever struck the earth" (Brinkley 2003). He relied on Harry Bennett's Service Department to keep unions out of his company. The Service Department had placed a network of spies and informers throughout Ford factories, and any worker who discussed unionization was fired. In May 1937, union organizers distributing pamphlets on a public overpass outside the Rouge plant were violently assaulted by a group of Service Department enforcers in what became known as the "Battle of the Overpass." The strong-arm tactics worked, at least in the short-term—Ford remained a non-union company long after GM and Chrysler had signed contracts with the UAW.

The Ford Campaign

In the late 1930s, the UAW renewed its campaign against Ford, using the provisions of the Wagner Act to increase the pressure on the company. It successfully argued that Ford had violated the Act by firing pro-union workers; the NLRB ordered them reinstated. Finally, on April 1, 1941, following Harry Bennett's firing of several union leaders at the Rouge, the UAW called its first ever strike against Ford. The strike lasted until the end of May. On May 26, the NLRB held an election in which Ford workers voted by an overwhelming margin to be represented by the UAW. A month later Ford signed a contract recognizing the union, agreeing to a basic eight-hour workday and forty-hour workweek, establishing a grievance procedure that settling disputes between individual workers and their supervisors, and agreeing to pay lost wages for more than 4,000 workers who had been illegally fired. Other concessions included the abolition of the Service Department and, most surprising of all, considering Henry Ford's views on unions, the establishment of a "closed shop" at the company. This meant that all workers would become members of the union no later than thirty days after their employment and would have union dues automatically deducted from their paychecks. Union officials in other companies had often been frustrated by the difficulty of actually collecting dues from the workers who benefited from the contracts they negotiated. The Ford system eliminated this "free rider" problem. The contract was a remarkable reversal of course for what had once been one of the most fiercely anti-union companies in the country.

Ford's willingness to recognize the UAW reflected a new context to collective bargaining in the United States. Although its entry into World War II was still some months away, the country was already shifting production to a wartime footing. The federal government had begun to increase its oversight of industrial relations because it did not want production during this crisis to be jeopardized by labor disputes. It set up a new organization, the National War Labor Board (NWLB), to supervise collective bargaining during the war. Under government pressure, and without even holding representation elections, the Little Steel companies agreed to recognize SWOC in 1942. The NWLB also

encouraged employers to adopt closed-shop practices such as the automatic union-dues check-off that Ford had endorsed. The result was that another 5 million new members were added to the union rolls during the Second World War, to go along with the nearly 5 million workers who had joined unions during the turbulent years between 1936 and 1939. By the end of the war, slightly more than one out of every three nonagricultural workers belonged to a union (Jacoby 1985).

The Impact of the Labor Movement

The effect of labor unionism was profound. The economic distinction between blue-collar and white-collar work, which had been so important at the beginning of the twentieth century, had shrunk considerably by the century's midpoint. Although production workers still lagged in status or prestige, their incomes, job security, and other benefits now rivaled those of their white-collar counterparts. Union contracts now specified that seniority would be used to determine the order in which workers would be laid off and rehired—the last to be hired would be the first to be fired. Seniority also became widely accepted as a principle for deciding who would have first priority for job openings within the factory or plant—companies established "bidding" systems that gave preference to those who had worked there the longest. Benefits that had been sporadically introduced in the 1920s—paid vacations, pension plans, health and hospitalization insurance, and paid sick leave—were now extended to the majority of blue-collar workers (Jacoby 1985).

The economic gains that blue-collar workers had achieved after fifty years of hard work and fierce conflict on the assembly lines and the

FIGURE 10.1 **Hourly earnings of production and nonsupervisory workers, 1947–2005 (2005 dollars).**

Source: Mishel, Bernstein, and Allegretto 2007.

waterfronts, in the steel mills and the rubber factories, as well as in many other workplaces, allowed
them and their families to attain a middle-class
standard of living. The years following the end
of World War II witnessed a new social contract
in the workplace that provided many American
workers with union oversight of their working
conditions, steady increases in their standard of
living, comprehensive health insurance, and generous pensions. For example, the average hourly
wage for nonskilled assembly-line workers in U.S.
automobile plants in 2005 was more than $30 an
hour; retirees from these plants with thirty years
of service received a pension of approximately

$3,000 a month. The automobile companies also
provided free health care for workers and their
dependents and, until 2005, for retirees and their
dependents (the companies and the UAW reached
an agreement that year, designed to control rising
health-care costs, that required retirees to cover
deductibles and co-payments up to a maximum
per family of about $750 a year) (Porter 2006).

Of course, not all workers enjoyed the benefits of this postwar accommodation between
employers and production workers; textile workers, garment workers, and farm workers were
among those whose gains were not as extensive. Nevertheless, as Figure 10.1 shows, the real

hourly wage of nonsupervisory workers rose consistently after the war, in the period from the late 1940s through the late 1970s. The question that we turn to next is why unions, which had been so successful in creating a prosperous working class, did not continue to flourish.

The Decline of Unions After World War II

Since the end of World War II, the percentage of American workers represented by labor unions has declined steadily. Union membership fell from a high of 35 percent of all nonagricultural workers in 1955 to 12 percent in 2007—a percentage that would have been lower still were it not for the 36 percent of all government workers who belonged to unions in 2007; in the private

sector only 7.5 percent of all workers were union members, as Table 10.1 shows.

Part of the reason for this decline has been a shift of employment from production jobs in manufacturing industries to management, professional, sales, and office jobs in service industries (see Table 3.2). These white-collar workers have proven more difficult to organize than blue-collar workers (with some exceptions, such as teachers), which is one reason why unionization rates have declined in Western Europe, Canada, and Japan as well (see Table 10.2). But as Table 10.2 also shows, the decrease in the United States has been far greater than in other countries, despite their having similar occupational structures to that of the United States. Economic factors, therefore, are just a small part of the declining unionization rate in the United States. The major reason

TABLE 10.1 Union Membership In Selected Industries, 2007 (numbers in thousands)

Industry	Total Employed	Union Members	Union Membership as a Percentage of Total Employment
Private sector	108,714	8,114	7.5
Construction	8,561	1,193	13.9
Education and health services	18,120	1,591	8.8
Food services and drinking places	7,575	70	0.9
Manufacturing	15,341	1,734	11.3
Telecommunications	1,186	233	19.7
Transportation and utilities	5,488	1,211	22.1
Wholesale and retail trade	18,89	990	5.2
Public sector	21,053	7,557	35.9
Federal government	3,423	916	26.8
State government	6,384	1,943	30.4
Local government	11,246	4,698	41.8

Source: Bureau of Labor Statistics 2008.

TABLE 10.2 **Wage and Salary Earners in Unions in Selected Countries**

COUNTRY	PERCENTAGE IN UNIONS		
	1950	1980	2000
Australia	56	48	25
Canada	26	35	28
Germany	36	35	25
Italy	48	50	35
Japan	46	31	22
United Kingdom	45	51	31
USA	28	22	13

Source: Wallerstein and Western 2000: 358; Pontusson 2005.

is political: just as political forces propelled the rise of unions, they have also led to their decline. To understand the drop in unionization in the United States, therefore, we need to take a closer look at the politics behind the union resurgence of the 1930s.

The growth of the union movement depended on two factors. The first was the willingness of workers to risk life and limb in defense of their right to representation. The second was the willingness of Congress and the federal government to support this right. Although World War II was a period in which unions added large numbers of members to their rolls—the membership of the UAW, for example, rose from 165,000 to 1,065,000 between 1939 and 1945—the war also triggered events that served to counter both factors. In particular, the war increased the union movement's dependence on the federal government. This meant, for example, that union expansion during the war years was due to the government's efforts to ensure that industrial conflict did not disrupt wartime production. It encouraged companies to recognize unions and to engage in peaceful collective bargaining, and it encouraged unions not to go on strike or to engage in other activities that would harm the war effort. The consequence was a union movement whose successes were compromised by its reliance on support from Congress and the federal government. The problem for the labor movement was that this support could be withdrawn, which is exactly what happened in 1947, when Congress passed an amendment to the Wagner Act, known as the Taft-Hartley Act. This act, which was strongly opposed by organized labor, dealt the movement a serious blow.

The Taft-Hartley Act

The 1946 congressional elections produced Republican majorities in both the House of Representatives and the Senate. The political mood in the country had become more conservative as the United States entered its long geopolitical and ideological rivalry with the Soviet Union—the Cold War. In this climate, unions became suspect. Some union leaders were accused of disloyalty, particularly in those cases where they were known to have belonged to or sympathized with the Communist Party, as some had done in the turbulent 1930s. In 1946, 4.6 million workers had gone out on strike, which the new Republican leadership in Congress took as additional evidence that union power needed to be curbed. The result was the Taft-Hartley Act of 1947, a bill that was passed over the veto of President Harry Truman and that continues to frustrate the labor movement to this day.

The proponents of Taft-Hartley believed that that the Wagner Act had tilted the balance of power in the workplace too far toward labor; the new act was an explicit effort to strengthen the hand of employers in their dealings with unions and workers. The Taft-Hartley Act (and subsequent amendments to it) made the following changes. It emphasized the right of workers *not* to join unions: states were permitted to outlaw the union shop, which gave workers in these "right-to-work" states the option of not joining any union that had been established in their workplace and of not paying union dues. (This last point proved especially important throughout the American South.) It prohibited the automatic check-off of union dues without the written consent of the employee. It permitted employers to voice their opposition to unions (although not to fire or to threaten workers who support unions). It allowed the President of the United States to end a strike or a potential strike by ruling that it had created a national emergency and then ordering these workers to return to work. It required elected union members to sign affidavits declaring that they were not members of the Communist Party. It made a union legally responsible—and liable for damages—if its members went on strike in violation of the collective bargaining agreement.

An immediate consequence of the Taft-Hartley Act was a split in the Congress of Industrial Organizations along ideological lines. The CIO leadership, although more liberal than that the American Federation of Labor, now turned its attention to the presence of communists and communist sympathizers in its ranks. In 1950 it expelled eleven unions from the federation on the grounds that they were communist-dominated. Among the expelled unions was the International Longshore and Warehouse Union (ILWU), the union that had emerged in the wake of the 1934 strike of West Coast longshore workers and that now represented workers in every port on the West Coast from California

to Canada. The CIO subsequently made up its differences with the AFL, which had now also embraced the principle of industrial unionism, and they were reunited in 1955 as the AFL-CIO.

There were three significant long-term consequences of the Taft-Hartley Act. First, it made collective bargaining between workers and their employers a more legalistic and bureaucratic process. There would be far fewer opportunities now for workers to take matters into their own hands, as they had during the 1930s, to settle disputes with employers. Disagreements would have to be resolved within the framework of the contract, and it was the union's responsibility, under penalty of law, to ensure that its members followed the contract. From this point onward, lawyers and labor law would play an increasingly prominent role in industrial relations, and labor organizations themselves became increasingly drawn into a bureaucratic web of rules (Brody 1980). Second, by legalizing "right to work" statutes, Taft-Hartley played a key role in the defeat of organized labor's effort to bring southern workers into the union fold. Since employers held substantial political power in the South, they were able to encourage the passage of labor laws that almost ensured the defeat of labor's efforts to organize southern workers (an effort known as "Operation Dixie," which began in 1946 but which had come to an unsuccessful end by 1953). Some analysts have argued that labor's failure to organize the South enabled employers to shift production toward a "union-free" zone, thus beginning the process of union decline (Griffith 1988).

A third consequence of the Taft-Harley Act may have been the most important of all, in that it encouraged management opposition to labor organizing, an issue we consider next.

Management Opposition to Unions

In the years since the passage of the Taft–Hartley Act, managers of U.S. corporations have made increasing use of the "free speech" provisions of the Act to express their opposition to unions. Speaking out against unions is, however, just one kind of anti-union activity. Freeman and Medoff (1984) point out that management opposition to unions has taken three forms. Some companies have engaged in "positive industrial relations," which means matching union contracts in terms of wages and, to a lesser extent, benefits paid to workers. These companies argue to their employees that they are providing them with the same rewards that they would get from union contracts and are saving them the costs of union dues.

Foreign auto manufacturers that have opened plants in the United States have used the matching strategy particularly effectively. For example, the average hourly wage in 2003 for an assembly-line worker at Toyota was $27, which was only slightly lower than the $31 that General Motors assemblers averaged that year. Toyota workers also receive medical, dental, and life insurance coverage and a traditional pension plan and a 401(k) plan, which raised the total compensation per hour to $48, compared to $55 at GM (McAlinden 2004; Maynard 2005). These wages and benefits are particularly attractive to workers in the South, where most of the foreign-owned auto plans are located. Unions have failed to organize workers in any of these plants—the UAW has lost every single representation election in a foreign-owned factory.

A second strategy is to conduct tough but legal campaigns against unions to convince workers that they should not support them. These campaigns include warning workers that unions do not represent their best interests, that they are simply interested in getting their hands on employees' dues money, that they are likely to harm the economic prospects of companies and workers, and that they will introduce conflict into the employer–employee relationship. This is the strategy favored by Wal-Mart, which has been a vigorous and effective opponent of labor unions.

Wal-Mart's anti-union campaign begins when employees are first hired. As part of their orientation, new employees are shown an anti-union video, as Barbara Ehrenreich describes in *Nickel and Dimed*:

> The theme of covert tensions, overcome by right thinking and positive attitude, continues in the twenty-minute video entitled *You've Picked a Great Place to Work*. Here various associates testify to the "essential feeling of family for which Wal-Mart is so well known," leading up to the conclusion that we don't need a union. Once, long ago, unions had a place in American society, but they "no longer have much to offer workers," which is why people are leaving them "by the droves." Wal-Mart is booming; unions are declining; judge for yourself. But we are warned that "unions have been targeting Wal-Mart for years." Why? For the dues money of course. Think of what you would lose with a union: first, your dues money, which could be $20 a month "and sometimes much more." Second, you would lose "your voice" because the union would insist on doing your talking for you. Finally, you might even lose your wages and benefits because they would all be "at risk on the bargaining table." (2001: 144–145)

Box 10.1 provides a recent example of Wal-Mart's effective use of anti-union tactics to thwart a union drive.

BOX 10.1 *At a Small Shop in Colorado, Wal-Mart Beats a Union Once More*

LOVELAND, Colo., Feb. 25—Joshua Noble, a 21-year-old who loves to snowboard, jolted Wal-Mart Stores last November when he got a majority of employees here at the Wal-Mart tire-and-lube shop where he worked to sign statements saying they wanted to vote on bringing in a labor union.

The unionization drive begun by Mr. Noble created a storm in this onetime ranching town at the foot of the Rockies—even the BBC covered it—and became a closely watched test of labor's efforts to unionize the world's largest retailer.

But on Friday the workers at the Wal-Mart Tire & Lube Express abandoned Mr. Noble, voting 17 to 1 against unionizing, another setback for organized labor at the very moment when its leaders are mapping a campaign to pressure the company to improve wages and benefits.

With Friday's vote, Wal-Mart can continue to say that not one of its 1.2 million American workers belongs to a union. Support for organizing dissipated here after the company repeatedly showed workers videos about what were portrayed as the shortcomings of unions, and transferred into the shop six new workers who, Mr. Noble said, had been screened by the company to ensure their antiunion sentiment.

Wal-Mart officials say the shop's work force simply concluded from all the information at hand that there was no need for representation by a third party.

Officials of the union involved, the United Food and Commercial Workers, counter by saying it lost because Wal-Mart struck fear in the workers with an intensive campaign. The union said it would challenge the outcome of the vote with the National Labor Relations Board, citing the lack of a union observer at the election and saying the six added workers had been brought in to dilute support for organizing.

Mr. Noble rounded up support for a union three months ago from 8 of his 16 co-workers—a majority, once he was included—who change tires, lubricate cars and install batteries, and who had complaints about wages, health insurance coverage and their treatment by managers.

The shop seemed fertile ground for organizing. Most of the workers were under 25. Some had a rebellious streak, some were college students, and some were single mothers struggling to make ends meet.

"We thought the only way they'd listen to us is to have a union," Mr. Noble said of management. "There's strength in numbers."

Wal-Mart responded to the organizing drive by flying in a group of labor experts from its headquarters in Bentonville, Ark.

Wal-Mart's team, several workers said, hammered away at a variety of themes: that unions only want workers' dues, that they cannot guarantee better wages or benefits, that they want to put Wal-Mart out of business, that they foment walkouts in which the strikers can lose their jobs.

"It wasn't a fair fight," Mr. Noble said. "Every day they had two or three antiunion people from Bentonville in the garage full time, showing antiunion videos and telling people that unions are bad."

BOX **10.1** *continued*

What angered him most, Mr. Noble said, was that after one union supporter was fired and two others moved away to attend college, Wal-Mart transferred in the six new workers, to undercut, he said, the union's chances of winning the vote.

Christi Gallagher, a Wal-Mart spokeswoman, said that the garage had merely been replacing the workers who had left, and adding a few for the sake of shop efficiency.

Of broader issues, Wal-Mart said Friday that results of the vote again showed its workers, whom it calls associates, to be satisfied and not eager for representation by the United Food and Commercial Workers.

"The U.F.C.W. has tried to organize our associates for years," said Terry Srsen, Wal-Mart's vice president for labor relations. "Many of our associates are former union members. They know better than anyone that the only guarantee a union can make is that it will cost the members money. And that is why they continue to reject the U.F.C.W."

The outcome here was just the latest turn in an intense battle between Wal-Mart and organized labor.

Two weeks ago, workers at a Tire & Lube Express in New Castle, Pa., voted 17 to 0 against unionizing. Fifteen months earlier, an administrative law judge ruled that Wal-Mart had illegally transferred pro-union workers out of that garage and added antiunion ones to skew the vote. Wal-Mart officials said the company had remedied those violations.

Wal-Mart decided this month to close a store in Quebec, one of its first to unionize in Canada. Wal-Mart said the store was barely profitable and not being closed in retaliation.

In 2000, meat cutters in Jacksonville, Tex., became the only Wal-Mart workers in the United States to vote to unionize. But soon afterward the company announced that it was replacing its meat-cutting operations in the South with pre-packaged meat.

Friends often told Mr. Noble that he was crazy to take on the big corporation and that he should look for a job elsewhere. But Mr. Noble, who has epilepsy, said he was reluctant to leave Wal-Mart, out of fear that he would have trouble obtaining health insurance elsewhere.

(Because he had a seizure on Friday, Mr. Noble did not make it to the polls until just before the balloting ended. The United Food and Commercial Workers complained that it had not been allowed to have an election observer stand in for Mr. Noble, the union's designate.)

Dan Wright, a technician in the tire and lube shop, voted against the union, he said, because he felt he could go straight to management with problems.

"My grandfather said that during World War II, unions were helpful—they had their place," Mr. Wright said. "But I don't feel I need one. This company treats me well. It's fair to its people."

Alicia Sylvia, a single mother of 10-year-old twins, was a big union booster at the outset.

"Compared to other stores, we don't even make what cashiers make," said Ms. Sylvia, who earns just under $9 an hour writing up service orders as cars arrive at the garage and says she cannot afford Wal-Mart's health insurance. In Colorado, full-time unionized supermarket cashiers generally earn $15.66 an hour after two years.

BOX **10.1** *continued*

"We should make more, since we work on vehicles and can get burned, and we have to stand out in the cold and heat," she said. "If you're working 10-hour days in the rain and getting your pants wet and freezing all day, it's not fun."

She acknowledged that the antiunion videos had helped turn her against unionizing.

"I really wish Wal-Mart would become better," she said. "But even if we get a union, it will be a long battle. Wal-Mart doesn't have to agree to anything. The message we got was, 'You're a small bunch of guys, and you can stand out there and strike, and we're going to replace you.' They'll never agree to a contract, out of pure stubbornness. I'm so confused."

Cody Fields, who earns $8.10 an hour after two years, said that he had originally backed the union "because we need a change" but that the videos had been effective. "It's just a bunch of brainwashing," Mr. Fields said, "but it kind of worked."

Source: Greenhouse 2005

A third strategy is to break the law by firing pro-union workers. Although this is a direct violation of the Wagner Act, the penalties that companies incur if they are found guilty of this "unfair labor practice" are minor: reinstatement of workers and the payment of back pay (minus whatever they earned in any other jobs that they took following their termination). It has become increasingly common for companies to fire pro-union workers, judging by the number of cases submitted to the NLRB. In fiscal year 2006, over 7,000 cases alleging illegal discharge were submitted to the NLRB (National Labor Relations Board 2006a). Freeman and Medoff have estimated that as many as one in every twenty workers who favor a union get fired. Companies that follow this strategy have apparently decided that it is worth the risk of being found guilty of an unfair labor practice if they can intimidate union supporters into withdrawing their campaign. According to Freeman and Medoff, this strategy works. Unions are successful in about 50 percent of NLRB representation elections today, compared to 65 to 75 percent in the 1950s; they attribute one quarter to one half of the decline to unfair labor practices committed by employers (1984: 237).

Finally, it should be noted that even if the employees in a factory or plant vote in favor of a union in a representation election, this does not assure them that they will gain a collective-bargaining contract. The Wagner Act obliges an employer to bargain but does not mandate that the two sides reach agreement. If there is no agreement and the union decides to strike, the employer may operate with replacement workers. The employer can even petition to hold a union decertification election one year after the original representation election in which the replacement workers are eligible to vote. If a majority votes against the union, it will be decertified. Freeman and Medoff estimate that one quarter of the workers who win representation elections do not gain a union contract (1984: 239–240).

Do Employees Want Unions?

The steady decline in American labor unionism over the past fifty years has led some observers to conclude that perhaps workers in this country, unlike their counterparts in the rest of the industrialized world, simply do not want unions. According to this argument, American workers are too individualistic and ambitious to rely on advancement through the collective effort of a union. They want to succeed or fail on their own merits.

There are two pieces of evidence, however, that suggest that American workers are not as union-averse as the preceding argument implies. First, as Table 10.1 shows, the level of unionism among public-sector employees, i.e., people who work for the local, state, and federal governments, is around 36 percent (compared to less than 8 percent in the private sector). One of the largest unions in the country, the Associated Federation of State, County, and Municipal Employees (1.4 million members), is a public-sector union. One of the reasons for this enormous difference in unionism levels is that public-sector employers, unlike those in the private sector, are far less likely to engage in the kinds of anti-union campaigns we have described.

Second, surveys of workers have found that a much higher percentage of workers want unions than actually enjoy the benefits of union representation. For example, Freeman and Rogers (1999) polled a sample of over 2,400 workers in union and nonunion workplaces. They were asked whether they would vote for or against a union if a NLRB election were held in their workplace. Ninety percent of the union workers said that they would vote for a union, as did 32 percent of the nonunion workers. Combining these two percentages, and adjusting for the fact

that union workers represent a small percentage of the overall workforce, Freeman and Rogers found that about 44 percent of workers want union representation—nearly four times the 12 percent that actually have it (1999: 89).

The desire to be represented by a union varies by race, gender, age, earnings, occupation, and income. Table 10.3, a survey of nonunion workers, shows that black workers are more likely to favor unions, as are women, younger workers, less educated workers, poorer workers, and blue-collar workers. What this indicates is that workers whose labor market position is the most vulnerable—whether due to discrimination or to a lack of human capital—are the most likely to want the support of an agent who bargains on their behalf. In addition to these factors, support for unions varies according to how well companies treat workers. The nonunion workers in Freeman and Rogers's sample were more than twice as likely to be in favor of a union if they rated relations between employees and management in their company as "poor" rather than "excellent" and if they had very little trust in their company's management rather than a lot of trust. They were about three times as likely to want a union if they gave their company's management an "F" grade for employee concern rather than an "A" grade and if they gave their management an "F" grade for its willingness to share power rather than an "A" grade (1999: 82).

The survey results suggest that American workers are as likely to be in favor of unions as their counterparts in other countries. The difference is that the Taft-Hartley Act, in combination with employer opposition to unions, makes it considerably more difficult for American workers to achieve union representation. The results also tell us that workers are likely to be in favor

TABLE 10.3 **Percentage of Nonunion Workers Who Want Unions**

Characteristic	Percentage in Favor of a Union*
Gender	
Men	27
Women	35
Age	
18–24	44
25–34	32
35–44	26
45–54	32
55+	24
Race	
Nonblack	28
Black	59
Education	
Less than high school	44
High school graduates	34
Some college	32
College graduates	21
Occupation	
Professional	25
Laborer	42
Weekly earnings	
Upper quartile	22
Lower quartile	45

* In response to the question: "If an election were held *today* to decide whether employees like you should be represented by a union, would you vote for the union or against the union?"
Source: Freeman and Rogers 1999: 71.

of unions if they feel disadvantaged, by virtue of race, gender, or economic status, or if they feel that their employers have little interest in their welfare. The reasons that workers want unions today are much the same as they have been for the past 100 years.

The Costs of Union Decline

Today about one in every thirteen workers in the private sector belongs to a union. The costs of union decline for workers can best be appreciated if we consider the benefits that unions provide to workers. There are two main advantages to union membership: better wages and greater influence over one's conditions of employment. Unions are well known for the first benefit—winning higher pay for their members. Less often recognized, however, is an important second benefit. Unions force employers to negotiate over work policies, such as job security or the speed of the assembly line, and they allow workers to challenge employers over workplace practices that they consider unfair, without the risk of being fired. This often means that union workers can act to protect their own dignity, while nonunion workers cannot.

The Union Wage Advantage

Unions increase workers' wages and improve their nonwage compensation. The decline of unions is one of the reasons that wages of nonsupervisory workers, who represent 80 percent of all workers, have stagnated since the late 1970s (see Figure 10.1). The average hourly wage in 2005 was only 10 cents an hour higher in real terms than it was in 1978, after almost doubling in the thirty years between 1945 and 1978. Another way of thinking about the impact of union decline on workers' wages is to examine the percentage of workers earning $20 or more an hour (in today's dollars). This is the amount that economists consider the minimum necessary to lift a family of four into the middle class. Union contracts raised the number of workers earning at least $20 an hour to a peak of 23 percent of the workforce in 1979; since then it has dropped to 18 percent (Uchitelle 2008).

A symbolic indicator of the change in fortunes of those at the top and bottom of the pay scale is the enormous difference between what the average worker earns and what the average chief executive officer of a corporation earns. In 1965 median CEO pay was 24 times the pay of an average worker; in 2005 the median CEO earned more than 262 times as much ($11 million per year compared to $42,000 per year). CEOs in the United States earned more than twice as much on average as CEOs in the thirteen other wealthy, industrialized countries for which there are equivalent data (Mishel, Bernstein, and Allegretto 2007).

How much does union membership increase workers' wages? In 2007, full-time workers who were not union members had median weekly earnings of $663. Full-time workers who were union members had median weekly earnings of $863, which was $200 a week or approximately 30 percent more (U.S. Bureau of Labor Statistics 2008). But union membership is only one factor among many that determines how much workers are paid. Other factors are workers' education and occupation, their race and gender, the industry in which they work, and the size of the firm for which they work. It is probable that some part of the $200 weekly difference between union and nonunion wages is due to these variables. Statistical models that take these variables into consideration—that "control" for them, in other words—have found that unions raise wages by around 20 percent (Mishel and Walters 2003). This is the union wage "premium" or advantage.

Unions also increase workers' nonwage compensation—what used to be called "fringe benefits"—such as health insurance, pensions, disability coverage, life insurance, and paid leave. Union workers are more likely than nonunion workers to have these benefits and to have better benefits. Take health insurance, for example. More than 83 percent of union workers have employer-provided health insurance compared to just 62 percent of nonunion workers—a difference of over 21 percentage points. But even when employers of nonunion workers provide health insurance, the coverage is not as good as that received by their union counterparts. Employers of union workers pay a larger share of the insurance premiums, and these workers have lower deductibles. If wages and fringe benefits are combined, the best estimate is that the union effect on total compensation is approximately 28 percent (Mishel and Walters 2003).

Most of the union wage premium goes to low-paid workers with a high school education or less. The premium is only 2 percent for white-collar workers and only 5 percent for people with college degrees. Compare these to the 23 percent union wage premium for blue-collar workers and the premium of over 35 percent for those who have not gone beyond high school. To appreciate how union membership can boost wages and benefits of workers in low-status service occupations, take the case of the 560,000 members of Culinary Local 226 of the Hotel and Restaurant Employees International Union in Las Vegas.

Culinary Local 226 represents casino and hotel workers—cooks, food and beverage servers, bellmen, dishwashers, porters, housekeepers, and hostesses. These workers have some of the lowest rates of union membership in the country as a whole. For example, only 4 percent of all workers in food preparation and serving jobs belonged to unions in 2004. Las Vegas is the exception. More than 90 percent of the workers on Las Vegas's famous Strip belong to the Culinary Union, including workers at the landmark Bellagio and MGM Grand hotels. Jobs such as dishwashing and housekeeping are low-wage, nonunion positions in most parts of the country, with pay averaging between $7 and $8 an hour and with few benefits. But Culinary Union workers earn an average of $12.80 an hour, they are guaranteed 40 hours' pay each week, they pay no health insurance premiums, they have an in-house pharmacy that offers free generic drugs, they pay just $10 for visits to the dentist, and they receive three weeks of vacation a year. These benefits were negotiated between the union and hotel owners following a series of strikes in the late 1980s and early 1990s, including one strike against the Frontier hotel that lasted over six years. Hotel owners came to the conclusion that striking workers were bad for the hospitality and entertainment business, whereas a contented and well-paid workforce would help to attract customers. Since the 1980s, the Culinary's membership has tripled and its contracts have been hailed as a model for how to bring a middle-class standard of living to the normally low-wage service sector (Meyerson 2004). Box 10.2 provides more details about this union and the workers it represents.

BOX 10.2 *Local 226, "the Culinary," Makes Las Vegas the Land of the Living Wage*

June 3, 2004

LAS VEGAS—Ask people here why Las Vegas is the nation's fastest-growing city, and they point to the thriving casino industry and to its ever-growing appetite for workers.

But there is another, little understood force contributing to the allure of Las Vegas, a force often viewed as the casino industry's arch-nemesis. It is Culinary Local 226, also called the Culinary, the city's largest labor union, an unusual—and unusually successful—union that has done a spectacular job catapulting thousands of dishwashers, hotel maids and other unskilled workers into the middle class.

In most other cities, these workers live near the poverty line. But thanks in large part to the Culinary, in Las Vegas these workers often own homes and have Rolls-Royce health coverage, a solid pension plan and three weeks of vacation a year.

The Culinary's extraordinary success at delivering for its 48,000 members beckons newcomers from far and wide. By many measures, the Culinary is the nation's most successful union local; its membership has nearly tripled from 18,000 in the late 1980's, even as the rest of the labor movement has shrunk. The Culinary is such a force that one in 10 people here is covered by its health plan, and more than 90 percent of the hotel workers on the Strip belong to the union. The union is also unusual because it is a rainbow coalition, 65 percent nonwhite and 70 percent female. It includes immigrants from Central America, refugees from the Balkan wars and blacks from the Deep South.

The Culinary's success cannot be separated from the industry's wealth. With the profits rolling in, the casinos have decided to be relatively magnanimous to their workers to ensure labor peace and a happy work force.

BOX 10.2 *continued*

"When you're in the service business, the first contact our guests have is with the guest-room attendants or the food and beverage servers, and if that person's unhappy, that comes across to the guests very quickly," said J. Terrence Lanni, chairman of the MGM Mirage, which owns the MGM Grand, the world's largest hotel, with 5,000 rooms and 8,200 employees. "These are people who are generally happy. Is it perfect? No. But it's as good as I've seen anywhere."

Under the Culinary's master contract, waiters are guaranteed $10.14 an hour before tips, the highest rate in the nation. In Las Vegas, unionized hotel housekeepers generally earn $11.95 an hour, 50 percent more than in non-union Reno. The Culinary contract guarantees workers 40 hours' pay each week, meaning housekeepers earn at least $478 a week, while in other cities housekeepers often work 30 hours and earn just $240. The Culinary's workers pay no premiums for health care, and they often pay just $10 for a dentist's visit, while non-union workers often pay upwards of $150.

"Our wages are higher, the medical benefits are great, and we have a guaranteed 40-hour week," said Marianne Singer, a waitress at the unionized MGM Grand. "Thanks to all that, I have a beautiful 2,000-square-foot home with a three-car garage."

The Culinary has struggled to shed a once-unsavory image. A half-century ago it worked closely with Bugsy Siegel and the other gangsters who built up Las Vegas. In 1977, its president, Al Bramlet, was found shot dead in the desert; some say the mob killed him because he opposed its efforts to take over the union.

The Culinary owes its successes to war and peace: first a war that most of the hotel casinos waged against it in the 1980's, and more recently, a broad partnership with the industry. The main war was a two-month strike in 1984 in which 900 picketing workers were arrested. Many casinos wanted to break the Culinary, but the union managed to pressure most into signing a good contract. The Culinary was badly shaken by the dispute, with six hotels refusing to sign a contract and eliminating their union presence. To gird itself for future battles, the union revamped, bringing in veteran organizers and young activists who organized vigorous rank-and-file committees in each hotel. The union also began doing strategic research on the industry, striking fear into some gambling companies by warning Wall Street that the casinos had dangerously high debt levels and could not withstand a strike.

Still smarting from the 1984 dispute and seeing that the union was a formidable force, the casinos made a strategic shift toward peace and partnership. In 1989, Steve Wynn, who transformed Las Vegas with his grandiose theme hotels, signed a groundbreaking agreement with the Culinary when he opened the Mirage, famed for its white tigers and erupting volcano.

Mr. Wynn vowed not to fight unionization, saying he would recognize the Culinary once a majority of the Mirage's workers signed cards saying they favored a union. In return, the Culinary gave Mr. Wynn two things he wanted. It rewrote archaic contractual language to whittle 134 job classifications down to 30. The union also pledged to use organized labor's lobbying clout to advance the industry's interests. Caesars Palace, Bally's, Circus Circus and other casinos soon signed similar labor agreements.

"The last thing you want is for people who are coming to enjoy themselves to see pickets and

BOX **10.2** *continued*

unhappy workers blocking driveways," Mr. Lanni said. "I swore then that we would never have such problems again."

Except for a few strikes at small casinos, the 1989 accords have ushered in 15 years of cooperation and prosperity. Management and union have worked hand in hand to improve service and to press the city's hospitals and doctors to hold down costs, saving the industry millions each year.

Twenty-four casinos help finance the Culinary Training Academy, hailed by many experts as the industry's finest job-training school. It teaches 2,500 students a year to step up to jobs as waiters, cooks or even sommeliers. Courses are free to

members of the union, while the unemployed can take courses with federal or state grants.

Steven Horsford, the academy's executive director, said the industry's needs for trained workers were so great that the academy would double its capacity to 5,000 students a year by 2006.

"In Las Vegas, more so than any place in the country, the hospitality industry and the union have realized it is not mere rhetoric to say, 'We're all in this together,'" said John W. Wilhelm, president of the Culinary's parent union, the Hotel Employees and Restaurant Employees International Union.

SOURCE: Greenhouse 2004

The union wage and benefit advantage for low-level jobs in the service industry explains why California supermarket chains and their employees were so threatened when Wal-Mart announced in 2003 that it planned to open 40 new supercenters in the state. Wal-Mart, the largest employer in the world, is well known for its low prices, low wages, and strong anti-unionism. Its sales clerks earn an average of $8.50 an hour; its health care coverage requires employees to pay premiums of $200 a month and deductibles of $1,000 a year. In contrast, the unionized stockers and clerks at California's three largest grocery chains, Albertsons, Vons and Pavilions (owned by Safeway), and Ralphs (owned by Kroger), earned $17.90 an hour in 2003 and paid no health insurance premiums (Greenhouse 2003a).

In October 2003, at the expiration of their contract with the United Food and Commercial Workers Union, which represented workers at these three companies, employers demanded concessions in the new round of negotiations. They wanted a two-year wage freeze, a lower pay scale for new hires, and for employees to start paying health insurance premiums. After a bitter strike and lockout of nearly five months, the union and the companies agreed to a new contract in which the union conceded to many of the employers' demands. The contract provided no pay raises and it required workers to start paying health insurance premiums of $5 to $15 a week in the third year of the agreement. The new contract also established a two-tier employment arrangement: new hires were to receive an average of $4 less in wages and benefits than

202 THE SOCIOLOGY OF WORK

current employees because they would be on a lower pay scale and would have to pay more for their insurance and pension coverage (LeDuff and Greenhouse 2004). This strike and its resolution demonstrated Wal-Mart's long shadow. The company's simple intent to enter the southern California supermarket industry had weakened the bargaining position of workers at other companies in that market.

The examples of the Las Vegas hotel workers and the southern California grocery workers show that low-level jobs in the service sector need not necessarily be low-wage work. In fact, these workers have one significant factor in their favor compared to their blue-collar counterparts in the manufacturing sector: their jobs cannot be shipped abroad. Without union representation, however, these workers are unlikely to reap the full benefit of their relative job security. Even if workers belong to a union, they are still vulnerable to the challenge of a nonunion competitor that pays wages below the union rate. The decline of unions, therefore, hurts workers in unions as well as those who lack union representation.

The Union "Voice" Advantage

Most studies of the consequences of union decline have focused on its impact on workers' paychecks. Less common is any discussion of how it has diminished workers' rights and freedoms on the job. Unions give employees a collective way of expressing their views to their employers over the wages and working conditions. Union contracts also specify what recourse employees have if they are dissatisfied with their treatment by their employers. These rights are what are known as "voice." In nonunion workplaces, employees are far less likely to have the voice option.

To illustrate what voice means in practice, take the standard language about strikes and work stoppages that is routinely included in every contract signed by the West Coast longshore workers' union (the ILWU) and the Pacific Maritime Association. Section 11.1 of the current contract states that there will be "no strike, lockout, or work stoppage for the life of this Agreement." But sections 11.41 and 11.42 note two exceptions: "Longshoremen shall not be required to work when in good faith they believe that to do is to immediately endanger health and safety.... Longshoremen on cargo handling operations shall not be required to work when in good faith they believe that to do so will result in an onerous workload." The contract goes on to note the Union's pledge not to misuse these provisions, i.e., not to use a safety or onerous work claim as a "gimmick" (*Pacific Coast Longshore Contract Document*, 2002: 62).

The effect of these provisions, even with the union promise not to misuse them, is to give longshore workers a highly effective voice. The waterfront has always been a dangerous working environment, so these workers can and do exercise their right to stop work or to engage in what Wellman (1995) has called "contractually defensible disobedience." Each port area on the West Coast has an arbitrator who rules on safety, onerous work, and other disputes. In the case of a dispute in which workers have stopped work, if the arbitrator rules in the union's favor, the workers will also be paid for the time in which they stood by. The contract also lists the penalties, ranging from brief suspensions to deregistration as a longshore worker (which effectively means being terminated from the industry), for offenses such as stopping work illegally, drunkenness, assault, drug abuse, pilferage, violation of the safety rules, and intentional damage to cargo and equipment. A joint (union and employers) Port Labor Relations Committee imposes the penalties; if the two sides are unable to agree on the appropriate penalty, the matter is turned over to the arbitrator for a final ruling.

In nonunion workplaces, employees' rights are provided at the discretion of the employer instead of through bargaining with a union. An employer may provide a disciplinary process to ensure that no employee will be discharged without just cause, but there is no legal obligation to create any such process. The legal foundation on which the relationship between employer and employee in the United States rests is "employment at will," which specifies that if there is no written employment contract, an employer can terminate an employee for "good cause, bad cause, or no cause at all." This means, for example, that an employer can fire a worker simply because he or she doesn't like that person. The worker has no recourse, provided that the firing did not occur because of the employee's age, race, sex, national origin, disability, or union activity. Aside from these protected categories, and in the absence of a contract, an employer can dismiss an employee for any reason and at any time. The consequence of employment at will is that any worker in a nonunion setting who challenges or even questions a supervisor's decision is risking his or her job.

The effect of union decline has been to divide the workforce into a small minority, who enjoy good wages, benefits, and working conditions, and a growing majority, whose pay is lower, who receive fewer benefits, and who work under terms largely dictated by their employers. This division has little effect on workers whose human capital has enabled them to enter the ranks of management (see Chapter 7) or the professions (see Chapter 8). Their education and skills protect and reward them. But the lack of a union is a severe disadvantage for less educated and low-skilled workers, for their hopes of climbing the socioeconomic ladder today, as for previous generations, rest on the availability of collective representation.

The Future of Unions

The immediate future of the labor movement does not appear to be bright. Unions have had great difficulty in organizing new workers—the continued failure to make any headway with Wal-Mart workers or to organize any foreign-owned auto plants are two of the most visible indicators of this failure—and past union strongholds, such as the domestic steel and automobile industries, have rapidly declined. For example, General Motors, Ford, and Chrysler are or have been in the process of cutting jobs and closing factories, which eliminated 140,000 jobs—one third of their entire North American workforce—between 2000 and 2008. In contrast, foreign automakers, which already employ 60,000 workers in their American factories, will be building new plants and adding workers during this period.

One of the paradoxes of the labor movement is that the successes of unions in the past, specifically their achievements in negotiating fringe benefits for their members, have come back to hurt them. The American auto companies are now supporting large numbers of retirees—GM has more than 400,000 retirees, about three for every one worker—and the costs of the retirees' pensions and health benefits have become a significant financial burden. GM estimates that providing health-care coverage for current workers, retirees, and their dependents adds $1,500 to the cost of every vehicle it makes in the United States. Executives at Ford have estimated that they actually spend more money on health care per car than they do on steel. By contrast, companies like Toyota and Honda have less than 0.05 retiree for every worker in the United States, and their employees and retirees in Japan receive government support for health insurance and pensions (Porter 2006). The distinctive feature of the social contract that was negotiated by American companies and unions after World War II is that it placed the burden of paying for health care and pensions on private employers and not on the state. At the time this was not seen as a liability, but it has become increasingly apparent that the state-funded health care provided to all citizens in European and Asian countries gives the companies headquartered there a significant competitive advantage because they do not need to offer health insurance to their employees. Recent rounds of bargaining in the auto industry have targeted this issue, but it seems unlikely that collective bargaining alone will provide a solution.

The labor movement is now also a divided one. Four of the biggest unions, the Service Employees International Union (SEIU), the Teamsters, UNITE HERE, and the United Food and Commercial Workers Union (UFCW), left the AFL-CIO in 2005 because of their dissatisfaction with the federation's organizing efforts and established a new labor alliance. All four of these unions have been quite effective in maintaining and even expanding their memberships in an era of shrinking union rolls. The SEIU, in fact, saw its membership increase from 625,000

in 1980 to over 1.8 million in 2005. Part of the reason for its success is that it organizes workers with jobs that cannot easily be sent abroad, such as caretakers, janitors, and nursing home aides. Part of the reason is that the union organizes workers on an industry-wide basis, so that individual companies are not faced with higher labor costs than their competitors if they sign a union contract. It is possible that the combination of the SEIU's approach and the growing rivalry between the new federation and the AFL-CIO for new members will spur a labor revival.

Summary

The number of workers belonging to labor unions rose from 3 million in 1933 to 15 million in 1945. Today there are still about 15 million union members, but these workers now represent just 12 percent of the nonagricultural labor force, compared to over 30 percent in 1945. The rise of the labor movement was due to a combination of political support from the White House and Congress—in the form of union-promoting legislation such as the National Industrial Recovery Act and the Wagner Act—and the willingness of workers to risk their lives to ensure that their employers accepted their constitutional rights to union representation. The decline of the labor movement was due in part to a shift from a manufacturing economy to a service economy but was mostly due to shifts in the balance of political power, which generated labor legislation (especially the Taft-Hartley Act of 1947), making union organizing increasingly difficult to achieve. The Act encouraged managerial opposition to unions, whether this opposition is legal (tough anti-union campaigns) or illegal (outright firing of workers who seek to use their legally protected labor rights). As a result, unions today are much less likely to win representation elections than they were in the past. The costs of union decline are felt not only in terms of lower wages, reduced fringe benefits, and reduced job security, but also in terms of the workers' loss of an independent voice in the workplace itself. It remains to be seen whether the American workers' movement can sustain a period of resurgence, especially in the context of industrial decline. The rise of government and service sector unionism is an important development, but one whose consequences remain to be seen.

Chapter 11

Gender and Work

The twenty-first century has seen a number of "firsts" for women in the United States, including the first African American female U.S. Secretary of State, the first female Speaker of the House, and the first female frontrunner for the Democratic presidential nomination. But even these accomplishments, while significant, are not the entire story. For instance, women in the United States are enrolling and graduating from college at a higher rate than men, and the gender pay gap for women of all economic levels and racial groups eroded steadily during the 1980s and early 1990s. Clearly, progress is occurring for women at work and in public life. At the same time, not all the evidence is so positive. While the gender wage gap has certainly closed significantly over time, the wage gap for college-educated women in mid-career (i.e., 36–45 years old) increased slightly between 1996 and 2006. Wal-Mart, the country's largest employer, is facing a class-action lawsuit contending that it has actively discriminated against women by restricting their access to management. And while more women are receiving MBAs than ever, women's presence in the top echelons of business is sparse (see Chapter 8).

Although the news may seem mixed, it all contributes to the story of gender, work, and inequality in the twenty-first century. Much has changed for the better in the workplace: in 2006, roughly half of all management, professional, and related occupations were held by women (Bureau of Labor Statistics 2007c). At the same time, persistent gender inequalities remain in wages and opportunity. For example, among hourly workers age 25 or over, twice as many women as men (1.8 vs. 0.9 percent) earned the minimum wage or less in 2006 (Bureau of Labor Statistics 2007c). In addition, the occupational structure remains "hypersegregated" by sex (Charles and Grusky 2004).

In this chapter we will take a look at these issues. We will explain what has changed and what has not; we will examine why change has been uneven, and speculate about what we can expect for the future. There are three parts to the discussion. We begin with a brief look at the U.S. economy and the forces responsible for married women's exploding rates of labor force participation during the last third of the twentieth century. Next, we turn our attention to the contemporary workplace, examining where women and men work and how much their work is worth. The final section looks at several issues facing women and men in the labor market.

FIGURE 11.1 Labor force participation rates for population ages 20–64 by sex, race, and ethnicity, 2005 (*, denotes non-Hispanic).

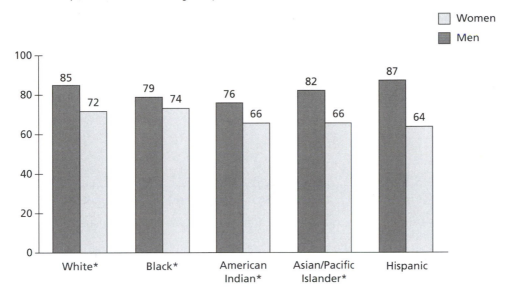

Source: Mark Mather, "Closing the Male-Female Labor Force Gap," Population Reference Bureau. (http://www.prb.org/Articles/2007/ClosingtheMaleFemaleLaborForceGap.aspx)

The Rise in Women's Labor Force Participation

The vast majority of women and men today work for pay, and majorities of both sexes are employed full-time (see Figure 11.1). Paid employment is typical for women and men of all racial groups. Just under 62 percent of African American women, 56.1 percent of Latinas, 58.3 percent of Asian American women, and 59.0 percent of white women worked for pay in 2006, as did majorities of men in each group (Bureau of Labor Statistics 2007c). Men and women work for pay even when they are parents; rates of labor force participation for both sexes during the primary childbearing years (i.e., 25–45) are over 70 percent. In 2005, 56.7 percent of women with at least one child under the age of 3 were employed. Overall, women comprised roughly 47 percent of the labor force.

During the last half of the twentieth century, men's rate of labor force participation declined, while women's rose (see Figure 11.2). This pattern, which was seen in some form in almost all industrial economies, "represented a major shift from earlier periods, since for most of the nineteenth century and early twentieth century, it was *men* who were moving into the paid labor force from joint production with their wives and from continuous involvement in the lives of their families" (Goldscheider and Waite 1991: 9). By far, the group most responsible for the increase in women's labor force participation was married women with children (Reskin and Padavic 1994).

FIGURE 11.2 Women's and men's rates of labor force participation, 1970–2006.

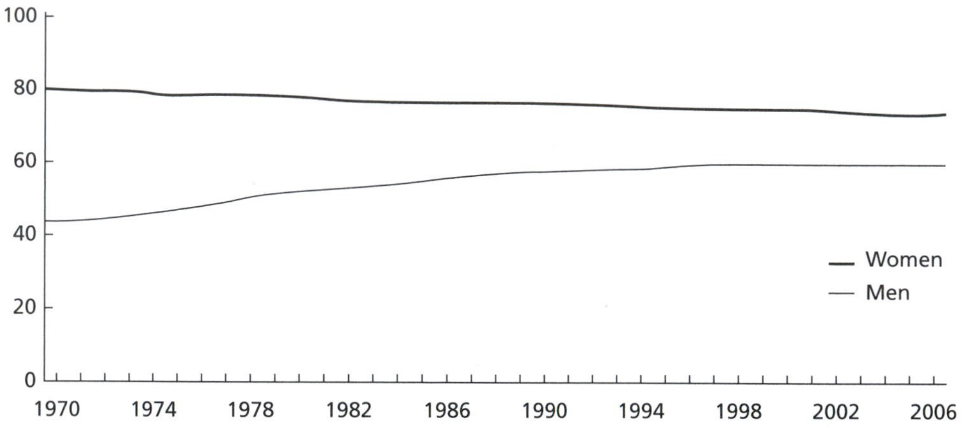

Source: Mark Mather, "Closing the Male-Female Labor Force Gap," Population Reference Bureau. (http://www.prb.org/Articles/2007/ClosingtheMaleFemaleLaborForceGap.aspx)

The factors that accounted for women's mass entrance into the paid labor force can be understood as a series of "pushes" and "pulls" (Gerson 1985). "Pushes" refer to those factors that make *not* working for pay increasingly difficult; hence, they reflect the costs of staying out of the labor market. "Pull" factors are those that attract people to the workforce; they represent the rewards of working for pay.

The forces pushing women out of the home were both economic and social. The major economic force was the declining wages of men. In the latter decades of the twentieth century, almost all groups of men saw their earning power eroded, increasing the labor force participation rates of women in all racial and ethnic groups. As men's wages fell, it became more and more difficult for them to support their wives and children. This economic reality helped to push many married women into the paid labor force. While women's paychecks were not equal to those of men's, women's salaries helped considerably to ease the

economic burdens on families. Indeed, households with two wage-earners continue to earn substantially more than households with only one employed adult (Casper and Bianchi 2002).

While economic forces were important, rising divorce rates and the consequent decline of stable marriage were also forces helping to push women into the labor force. Divorce causes economic uncertainty for women, creating an economic incentive for them to enter the labor force. Second, regardless of people's own circumstances, as divorce became more common, it likely figured into the ways that young people— even those yet to marry—assessed their options. Relations between divorce rates and women's employment are complex, however. Not only may higher divorce rates lead people to plan their futures differently, but paid employment itself may contribute to divorce.

The costs of staying home increased for women, but so too did the rewards of going to work for pay. Prior to the 1970s most employed women worked in a narrow range of low-paying, predominantly female occupations. Restricted opportunities in the workplace reduced the rewards women could obtain from the labor market. Most women worked for pay only when they were compelled by circumstances such as poverty or divorce, or when they were young and unmarried.

Women's opportunities for paid employment expanded greatly during the 1960s and 1970s, however. Legislation such as the 1963 Equal Pay Act, Title VII of the 1964 Civil Rights Act, and the 1972 Education Amendments, as well as various Supreme Court decisions, began to break down some of the legal barriers to paid employment for women. Opportunities expanded accordingly as women found jobs in fields previously closed to them.

In addition to legal changes, other social forces were reshaping work opportunities for women. As we saw in the previous chapter, the expanding service economy created many opportunities for employed women. In 2004, women made up at least half of all workers in education and health services, leisure and hospitality, financial activities, and other services. Opportunities for women in the service sector were not confined to lower-paying, personal service occupations, but also involved the professional ranks. In 2004, half of all management, professional, and related occupations were held by women. The loosening of legal and cultural barriers to professional schools enabled women to enter fields such as law and medicine, which had previously been much harder for them to pursue.

Another factor contributing to women's expanded job opportunities involved education. As noted, women's entrance into the professions was made possible in part by legal challenges to sex discrimination in education. The percentage of women with college degrees has risen substantially since the early 1970s, while the percentage of men with college degrees has stayed about the same; Only one out of ten employed women held a college degree in 1970, whereas three out of ten did so in 2004 (Bureau of Labor Statistics 2007a). Women received 58 percent of all bachelor's degrees awarded in 2003, 59 percent of all master's degrees, and 47.1 percent of all doctoral degrees (U.S. Department of Education 2004). With expanded educational opportunities have come more options in the paid labor market. By 2004, a higher percentage of women than men in the labor market were college graduates.

A final factor "pulling" women into the labor market was the women's movement, which was gaining momentum during the 1960s and early 1970s. Middle-class women, in particular, began to encounter gender egalitarian ideologies in college. Some gravitated to feminism as a direct result of their participation in the civil rights or antiwar movement, while others were attracted to the ideals of women's liberation itself. While many young white and middle-class women participated in the women's movement directly, other women (and men) were exposed indirectly to the movement's goals and philosophies. Economic independence and equal opportunity in the workplace were among the most important of these. In addition, each of the previous factors—including the declining wages of men, rising rates of divorce, equal opportunity legislation, increased numbers of women in college, and women's employment itself—contributed to a new cultural landscape. Employment outside the home became normative for women, even those who were not desperately poor and those who were married and had children.

Many analysts expect women's labor force participation to flatten out and perhaps even decline slightly over the next few decades, as another set of "pushes" and "pulls" exert their effects. For example, between 2006 and 2016 the number of women in the labor force is expected to grow at a slightly higher rate than the number of men, but a weakening economy means that the women's growth rate will be lower than in recent decades (Mather 2007). Others argue that women's continuing need to balance paid work with family responsibilities places limits on their rates of labor force participation. These limits could be overcome, however, if the United States became more like most other industrialized economies and began offering more generous parental leaves and childcare benefits.

Sex Segregation of Jobs and Occupations

The rates of male and female labor force participation are only part of the story, however. To better understand the ways in which gender structures employment, we need to examine the kinds of work performed by women and men and their distribution across occupations and jobs. In virtually all societies, times, and places, sex has been an important basis of work organization and remains so today. Although women represent close to half of those participating in the paid labor force (46 percent in 2006), women and men are employed in different occupations, firms, and jobs. Sex segregation, defined as the concentration of women and men in different occupations, firms, and jobs, is a pervasive, entrenched feature of the American workplace and one that shapes women's and men's work lives in multiple ways.

One widely used measure of sex segregation is the *index of dissimilarity* (also referred to as the index of segregation). The index of segregation ranges from 0 to 100. A score of 100 indicates complete segregation; jobs or occupations are all either 100 percent female or 100 percent male. A score of 0 indicates complete integration; every occupation or job has the same proportion of women and men in it as the labor force as a whole.

To apply this formula, we start with the fact that the U.S. labor force is approximately 46 percent female and 54 percent male. Thus, if all occupations were completely sex-integrated, every occupation would be exactly 46 percent female and 54 percent male. On the other hand, if the labor force were completely sex-segregated, then all occupations would be either 100 percent female or 100 percent male. The actual value of the index of dissimilarity in the United States is approximately 52 (Cotter et al. 1995). This means that 52 percent of either women or men—more than half of either category—would have to move to another occupation in order to bring about an occupationally sex-integrated labor force.

Occupations and jobs are also segregated by race (Padavic and Reskin 2002). Due to data limitations, most studies of racial segregation in employment focus on segregation between African Americans and whites. This research shows that levels of occupational segregation by race are lower than levels of occupational sex segregation. Women and men thus are more likely to work in different occupations than are blacks and whites. Moreover, sex segregation among both blacks and whites is greater than racial segregation among women and among men. Black men and black women are as likely to be segregated from one another as white women are to be segregated from white men. The indices of racial segregation among both women and men were around 30 at the beginning of the twenty-first century, while the indices of sex segregation among whites and among African Americans were each just over 50. Occupational sex segregation was relatively stable during most of the twentieth century, and then began to decline in the 1970s. This stability is remarkable considering all of the other social, economic, and cultural changes that occurred during the twentieth century.

From a historical perspective, one of the fascinating aspects of occupational sex segregation is the way in which many occupations have changed their sex label over time. In other words, while the overall level of occupational sex segregation has been relatively stable, some occupations have altered their sex composition. Librarians, clerical workers, teachers, and bank tellers are examples of occupations that used to be mostly filled by men, but are now dominated heavily by women. The feminization of occupations—the movement of women into fields dominated by men—is primarily responsible for the decline in aggregate levels of occupational sex segregation that occurred during the 1970s (Reskin and Roos 1990). The feminization of occupations continues. For example, while women students were rare in schools of veterinary medicine in the 1960s, they are now in the majority (Gose 1998). Although most practicing veterinarians are men, the high enrollment of women in veterinary schools suggests that this field's sex composition is changing rapidly.

Interestingly, there are far fewer examples of occupations that have shifted in the other direction—from mostly female to mostly male.

Hence, while Reskin and Roos (1990) identified thirty-three occupations that feminized in the 1970s, they could find only three (cooks, food-preparation kitchen workers, and maids and housemen) where the percentage of men significantly increased. Despite these changes, however, it is important to note that the sex composition of the vast majority of occupations remained fairly stable during the time period studied by Reskin and Roos. The processes that create and maintain a sex-segregated occupational structure are ongoing, and the sexual division of labor is maintained even as particular occupations experience changes in their sex composition.

Researchers have also compared levels of occupational sex segregation across societies. This is a difficult task, given the tremendous variability across countries in the quality and availability of occupational data. Nevertheless, these studies show that the occupational sex segregation is a feature of all industrial societies, with some of the highest levels found in countries such as Sweden and the lowest levels in Japan (Roos 1985). In general, research suggests that a country's level of occupational sex segregation depends upon a variety of economic, social, and cultural factors. Women tend to have greater access to predominantly male occupations in countries with low birth rates and strong egalitarian belief systems, while sex segregation is increased when countries have large service sectors (Charles 1992).

Gendered Jobs and Gendered Workers

Both women and men typically work in jobs and occupations that are dominated by members of their own sex. Demographically speaking, then, most occupations tend to contain large numbers of men or women, but not both. As a result of this segregation, jobs and occupations slowly take on the characteristics of those who typically perform them. Consider nursing—as women filled these jobs, nursing came to be seen as an occupation that demanded "feminine" qualities, such as empathy. This assumption, in turn, helps perpetuate the traditional sex composition of nursing since it implies that women as a group are inherently better suited than men for this occupation. These processes also apply to jobs held disproportionately by men (Pierce 1995; Cheng 1996; Maier 1999). Many predominantly male jobs implicitly and explicitly require workers to display traditionally masculine behaviors, such as aggressiveness (Pierce 1995). Maier (1999: 71) argues that managerial practices and organizational cultures—not merely specific jobs— embody a "corporate masculinity" that privileges individualism, competitiveness, and technical rationality.

That jobs dominated by a particular sex come to be seen as most appropriate for that sex may seem unproblematic and inevitable, but this association is produced through a complex process of social construction. As Reskin and Roos (1990: 51) note, virtually any occupation can be understood as being more appropriate for one sex or another "because most jobs contain both stereotypical male and stereotypical female elements." Indeed, jobs and occupations that are predominantly female-identified in the West are not necessarily held by women in other parts of the world and vice versa. For example, in Sengal and Tunisia approximately half of all nurses are men (Anker 1998). Similarly, during World War II when it was necessary to quickly fill jobs traditionally dominated by men with female workers, many predominantly male jobs were redefined to emphasize their association with traditionally female qualities and tasks (Milkman 1987).

Maintaining Barriers Between "Women's" and "Men's" Jobs

As Box 11.1 shows, beliefs about who should engage in what type of work and the appropriateness of particular jobs for women or men were once part of the official descriptions of jobs. For many years, these beliefs were also enshrined in law, providing a legal justification for sex segregation. Such "protective" legislation justified restrictions on women's work activity on the basis of the need to protect their procreative abilities or their morals. For example, in 1948 the Supreme Court upheld a state law that forbade the licensing of female bartenders unless they were the establishment owner's wife or daughter. Protective legislation also influenced the type of jobs available to women by restricting the number of hours or time of day when they could work.

....

BOX 11.1 *A Brief History of Gender Stereotypes in the Occupational Outlook Handbook*

In a September 1, 1948, letter of transmittal to Secretary of Labor Maurice J. Tobin, Commissioner of Labor Statistics Ewan Clague announced that an *Occupational Outlook Handbook (OOH)* was "being made available through public sale" [*Occupational Outlook Handbook*,

BOX **11.1** *continued*

Bulletin 940, Bureau of Labor Statistics, 1949, p. ii]. The first of 23 editions was published in 1949. . . . A detailed examination of the coverage and content of various editions over the course of 50 years, however, reveals significant changes. . . . [These changes] illustrate the ever-shifting occupational structure and social environment over the 50-year period.

. . . From the outset, analysts preparing the *Handbook* relied heavily on the Bureau of the Census for employment data and the *D.O.T.* for descriptions of work. Because the occupational classification system used by each of these sources contained sexist titles, they naturally found their way into the *Handbook*. Thus, the 1949 edition presented separate reports on airplane hostesses and flight stewards. Under a description of the duties of these two occupations, readers learned that "when a hostess and steward work together, as is often the case on big planes, the former tends to specialize in service to the women and children aboard, [while the latter] tends to handle the heavier work" (p. 163). Under "Qualifications and Advancement," one learned that "as a general rule, only single women (or widowed or divorced women without children) are eligible for jobs, and their continued employment is conditioned upon their remaining unmarried" (p. 163). Further, "about 1 out of 10 of all present stewardesses are nurses, [and] girls without this qualification must, as a rule, have at least 1 or 2 years of college education" (p. 163). In early editions of the *Handbook*, it is not unusual to find third-person singular pronouns (he, his, she, her, and so forth) used in describing the nature of work in occupations in which most workers were either men or women. Equal employment legislation such as the Civil Rights Act of 1964 and the Age Discrimination in Employment Act of 1967 prohibited the use of sex- and age-specific language in inappropriate contexts by the public employment service. To conform to these regulations, the U.S. Department of Labor issued a publication in 1975 revising nearly 3,500 job descriptions in the *D.O.T.* that were considered potentially discriminatory with regard to sex or age. For example, terms circumscribing a person's age, such as "boy," "girl," "junior," and "senior," were eliminated, as was sex-stereotyping language, such as "man," "woman," "lady," and suffixes like "-ess," denoting females. Thus, "foreman" was replaced by "supervisor" and "draftsman" by "drafter." The Bureau formally adopted the use of nonsexist job titles in the 1976–77 *Handbook*, with the sole exception of "able seaman," which, for reasons unknown, was retained. Only scattered references to the number of women employed in various occupations appeared in the 1949 *OOH*. Beginning with the 1957 *Handbook*, however, the Bureau made an effort to provide more information on the employment of women. Eventually, though, the authors became dissatisfied because they felt that numbers showing very small or very large percentages of women employed in certain occupations constituted sex stereotyping. . . . By the mid-1970s, the Bureau believed that, from a career-counseling standpoint, the negative effects of sex stereotyping far outweighed the merits of presenting employment data on women in the *Handbook*. Consequently, the authors dropped all references to the employment of women beginning with the 1978–79 edition.

SOURCE: Pilot 1999

The legal basis for sex segregation began its slow erosion with the passage of the 1964 Civil Rights Act, which banned discrimination on the basis of sex, race, color, religion, and national origin in hiring, firing, compensation, and other aspects of employment. In theory, this law made it illegal for employers to reserve some jobs for men and some for women. Court challenges continue to this day, however. And while some of the forces that reproduced sex segregation have diminished, others reinforce these patterns. To understand how segregation is reproduced, we must consider two sets of factors.

One set of factors involves "supply side" characteristics, such as male and female workers' preferences, skills, and abilities. These characteristics are typically understood as being formed prior to women and men entering the labor market. In this view, women and men are assumed to seek and be qualified for different kinds of occupations and jobs. Alternatively, a second set of factors focuses on the "demand side." Here, segregation is explained by processes that operate inside the workplace as workers are hired for and assigned to jobs. In this view, employers' actions—either intentionally or unintentionally—reinforce segregation. Though both sets of factors are undoubtedly relevant, most sociologists believe that gender differences in preferences, skills, and abilities are less important than what happens on the job.

Workers' Preferences, Values, and Abilities

The sex composition of an occupation or job may reflect sex differences in preferences, values, and abilities. These differences are presumed to take shape as women's and men's lives unfold from birth. To the extent that each gender has different experiences and interactions, they would be expected to approach work differently, make different kinds of choices, and consequently end up in different kinds of occupations.

While intuitively appealing, these explanations are not completely satisfactory and receive only mixed empirical support. For example, while children's occupational aspirations are highly gender-typed, these differences get smaller as children age and enter adulthood. In addition, young women's occupational aspirations have changed dramatically over time. In a study of several age groups, Shu and Marini (1998) found that younger women were less likely than older women to aspire to predominantly female occupations and were more likely to aspire to occupations with higher earning potential. These changes occurred among all social classes and racial groups, to some extent, but were particularly strong among women from higher socioeconomic backgrounds. Men's occupational aspirations remained relatively stable across the birth cohorts in Shu and Marini's study.

Research on individual careers also challenges the notion that sex segregation reflects sex differences in job preferences. Jacobs (1989), for example, found that women's and men's aspirations, college majors, and occupations show considerable "sex-type mobility." Moreover, among both women and men who change aspirations, college majors, or occupations, there is only a weak relationship between the sex type of the original position and the destination position. In other words, while women's and men's occupational aspirations, skills, and choices may be influenced by sex, "sex-typed preferences are neither fixed for life nor fully deterministic of the sex type of workers' jobs" (Reskin and Hartmann 1986: 37).

Empirical support for sex differences in the area of work-related values is also relatively weak.

Rowe and Snizek (1995) examined data from twelve national samples of the U.S. population, spanning the years 1973 to 1990. Survey respondents were asked to rank five work values, ranging from most to least preferred in a job. Rowe and Snizek found that women and men ranked each value in exactly the same order of preference: feeling of accomplishment, high income, chance for advancement, job security, and short working hours (from most to least preferred). Moreover, these researchers found no real changes over time in the magnitude of sex differences. Work values, as measured in this study, had more to do with factors such as age, education, and occupational prestige than sex.

The above accounts of occupational choice emphasize people's experiences and patterns of social interaction with parents, peers, and others. Economists treat issues of occupational choice much more narrowly. They argue that people are motivated primarily by an economic calculus, seeking to reduce costs and increase rewards by choosing one occupation over another. To understand how this applies to issues of gender, we must consider the concept of *human capital*. Human capital refers to those things that increase one's productivity.

Human capital theorists suggest that people invest in their own human capital—through actions such as going to college or acquiring on-the-job-training—with the expectation that this investment will eventually pay off for them economically. Two people who make different kinds of investments thus will acquire different types and amounts of human capital. Further, these theorists assume that people are economically rational—that is, they will try to avoid bad investments and gravitate toward those where the rewards of the investment outweigh the costs. Human capital

theorists believe that women and men, on average, make different kinds of human capital investments. As a result, men and women are not really "substitutable" for one another in the labor market; they look different to an employer and thus end up working in different kinds of jobs.

A central problem with human capital accounts of sex segregation is the validity of its claims regarding sex differences in levels of human capital. Most researchers recognize years of education as one useful measure of human capital. Even at the highest levels of education, however, the gap between women and men on this measure has virtually closed, with women surpassing men in the percentages of bachelor's and master's degrees awarded and close to parity in the awarding of doctoral degrees. If differences in human capital explain sex segregation, however, we would have expected sex segregation to decline by a much more significant amount than it has declined. Other traditional measures of human capital, such as years of work experience, show similar trends. Women and men are much more alike with respect to the kinds of things that make them productive employees than they were twenty years ago.

The Opportunity Structure at Work

The factors examined previously imply that women and men are different from one another when they enter the labor market. Employers are presumed to respond to these differences, but do not create them. However, little evidence supports the claim that sex segregation in paid employment primarily reflects sex differences in job-related preferences, skills, and abilities. Explaining how and why people get the jobs they do thus may have less to do with workers' choices and more to do with what happens on the job.

Employers play important roles in creating and maintaining sex segregation because employers—in the form of personnel managers or other gatekeepers—are the ones who hire and assign workers to jobs. To understand how this occurs, we must consider the hiring and staffing process. The hiring process brings together job applicants with prospective employers. A successful job search can be thought of as a match between a worker and a job (Marsden 1996). The ways in which this match is made are important; they shape which individuals are hired for which jobs. One aspect of the hiring process that seems to play a role in reproducing sex segregation is employee recruitment.

Recruitment can occur through various mechanisms. Employers can place advertisements in newspapers or on websites; they can rely on "headhunters" or employment agencies; they can recruit informally by accessing their own or their employees' social networks. Employers typically prefer more informal methods, such as personal contacts or employee referrals, to recruit new employees (Granovetter 1974; Kalleberg and Schmidt 1996). These are regarded as more efficient and more effective than more formal recruitment methods, such as placing advertisements. Informal recruitment methods tend to produce job applicants who are the same gender as those already employed, however (Marsden 1996). This results from the fact that people's social networks—those with whom they interact and share information—tend to be homophilous; that is, they contain people similar to themselves (McPherson, Smith-Lovin, and Cook 2001).

Other aspects of the hiring process also help to maintain sex segregation. For example, employers may use various means to assess a prospective employee's skills and abilities. Some employers rely on formal tests or other structured techniques to evaluate applicants, while others operate much more informally. In general, research suggests that informal staffing methods are more exclusionary to outsiders or those deemed "nontypical" than more formal methods.

When recruiting or hiring workers, sex segregation is maintained when employers rely on gender stereotypes as the basis for their decisions. One way in which stereotypes can influence decision making is via statistical discrimination. This form of discrimination occurs when an individual applying for a job is treated as if he or she possesses the qualities and characteristics "typical" of his or her gender. For example, there is a small, average difference between the height of women and men in American society. As a result, employers needing to fill a job with people who at least six feet tall could decide to exclude all women from consideration on the assumption that the average woman is less likely to meet this height requirement than the average man. Employers who used sex as a device to screen prospective employees on height would likely be able to find qualified job candidates. Some men they considered would not be tall enough, and they would exclude from consideration some women who met the height requirement. Overall, however, they would not be excluding very many qualified candidates or including many applicants who were unqualified.

When employers statistically discriminate, they are assumed to be *correctly* assigning group averages to individuals. This distinguishes statistical discrimination from discrimination resulting from employers' use of incorrect, exaggerated, or unsubstantiated stereotypes to hire or assign jobs to workers. Statistical discrimination, like other forms of sex discrimination, is illegal. However, employers who engage in this type of discrimination have an economic motive to treat male and female workers differently.

Hiring and staffing processes that systematically channel women into different jobs than men are illegal according to the Civil Rights Act. Yet, as numerous court cases reveal, sex discrimination has not disappeared. For example, in California, female employees of the Publix supermarket chain recently reached an $81.5 million dollar settlement with the company. This class action suit alleged that women were segregated into stereotypical "female" jobs and prevented from higher-paying management positions (National Women's Law Center 2000). Another case still pending involves Costco Wholesale Corp. Although its workforce is roughly half female, only 2 out of 35 senior executives at Costco are women (Harris 2006). Wal-Mart faces a similar court challenge (Besen and Kimmel 2006).

Despite these examples, it is exceedingly difficult to uncover and document discriminatory practices. As Petersen and Saporta (2004: 860) explain, "Those not hired and possibly discriminated against will rarely know what occurred, and even when they do, it may be impossible to gather the relevant evidence. And those turned down often have applied for other jobs and may have gotten those, in which case the incentives for complaining or filing suits are small, in particular when this kind of discrimination typically requires litigation." As a result, recruitment or staffing practices that help perpetuate sex segregation tend to be reproduced over time, taking on a life of their own, regardless of the lack of discriminatory intent.

Being Different: The Experiences of the Token

Thus far, we have looked at the factors that maintain sex segregation in the labor market. Barriers between "men's" and "women's" jobs are not insurmountable, however. While their numbers are small, roughly 6 percent of all registered nurses are men. Understanding the experiences of men and women who work in gender-atypical occupations is important as it will help us identify some of the ways that interactions between workers help to maintain barriers between women's and men's jobs.

In her 1977 classic, *Men and Women of the Corporation*, Kanter argued that one key to understanding people's experiences at work was how many of their "social type" was present. Kanter (1977a: 207) proposed that that the relative proportions of different "social types" in a group shape members' social relations. "As proportions shift," she suggests, "so do social experiences." Proportions have this effect because they influence how people perceive one another.

Kanter (1977a: 208) was particularly interested in what she called "skewed groups." In these groups, one social type is numerically dominant and the other is a very small numerical minority (15 percent or less). Kanter's focus on this type of group stemmed from the fact that this is likely to be the situation experienced by "newcomers" to a social setting. Women who enter jobs or workplaces historically dominated by men, for example, are apt to enter as a minority of this type, as are people of color who enter jobs historically dominated by whites. Because it is unlikely that an employer would hire large numbers of women or people of color at one time, sex (and race) integration happens slowly, one or two people at a time. Members of the numerical minority in skewed groups are called tokens. For Kanter, this term is not pejorative, nor does it refer to people who are assumed to have been hired because of their sex or race. Instead, the term "token" is a neutral label, referring to those whose "social type" constitutes 15 percent or less of a group.

Kanter argues that relations between tokens and dominants in skewed groups are shaped by three perceptual tendencies: visibility, contrast, and assimilation. First, tokens—because they are different from the majority—are easily noticed; their behavior is often attributed more to their social category membership than to their own individual characteristics. The second perceptual tendency associated with tokenism, contrast, involves dominants' attempts to exaggerate and affirm their differences from tokens, a set of behaviors Kanter (1977a: 229) refers to as "boundary heightening." The third perceptual tendency associated with tokenism is assimilation. Dominants see tokens less as individuals and more as representative members of their social category. Moreover, because the characteristics dominants associate with a token's social category are often overly simplified or inaccurate stereotypes, assimilation contributes to the dominants' misperceptions of the token.

Tokens are threatening to dominants because their presence creates uncertainty. Norms, beliefs, and styles of communication that dominants take for granted may be challenged or misunderstood. Dominants' uncertainty and discomfort may result in hostility directed toward tokens or, in more extreme cases, sexual harassment. Tokens may leave or be driven out of their jobs as a consequence of this treatment, thereby preserving the dominance of the majority.

Kanter's ideas were derived from her research on women working in white-collar positions dominated by men. Since Kanter, there have been many more studies of women's experiences in predominantly male jobs. We know less about men's experiences in predominantly female work settings.

Men Doing "Women's Work"

Although Kanter's research focused on female tokens, she believed that the processes associated with tokenism would operate regardless of whether tokens were male or female. In the years since Kanter first made these arguments, researchers have concluded that the consequences of tokenism may be very different for women and men. For example, Williams (1992) found that while relatively few men seek out predominantly female occupations such as nursing or elementary school teaching, those who do are likely to be successful and more highly economically rewarded than their female co-workers. In the case of male elementary school teachers, Cognard-Black (2004) found that they were significantly more likely than comparable female teachers to move up to a principal or assistant principal position.

Because "femaleness" is less highly valued than "maleness," women entering predominantly male occupations must struggle to fit in and demonstrate their competence. Men entering predominantly female occupations, on the other hand, carry no such burden. Maleness is positively regarded, in general, and thus men in predominantly female occupations may strive to demonstrate these qualities and preserve their distinctiveness from women. Hence, men are likely to benefit from their token status in ways that women do not. While female tokens must prove themselves capable of doing "men's work," male tokens often find themselves on *glass escalators*, with invisible and sometimes even unwanted pressures to move up in the workplace (Williams 1992).

Along with research comparing the experiences of male and female tokens, there have been studies looking more generally at the experiences of women and men in gender-atypical jobs. For example, in their study of male clerical temporaries, Henson and Rogers (2001) ask: How do men "do masculinity" in a predominantly female job? The vast majority of clerical workers are women, and this is also true among those in temporary jobs. Henson and Rogers note that prior to the 1960s, most temporary employers of clerical workers did not even accept male applicants. Not surprisingly, then, men who become clerical temporaries are likely to face questions, surprise, and disapproval from their peers and co-workers. As one man interviewed by Henson and Rogers commented:

> "People are looking at me like, 'What are you doing here?' Like they're thinking, 'Gee, what's the deal? Shouldn't you be, I don't know, doing something else?' I mean it's sort of fine if you're just out of school. They kind of expect well, you're just doing this until you get a regular job" (2001: 223).

In response, male clerical temporaries reasserted their masculinity using several strategies designed to set them apart from and superior to women. For example, they reframed the work, replacing the term "secretary" with more masculine or gender-neutral descriptions, such as bookkeeper or word processor (Henson and Rogers 2001). They used "cover stories" to create an alternative occupational identity, such as actor or writer, and minimized

the significance of their temporary job. The male clerical temporaries in Henson and Rogers' study also asserted their masculinity by refusing to show the deference (see Chapter 9) typically required of subordinates—especially women (Pierce 1995).

From these studies, we see that sex segregation is a persistent feature of the workplace and seems to be continually reproduced. When women enter occupations traditionally dominated by men, men begin to avoid those fields, leading to a resegregation of that occupation. When occupations or jobs integrate by sex, as we have seen, other kinds of sex distinctions often emerge.

The Gender Pay Gap and the Worth of Jobs

An important link between the gendering of jobs and gender inequality appears when we examine the relative values attached to different kinds of work. The higher societal value placed on males and masculinity over females and femininity is reproduced within the workplace. In this setting, the relative worth of activities can be assessed economically—in the form of wages—and symbolically—in the form of status and prestige. On both counts, men and masculine activities are more highly valued than women and feminine activities.

Women workers, on average, earn less than men, and this has been true ever since the United States began keeping track of the relative earnings of each sex. Moreover, the wage disparity between women and men persists "regardless of how you define earnings (e.g., annual vs. weekly, mean vs. median), in all race/ethnic groups, across educational categories, over the life cycle, within detailed occupational categories, and across cultures" (Roos and Gatta 1999: 95).

FIGURE 11.3 Median weekly earnings of full-time workers by gender, race, and ethnicity, 2006.

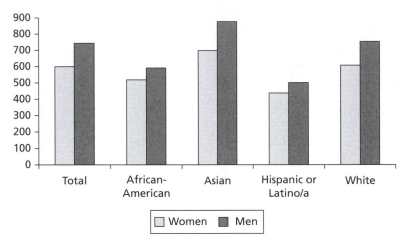

Source: I/S/Bureau of Labor Statistics 2007b.

The gender wage gap is typically expressed as a ratio of women's earnings to men's earnings. Usually, this ratio is measured in terms of the median earnings of women and men who work full-time, year-round. In 2006, women's median weekly earnings (among those employed full-time) were 80.7 percent of men's (Bureau of Labor Statistics 2007c). Women earn less than men in all racial and ethnic categories (see Figure 11.3) and in all major occupational groups, including those containing high percentages of women (see Table 11.1).

Figure 11.4 shows that the gender wage gap has fluctuated somewhat over time, declining since the mid-1970s, but rising between 1995 and 2000. This decline in the gender wage gap has occurred among African Americans and Hispanics. For example, in 1970 African American women working full-time, year-round earned 66.9 percent of what African American men earned; this ratio had risen to 81.0 percent by 1990 (Roos and Gatta 1999). A similar trend can be seen among Hispanics and whites. In the past five years, however, all racial-gender groups have lost ground relative to white men, who continue to have the highest earnings of any group.

The gender wage gap varies by age. The earnings of younger women are closer to the earnings of younger men than is the case among older workers. In 2006, for instance, women between the ages of 25 and 34 (employed full-time, year-round) earned 88 percent of what men in this age group earned; by contrast, women between the ages of 45 and 64 earned only 73 percent of men in this age group (Bureau of Labor Statistics 2007c).

Researchers suggest two reasons to explain why the gender wage gap varies by age (Roos and Gatta 1999). The first involves cohort differences; younger workers are beginning their careers in a more gender-equal world than the one in which older workers began theirs. In addition, these variations in the gender wage gap in part reflect life cycle differences in women's and

TABLE 11.1 Median Weekly Earnings of Full-Time Workers by Major Occupational Group and Sex, 2006

OCCUPATION	WOMEN	MEN	WOMEN'S EARNINGS AS PERCENT OF MEN'S EARNINGS
Management, Business, and Financial Occupations			
Management	$926	$1,264	73.3%
Business and financial operations	828	1,134	73.0%
Professional and Related Occupations			
Computer and mathematical	1,043	1,231	84.7%
Architecture and engineering	972	1,181	82.3%
Life, physical, and social science	872	1,121	77.8%
Community and social services	703	792	88.8%
Legal	901	1,734	52.0%
Education, training, and library	763	969	78.7%
Arts, design, entertainment, sports, and media	733	942	77.8%
Healthcare practitioner and technical	860	1,098	78.3%
Service Occupations			
Healthcare support	417	502	83.1%
Protective service	557	737	75.6%
Food preparation and serving related	355	389	91.3%
Building and grounds cleaning and maintenance	363	445	81.6%
Personal care and service	388	506	76.7%
Sales and Office Occupations			
Sales and related	487	761	64.0%
Office and administrative support	557	619	90.0%
Natural Resources, Construction, and Maintenance Occupations			
Farming, fishing, and forestry	342	401	85.3%
Construction and extraction	533	621	85.8%
Installation, maintenance, and repair	697	744	93.7%
Production, Transportation, and Material Moving Occupations			
Production	432	621	69.6%
Transportation and material moving	414	581	71.3%

Source: U.S. Bureau of Labor Statistics 2007b, Table 39.

FIGURE 11.4 Median usual weekly earnings of full-time workers in constant (2006) dollars by sex, 1979–2006: annual averages.

Source: U.S. Bureau of Labor Statistics 2007c. p. 4.

men's careers. Women's and men's earnings may be more similar at the beginning of their careers than later in adulthood after other life events—such as marriage and childbearing—have taken place. Together, these explanations imply that, while gender-based wage discrimination may have decreased, women's and men's earnings continue to be differentially affected by changes over the life course.

Men earn more than women in every country in the world, although the size of this gap varies. In 1997, for example, women in Sweden earned 89 percent of what men earned, as compared to Greece and the Netherlands, where the gender wage gap was around 71 percent (Van Der Lippe and Van Dijk 2001). These patterns reflect several factors, including cross-national differences in levels and types of sex segregation, government policies, occupational structures, and cultural beliefs.

Explaining the Wage Gap

To understand why women earn less than men, we must first return to the issue of sex segregation, discussed earlier in this chapter. Sex segregation contributes substantially to the wage gap. Women earn less than men in part because women and men work in different jobs; jobs held disproportionately by women pay less than comparable jobs held disproportionately by men.

That jobs performed by women receive lower average wages than comparable jobs performed by men has become a well-established research finding (Catanzarite 2003). Moreover, it is important to note that both women *and* men suffer wage penalties when they work in predominantly female jobs, and the wages of both sexes benefit from employment in jobs held predominantly by men (Budig 2002). More generally, Catanzarite (2003) shows that occupations in which subordinate groups are overrepresented tend to be more vulnerable to wage deterioration over time than those populated by higher-status groups. In other words, wages are more likely to erode over time in occupations that have disproportionately high percentages of women or people of color.

Although these links between a job's sex (and race) composition and its wages are complex, they suggest that pay rates are determined in part by cultural understandings regarding the "worth" of jobs and the values that should be given to various kinds of skills. In societies that have traditionally placed higher value on male achievements and masculinity than on the achievements of women and femininity, it is not surprising that insofar as cultural values enter into wage setting, they will result in a higher value placed on jobs and activities associated with men.

The efforts of workers and their organizations also influence the wages of many kinds of jobs. The more powerful the workers, the more likely they are to successfully influence the wages their jobs receive, not only in the context of labor unions, but in nonunion settings as well (where social networks and organizational processes often operate to the disadvantage of women and minorities; see Nelson and Bridges 1999). Historically, male workers have been better organized and thus a more powerful force in negotiating wages with employers than women. Although women have a long history of labor activism, craft unions representing skilled workers

in predominantly male manufacturing jobs have been among the most powerful throughout the twentieth century. As a result, some argue that men—particularly white men—have been better able to organize for and demand higher wages than their female counterparts, regardless of skill level and market forces. In recent years, women and racial minorities have had more opportunities to engage in collective action in the public sector. Hence, it is not surprising that public-sector unions have been among the strongest supporters of gender pay equity.

Yet the wage gap between women and men cannot be explained entirely on the basis of sex segregation. Even within jobs, men are paid more than women with comparable qualifications (Budig 2002). Bayard et al. (2003) estimate that about one half of the wage gap is due to pay differences between women and men employed in the same occupation and establishment. Budig (2002) argues that this within-occupation wage gap reflects powerful forces of statistical discrimination. Employers hire men at higher average wages and reward them with promotions and raises at faster rates than women because the average woman has greater nonwork obligations than the average man. In this view, the workplace is structured in ways that penalize femininity, especially its stereotypical association with caregiving and family responsibilities.

Studies of the "motherhood wage gap" lend some support to this view. While women earn less than men, on average, women who are mothers in their childbearing years earn about 7 percent less than other women (Budig and England 2001), an effect that has also been found in some other industrialized countries (Harkness and Waldfogel 1999). Mothers earn less than other women in part due to having fewer years of work experience, more part-time work, and more breaks in employment than nonmothers. However, these differences explain only part of the motherhood wage gap. We do not know how much of the remainder stems from other employment-related differences between mothers and nonmothers and how much may result from employers' differential treatment of similarly qualified and productive mothers and nonmothers. Yet, some studies suggest that differential treatment may be a contributing factor (Cuddy, Fiske, and Glick 2004; Fuegen, Biernat, Haines, and Deaux 2004). Even when similarly qualified, mothers are viewed as less desirable employees than fathers or women who are not mothers.

The Future of Gender Inequality at Work

Researchers' understanding of gender inequality at work, including how it occurs, how it has changed over time, and its variations among women and among men have become increasingly more complex and nuanced (Blau and Kahn 1992; Bernhardt, Morris, and Handcock 1995; Charles and Grusky 2004). For example, some research attempts to relate gender-based wage inequality to wage inequality more generally as well as to other forces that are transforming the workplace, including the changing relations between work and family (see Chapter 14). Wage inequality in the United States has increased in recent decades—a pattern that reflects industrial and occupational restructuring, changing labor force demographics, globalization, and political trends (Morris and Western 1999). This widening inequality reflects not only earnings differences between women and men, but also differences *among* women and *among* men.

Similarly, researchers studying sex segregation have concluded that this issue is more complicated than it seems. Egalitarianism is a strong social force in modern (and postmodern) societies, and progress toward gender equality, in particular, has been dramatic in several arenas, such as educational attainment and labor force participation. At the same time, levels of segregation have not appreciably declined, especially when compared to these other areas (Charles and Grusky 2004). Charles and Grusky (2004: 298) suggest that a hypersegregated occupational structure, in which "women are presumed to excel in personal service, nurturance, and social interaction (nonmanual pursuits) and men are presumed to excel in technical tasks, outdoor work, and strenuous physical labor (manual pursuits), is a type of gender inequality that is especially resistant to change and is compatible with "equal opportunity" reforms.

It is also important to understand that gender is not the only important distinction among workers. The 150 million members of the U.S. labor force differ by race, ethnicity, nationality, age, sexual orientation, and many other characteristics. Researchers who study workplace diversity are interested in how *all* of these differences—acting together and alone—shape people's interactions on the job and their responses to work (Chemers, Oskamp, and Costanzo 1995; Tsui and Gutek 1999). This research suggests that differences between people—such as those deriving from gender or race—are not always a source of conflict in the workplace. For example, Chatman et al. (1998) found that a more collectivistic organizational culture that emphasizes teamwork and encourages people's sense of a shared fate can create cohesiveness even among diverse groups. How a particular work group is affected by diversity among its members depends on several other aspects of the work group and the organization of which it is a part. For example, based on their analyses of culturally diverse work groups in three firms, Ely and Thomas (2001) conclude that work groups often have different orientations to diversity and that these orientations—not the type or amount of diversity alone—affect the impact of diversity on group functioning. Diversity researchers challenge employers in the twenty-first century to create workplaces where people who are different can work together.

Conclusion

This chapter shows some of the many ways in which gender has been incorporated into the workplace. Our understandings of work, workers, and jobs incorporate assumptions about gender. The clearest evidence for this comes from studies of sex segregation, which show how and why women and men end up in different jobs. Studies of wage setting reveal how gender shapes the "worth" of jobs and the power of workers to demand and receive high wages.

One of the most important aspects of these features of the workplace is their highly institutionalized character. An arrangement that is highly institutionalized is one that is so taken for granted that it seems to reproduce itself. It is much more difficult to alter something that is highly institutionalized than it is to perpetuate it. As a result, highly institutionalized arrangements do not require coercion to sustain them, making participation appear voluntary and easily justifiable. The gendered aspects of work described in this chapter clearly fit this description; they are often unintended, taken for granted, and operate so subtly that they rarely are scrutinized. In this respect, gender is a highly institutionalized feature of the modern workplace.

Managing Diversity: Racial and Ethnic Divisions at Work

Imagine for a moment that you took a job at the Smithfield Packing Company in Tar Heel, North Carolina. This is the largest pork-processing plant in the world, and it puts meat—bacon, ham, sausage—on millions of breakfast tables every day. The counties surrounding Tar Heel provide relatively few job opportunities, but this plant has a staggering turnover rate, largely because the work is so dangerous, dirty, and painful. Workers at the Tar Heel plant are expected to work as rapidly as possible; many go home with swollen hands from the pace of cutting meat from bone. As one participant observer put it, "the first time you stare down at that [conveyer] belt, you know your body is going to give in way before the machine ever will" (Le Duff 2000: A1). It's physical work a highly demanding form—but what may be the most remarkable aspect of this plant are its the racial and ethnic lines, which are as sharply drawn as the knives workers use.

A *New York Times* reporter Charlie Le Duff went to work at this plant for three weeks in 2000, documenting the conditions he saw in this plant. So gripping were his articles that Le Duff eventually won a Pulitzer Prize. What this journalist saw was a plant in which virtually all aspects of social interaction depended on the color of one's skin. Which job people were assigned, what "place" they held in the social hierarchy, and even where they drank or who they fought with after work—all these things depended in complex ways on whether they were white, black, red, or brown. In the racial hierarchy that developed at this plant, whites and Native Americans occupied the top positions, blacks were a significant rung below them, and Mexicans, joined by prison inmates on work release, held positions at the bottom of the hierarchy. Jobs were assigned on the basis of this status ranking, with very few workers employed alongside members of another ethnic group. Although there were plenty of problems the workers wanted management to address—the harsh and unsafe working conditions, the low pay, and often arbitrary treatment by supervisors, to name a few—efforts to stand up to the company typically came to naught. As Le Duff found, "more than management, the workers see one another as the problem, and they see the competition in skin tones." Despite Le Duff's reporting from the shop floor and his commentary on the razor-sharp pattern of race-typing of jobs, Smithfield Packing Company denies any pattern of racial discrimination.

These circumstances seem extraordinary in the contemporary world, in that most Americans find this kind of race-typing to be wholly repugnant. Yet a century ago, the pattern that Le Duff reported would have elicited little if any surprise. In the steel mills of Pennsylvania or the Chicago meat packing industries, for example, the workplace was marked by a deeply established racial hierarchy that reserved skilled and supervisory jobs for native-born whites, while blacks, Italians, Poles, and Hungarians were eligible for only the dirtiest and most dangerous jobs in the nation's plants. In southern textile mills, black workers were largely excluded until the civil rights movement of the 1950s and 1960s. In the auto industry, even as recently as World War II, many white workers from the South conducted work stoppages—newspapers called them "Hate Strikes"—in protest against having to work alongside African Americans even as the nation geared up for war.

Thus the racial fault lines at Smithfield represent nothing new in U.S. economic institutions. Indeed, what seems extraordinary about the Smithfield case today is that such salient color lines can still exist, and so brazenly. But the Smithfield case is sociologically interesting, for it prompts us to ask any number of important questions about racial and ethnic relations on the job. How far *have* racial and ethnic relations at work progressed since the middle of the twentieth century? Is the Smithfield plant an aberration? Or does it reveal, in an unusually clear manner, aspects of the American workplace that are simply less easily seen in large cities and corporations, where economic activities are geographically dispersed? What can we learn from the steady stream of allegations—often with testimony that is as damning as it is detailed—of racial discrimination at prestigious corporations

like Microsoft, Coca-Cola, Kodak, and Texaco (among many others)? Where sharp disparities in hiring, pay, and promotions persist, how can they be explained? And how effective have corporate and government policies been in the effort to address racial and ethnic discrimination at work? These questions cut to the core of what equal opportunity really means, and how our society might safeguard the rights of all groups to equal treatment within the world of work.

In this chapter we explore the major findings that the sociology of work has produced in an effort to address precisely these questions. The issue of racial and ethnic relations at work has particular relevance for a number of reasons: first, because of the centrality of work as an institution that confers income, power, and prestige; second, because of the history of racial tension that has characterized U.S. society; and third, because of the rise of immigration in the last two decades, which has left the workforce more complex and diverse than ever before (see Chapter 13). Especially in the post-9/11 world, understanding ethnic diversity in the broadest possible terms is a matter of great importance and an issue that holds continuing importance for public debates in the contemporary world.

Race, Ethnicity, and the Sociology of Work

Beginning with the Chicago School at the beginning of the twentieth century, sociologists have long sought to understand the work experience of marginalized racial and ethnic groups. Led by such students of urban communities as Park and Burgess, the Chicago sociologists often explored immigrant settlement patterns and the formation of ethnic communities within industrial cities.

A second generation of Chicago sociologists extended this ecological focus to the workplace and explored the ways in which different racial and ethnic groups formed at work and affected the behavior and standing of each group's members. In a classic study of race relations at a metal polishing and finishing plant, Hughes (1946) began to show how the fabric of workplace life operated to keep minority groups within their traditional "place," erecting subtle constraints on their member's actions that were difficult for the dominant group to understand.

Influenced by the leading anthropologists of the day, the Chicago sociologists also studied the experience of black workers who were assigned work that other groups regarded as "dirty" or "unclean," much as was the case for Untouchables under Hinduism in India. This focus on marginal work has retained its significance even today, as some sociologists have studied the position of the "underclass," whose members are excluded from mainstream economic life. Recently, researchers have broadened their focus well beyond groups at the bottom of the social structure, exploring the ways in which the unequal distribution of opportunity can affect even well-educated groups seeking access to middle class pursuits (Feagin 1991). They have also recognized that race relations are increasingly complicated, with diversity that far transcends interaction between blacks and whites.

Detecting Racial and Ethnic Disparities at Work

It is undeniably true that U.S. society has taken important steps in the direction of equality of opportunity within most of its institutions. This progress is apparent with respect to the opportunities enjoyed by racial and ethnic groups at work. For example, despite the legacy of slavery and segregation, African Americans have taken tremendous strides toward full inclusion within the occupational structure, and this is evident in almost all social and economic indicators. The proportion of blacks living in poverty has dramatically declined since the 1950s; the educational gap between blacks and whites has rapidly closed; and levels of income for African Americans have shown dramatic increases in absolute terms. Significant progress has occurred in the proportion of jobs that blacks hold in management, the professions, and well-paying skilled construction trades, among other rewarding positions. As late as 1960, the modal (or single largest) occupation for black women was that of domestic service. By 1980 an important shift toward office employment had taken place, with the largest proportion of African American women in administrative support occupations, much as was true among women who were white.

Yet it would be a real mistake to conclude that work organizations have become race-neutral distributors of opportunity. When one looks more closely at the data, a disturbing pattern of continuing racial and ethnic disparities in employment opportunity begins to come into view. This disparity is found even among African American men who are employed full time and who hold qualifications that are comparable to their white counterparts. To say this is not to accuse white employers of racist or discriminatory practices (although this certainly does occur). Rather, it is to suggest that deeply institutionalized patterns of inequality have persisted to this day, and they remain far more prevalent than is commonly assumed.

Such inequalities begin to emerge when we examine the occupational distribution of workers by race and ethnicity groups in the United States. Table 12.1 shows how white, black, Latino, and

TABLE 12.1 Occupational Distribution by Race and Ethnicity (in Per Cent), for both Men and Women, 2007. Employed Persons 16 years of age and over

Occupational Category	Gender and Racial/Ethnic Group							
	Men				Women			
	Whites	African Americans	Latinos	Asian Americans	Whites	African Americans	Latinos	Asian Americans
Management and Professional Occupations	33.2	22.3	14.3	49.3	39.5	31.2	23.1	46.8
Service Occupations	12.4	19.2	19.7	13.5	19.3	26.8	30.7	18.9
Sales and Office Occupations	16.7	18.7	13.2	18.4	34.4	32.7	33.1	26.0
Construction, Maintenance, and Natural Resource Occupations	20.4	14.0	31.0	7.4	1.0	0.8	1.8	0.9
Production, Transportation, and Material Moving Occupations	17.3	25.7	21.7	11.4	5.7	8.5	11.3	7.4
Total	100%	100%	100%	100%	100%	100%	100%	100%

Source: U.S. Bureau of Labor Statistics, Labor Force Statistics from the Current Population Survey, Table A10.

Asian-American employees are distributed into five broad occupational categories, with the data broken out for men and women separately. In reading this table, it is important to keep in mind the fact that these occupational categories (defined by the U.S. Census) are extremely broad, encompassing jobs that are themselves heterogeneous. Still, even using these relatively broad categories, the table reveals a number of important points.

First, whites remain much more likely to hold the most prestigious and rewarding jobs in the labor force than are either African Americans or Latinos. The modal occupational category for white men is that of management and professional work, which accounts for just under a third (33.2 percent) of all jobs held by this group. Only 1 in 6 white men (or 17.3 percent) hold jobs in production, transportation, and material moving occupations. This means that white men are roughly two times more likely to hold managerial and professional jobs than to work as production workers or truck drivers. Asian Americans, too, seem overrepresented in jobs providing the highest levels of job rewards (though other studies suggest that they often find themselves tracked into technical staff positions).

Second, and in sharp contrast with the positions held by whites, both African American and Latino males are significantly over-represented in manual jobs. Thus the single largest occupational category for African Americans is the production, transportation, and material moving category – the very semi-skilled, manual occupations that are relatively uncommon for white men. Latinos, finally, are clustered in the "construction, maintenance and natural resource" category (especially, in positions as laborers). Much the same pattern of racial and ethnic disparities

exists among women, although not quite in so pronounced a form.

The most obvious way of accounting for these occupational disparities is to point toward differences in each group's levels of education and training. This approach is especially emphasized by economists who use what is called the "human capital" perspective. In this approach, occupational attainments (and the earnings they provide) are viewed as a function of the social choices which individual employees have made, especially with respect to their willingness to invest in education, training, and marketable expertise. The argument here is that these unequal levels of representation across racial and ethnic groups might well be attributed to inequalities in the levels of human capital each has attained.

One problem with this perspective is that it focuses on the characteristics of the labor *supply–* that is, the qualifications of the workers themselves. In so doing, it tends to neglect influences rooted in the *demand* for labor (in other words, influences rooted in the work organization and the practices of employers). And indeed, the literature provides several reasons to believe that the occupational disparities under discussion here cannot be explained through attention to levels of human capital alone.

To begin with, studies have consistently revealed racial disparities in the distribution of job rewards such as hiring, pay, and promotions, even when job qualifications are held constant. This point is evident in a number of ways. For example, data suggest that the hiring process varies in subtle ways for blacks and whites. Whites are more likely to find jobs through informal "sponsorship networks" that place little emphasis on formal credentials, while black applicants tend to be evaluated more strictly on the basis of their educational credentials and experience (Wilson 1997; Royster 2003). "Audit" studies conducted by the Urban Institute, a policy-oriented think tank, sent carefully trained white and minority (including Latino) researchers to apply for jobs using equivalent applications, dress, and behavior, with Chicago and Washington, DC serving as the sites for these tests. The results revealed that in roughly 80 percent of the cases, white and minority applicants received approximately equal treatment —that is, similar proportions of whites and minorities were given job applications, called back for interviews, or actually offered positions. Yet in roughly one in six job applications, the white applicants enjoyed opportunities that were denied to their equally qualified minority counterparts (receiving applications, getting interviews, or actually being hired when similarly qualified minorities did not). In 14.8 percent of the audits, the white job seeker was offered a job while the minority job seeker was not. In only 5.3 percent of all applications was the minority applicant favored in this way (Heckman and Siegelman 1992). Some recent studies have even found that job applications using "African American" sounding names receive less favorable treatment than applications filed with racially neutral names, even when qualifications have been held constant (as discussed in Chapter 3). Accumulated over the course of months and years, such disparities in access to opportunity can have substantial effects on personal careers, earnings, exposure to unemployment, and perceptions of fairness as well.

Data also suggest that, once hired, minority workers enjoy less access to positions that confer authority—for example, jobs supervising or managing other employees—than do whites with similar experience and credentials. This pattern was first identified by Kluegel (1978), who found that black workers were significantly less likely to receive promotions to positions of authority, even when education, experience, and skill had been statistically held constant. This bias against minorities seemed to grow more pronounced at the higher levels of the work organization. Kluegel went so far as to suggest that one third of the income disparity between white and black men stemmed from this unequal access to positions of authority. More recent research by Smith (1997) has extended Kluegel's initial results. Using nationally representative survey data over time, Smith has found that minority workers are only half as likely as similarly qualified whites to receive promotions to supervisory or managerial positions. Smith also found no change in this disparity during the period from 1972 to 1994. As did Kluegel, Smith found that racial disparities seemed most pronounced at the upper reaches of the job structure: at the lower rungs of the organizational ladder, the income benefits received by white and black workers in supervisory positions were roughly comparable. As one rises in the job structure, however, authority wielded by whites seems to provide much sharper income returns than is the case for minorities. These disparities often seem more pronounced in private firms than in public or civil service organizations. Likewise, in firms and industries that do significant business with government (and thus come under closer scrutiny), these disparities are reduced (Baldi and McBrier 1997; Smith 1997, 2001, 2002; Maume 1999).

Additional evidence about the prevalence of occupational segregation by race is found in a recent study by the economist Darrick Hamilton (2006), who sought to use much more detailed occupational categories than are found in Table 12.1, and which again took human capital variables into account. Hamilton used Census data on the racial composition of 475 detailed occupational categories in the year 2000. He calculated the degree to which minorities were under-represented, fairly represented, or over-represented in each job, relative to the number of black men whose levels of education and training would have made them eligible for employment in each of these job categories. His findings revealed several important points. First, black men tend to be sharply under-represented in (in Hamilton's terms, "crowded out" of) the most highly rewarding occupations. This pattern affected roughly 45 percent of the jobs in Hamilton's study. A second and almost equally pervasive pattern is one in which black men are significantly *over*-represented in (or "crowded into") particular occupations, especially among jobs which have become race-typed. This pattern accounted for roughly 40 percent of all jobs in the labor force. The third pattern, in which black men were represented in rough proportion to their numbers in the eligible labor supply, was relatively rare, accounting for only 14 percent of all occupations in the United States. Much as with residential neighborhoods, it seems, occupational integration across the color line is more the exception than the norm.

A final point to consider here is that even when white and minority employees "make it" into the same occupation, substantial differences may still exist with respect to career opportunities. This point emerged in several studies by Sharon Collins (1989, 1997), who found that when African Americans gain entry into management positions, the tendency is for blacks to hold positions that are implicitly "racialized"

(that is, confined to dealing with minority issues or minority clientele). Studying the careers of African American managers in leading Chicago corporations, Collins found a strong tendency for blacks to hold jobs on the periphery of corporate job structures. Often, African American managers had been asked to accept positions that were designed to signal the firm's commitment to equal opportunity. Such jobs typically involved community relations or urban affairs positions, or the handling of accounts with black clients and communities. Although these jobs did provide a route into management for a previously excluded group, Collins found that these positions rarely provided blacks with the same chances of promotion to the uppermost echelons of power and authority within the firm as white managers enjoyed. If the structure of corporate management is viewed as constituting a core and a periphery, with core jobs providing more abundant opportunities, the tendency Collins found was for minority managers to occupy positions on the periphery of corporate management (Federal Glass Ceiling Commission 1995).

Much remains unknown about the workings of race and ethnicity within the labor market. Yet a number of suggestions and observations are beginning to emerge. First, although studies of the work situations and opportunities experienced by Latino and Asian workers are only now receiving systematic attention, there are indications that these groups too encounter forms of unequal treatment, though in different ways. Even after allowing for any differences that may flow from language abilities or levels of education, Latinos—themselves heterogeneous by nationality (see Chapter 13)—seem to encounter some of the same obstacles to equal employment opportunity as do African Americans. Although Asians have achieved remarkable success (as shown in Table 12.1), they can nevertheless encounter subtle stereotypes which exclude them from the uppermost reaches of corporate life. A large proportion of the Asian American population which has made it into the ranks of senior executive positions are in stereotypically "Asian" sectors of the economy, such as in high technology.

A second suggestion that is emerging among researchers concerns the importance of socially dominant conceptions of the groups that are viewed as "appropriate" holders of given occupational positions. The notion here is that both employers and the public form taken-for-granted conceptions of who "ought" to hold high-status positions; hence, members of groups that clash with these conceptions are less likely to gain admission into such jobs. This line of thinking is confirmed by Kaufman's national study of the representation of blacks and whites in 1,917 occupations, which concluded that variations in the racial (and gender) composition of jobs stemmed from "widespread employer stereotypes about the race- or sex-typed nature of specific skills and working conditions" (2002: 567). For example, corporations that operate high-status hotels or restaurants may seek to project a particular image of themselves to the public, and thus conceive of the "ideal" employees along high-status lines. Such an image can implicitly exclude minority workers, confining them to positions out of public view. Said one African American man who had applied for many jobs waiting tables in high-status restaurants: "I faxed my qualifications to restaurants and they expressed excitement. Then they saw me in person and the whole conversation changed" (Collins 2000 B1). Certainly, gender seems to affect hiring in restaurant jobs: Neumark (1996: 933) found that the higher a restaurant's prices, the more likely it was that serving jobs would be offered to men, not women.

Third, evidence has accumulated to indicate emerge that the passage of time alone need not address these disparities. Change, it seems, does not follow a linear course. Thus, dramatic strides toward equality were made in the wake of the 1964 Civil Rights Act (which barred discrimination in public accommodations and employment for employers with at least 50 workers), and these gains gathered force through the 1970s. But the decade of the 80s was notable for slowed progress (and even some erosion of gains in employment opportunity; see Smith 2001 for discussion). The most careful analysis of trend lines in racial segregation within work establishments, conducted by Tomaskovic-Devey and his colleagues (2006), finds that although rapid gains were made in the decade and a half following the Civil Rights Act, "black–white workplace desegregation essentially stops after 1980." In fact, there is "some disturbing evidence of resegregation after 1995 in old economy sectors" such as manufacturing and construction (2006: 584).

The reasons for this pattern are still debated, with some theorists stressing economic trends in the mix of jobs while others point to shifts in the political and legal climate (which weakened the enforcement of antidiscrimination laws). Most researchers agree that racial inequality cannot be assumed to disappear on its own account.

A fourth and final point that researchers stress is that racial disparities often flow from social and organizational processes that are quite different from and much more complex than direct discrimination (that is, the denial of equal treatment on the basis of overt prejudice). As shown below, theorists disagree on the precise mechanisms that account for the persistence of racial and ethnic disparities. Despite this disagreement, analysts generally agree that racial disparities in the distribution of opportunity are so deeply rooted in the structure and culture of work organizations as to outstrip the capacity of individuals to grasp the biased consequences of the firm's practices. In a sense, racial disparities are often invisible to the actors involved, who may in fact misperceive the dynamics in which they are immersed.

An example of this last point can be found in the influential work of William Julius Wilson (1996), mentioned previously. A massive study of race and work within the Chicago metropolitan area, part of Wilson's study surveyed 179 employers in the inner-city areas of the city. Wilson's data indicated the presence of widespread stereotypes about African American workers, whom employers often viewed as lazy, irresponsible, and untrustworthy. Many employers also viewed black workers as unresponsive to organizational needs and resistant to directions from their supervisors. Wilson concluded that this pattern involved more than simple racism or discrimination, however. For one thing, it was not only white business owners but also black employers who expressed these perceptions. Moreover, Wilson's data suggested that a complex pattern of socioeconomic trends has fostered what seems to be an often-troubled relation between companies and inner-city blacks. Faced with the steady loss of traditional manufacturing jobs to suburban locales and their need to resort to low-wage, high-turnover service jobs, inner-city black workers often develop a sense of falling further and further behind their white and Latino counterparts, and understandably, they grow "resentful in the face of their employment prospects and often manifest or express these feelings

in their harsh, often dehumanizing, low-wage work settings" (1996 144). This tends to "create the widely perception that they are undesirable workers"—in turn fueling the very resentment that employers are likely to perceive.

Explaining Racial and Ethnic Disparities

How then can we explain the prevalence and the persistence of racial and ethnic inequalities at work? Although no comprehensive or agreed-upon theory of such inequalities has yet been devised, a number of middle-range theories have been advanced that have received substantial empirical support and that seem to capture many of the most important conditions that account for the persistence of racial and ethnic inequality at work.

Race and Relative Proportions: The Role of Numbers

One abiding approach in this field has viewed racial and ethnic inequalities as a function of variations in the relative proportions of dominant and minority workers within the firm. Much of this literature has appealed either to Kanter's theory of relative proportions (1977a) or to Blalock's theory of group threat (1967 see also Blumer 1958). As was discussed in the preceding chapter on gender, Kanter's theory would expect to find that the social and cultural barriers to minority worker attainment will be greatest within "skewed" groups (where minority workers comprise only 10 to 15 percent of the total), for under these conditions the dominant group is likely to become aware of any intergroup differences, to exaggerate them, and to impose stereotypes on individual workers even if such preconceived notions don't readily fit. Kanter calls this syndrome the "dynamics of tokenism" and argues that it tends to undermine the likelihood that minority workers will succeed. Thus, heightened visibility will multiply the performance pressures that minority workers face, obliging them to "prove" their worth in ways that dominant group workers must seldom do. Kanter also contends that these dynamics are likely to grow faint as the minority composition becomes more evenly "balanced," for minority workers will enjoy the power of increased numbers, the possibility of refuting ill-fitting stereotypes, and the chance to form alliances among their own ranks. She therefore contends that managers should pay particular attention to the achievement of a critical mass of minority group employees within a given organizational unit, for doing so will open the way for more equitable forms of social interaction that promise to undermine the vicious circle of disadvantage that often engulfs minorities at work.

The group threat view takes a very different approach to the role of relative proportions. Indeed, in this second view, the larger the minority composition in a given work organization or community, the greater will be the resistance to social change. That is, growth in the minority composition of a firm or occupation is expected to produce increased resistance by the dominant group, thus heightening the barriers to minority group attainment. Growth in the minority composition of an occupation can also engender out-migration by dominant group members, resulting in a pattern of race typing and a general devaluation or reduced rewards for the occupation and its new incumbents (much as happens within neighborhoods that undergo white flight).

Although a number of studies have addressed these predictions, the resulting evidence remains complex and contradictory. Reskin, McBrier and Kmec (1999) discuss evidence indicating that minority workers are most harshly evaluated where their relative proportions are low, much as Kanter would predict. Yet other studies seem to favor the group threat perspective, finding, for example, that the larger the minority representation in a given organizational unit, the less favorable are the evaluations of minority workers' skills (Braddock and McPartland 1987; Tienda and Lii 1987) and the lower is the chance of its members gaining a promotion (Baldi and McBrier 1997; Maume 1999). The matter remains unresolved and may be at least partly misleading. Arguably, these two perspectives may not be mutually exclusive possibilities, but may simply identify two distinct forms of racial inequality that emerge at low and high levels of minority composition. In other words, the *form* but not the *level* of racial disparities may vary in accordance with minority composition. Thus, within skewed groups, a pattern of "paternalistic" treatment may arise, while more highly diverse or balanced groups, a more sharply "competitive" or openly conflict-ridden situation may arise (van den Berghe 1967). Whether or not this turns out to be true, the ongoing debate over relative proportions serves to sensitize us to the ways in which structural influences—in this case, the social composition of organizations—can affect patterns of interaction at work across racial and ethnic groups.

"Birds of a Feather": Homophily and Homosocial Reproduction

In his classic study of managers in the 1950s, sociologist Melville Dalton (1959) noted similarities between the social and cultural backgrounds of both senior managers and the assistants they selected for positions as future managers and executives. In a bit of wry humor, Dalton called this process "homosocial reproduction"—a term he coined to refer to the process by which dominant group members tend to recruit newcomers who share in-group characteristics, such as speech patterns, manners, dress, and social background. Two decades later, Kanter (1977a) extended Dalton's reasoning, developing a theory of "homophily"—the preference for one's own group—that has received much discussion and research (see Chapter 7).

Managers must perform tasks that are highly complex, involving decision making under highly ambiguous or uncertain conditions. As a result, they tend to seek out assistants and co-workers who share their orientations and assumptions, thus increasing the level of understanding, trust, and comfort they can take for granted. What results is a kind of cultural exclusivity that works against members of outgroups, whose backgrounds are different from those of the dominant group. Quite apart from any question of merit or qualification, Kanter argued, members of established groups often manifest an in-group preference that, unless disrupted, operates to reinforce or reproduce the unequal distribution of opportunity at work. This is especially true, the theory runs, where hiring and promotions are conducted on the basis of informal or nonbureaucratic procedures, for then friendship networks will influence who gets the really good jobs.

Kanter's argument was framed in terms of the selection of employees for elite positions, but it has broader applicability. Levels of trust and familiarity are likely to affect the distribution of opportunity, from the hiring process to performance on the job itself, even when actors are unaware of their in-group preferences. When hiring depends on informal referrals (a practice that firms often use as a cheap and reliable conduit of information about prospective employees), minority group employees are likely to be excluded (Mouw 2002). Racial boundaries seem to affect the interview process, too: in one study, white interviewers were found to be significantly more anxious when interviewing black job applicants, and sat further away from them than they did from white applicants. Applicants exposed to such discomfort in turn performed less effectively, thus reinforcing disparities in the hiring process (Word, Zanna, and Cooper 1974). Tsui and O'Reilly (1989) found that workers whose racial and ethnic status is different from that of their supervisors are likely to receive lower evaluations than would otherwise be the case, not so much because of overt prejudice, but rather because of intergroup tensions and misunderstandings. Finally, a number of studies have found that paths to promotion are differentially shaped for dominant and minority group employees. For minority group members, attaining a supervisory position seems to depend much more heavily on formal educational credentials and experience than is the case for whites (Wilson 1997; Smith 2001).

Informal Networks and Access to Employment Opportunity

Implied in the foregoing discussion is an important point that sociologists of work have long taken stressed: people do not enter into jobs as isolated individuals. Rather, finding a job and performing well within it (which often means counting on social support of one's co-workers) is often influenced by the social networks and groups in which one is embedded (see Ch. 1). This makes perfect sense. Think about the jobs you have held, and chances are that someone you knew—a relative, an acquaintance, a neighbor—played some role in your hiring, whether by providing information at just the right time, helping to arrange an interview, or singing your praises to a person in a position of some authority. The point here is that not everyone is equally positioned to benefit from such informal affiliations. Some of us are placed at a further distance than others from key sources of information and influence.

A recent study by Royster (2003) illustrates how informal networks play a role in generating racial and ethnic disparities. Royster studied a cohort of working class youth who had been graduated from Glendale Vocational High School in Baltimore, Maryland. This school, like many others, seeks to provide young students with the job skills needed to win secure, well-paying jobs in skilled manual occupations—the stuff of the American dream. Following up students who completed their schooling in 1990, Royster compared the work and career experiences of white and black students holding the same qualifications (and, it turns out, similar grades, attitudes toward work, and behavioral records at school and thereafter). She finds stark differences in the labor market experiences of the two racial groups: black youth took longer to make the transition into jobs, experienced more frequent and longer bouts of unemployment, and generally enjoyed much less success in securing good jobs than did whites. The reason had little to do with the attitudes or preferences of the workers: all held much the same values and aspirations. Rather, a key reason for these racial differences was rooted in the social networks in which these young job

seekers were embedded. White workers enjoyed more supportive relations with school counselors and teachers and were more strongly positioned within networks that linked them to information about and ties to prospective employers (many of whom had themselves attended schools much like Glendale). Having been historically excluded from the nucleus of economic institutions, the families and communities in which black youth were embedded simply lacked the connections that white youth enjoyed. Worse, many of the whites in Royster's study were convinced that government intervention had stacked the deck against *them*—that is, against white workers—and thus tended to view what advantages they held as morally justified, in that they served to correct a playing field they believed was no longer truly level.

Royster's study and others like it illustrate many important points. First, most Americans seem to believe that, left to themselves, labor markets tend to operate in a racially neutral fashion, with the "invisible hand" of the marketplace distributing opportunities in accordance with merit and determination. In this view, the only "visible" hand is that of the government, which seeks to redistribute opportunity in a predetermined way. Yet the data indicate that things are not quite this simple. How workers fare within labor markets and work organizations depends in significant ways on the ability of their groups to provide strategic resources (such as information about jobs, informal affiliations with employers, and support for the acquisition of skills once on the job). And research repeatedly finds that these resources are by no means distributed equally (MacLeod 1995; Mouw 2002). Instead, they continue, in subtle yet significant ways, to reflect the legacy of the past.

Government Efforts to Uproot Racial and Ethnic Disparities

A large body of research has shown that the passage of civil rights laws beginning in the 1960s dramatically changed employment practices in many quarters of the United States. The overall effect has been to reduce the most egregious forms of overt discrimination, opening up greater opportunities for minority groups and, in turn, accounting for many of the economic and social gains experienced by minorities in the latter half of the twentieth century (Heckman and Payner 1989; Burstein and Edwards 1994). Yet beyond these general comments, the story becomes more complex and more intriguing.

Civil Rights and Affirmative Action

The first thing to note about the civil rights policies that crystallized in the 1960s is that they largely reversed long-standing federal tolerance for racial segregation on the job. Partly reflecting political pressure from conservative southern Democrats, U.S. presidents had been loath to challenge the Jim Crow laws that excluded many African Americans from well-paying jobs. Even the New Deal legislation of the 1930s, which sought to provide an economic floor beneath many economically vulnerable groups, specifically excluded from coverage jobs held by many African Americans. Indeed, it was only with the emergence of large-scale civil rights demonstrations that President Franklin Roosevelt signed an executive order supporting equal employment rights in 1941. Until the 1960s, the federal government largely permitted labor organizations to maintain racially segregated local unions (a fact that in effect worked to exclude many black workers from skilled manual occupations). As

the civil rights movement gained momentum, and as pressures grew in support of policies protecting racial equality, federal policy changed significantly.

One key step was passage of the 1964 Civil Rights Act, Title VII of which banned employment discrimination on the basis of race, sex, and national origin, with similar provisions extended to include age, religion, and disabilities. The Act also established the Equal Employment Opportunities Commission (EEOC), which was charged with collecting data on workplace opportunities and enforcing the Act. In conjunction with a series of executive orders tightening the EEO rules established by the Office of Federal Contract Compliance, the Civil Rights Act ushered in significant changes in the nature of corporate practices and labor markets, prompting large corporations to restructure their hiring and promotion policies, thereby signaling their intent to provide fair and equitable treatment for employees regardless of ascribed statuses such as race, ethnicity, and gender (Edelman 1990; Sutton et al. 1994). This was indeed a significant shift.

Yet a number of factors have acted to limit the changes achieved by the new civil rights policies. One is that the Civil Rights Act itself specifically excludes many small businesses: those that employ fewer than 50 workers are exempt from its provisions. A second is that while in theory the EEOC has the capacity to bring employers to court for violating civil rights law, in practice the Commission rarely does so, partly because it lacks the legal staff and resources to bring more than a fraction of the transgressors to court. In the late 1990s, the EEOC litigated only a small fraction of the 80,000 complaints filed under its auspices. Third, judicial rulings have tightened the legal standards of proof and evidentiary rules needed to demonstrate that firms have violated civil rights law. Courts have increasingly ruled that even glaring statistical disparities in the allocation of job rewards are insufficient in themselves; needed is direct evidence of unequal treatment or prejudicial intent—an extremely difficult test to meet (see Reskin 2003: 11–12). Finally, the courts have ruled that such evidence must be presented immediately after any alleged instances of discrimination have occurred. Thus *Ledbetter v. Goodyear*, a 2007 ruling by the U.S. Supreme Court imposed tight guidelines on the time period during which discrimination allegations can be filed, instituting a six-month time period that significantly narrows the possibility of filing suit.

Perhaps the most hotly debated aspect of civil rights policy has centered on affirmative action, a term first introduced as part of Executive Order 11246 issued by the Johnson administration in 1965, which directed federal contractors to "take affirmative action to ensure that applicants are employed . . . without regard to their race, creed, color, or national origin." The order was part of a federal effort to encourage employers and educational institutions to formulate actual plans of action, rather than mere rhetoric, to achieve demonstrable progress —not only with respect to race and ethnicity, but *also* to gender inequalities as well.

Affirmative action has served as a lightning rod for criticism in recent years as opponents and advocates have engaged in sharp debate over the morality and fairness of this policy. Specifically, accusations of reverse discrimination have mounted, producing litigation and state referendums that have sharply narrowed the scope of affirmative action policies. Unfortunately, there seems to be a large gap between public views of affirmative action and the evidence that scholars have generated with respect to its actual impact. Although large proportions of the American public view affirmative action as having an unfair and adverse effect on employment opportunities for members of the dominant group, there is little empirical evidence of such adverse effects. Data suggest that, apart from a handful of highly celebrated cases, a very small proportion of dominant group populations has been adversely affected by the policy. Fewer than 2 percent of the 91,000 EEOC cases filed in 1999 alleged reverse discrimination, and surveys find that few white respondents have themselves experienced adverse effects attributable to affirmation action. Moreover, the beneficial impact of affirmative action has been limited to a small stratum of employees who were well positioned to take advantage of its effects. This set of circumstances—a policy that has had modest effects, yet has provoked a massive controversy—led Jennnifer Hochschild (1997) to suggest that affirmative action has become part of the larger culture war in the United States. Precisely because the policy's effects are so ambiguous, it provides the perfect issue with which groups advocating different values can demarcate their opposing views.

Although much research remains to be done on the corporate practices that actually lead to equality in the distribution of job opportunities, one recent study has produced an interesting pattern of findings. Kalev, Kelly, and Dobbin (2006) conducted one of the most systematic comparisons of the efficacy of different corporate approaches toward racial and ethnic equality and reported an interesting pattern of results. Using official reports on the composition of management jobs at U.S. establishments during the years 1970 to 2002, and combining these data with surveys on the practices that corporations use to achieve greater diversity, Kalev and colleagues found that some of the most prevalent human resource practices either provide no benefit at all or else actually set back the cause of racial diversity. Diversity training (which tries to overcome managerial biases) did surprisingly little to equalize access to management jobs. Efforts to establish mentoring and networking programs likewise had little positive effect. What seemed to produce meaningful change in the social composition of management ranks were efforts to build responsibility for equal opportunity into particular committees, departments, or task forces. When responsibility for achieving gains in equal opportunity is built into the organizational structure, with provisions for holding distinct units of the firm accountable for the result, the subsequent pattern is one of significantly greater racial and gender equality.

Corporate Change and the Management of Diversity

Partly because of public reluctance to embrace the concept of affirmative action, and partly due to the newly competitive climate that has enveloped the business world, corporate approaches to racial and ethnic disparities have evolved in new directions since the late 1980s. Empirical study of management journals, for example, begins to track a shift that leads away from a concern with civil rights and its legal expectations toward a somewhat more ambiguous concept of "diversity," defined in such a way as to include not only racial and gender differences but also differences based on age, lifestyle, occupational background, and even cognitive style. Advocates of this shift have often claimed that greater workforce diversity tends to promote

higher levels of performance on the part of the work groups involved. The logic here expects that diverse work groups will be able to consider multiple approaches toward particular tasks, to understand their tasks more fully, and thus avoid the parochial approaches that may confine the thinking of socially uniform groups (Ancona and Caldwell 1992; Williams and O'Reilly 1998; van Knippenberg et al. 2004). Conscious of the need to signal broad acceptance of progressive ideals, corporations have used the diversity concept in their advertising, promotional materials, and internal documents regarding employee philosophy.

Although much remains to be established about the management of diversity, several conclusions have begun to emerge in the empirical research. First, it seems clear that the impact of diversity on organizational effectiveness is much more complex than was initially assumed. Although some studies have indeed found that diverse work groups perform at higher levels than uniform or less heterogeneous ones, other studies have reported the opposite results. At times, diversity in terms of race, gender, or job tenure has actually hampered the performance of the work group, for example, by lowering the level of group cohesion, or by making it more difficult for group members to reach consensus about key tasks or to exchange important information. Diversity has at times also increased the frequency of social conflict among the members of the group (Lichtenstein et al. 1997; Knight et al. 1999; Townsend and Scott 2001). In one study of banking employees, diversity had *beneficial* effects among work groups where the companies were expanding their operations—but *negative* effects within companies that were laying off employees (Richard 2000). Clearly, the effects of diversity are complex and will depend on the social and organizational context in which employees are embedded.

A second point that has emerged in the literature concerns the concept of diversity itself. Rather than taking this concept as a given, a recent study by Lauren Edelman and her colleagues has asked why the diversity concept has been embraced so widely within the corporate world (see Edelman, Fuller, and Mara-Drita 2001). To explore this concept, Edelman et al. compiled a data base of all articles published in 18 leading management journals from 1975 to 1996. Their findings are revealing. First, beginning in the early 1980s they find a broad downward trend in managerial references to civil rights concepts and concerns. Second, they find a sharply rising emphasis on "diversity," defined in a way that is not only more ambiguous, but that is also only partially related to legal rights and obligations. In a sense, the diversity concept is a "managerialized" version of civil rights concerns, in which human resource concerns have taken the place of legally enforceable rights and obligations. Third, the corporate approach toward diversity has often been tied the pursuit of diversity to the pursuit of lucrative markets—an approach in which diversity is defined as enhancing corporate access to certain categories of clients and to market niches that diversity can provide. In practice, this has often meant that corporations have defined diversity in highly instrumental terms—that is, not as a value in its own right, but as a necessary step that the corporations must take if they are to gain access to desired markets for their goods. The mixed message this sends to employees who are different can be sensed in the following statements reported by Edelman et al. (2001: 1614):

While society has not succeeded in producing a true melting pot, employers have no choice [but to do so]. It is not a question of political correctness; it is a matter of survival.... Simply put, there are not enough white males to fill all of the jobs available in the American economy.

"Managing diversity" is fast becoming the corporate watchword of the decade—not because corporations are becoming kinder and gentler toward culturally diverse groups but because they want to survive.

The notion here is that cultural conceptions have not changed, but that business imperatives require a shift in hiring practices, however reluctantly and (at times) out of financial necessity.

Evidence has begun to emerge that such mixed messages can have an adverse effect on the quality of employment that minority group employees encounter on the job. Thus, Robin Ely and David Thomas (2001) developed case studies in three different business contexts—a public interest law firm, a financial services firm, and a business consulting company. They found starkly different perspectives toward the value of diversity. In the law firm there was a genuine appreciation for the cultural lessons and breadth of understanding that flowed from an inclusive approach toward minority hiring. This diversity perspective—which the authors called an "integration and learning" approach—involved minority employees (professionals and staff alike) in the life of the firm in highly meaningful ways. In the financial services firm, by contrast, diversity was largely defined as a business asset—that is, as a tool with which to win the business of minority customers. This second perspective—an "access and legitimacy" perspective—implicitly led toward segregated business operations. Financial analysts handling black or Latino accounts were themselves minority employees, while those handling the most lucrative, elite accounts tended to be white. The final diversity perspective that Ely and Thomas found—a "discrimination and fairness" approach—defined diversity in numerical terms. Here, having high numbers of minority employees was viewed as a sign that any racial barriers had been overcome and that a race-blind workplace had been achieved. The irony here was that this last approach toward diversity tended to foster a pattern of racial conflict and competition, even as the notion of a race-blind workplace prevented employees from openly discussing the meaning of racial diversity. What this study suggests, and what the literature on diversity has begun to show, is that how organizations define the meaning and the value of diversity will have highly significant effects on the patterns of social interaction that develop among different groups of employees.

Economic Restructuring and Racial Inequality

One concern that deserves wider debate than it has received concerns the growing danger that economic trends have powerfully counteracted government and corporate efforts to achieve greater equality of employment opportunity. Thus, the suburbanization of capital investments, the erosion of manufacturing jobs in older urban areas, and the increasing tendency for economic growth to occur in exurban areas, may all combine to generate trends that place minority employees at a particular disadvantage. Thus, some theorists have suggested that the labor market has been characterized by a widening "spatial mismatch," in that the demand for labor is structurally distant from regions in which job seekers

are found in abundance (Wilson 1987). As capital migrates to areas not easily accessible from metropolitan areas, geographic barriers intrude, creating problems in balancing labor supply and demand which the market alone cannot easily solve.

This argument, which has fueled much research, has gained increasing urgency with the growth of high-technology firms, industries, and occupations, inasmuch as these sectors— e.g., information technology, communications, software engineering, science intensive industries, and other fields—have long been disproportionately composed of dominant group employees, or else of highly educated employees who are imported from abroad. As these science-intensive areas gain strategic importance, and as other sectors of the economy suffer either from fierce global competition (as in manufacturing) or from depressed wage levels (as in many service industries), the danger is that an increasing gulf will open up between dominant and minority groups, undoing the gains of the last few decades. Moreover, given the trend toward "team" based systems of work organization (discussed in Ch. 15 below), employers often demand not only "hard skills" (technical proficiency in a particular field) but also "soft skills" (the ability to interact well with others or to avoid conflict). The issue, as emphasized by Moss and Tilly (2001), is that the ambiguous meaning of "soft skills" can open the door to the use of stereotyped conceptions of workers and their abilities. In their multi-industry study of employers in four different cities, Moss and Tilly found that employers have highly detailed conceptions of the abilities of different groups of employees and often link these to hiring preferences. The danger is that as new forms of skill are required, an ambiguity in job definitions arises that may operate to exclude job seekers in subtle yet highly significant ways.

Conclusion

In this chapter we have discussed the ways in which racially exclusive arrangements have operated to limit the employment opportunities for racial and ethnic minorities. In a sense, the literature we have reviewed is indicative of a huge gulf in thinking about race and work. Overwhelmingly, people seem to get along well with one another at work, and, indeed, the workplace is likely one of the most important sites in which social interaction occurs across racial and ethnic lines. But in the public arena, there is a wide disparity in the beliefs that people bring to bear on social policies designed to equalize the playing field. Indeed, a majority of dominant group employees feel that the major problem we face is one of reverse discrimination—the notion that racial preferences have moved so far in the direction of minority groups as to disadvantage innocent whites.

As this chapter suggests, there is little evidence in support of this notion—and much evidence that hidden biases have continued to operate at work, whether in hiring, promotions, job evaluations, or pay. Such biases are at times built into the relative proportions of work groups and organizations or into the tendency toward homophily which workers often exhibit. They may be rooted in a sense of group threat that dominant groups experience. Often they operate invisibly, fostering resentment and discontent that are difficult to detect. The emergence of new conceptions of social difference—most notably the concept of diversity—represents organizational developments that may have certain virtues. Thus, by adopting broad notions of cultural difference, the concept of diversity may operate to blur racial and ethnic boundaries that might otherwise seem salient or even inflamed. On the other hand, the concept of diversity may represent a corporate retreat from the commitment to the ideals that drove the civil rights movement. Only time—and systematic research on these questions—will tell.

Chapter 13

Immigrant Workers: Marginal Work, Networks, and Entrepreneurship

To a greater extent than any other industrialized society, the United States has been and remains a country of immigrant workers. In the ten years before World War I, for example, an average of 1 million people a year entered the United States (many of whom ended up working at companies such as Ford Motors). Although immigration dropped sharply in the years between World War I and World War II, today more than a million people a year continue to migrate to the United States. The result is that nearly 12 percent of the U.S. civilian population—around 36 million people—are foreign-born.

Although immigration is one of the defining features of the American experience, the surge in immigration since 1970 is unprecedented even by U.S. standards. In 1970, there were fewer than 10 million foreign-born inhabitants in the country, representing less than 5 percent of the total population (Gibson and Lennon 1999). Today there are over three times as many foreign-born residents in the country as there were in 1970, and their share of the total population is twice what it was. Much of this immigration has taken place since 1990: over 15 million legal immigrants entered the country between 1990 and 2006, approximately two thirds from Latin America and Asia.

A third of all legal immigrants came from just four countries: Mexico, the Philippines, China, and India (U.S. Census Bureau 2008). Half of the foreign-born persons live in California, Texas, and New York, but the biggest percentage increase in the foreign-born population has occurred in the South, especially Georgia and North Carolina (Nolan, Baluja, Costanzo, and Davis 2003).

Many foreign-born inhabitants have either entered or remained in the country without authorization. Some crossed the U.S.–Mexican border on foot; others entered the country legally—on tourist or student visas, for example—and remained after their visas have expired. The Census Bureau has estimated that 10.5 million immigrants were in the country illegally in 2005 (U.S. Census Bureau 2008). Today there may be as many as 12 million unauthorized immigrants living in the United States, and it has been estimated that an additional 400,000 to 500,000 enter the country each year (Passel 2005).

Illegal immigrants—also known as undocumented workers—perform many of the low-wage, physically demanding jobs that citizens and legal immigrants avoid. They build houses, install roofs and drywall, process pork and poultry, plant, tend, and harvest fruits and vegetables, mow lawns and landscape yards, wash dishes and clothes, and clean rooms and care for children. Without the legal right to live and work in the United States, with little knowledge of the rights they do have, and with limited English skills, these workers are often at the mercy of their employers. The following portrait of laundry workers in New York City in 2004 demonstrates how easy it is for employers to take advantage of such immigrants:

For the many New Yorkers who dread spending two hours in a noisy, often smelly laundry washing and drying their clothes, it is a godsend that most laundries will handle that unpleasant chore for them and for as little as $5 a load.

But few customers pay attention to the thousands of "wash and fold" workers—most of them women from Mexico—who actually handle their laundry. They are among the most anonymous laborers in New York. In humid basements and backrooms around the city, they shovel clothes in and out of washers and dryers, matching socks and folding hundreds of towels and undergarments each day.

Most laundry workers earn less, often far less, than the minimum wage of $5.15 an hour. Gabriela Mendez, a veteran of six Manhattan laundries, said one paid her $230, or $3.19 an hour, for a 72-hour week, while at another she earned $220, or $2.45 an hour, for a 90-hour week.

She and other workers boil over with tales of oppressive conditions or abusive bosses. Some said their employers hit them for taking a long lunch or fired them for being out sick for a day; others said they saw co-workers collapse from the heat. "The laundry pays us less because they're able to," said Inriqueta G., an illegal immigrant who works at a laundry in the Brighton Beach section of Brooklyn. (Greenhouse 2004a)

The treatment of workers described here is not in fact legal. Undocumented workers are still protected by most U.S. labor laws, even if they are in the country illegally. Owners of laundries, garment factories, and other businesses may be able to get away with paying their workers less than the minimum wage and no overtime—indeed, according to government reports, sweatshop conditions have become widespread in some workplaces in Los Angeles and New York (Bonacich and Appelbaum 2000)—but such treatment is against the law. The Fair Labor Standards Act, for example, requires workers to be paid at the overtime rate of 1.5 times their regular rate of pay after they have worked 40 hours in a workweek.

Although it is the presence and treatment of undocumented workers that has generated most of the discussion of U.S. immigration policy, there is another group of foreign-born workers at the other end of the socioeconomic spectrum whose contribution to the American economy is equally noteworthy. Over 27 percent of foreign-born individuals have at least a bachelor's degree (exactly the same percentage as that of the native-born). The foreign-born are just under 12 percent of the population, but they are more than 14 percent of all dentists, nearly 16 percent of pharmacists, and nearly 25 percent of all physicians and surgeons (Lowell and Gerova 2004). Some recent studies have suggested that a large proportion of high-tech businesses are started up by immigrant entrepreneurs.

The above statistics suggest that immigration into the United States is not random. In fact it takes two forms. At the bottom of the occupational ladder are immigrants from Central America and the Caribbean, often from rural areas of such countries as Mexico, the Dominican Republic, El Salvador, and Guatemala. Most have less than a 9th-grade education, and many have entered the country illegally. Slightly more than half (52 percent) of the 36 million foreign-born inhabitants of the United States were from Latin America and the Caribbean. At the top of the occupational ladder are immigrants from Asia, Europe, and Africa. The Asian-born account for just over one quarter (26 percent) of all immigrants; the remaining 22 percent were born in other countries and regions including Canada, Europe, Africa, and Oceania (Larsen 2004). Most of the immigrants in this second category have some education beyond the high-school level. About half of those from Asia have a college degree, as do about one third of those born in the other regions (Larsen 2004).

The desire of many educated people all around the world to live and to work in the United States explains why the country benefits from a significant "brain gain": far more skilled workers (those with a postsecondary education) enter it than leave it. The net U.S. brain gain as of 2000 stood at nearly 10 million workers; next highest was Canada with a net gain of a little over 2 million workers. To put it another way, at the present time about half of all skilled migrants in the world live in the United States (Docquier and Marfouk 2006).

The differences in educational levels between Latin America immigrants and those from Europe and Asia are reflected in the occupations they enter once in the United States. As Table 13.1 shows, immigrants from Europe, Asia, and other parts of the world are more likely to be managers and professionals than are Latin American immigrants—they are actually more likely to be in these jobs than are U.S.-born workers. Conversely, Latin American immigrants are more likely to be operators, fabricators, laborers, and farm workers than are immigrants from any other region or U.S.-born workers.

In this chapter we will examine both kinds of immigrants—those with little education and those who are highly educated. We start by asking why migrants want to leave their native countries and why American employers want to hire them. Second, we consider where immigrants go once they get to this country and how they are recruited to the jobs they hold. Third, we examine those immigrants who are entrepreneurs, i.e., those

TABLE 13.1 Percentage Distribution of Occupation of Employed Persons in the United States by World Region of Birth, 2000

OCCUPATIONAL GROUP	U.S.-BORN	EUROPE	ASIA	LATIN AMERICA	OTHER
Managers and professionals	31.0	37.9	38.9	11.8	36.3
Technical, sales, and administrative support	30.7	24.0	27.3	16.3	21.5
Service	13.1	15.1	15.0	22.7	16.7
Precision production, craft and repair	10.5	12.2	6.0	16.2	7.3
Operators, fabricators and laborers	12.6	10.2	12.1	25.1	15.9
Farming, forestry, and fishing	2.1	0.6	0.7	7.9	2.4

Source: Hagan 2004.

who have opened their own businesses following their arrival in the United States.

Migration of the Poor: Mexicans, Central Americans, and Filipinos

The Roots of Migration: Geography, History, and Poverty

Geographical proximity, historical and familial ties, and economic opportunities all determine if the poor will migrate and where they will go. Consider, for example, the relationship between Mexico and the United States. The long and porous border between these neighbors, combined with their intertwined histories, enables and encourages people to move from one country to the other. The higher wages and better employment prospects available in the United States, in addition to family and other connections to those already in the country, mean that poor Mexicans have a strong incentive to migrate northward. Finally, the North American Free Trade Agreement (NAFTA) has opened up the Mexican economy to American trade and investment, often displacing Mexican workers in agriculture and sometimes in manufacturing, pushing workers northward in search of jobs. Given all of these factors, it is not surprising that Mexican migrants constitute such a large share of the legal and illegal immigrant population. The Mexican-born make up one third of the total foreign-born population and more than two thirds of all unauthorized immigrants (Borjas and Katz 2005; U.S. Census Bureau 2008). A similar combination of factors accounts for the presence of many poor North Africans in Europe as well as the absence of poorly educated Mexicans from Europe and of poorly educated North Africans from the United States.

Mexicans and Central Americans have come to the United States to escape poverty. They are mostly young men with less than a high-school education from villages and rural areas, although an increasing percentage of migrants are women (see Box 13.1). They may have had to pay as much as $1,500 to a "coyote" or smuggler to get them into the United States, a dangerous and sometimes deadly trip, particularly if they make the border crossing through the Arizona desert. Nearly half of all Mexican male migrants have in recent years found employment as operatives and laborers, farm workers, gardeners, and cooks. About half of all female migrants work as operatives, domestic servants, clerical workers, farm workers, and cooks (see Table 13.2). These jobs are often hard, dirty, and low-paying. They include, for example, carpet manufacturing, poultry processing, and citrus- and tomato-picking. Nevertheless, they pay far better than jobs in Mexico where workers might make $5 a day—one tenth of what they can earn in the United States.

In some cases, migration to the United States reflects history more than geography. The second largest group of immigrants to the United States over the last twenty-five years has been Filipinos, a fact that can be attributed to the long and close relationship between the United States and the Philippines. The United States acquired the Philippines from Spain in 1898 as part of the settlement of the Spanish-American War. The country remained a U.S. possession until 1934, when it acquired commonwealth status; during this period Filipinos were free to migrate to the United States. In 1946, the country gained full independence. Immigration from the Philippines, which had declined sharply after 1934 due to the country's changed status and to anti-Asian immigration

BOX 13.1 *More and More, Women Risk All to Enter U.S.*

It took years for Normaeli Gallardo, a single mother from Acapulco, to drum up the courage to join the growing stream of Mexican women illegally crossing the border on the promise of a job, in her case working in a Kansas meatpacking plant for $5.15 an hour.

First, she had to grapple with the idea of landing in an unfamiliar country, all alone, with no grasp of English and no place to live.

Then she had to imagine crossing the Arizona desert, where immigrants face heat exhaustion by day, frostbite by night and the cunning of the "coyotes"—smugglers who charge as much as $1,500 to guide people into the United States and who make a habit of robbing and sexually assaulting them.

And finally, Ms. Gallardo, 38, who earned $50 a week at an Acapulco hotel, had to contemplate life without her two vivacious daughters, Isabel, 7, and Fernanda, 5. That once unimaginable trade-off—leaving her children behind so they could one day leave poverty behind—had suddenly become her only option.

She simply did not earn enough money, she said. If she paid the electric bill, she fell behind on rent; if she paid the water bill, she could forget about new clothes for the children.

"My heart broke; my heart broke," said Ms. Gallardo, who crumbled as she recounted her decision to leave her girls with her sister and make the uncertain journey across the border. "But I had to give them a better life. I told them I would go and work, and we could buy a small plot of land and build a little house and have a dog."

Undaunted by a backlash against illegal immigrants here, Ms. Gallardo is part of what some experts say is a largely unnoticed phenomenon: the increasing number of women, many without male companions, enduring danger and the risk of capture to come to the United States to work and to settle.

As many as 11 million illegal immigrants are thought to be living and working in the United States, though estimates vary.

No one knows how many people illegally cross the Mexico-United States border, trekking through the desert, hiding in cars and trucks, or walking through points of entry with false papers. But academics, immigration advocates and Border Patrol agents all agree that the number of women making the trip is on the rise.

Katharine Donato, an associate professor of sociology at Rice University in Houston who studies Mexican migration to the United States, estimates that as many as 35 percent to 45 percent of those crossing the border illegally today are women. Twenty years ago, fewer than 20 percent of the people crossing illegally were women, she said.

The increase, which has occurred gradually, comes at a time when anger over illegal immigration is on the upswing, especially in states near the border. Some of that anger is directed at women who have babies in American hospitals and send their children to public schools.

The House recently passed a hard-hitting bill that seeks to beef up border enforcement and make it a federal crime to live in the United States illegally.

But to most of the women who cross the border, the debate over illegal immigration and the ire of taxpayers has little bearing, if any, on the difficult decision they make to undertake the journey. "'Vale la pena,'" said Kat Rodriguez, an organizer for the Human Rights Coalition

BOX **13.1** *continued*

in Tucson, echoing a refrain among the women. "'It's worth it.'"

Some women cross simply to keep their families together and join their husbands after long separations, a situation that has grown more pronounced since the Border Patrol agency began stepping up enforcement 10 years ago. With the border more secure in California and Texas, many people are now being funneled into the rugged territory of Arizona—an effort that virtually requires the help of an expensive coyote to cross successfully.

Yet a growing number of single women, like Ms. Gallardo, are coming not to join husbands, but to find jobs, send money home and escape a bleak future in Mexico. They come to find work in the booming underground economy, through a vast network of friends and relatives already employed here as maids, cooks, kitchen helpers, factory workers and baby sitters. In these jobs, they can earn double or triple their Mexican salaries.

"It remains a story about family reunification, but the proportion of women coming to the U.S. who are not married and working full time has gone up substantially," Professor Donato said. "So we see the single migrant woman motivated by economic reasons coming to the United States that we saw very little of 30 years ago."

Still, the promise of a sweeter future often goes unfulfilled.

Ms. Gallardo never made it to Kansas. She never made it beyond the desert. After walking eight hours at night and committing $500 to a coyote, she stumbled down a rocky hill near Tucson and broke her ankle. The coyote left her sitting on a nearby highway in the desert, where the Border Patrol eventually found her, took her to a local emergency room and deported her to Nogales, Mexico, the next day.

A Mexican immigrant group, Grupo Beta, took her to a Mexican hospital where she was told she needed surgery on her ankle at a cost of 3,000 pesos, or seven weeks' salary. She also owes the friends who gave the coyote $500.

A month and a half earlier, Margarita Ximil Lopez, 20, had her hopes dashed, too. She sat in a dismal holding cell at the United States Border Patrol station in Nogales in October and tried to hide her tears from her son, Edel, who is about to turn 6.

It was for his sake, she said, that she illegally crossed the border, only to be abandoned by the coyote and picked up at a motel by American immigration officers. Ms. Ximil, from Puebla, a large city southeast of Mexico City, had hoped to join her sister, who had lined up a job for her as a waitress in Los Angeles.

Here in Arizona, a tide of anti-immigrant sentiment has swelled along with the number of border crossers, some of it directed particularly at women. Many taxpayers say they resent that their tax dollars are being spent to educate these women's children and pay for their delivery costs at local hospitals....

The nation's roiling immigration debate weighs little on the minds of the women who cross here. Nor do the dangers of the crossing itself, which they know routinely include sexual harassment or assault. As the borders have become tighter, the coyotes have become more violent and desperate, law enforcement officials and immigration advocates say.

"These poor aliens are nothing but product to these animals," said Mr. Hawkins, adding that

BOX **13.1** *continued*

many women are raped, robbed and abandoned at the first sign of trouble and are given amphetamines to keep them moving faster at night.

Since most women do not come forward to report the crimes—because they don't speak the language and are illegal, ashamed and scared of deportation—few hard numbers exist. But there is ample anecdotal information to bolster the claim.

Maria Jimenez, 29, who is from Oaxaca and came here to work and join her husband, has experienced most of what can go wrong. The first time she crossed into Arizona three years ago, she was told by a coyote to expect a three-hour evening walk across the desert. She packed no water. The journey took two nights and three days, and Ms. Jimenez grew desperately dizzy and disoriented.

Then the coyote, an American, tried to sexually assault her and her sister-in-law, she said. "I told him no," Ms. Jimenez said. "I started to cry." He left her alone, but robbed her of the $300 in her pocket. Then just as they neared a highway, the Border Patrol arrested the group.

She tried again a month later carrying drinks with electrolytes but no money in her pocket. She made it, joining her husband in Tucson, where she got a job at a restaurant and had a baby, Stephanie. A family emergency in Oaxaca forced her to return home last year. But in November, she came back into the country, this time with a group of eight people—four of them women she met in Nogales.

During the trip, Ms. Jimenez slipped and fell, spraining her ankle. She wrapped it in discarded clothes strewn across the desert by other immigrants, and she hobbled on.

After a night of walking, they reached the railroad tracks and hopped a freight train to Tucson. Her husband paid the coyote $1,000.

Ms. Jimenez, her husband and baby now share a house with another family. She found work quickly in a restaurant kitchen for $5.25 an hour, no breaks, no sick days.

"We are all scared when we cross," she said. "But the thought that we can help people back home makes it worth it."

SOURCE: Alvarez and Broder 2006.

legislation in the United States, resumed after the passage in 1965 of the Immigration and Nationality Act. This act removed the restrictions on Asian immigration and established family unification as an immigration priority.

An unusual aspect of Filipino immigration to the United States is that it is a microcosm of immigration to the country as a whole. It includes English-speaking professionals who, like other Asians, qualify for entrance because of their occupational skills, and it includes unskilled non–English-speaking workers who are permitted entrance because of family ties. The former normally settle in New York, New Jersey, and California. The latter generally migrate to Hawaii, where the pre-1934 Filipino immigration was concentrated—the original migrants were workers in the sugar fields of that state (Liu, Ong, and Rosenstein 1991).

To explain the employment of Mexican or Filipino immigrants with low levels of education and a lack of proficiency in English, we need to

TABLE 13.2 Top Five Occupations Ranked According to Percentage Share of Employment of Mexican Immigrants

Occupation	Year			
Men	1970	1980	1990	2000
Operatives	18.2	20.1	16.0	15.5
Laborers	11.1	11.7	11.9	11.7
Farm Workers	14.9	10.5	9.5	6.3
Gardeners	2.9	2.6	4.8	5.8
Cooks	1.7	3.3	4.9	5.4
Top 5 total	48.8	48.2	47.1	44.7
Women	1970	1980	1990	2000
Operatives	34.9	35.8	26.9	21.2
Domestic servants	5.4	2.8	4.2	9.0
Clerical workers	2.8	5.1	5.4	7.6
Farm workers	7.4	8.7	7.7	5.0
Cooks	1.8	2.4	3.7	4.9
Top 5 total	52.3	54.8	47.9	47.7

Source: Borjas and Katz 2005.

answer a basic question: Why do employers hire unskilled migrants? Or, to pose the question the other way around, why isn't immigrants' lack of English and formal education a barrier to their securing employment? The answer is that hiring non–English-speakers is less of a liability than is often assumed and has a number of distinct advantages.

Let's examine the apparent cost of hiring a worker who does not speak English. This would be a problem for an employer in a workplace in which the other workers were all English speakers or in which they were required to communicate with English-speaking customers or clients; under these circumstances, there would be a considerable disincentive for any employer to hire such an employee. But there are many workplaces where speaking English is not a requirement. The most obvious examples are ethnic businesses, i.e., businesses that serve members of a particular non–English-speaking community. In these cases, employers need employees who speak their customers' language. Mexican bakeries, therefore, hire Mexican immigrants (Rodriguez 2004). Even in nonethnic businesses, however, there may be departments or units where workers are isolated from other workers or customers, so their inability to speak English will not hamper their ability to do their jobs. For example, housekeeping, stewarding, and landscaping jobs in hotels are performed backstage, away from customers. Customers may see the housekeepers and stewards at work—cleaning rooms, loading dishes onto carts, and trimming bushes—but they seldom speak to them. Consequently, employers are willing to hire non–English-speaking immigrants from Central America or the Philippines for these jobs (Waldinger and Lichter 2003; Adler and Adler 2004).

The fact that a workplace can function quite well with non–English-speaking workers, as long as they share a common language, does not explain why an employer would choose to hire them. Why do many businesses employ Mexicans, Central Americans, and Filipinos? The answer is that employers realize that they make ideal employees: they put out a high level of effort, they are highly motivated, and, in the case of undocumented workers, their legal vulnerability forces them to accept low wages and to tolerate harsh and even dangerous working conditions without protest.

Hard Work and High Motivation

Employers believe that immigrants appreciate low-wage jobs more than native workers do and that they work harder than their native counterparts. Evidence of this attitude can be found in Waldinger and Lichter's (2003) study of the hiring of low-skilled workers in Los Angeles County. The employers whom they interviewed consistently rated Latino and Asian immigrants more favorably as prospective employees than native white and African American workers. They saw immigrants as willing to perform hard, physical labor for low wages without complaint. Immigrants were also eager for any opportunity to work overtime. Here's how a fast-food manager in the study described his Mexican workers:

> Yes, the immigrants just want to work, work long hours, just want to do anything. They spend a lot of money coming up from Mexico. They want as many hours as possible. If I called them in for

four hours to clean latrines, they'd do it. *They like to work.* They have large families, a big work ethic, and small salaries [emphasis in original].

A coffee shop manager said:

> Immigrants are here to work, and they're not afraid of hard work. There are a lot of young Americans who don't want to work....Immigrants will work for minimum wage and *won't complain, even if you keep them there forever.* They're used to this kind of job [emphasis in original]. (Waldinger and Lichter 2003: 161)

It would be easy to dismiss these statements as prejudice on the part of employers, reminiscent of the way employers in the early twentieth century stereotyped Polish workers as strong, Jewish workers as dexterous, and African American workers as unable to operate machinery (see Chapter 5). Certainly prejudice is present in hiring decisions at all levels, as we have seen in Chapters 11 and 12. There are, however, good reasons to accept the proposition that immigrants are a highly motivated group of workers. One indication of this is the trouble and expense they have taken to get to the United States, whether legally or illegally. As Box 13.1 showed, immigrants who cross into the country without documents risk their safety and even their lives.

Once in the United States, immigrants are renowned for saving as much of their income as possible to achieve tangible and specific goals, such as repaying a coyote, acquiring a house, reuniting their families, supporting those they have left behind, and, for those who planned to return, buying land in their country of origin. They attain these goals by working long hours and multiple jobs. Take as an illustration Adler and

Adler's description of the Filipino immigrants who occupy the low-level housekeeping, landscaping, and stewarding jobs in Hawaiian resort hotels:

> Employed as laborers, new immigrants were admired by management for their high job performance.... They executed tedious jobs— cleaning the guest rooms, maintaining the landscaping, buffing, polishing, and sweeping the lobby, garden, and restaurant areas—keeping the Ali'i hotels in immaculate condition over long hours for very low pay.... In addition to working low-status, low-paying difficult jobs, new immigrants often worked multiple jobs. It was not uncommon for individuals to work a forty-hour week at one job and then hold another job, either part-time or full-time, as well. (2004: 45)

Adler and Adler suggest that the motivation for this extraordinary effort is the traditional desire of immigrants to improve their economic status:

> Their goals and values strongly motivated new immigrant workers. Instrumental in their orientation, they supported the extended family unit, working hard to advance themselves. They wanted to buy land, to acquire the material possessions that were part of the American dream, and to make themselves a part of their new country. Key to this goal was buying a house. With land and housing prices astronomically high, as in most resort areas, new immigrants slaved to accrue a down payment for a house and to make the monthly payments. (2004: 46)

For some immigrants, however, there is a less heartwarming reason for their willingness to work hard. Their "motivation" is based on their legal vulnerability. We are referring here to undocumented workers. Workers without the legal right to live in the United States are hesitant to challenge employers who expose them to workplace dangers, require them to work excessive hours, or underpay them, because they fear deportation. They are also not covered by the National Labor Relations Act (see Chapter 10), which makes it a violation of labor law to fire workers who want a union. A recent survey of 2,660 day-laborers in 20 states and the District of Columbia—these are workers who gather at open-air hiring sites in cities and negotiate employment with prospective employers for the day—paints a vivid picture of the consequences of legal vulnerability.

Day-laborers take jobs as construction laborers, gardeners, landscapers, painters, roofers, and drywall installers. The survey found that three quarters of them were undocumented, with nearly 90 percent coming from Mexico and Central America. Employers mistreated them in a variety of ways. One form of employer abuse was injury: day-laborers were exposed to hazardous conditions, such as chemicals and dust, were expected to use poor-quality equipment, and were provided with little protective gear. The result is that one in five reported being injured on the job, with two thirds continuing to work despite being in pain. Another abuse was wage theft: about half reported not being paid for work they had done. A third form of abuse was being overworked: nearly half were denied food, water, and breaks during their working day, and one third were required to work more hours than they had agreed to. The authors of the study concluded that the abuses are primarily due to the day-laborers' illegal status:

> The high incidence of labor rights violations is directly related to the status of most day-laborers

as undocumented immigrants...Employers are often able to deter workers from contesting these violations by threatening to turn them over to federal immigration authorities. Even when employers do not make these threats overtly, day-laborers, mindful of their status, are reluctant to seek recourse through government. (Valenzuela, Theodore, Meléndez, and Gonzalez 2006: 22)

The exploitation of undocumented workers is not restricted to the margins of the U.S. economy, nor are Latinos the only immigrants who are abused by employers. In the apparel industry, both Latino and Asian workers commonly experience conditions that are either unsafe or unhealthy or which violate federal labor laws (Bonacich and Appelbaum 2000). Even as large and prominent a company such as Wal-Mart—the largest corporation in the world—has been linked to the hiring of undocumented workers. Between 1998 and 2003 federal agents raided Wal-Mart stores around the country and discovered hundreds of undocumented immigrants working there as janitors. These workers, many from Eastern Europe, had been hired by contractors to whom Wal-Mart had contracted the cleaning of its stores. The contractors' labor-law violations included requiring janitors to work seven days a week, not providing breaks during the workday, and not paying overtime wages. Box 13.2 shows that Eastern European migrants have similar ambitions to those from Mexico and Central America and experience the same treatment: they are willing to do jobs that American workers don't want and are forced to tolerate working conditions that legal residents wouldn't accept.

BOX 13.2 *Illegally in U.S., and Never a Day Off at Wal-Mart*

They came from Russia, Poland and Lithuania, and their tales of washing and waxing Wal-Mart's floors for seven nights a week sound much like Pavel's.

Last February, Pavel responded to an intriguing Web site that boasted of cleaning jobs in the United States paying four times what he was earning as a restaurant manager in the Czech Republic. He flew from Prague to New York on a tourist visa and took a bus to Lynchburg, Va., where a subcontractor delivered him to a giant Wal-Mart.

Pavel immediately began on the midnight shift and said he soon learned that he would never receive a night off. He said he worked every night for the next eight months. In this way, Pavel, who refused to give his last name, became one pawn among hundreds employed by subcontractors that clean Wal-Mart stores across the nation, paying many workers off the books.

Pavel's unhappy stay in the United States ended with a shock when federal agents raided 60 Wal-Marts on Oct. 23 and arrested him and 250 other janitors as being illegal immigrants. Yesterday, the company acknowledged that it had received a target letter from federal prosecutors accusing it of violating immigration laws and saying that Wal-Mart faced a grand jury investigation.

The 21-state raid last month exposed an unseemly secret about Wal-Mart, the world's largest retailer: Hundreds of illegal immigrants worked at its stores, and its subcontractors appear to have violated overtime, Social Security and workers' compensation laws.

BOX **13.2** *continued*

Company officials deny having known that illegal immigrants worked in their stores, saying they required their cleaning contractors to use only legal workers.

But two federal law enforcement officials said in interviews that Wal-Mart executives must have known about the immigration violations because federal agents rounded up 102 illegal immigrant janitors at Wal-Marts in 1998 and 2001. In the October raid, federal agents searched the office of an executive at Wal-Mart's headquarters, carting away boxes of papers. Federal officials said prosecutors had wiretaps and recordings of conversations between Wal-Mart officials and subcontractors.

The use of illegal workers appeared to benefit Wal-Mart, its shareholders and managers by minimizing the company's costs, and it benefited consumers by helping hold down Wal-Mart's prices. Cleaning contractors profited, and thousands of foreign workers were able to earn more than they could back home.

But the system also had its costs—janitors said they were forced to work seven days a week, were not paid overtime and often endured harsh conditions…

"We Czechs are willing to sacrifice and work hard, but we definitely weren't earning enough money," said Pavel, 33, in a telephone interview from the Czech Embassy before he was deported last Friday. He said he received $380 in cash for his 56-hour workweeks. That came to $6.79 an hour, and he did not receive time-and-a-half for overtime.

In interviews, federal law enforcement officials, cleaning contractors, industry experts and seven illegal immigrant cleaners at Wal-Mart, including Pavel, said subcontracting allowed Wal-Mart to benefit while enabling it to deny responsibility…

One subcontractor, Stanislaw Kostek, whose company, CMS Cleaning, cleaned more than a dozen Wal-Marts in New York, Pennsylvania and Virginia, acknowledged that he had hired illegal immigrants.

"It's a degrading job; very few people want to do it even though the salary is at least $2 above the minimum wage" of $5.15 an hour, Mr. Kostek said. "But there are workers who want to do the job."

Those workers, he said, come from not just Eastern Europe but also Mexico, Mongolia, Uzbekistan and other distant lands. Some take the jobs hoping they will be the first step in their climb to the American dream, while others view it as a way to earn cash before returning home…

Victor Zavala Jr., who cleaned Wal-Marts in New Jersey seven nights a week, explained the lure of the job.

"When I talk on the phone to friends in Mexico, they ask me how the pay is, and I say, 'We're getting $350 a week,'" said Mr. Zavala, a native of Mexico City who was rounded up in the Oct. 23 raid. "They say, 'Wow, in Mexico we're earning 300 pesos a week.' That's just $30 a week. So compared with Mexico, it's good money."…

Denis, who refused to give his last name, said he got a medical degree in Russia before taking a job at a Wal-Mart in Lexington, Va. He said the store manager knew that illegal immigrants were cleaning the floors.

"It's obvious," he said. "They knew the whole crew consists of foreigners who don't speak English."

BOX 13.2 *continued*

Denis said it was exhausting to work seven nights a week, with just a 15-minute break. "There were no benefits, no health insurance, no nothing," he said.

Robert, a Czech who runs a Web site to attract Eastern Europeans to janitorial work, said using foreign cleaners was good for Wal-Mart and for American consumers.

"No American wants to do this job," he said. "If they hired Americans, it would take 10 of them to do the work done by five Czechs. This helps Wal-Mart keep its prices low."

Source: Greenhouse 2003b.

Immigrant Hiring: Networks and Gateways

A casual observer of workplaces in which immigrant workers are employed may have noticed two trends. First, it is quite common to find that workers who do the same job come from the same country. Mexicans work alongside other Mexicans, El Salvadorans with others from El Salvador, and Filipinos with other immigrants from the Philippines. Second, many of the factories located in small towns and rural areas that once employed whites and African Americans only (such as the Smithfield pork processing plant described in Chapter 12) now have increasing numbers of Latino and Southeast Asian immigrants working in them. These factories include carpet makers and poultry- and pork-processing plants. Both of these trends are due to to employers' reliance on hiring through networks, to changes in the ways in which unskilled immigrants move about the country, and to employers' search, in an era of increasingly intense global competition, for the cheapest sources of labor. In the next section of this chapter we will consider these developments in greater detail.

Recruitment and Networks

In some businesses, such as landscaping, all the workers often come from a single country. In other businesses, such as resort hotels, immigrants and the U.S.-born work for the same organization but in different jobs. Adler and Adler (2004) point out that the ethnic segregation of jobs is a common feature of hotel work. In Hawaii, the stewards are Filipinos and Tongans (they assemble and bring all dishes, glasses, and silverware to the serving area, and they wash everything and clean the kitchen after the meal), the housemen are local Hawaiians (they set up the tables, chairs, buffets, and bars before the meal and put them away afterwards), and the banquet servers are whites from the mainland (they prepare the tables, serve the meals, and remove the plates). This system of "occupational funneling"—equivalent versions of which are found in other regions of the country—corresponds to the degree of physical effort involved: stewards, the positions invariably held by the newest immigrants, have the most demanding and dirtiest jobs, followed by the housemen, who are usually more established immigrants and minorities, and then the servers, who are mostly white (Adler and Adler 2004: 140–144).

These patterns do not occur by chance. When hiring immigrants, employers often select workers from the same country and sometimes from the same region or ethnic group within a country. There are a number of reasons why employers choose to do this. First, it saves them from having to spend money on recruiting new workers—they may not even have to advertise for job applicants when there are vacancies because immigrants know others, either friends or family, who they will recommend for the positions. A manager of the laundry, wardrobe, and housekeeping departments at one of the hotel resorts in Adler and Adler's study stated that he barely had to advertise for new workers:

> When something opens up here, we hardly even have to post the job. Everyone knows when someone is leaving. They take care of filling the positions with their friends and relatives. Even before the person leaves, they have their relative come in on their day off to train under them. Then, when the job is officially open, the new person just steps into it. They like it, because they can take care of their own. We like it because if new people give us any problems, we just talk to our long-time employees and they handle it. (Adler and Adler 2004: 144)

Sociologists call this kind of recruitment process "network hiring." In recent years, they have attested to the importance of networks in a wide variety of settings; immigration, and the hiring of immigrants, is one area of social life where the concept of network ties is particularly useful (see, e.g., Tilly 1998; Massey, Durand, and Malone 2002). As we can see from the above

quotation, the benefits of network hiring for employers go well beyond the low cost of finding new employees.

A second benefit is that job candidates are produced extraordinarily quickly. Many employers have commented on the fact that every immigrant appears to know someone who needs a job and is instantly available when there is a vacancy. News of these vacancies quickly spreads through word of mouth to others in the immigrant community, and in a very short time a pool of potential candidates has formed.

A third benefit is that network hiring produces high-quality candidates with little need for employers to do any screening or testing of them. Employers assume that employees are unlikely to recommend someone who will not reflect well on them—their assumption is that the better the employee, the better the candidate because the employee's reputation and credibility is on the line. Employees will also help those they have recommended to fit in by explaining how the organization functions, introducing them to other workers, showing them how to do the job, and, if necessary, providing informal discipline if the new hire fails to perform up to expectations. Network hiring pays off for employers by turning existing employees into the recruiters and mentors of new hires (Waldinger and Lichter 2003: 103–107).

Network hiring has a number of advantages for employees as well. It allows job occupants to decide who has access to work opportunities, thus enabling them to assist friends, family members, and others from their region of origin or ethnic group and to exclude anyone who lacks any of these ties (a process that Tilly [1998] refers to as "opportunity hoarding"). It means that they can work alongside people they know well and like. It strengthens their ties to other members of their community and creates obligations that they can draw on in the future. Finally, employers sometimes pay bonuses to employees who recruit new workers who stay through the 30- to 90-day probationary periods that new hires typically serve. These payments are common in pork and poultry plants (Grey 1995; Griffith 1995).

The result of network hiring is what Griffith (1995) has called the "colonization" of many small-town industries in the South and Midwest by immigrants, mostly from Mexico and Central America. These immigrants gained a foothold in industries such as textiles and meat processing in the late 1980s and early 1990s; their presence quickly expanded as they drew other immigrants into these workplaces and they replaced the African Americans and whites who had traditionally worked the grueling, repetitive jobs of killing and cutting up hogs and chickens. This still leaves two questions. First, what has drawn immigrants to the small towns of the South and the Midwest, which are quite far from the border states and the large urban areas that historically had provided the immigrants' gateway to the United States? Second, why did employers replace native-born workers with immigrants? We consider these two questions next.

Immigrant Gateways

For many of us the pictures of immigrants and immigration that we have in our minds are from the past: the arrival of thousands of Europeans at Ellis Island in New York City at the beginning of the twentieth century and their dispersion to Pittsburgh, Detroit, Cleveland, Chicago, Milwaukee, and the other large cities of the industrial Northeast and Midwest. If we think of more recent immigrants, the presence of Mexicans and Central Americans in the states

of Florida, Texas, and California is what will probably come to mind. But these traditional gateways to the United States are not the locations that have seen the most rapid growth of immigrant populations in recent years. The five states with the greatest percentage increase in the foreign-born population between 1990 and 2000 were North Carolina, Georgia, Nevada, Arkansas, and Utah. In 1990 there were fewer than 500,000 foreign-born inhabitants living in all five states combined; by 2000, they had more than 1.5 million foreign-born inhabitants, a threefold increase. The foreign-born population of Georgia alone grew by 600,000. Nearly half of the new immigrants in the five states were from Mexico.

Table 13.3 lists the 10 states with the biggest percentage increase in the foreign-born population in the ten-year period between 1990 and 2000. All of these states have become increasingly popular as gateways—or points of initial settlement—for immigrants entering the United States, although the number of immigrants residing there is still dwarfed by the number in traditional gateway states like California (8.9 million), New York (3.9 million), Texas (2.9 million), and Florida (2.7 million) (Malone et al. 2003). It is in these four states that most immigrants still live. Nevertheless, the enormous growth of immigrants in the new gateway states is a striking departure from traditional patterns of migration and goes a long way toward explaining why immigration has become such a pressing national concern in recent years.

In every state listed in Table 13.3, Mexicans made up the largest group of new arrivals. Why have Mexicans migrated recently to states where in the past they almost never settled? There are two main reasons. The first is that they gained

TABLE 13.3 Ten States with the Biggest Percentage Increase in Foreign-Born
Population Between 1990 and 2000

STATE	FOREIGN-BORN POP. 1990	FOREIGN-BORN POP. 2000	% GROWTH 1990–2000
North Carolina	115,077	430,000	273.7
Georgia	173,176	577,273	233.4
Nevada	104,828	316,593	202.0
Arkansas	24,867	73,690	196.3
Utah	58,600	158,664	170.8
Tennessee	59,114	159,004	169.0
Nebraska	28,198	74,638	164.7
Colorado	142,434	369,903	159.7
Arizona	278,205	656,183	135.9
Kentucky	34,119	80,271	135.3

Source: Waters and Jiménez 2005.

legal status in the United States after the passage of the Immigration Reform and Control Act (IRCA) in 1986. Congress passed IRCA in an attempt to prevent further Mexican immigration to the United States. The Act established penalties for employers who knowingly hired undocumented workers; it also provided amnesty for undocumented workers who had lived and worked in the United States prior to January 1, 1982. More than 2 million Mexican immigrants took advantage of the act to acquire resident-alien status (Waters and Jiménez 2005). They were now free to move from states such as California and Texas to North Carolina and Georgia without the threat of being arrested and deported: they no longer had to remain in communities where their safety from the authorities lay in their numbers.

Second, Mexican workers and other immigrants have been drawn by the increased economic opportunities in states in the South and the Midwest since the mid-1980s. For example, the emergence of Atlanta as a major metropolitan area resulted in a construction boom in the region that in turn lured thousands of immigrants from other states as well as new immigrants from across the border. Many of these new immigrants had not lived in the United States previously; they made Georgia their destination instead of Texas or California because they now had Georgian ties—the immigrants who had moved there after being granted amnesty under IRCA (Hernández-León and Zúñiga 2000). The immigrants who followed those who had gained legal-resident status were often undocumented workers, although IRCA had imposed fines on employers for hiring illegal workers. But these penalties were seldom enforced because it required the federal government to show that an employer had knowingly hired an undocumented worker—as long as a worker showed an employer some proof of his or her right to legal residence, whether forged or not, the employer could claim to be in compliance with the law.

Research on the ties between Mexicans in Mexico and those in the United States demonstrates just how intertwined the two groups now are. Phillips and Massey (2000) analyzed data from 38 communities in western Mexico and found that almost three quarters of the household heads knew someone (a family member or friend) living in the United States. On average they knew nineteen people living north of the border. As Phillips and Massey note, this is an impressive number of potential contacts "for advice on crossing the border, getting a job, or making one's way in the United States" (2000: 42).

Global Competition and Low Wages

Global competition has also played a role in creating economic opportunities, encouraging migrants, and forming new immigrant gateways. In the 1980s and 1990s, large corporations began to enter local industries such as meatpacking, poultry processing, and textiles, which had previously been dominated by small, often family-run firms. Many of these firms went out of business or were bought by their larger competitors. The corporations that now ran these businesses brought their cost-cutting methods with them. In particular, they saw the advantage of a low-wage labor force and they began actively to recruit and hire immigrants. The result was a demographic transformation of the small towns and rural areas in which meatpacking, apparel, and textile factories were located. Consider, as an illustration of this process, the case of the Storm Lake, Iowa, meatpacking plant. (Our account is taken from Grey [1995].)

The plant's operations began in 1935, when the Storm Lake Packing Company built the first plant there. In 1953 the plant was bought by Hygrade Food Products, which operated it for the next three decades. The workers were mostly white and male. They belonged to a union (Local 191 of the United Food and Commercial Workers) and were well paid, with average annual incomes in the late 1970s of around $30,000. In 1981, however, Hygrade demanded that workers accept a $3 per hour pay cut. When the union refused, Hygrade closed the facility and laid off its 500 production workers and 50 managers.

In April 1982, six months after the plant had closed, it was bought by IBP, a large multinational corporation with global operations—and with an anti-union reputation. IBP reopened the factory in September 1982. The factory's workforce and approach to labor management had been completely changed. There was no union and beginning wages were only $6 an hour—a fraction of the previous pay rates. Many of the workers who were hired were newcomers to Iowa and to meat processing; they included refugees from Laos and immigrants from Mexico. By 1992 the 300 Lao and the 80 Latinos at IBP made up 25 percent and 7 percent, respectively, of its workforce.

The Lao workers moved to Storm Lake from other parts of the state and the country because of their patron–client or kinship ties to an initial group of refugees who had been resettled in the area in the mid- to late 1970s. Established Lao residents served as patrons for newcomers by encouraging them to move to Storm Lake and then helping them to find work at IBP and housing in the town. The Mexican workers were later arrivals. IBP began to recruit them in the early 1990s by running Spanish-language television commercials in Texas, California, and Mexico.

By the mid-1990s, Latinos had become the largest single group of migrants in this once ethnically homogeneous Iowa community. The change that we have described—meatpacking companies' replacement of their unionized workforces with nonimmigrant and Latino workers—was replicated in dozens of beef- and pork-processing plants in small towns across the Midwest. The result was a significantly larger Latino presence in these communities (for example, Latinos make up more than 30 percent of the population in five rural counties in western Kansas that have large meatpacking plants) and a decline in real wages paid to these workers. Real average hourly wages in the meatpacking industry decreased from $10.30 in 1980 to $6.46 in 2002 (Champlin and Hake 2006).

In the South, the region that dominates poultry processing, a similar process has unfolded, but with some important differences. Here, immigrants replaced African Americans and women in new destination states such as North Carolina, Georgia, Arkansas, and Virginia. The poultry firms' recruitment of Mexican workers in the late 1980s was consistent with their emphasis on low-wage, high-speed production that had led them to concentrate their operations in the South in the first place. A survey of poultry personnel managers in 1988 found that most were targeting Latinos in their recruitment efforts, using network recruiting and the payment of bonuses to workers who brought in new hires. In some plants over 80 percent of workers were hired through networks (Griffith 1995).

An added attraction of Latino workers to employers in the South has been that they are less familiar with their rights as employees and are more fearful of losing their jobs than were U.S.-born workers. Poultry plants run their lines

fast—from seventy to ninety birds a minute—and workers perform the same cutting actions over and over again a day, thousands of time a day. The result is repetitive motion injuries, such as carpal tunnel syndrome. Griffith (1995) reports that poultry employers encourage workers to continue working even if they are in pain in order to keep reported occupational injury rates low. He states that in some cases employers have paid workers to come to work, even if they were unable to do their jobs, to avoid reporting the injury and thus keep compensation and insurance rates down.

Thus the processes of global competition have transformed the small towns of rural America in two ways. First, national and international corporations have replaced local businesses in many industries. Second, some of these companies have intentionally recruited a docile immigrant workforce to perform the low-wage jobs that they have created. Clearly, these processes can fuel sharp labor market competition across ethnic lines, which is why immigration has become so heated a political issue in recent years.

Many immigrants don't want these kinds of jobs, however. For them there remains one other option—becoming an entrepreneur.

Immigrants and Entrepreneurship

Patterns of Self-Employment

In the final section of this chapter we turn our attention to a different form of participation in the American economy: self-employment. We define self-employment in the broadest possible sense as anyone who works for himself or herself, regardless of whether this person has any employees or not. Throughout the immigrant era many newcomers have chosen to work for themselves rather than to become employees of others. Even if the "rags to riches" stereotype of the immigrant entrepreneur is an exaggeration, it is important to acknowledge the relatively high rate of self-employment among immigrants. Historically, the self-employment rate among immigrants has consistently been higher than that of the native-born. In 2000, for example, while the self-employment rate among the U.S.-born was 8.2 percent, among some foreign-born newcomers such as Koreans and some Latino nationalities, self-employment rates reached 25 percent and higher (Toussaint-Comeau 2005).

Data on the overall self-employment rate among immigrants hide the substantial differences among immigrants from different parts of the world. Self-employment rates across ethnic groups vary widely, just as they did in the past when entrepreneurship was concentrated among Jewish and Italian immigrants. More recently the highest levels of self-employment have been found among Korean and Middle Eastern immigrants, although the percentage of workers from these regions who are self-employed declined between 1990 and 2000. Table 13.4 uses U.S. Census data to compare self-employment rates for immigrants from different regions of the world from 1980 to 2000. It indicates that Middle Eastern immigrants have had the highest rates of self-employment since 1980.

TABLE 13.4 Self-Employment Rates in the United States by
Country/Region of Origin

COUNTRY/REGION	SELF-EMPLOYMENT RATE (%)		
	1980	1990	2000
U.S.-born	6.8	7.8	8.2
All immigrant	7.9	9.5	9.3
Middle East	15.7	18.3	16.0
Cuba	9.5	12.6	12.5
Europe	10.4	12.3	12.5
Northeast Asia (Korea, China, Japan)	11.1	14.6	10.7
India and Pakistan	7.9	10.1	10.2
Latin America (excluding Mexico, Cuba, and Puerto Rico)	5.4	7.7	9.2
Africa	7.5	9.9	8.4
Southeast Asia (Indonesia, Philippines, Malaysia, Thailand, Laos, Vietnam, Cambodia)	4.1	6.0	7.0
Mexico	3.5	5.6	6.8
Caribbean	3.1	5.7	6.2
Puerto Rico	3.2	4.4	4.7

Source: Toussaint-Comeau 2005.

The data in Table 13.4 do not capture the full extent or importance of immigrant entrepreneurship, however. The impact of immigrant entrepreneurs was recently demonstrated in a study of engineering and technology companies started in the United States between 1995 and 2005. These companies, representing some of the most modern sectors of the economy such as bioscience, computers and communications, innovation and manufacturing-related services, semiconductors, and software often have an immigrant founder: the percentage of companies with one or more immigrant founders ranged from 20 percent in bioscience to over 35 percent in semiconductors. Immigrant-founded engineering and technology companies now operate in every region of the country and have become major employers—they employed nearly 450,000 workers in 2005. The study's authors conclude that "[it] is clear that immigrants have become a significant driving force in the creation of new businesses and intellectual property in the U.S.—and that their contributions have increased over the past decade" (Wadhwa, Saxenian, Rissing, and Gereffi 2007: 5).

Look around any American city and you will notice that there are distinct patterns to immigrant entrepreneurship, with different ethnic groups being concentrated in different kinds of business. Chinese immigrants have traditionally specialized in the restaurant and laundry businesses, for example. Koreans operate laundries, groceries, and liquor stores. Mexican immigrants are concentrated in landscaping, construction, child daycare, and restaurants, while Cuban immigrants are more likely to be found in finance, insurance, and real estate. Vietnamese immigrants are heavily represented in personal care businesses, such as beauty salons and nail salons, whereas Indian and Pakistani immigrants run motels and hotels, gasoline stations, and taxi and limousine services (Toussaint-Comeau 2005). Immigrants with professional degrees or technical skills are an exception to this pattern of ethnic specialization because they are likely to open businesses in the occupation in which they have been trained, regardless of their nationality. The medical profession is a good example—doctors from all around the world have opened practices in the United States.

Causes of Self-Employment

What explains why immigrants open their own businesses and why these vary by country or region of origin? These are questions that have received considerable sociological attention for over thirty years. The consensus of this research is that immigrants are most likely to pursue self-employment when they are at a disadvantage in the labor market (a phenomenon known as "blocked mobility"), when they have the resources to open their own businesses, and when there are economic opportunities of which they can take advantage (Waldinger, Aldrich, and Ward 1990; Yoon 1997). Let's consider each of these factors in turn.

Labor Market Disadvantages

Immigrants may be disadvantaged in a number of ways in the labor market. First they may experience discrimination if employers choose not to hire them because of their foreign origin. Second, they may lack legal documents allowing them to work. Third, their educational credentials may not be viewed as legitimate or applicable in the host society. Fourth, a lack of fluency in English may result in their not being hired for jobs for which they would otherwise be qualified

(Light 1979). Self-employed immigrants from Cuba, Mexico, Latin America, and Asia are the most likely to report that they speak English not well or not at all, as Table 13.5 shows. Regardless of the reason, the effect of disadvantage is that many immigrants conclude that they will be better off financially if they are self-employed (Tienda and Raijman 2000; Valenzuela 2001).

Although some employers hire (and in industries like meat processing, even prefer) workers whose knowledge of English is limited, this is much less likely to be true of employers of white-collar workers. Yoon's (1997) study of Korean business owners in Chicago and Los Angeles provides a good illustration of how a limited proficiency in English encourages self-employment among workers who would otherwise compete for white-collar jobs. More than 60 percent of the Koreans in his sample were college graduates and about 40 percent of them had worked in white-collar positions in Korea prior to their leaving the country. Their primary reason for emigrating was economic—they had come to the United States in pursuit of better economic opportunities. They had difficulty in securing equivalent positions in the United States because

TABLE 13.5 English Proficiency and Education of Self-Employed by Country/Region of Origin (Percentages)

COUNTRY/REGION	SPEAKS ENGLISH NOT WELL OR NOT AT ALL	LESS THAN HIGH SCHOOL	COLLEGE OR MORE
U.S.-born	0.4	6.5	36.2
All immigrant	23.2	24.1	28.4
India and Pakistan	5.8	7.8	62.1
Africa	4.3	7.0	46.3
Northeast Asia (Korea, China, Japan)	26.4	11.4	46.3
Middle East	4.9	8.3	45.8
Europe	5.4	11.1	34.6
Southeast Asia (Indonesia, Philippines, Malaysia, Thailand, Laos, Vietnam, Cambodia)	19.7	17.2	31.8
Cuba	30.0	20.2	23.5
Puerto Rico	15.3	26.4	18.1
Latin America (excluding Mexico and Puerto Rico)	30.5	29.3	18.1
Caribbean	18.5	22.8	16.0
Mexico	44.2	59.1	5.7

Source: Toussaint-Comeau 2005.

of their limited English; most started off in low-level production and service jobs before beginning their own businesses. These businesses were mostly in the retail sector—general merchandise, wig, clothing, and shoe stores, liquor, grocery, fruit and vegetable stores, laundries and dry cleaners, and gas stations. The immigrants' hope was that long hours and hard work would bring financial success, as Yoon explains:

> Many respondents said that if white-collar jobs had been available, they would have chosen them, but the language barrier precluded such a possibility. Many of them found that they had to start off as factory workers, dishwashers, or pumpers at gas stations. Given such bleak employment prospects, small business ownership was viewed as the best choice. (1997: 123)

The desire to operate his or her own business to offset labor-market disadvantages is just the first step for any immigrant on the road to self-employment. If the entrepreneurial dream is to become a reality the immigrant must have the means to achieve it. Immigrants depend upon a mixture of ethnic, class, and family resources to provide the necessary means (Yoon 1997).

Resources

Ethnic resources are the benefits that accompany membership in a particular ethnic group. One kind of ethnic resource is employment opportunities—immigrants are frequently hired by other members of their ethnic group, as researchers have noted (Tilly 1998). Employment provides more than a job, however. It gives new immigrants the skills, the know-how, and the contacts that are indispensable for entrepreneurship (Portes and Bach 1985). Take, for example, a Korean immigrant who lands his first job in a Korean-owned laundry. If he follows a common pattern, he will work for three to five years saving money for a down payment on his own laundry. In most cases he will buy it from another Korean (two thirds of the Los Angeles business owners in Yoon's study bought their business from a Korean). He may, in addition, borrow the money to cover the rest of the purchase price from a Korean rotating credit association or *kye*, which makes short-term loans to its members (more than one quarter of the Chicago business owners borrowed money from this source). Thus he is able to finance his business using another kind of ethnic resource: access to informal credit.

Kyes operate on the basis of trust. Each member—there are typically ten to twenty—contributes money to the fund, which then lends these funds on a rotating basis. The loan amounts ranged from $10,000 to more than $30,000. All members must continue to contribute monthly payments until everyone has received a loan, which are normally provided at high rates of interest. A loan from a kye is not like a loan from a bank where a person puts up his or her business as collateral against the risk the bank is assuming for nonpayment. The kye is based on the members' trust in one another, which is also an ethnic resource (Yoon 1997: 129–144).

Class resources are the immigrants' level of education, their occupations prior to emigrating, and the amount of money they brought with them. Immigrants who are well educated, who were self-employed in their native countries, or who are affluent are more likely to open their own businesses than those who are not. As we can see from Table 13.5, immigrant entrepreneurs from India and Pakistan, Africa, Northeast Asia, and the Middle East are particularly likely to have college degrees. Many, in fact, have graduate degrees in fields such as genetics, computer science, mathematics, physics, and engineering and are thus well qualified to start companies in fields such as biosciences, computing, and software development. Sergey Brin, one of the two founders of Google, offers a famous illustration of the relationship between education and software entrepreneurship. Brin was born in Russia and was a graduate student in computer science at Stanford, where he and Google co-founder Larry Page developed the search algorithm that was the foundation of their company's extraordinary commercial success.

Family resources come in the form of capital and labor. The aspiring immigrant entrepreneur will turn to family members for loans to start the business and for labor, often unpaid, to keep it going. According to Bates (1997), more than 40 percent of Korean and Chinese entrepreneurs in the United States have borrowed money from family members for their businesses. Equally important is family labor. The typical immigrant business, especially in the retail sector, is a mom-and-pop operation. Well over half the Korean business owners in Yoon's sample relied on spouses to work in their stores. He estimates that family members provided between forty and forty-five hours of unpaid labor a week (1997: 157). In addition to being inexpensive, family members are reliable, trustworthy, and willing to work the very long hours that are necessary to make a success of any small retail business.

Opportunity

The availability of economic opportunities is the third factor that determines whether immigrants pursue self-employment. Immigrant entrepreneurs seldom compete directly with the large established firms that dominate the U.S. economy. They are most often to be found in markets that other firms have ignored or in which they have chosen not to compete. One such overlooked market is supplying ethnic goods and services to immigrants. The Korean entrepreneur who establishes a video store to rent Korean videotapes and DVDs or the Mexican baker who sells Mexican pastries are catering to immigrants' continuing desire for products from their home countries. This market, which is too small and specialized to interest the typical American company, has provided one of the most common routes to self-employment over the years. Immigrant businesses that serve their ethnic communities are most likely to flourish in neighborhoods, sometimes described as "ethnic enclaves," where there is a high concentration of inhabitants with roots in a particular country or region (Portes and Bach 1985). Examples of such enclaves are the Chinatowns in New York and San Francisco, the Mexican-dominated Little Village neighborhood of Chicago, and the Little Havana Cuban neighborhood in Miami.

Immigrant entrepreneurs enter other markets because bigger businesses have decided for one reason or another not to compete there. For example, large grocery chains are often reluctant to establish stores in urban locations because of the high cost of buying or renting land and the high cost of labor; this gives the smaller store, run by a husband and wife who are willing to work very long hours, a chance to establish a foothold. This explains why densely populated cities have so many small stores, including many immigrant businesses. It also explains, as Waldinger, Aldrich, and Ward point out, why so many taxis are owned and operated by immigrants:

Another case in point is the taxi industry in the United States, where immigrants have been able to move rapidly into ownership positions. What is distinctive about the taxi industry is that virtually no advantages accrue to the large firm. Because the owner-operator of a single cab operates at essentially the same costs as a fleet of 20 to 30 cabs, the key to cost reduction is keeping the vehicle on the road for the longest possible time. Thus if immigrants are amenable to self-exploitation or, better yet, can pool resources to buy a taxi and then split shifts so that the cab is in use 24 hours a day, they can effectively compete with native-owned firms. (1990: 26)

Finally, there are the markets from which mainstream businesses have withdrawn. Inner-city or ghetto neighborhoods are the classic example. The "white flight" of residents from cities such as Chicago and Detroit during the 1960s and 1970s as African Americans moved into what were formerly white neighborhoods was followed by a flight of white businesses; their owners complained of increasing crime rates and falling profits. Korean and Middle Eastern entrepreneurs moved into this vacuum. Yoon argues that the immigrant entrepreneurs saw the problems associated with an inner-city location as an advantage, since it would make it cheaper to establish their business and would make their clientele more tolerant of the business owners' limited English.

We conclude on a note of caution. In considering why immigrants favor self-employment, we do not mean that it is necessarily a successful strategy in achieving the upward mobility that so clearly motivates it. Sociological research has overwhelmingly focused on why immigrants become entrepreneurs and has devoted little time to following their careers as entrepreneurs over time. We don't know a great deal about their performance over the long term, for example, although we do know that small businesses in general have a notoriously high failure rate. We also don't know the extent to which immigrants tire of the demands of business ownership, perhaps concluding that the rewards are too scanty to justify the efforts that are needed. It is possible that immigrant entrepreneurship is just a stage, to be abandoned once the immigrant improves his English or finds an occupation in which the reward-effort trade-off is more appealing. There is still much that we have to learn about immigrants and their businesses. Regardless of whether individual immigrants succeed as entrepreneurs or not, however, their willingness to come to the United States and to embrace the risks and demands of starting a business remains one of the most striking aspects of international migration.

Summary

There has been a substantial increase in immigration to the United States since 1970, much of which has occurred since 1990. There are today nearly 36 million foreign-born people in the country, representing about 12 percent of the total population. An estimated 12 million of the foreign-born are undocumented workers, the majority of whom have crossed the Mexico–U.S. border illegally. Undocumented workers perform a variety of low-wage, physically demanding jobs. The growth in the number of foreign-born inhabitants is also due to the large number of highly educated immigrants from Asia, Africa, and Europe who have settled in the country over the last two decades.

Immigrants from Mexico and Central America have come to the United States in search of work and to escape poverty. They have risked their lives crossing the border to take some of the dirtiest and toughest jobs in the country, which include pork and poultry processing, construction, and picking fruits and vegetables. Employers favor immigrant workers over the native-born because they see immigrants as hard working, uncomplaining, and highly motivated. Employers can also take advantage of undocumented workers who, because of their legal vulnerability, are often forced to tolerate dangerous working conditions and other on-the-job abuses.

Much of the hiring of immigrants takes place through networks. Employers rely on immigrants to recruit their family and friends to their workplaces, which keeps down the cost of recruiting and screening new employees. This process of network hiring has enabled immigrants to "colonize" industries such as textiles and meat processing, as employers in these industries shifted to a low-wage, high-productivity strategy in the 1980s and 1990s. The initial recruitment of one or two immigrants was followed by an influx of others from the same community. The result has been the opening of new immigrant gateways—states such as North Carolina, Georgia, Nevada, and Arkansas—in regions where the immigrant population had previously been quite small.

Finally, over the years many immigrants have started their own businesses in the effort to achieve economic prosperity in their new country. Today the highest levels of self-employment are found among immigrants from Korea and the Middle East. Immigrants are most likely to pursue entrepreneurship when they encounter labor-market disadvantages, when they have the necessary ethnic, class, and family resources, and when there are market opportunities of which they can take advantage. Korean entrepreneurs, who have been especially active in establishing retail businesses, illustrate the role played by all three of these factors. Their lack of proficiency in English is a significant disadvantage in the labor market, they have access to credit from other members of their community, they are highly educated, they can count on unpaid labor from family members, and they are willing to work long hours operating stores in urban and inner-city neighborhoods in which larger firms choose not to compete.

PART V

❦

THE FUTURE OF WORK: KEY ISSUES AND SOCIAL CHOICES

Chapter 14

Work and Family

In October, 2003, the *New York Times Magazine* published an article titled "The Opt-Out Revolution" (Belkin 2003). According to the *Magazine*'s editors, this article generated "record-breaking mail" as readers reacted to Belkin's piece. What topic inspired such a response? "The Opt-Out Revolution" focused on a group of women who left high-powered, high-paying jobs in order to stay at home and raise their children. The article explored the reasons behind the women's decisions and reflected more broadly on the question of gender differences in the meaning of success and the definition of personal fulfillment. This article has not been without controversy. Analyzing data on the labor force participation rates of women with and without children, Boushey (2005) refuted the "opt-out" premise of the *Magazine*'s story. More recently, Williams, Manvell, and Bornstein (2006) examined press coverage of work–family conflict, concluding that these stories are much more likely to frame the issue in terms of women making choices to leave the labor force than investigate the factors operating inside the workplace that push women out.

The debate surrounding "The Opt-Out Revolution" illustrates several important themes that will frame this chapter's discussion of work and family. First, how people resolve issues of work and family in their lives is intensely emotional. For most, the effort to achieve some sort of work–family balance involves more than allocating time, but forces people to think about the kind of person they are or want to be. People are strongly and emotionally committed to work and family. Second, gender, work, and family are inextricably intertwined; changes in work and family give rise to changes in gender relations, and changes in gender relations give rise to changes in family and work. Third, as with most other issues in the sociology of work, the opportunities for reconciling work and family life are unevenly distributed. The affluent, well-educated women in "The Opt-Out Revolution" have options unavailable to the average worker—woman or man. Finally, work–family conflict is more than an individual matter. We cannot understand people's "choices" without taking into account the larger structural and institutional context within which they are made.

The Rise of Domesticity

Work and Family in Historical Perspective

In order to understand the relations between work and family in the twenty-first century, we must return briefly to the forces at work during the Industrial Revolution. As we saw in Chapter 4, work and family life were highly intertwined during the preindustrial era. But the advent of industrial capitalism brought with it the separation of these two spheres (Cowan 1983; Haraven 1990). During the mid- to late nineteenth century, men's responsibilities became centered on the paid workplace, while the "ideal" woman was one whose life revolved around home and family.

Williams (2000: 20) conceives of these social arrangements, with men defined as "ideal workers" and women as mothers and caregivers, as essential features of the system of "domesticity." Domesticity, she argues, is comprised of three elements: "[e]mployers' entitlement to demand an ideal worker with immunity from family work;" "husbands' right, and their duty, to live up to this work ideal;" and the view that mothers' lives "should be framed around caregiving."

In addition to a strictly demarcated gender division of labor, domesticity involved a set of cultural beliefs that defined women and men as categorically different, possessing talents and skills best suited to different domains. In this view, men were "naturally" better equipped for paid work, while women's essential natures received fullest expression at home, surrounded by children. Domesticity thus attached gendered meanings not only to individual characteristics, but also to institutions and entire realms of human expression (Williams 2000).

Domesticity was not the only feature of industrialization that contributed to a growing separation between work and family. The organization of work was also changing in ways that reinforced its distinctiveness from family life and the world outside the workplace. The most important of these involved the rise of mass production and the growth of large, bureaucratic, hierarchically organized firms (Jacoby 1985; Perrow 2002). Accompanying these changes was a view of work and work organization as increasingly subject to impersonal forces, such as market competition, technology, and capitalism. These forces shaped work directly in the form of organizational structures and technological innovations, and they led to the creation of new roles in industry for those trained to apply "scientific" techniques to ever more expanding areas of the workplace, including the social relations of work and the management of workers (Taylor 1911; Mayo 1933).

Employers attempted to minimize the effects of outside influences on the workplace in more direct ways as well. For example, anti-nepotism laws sought to prevent family ties from interfering with organizational authority and discipline. For more affluent white-collar workers, zoning laws and the growth of suburbs created a real geographic separation between work and home, further severing ties between these realms (Kanter 1977a).

Domesticity and Sociology

As a set of cultural beliefs, domesticity conceived of paid work as separate and distinct from family life. These ideas became an important centerpiece of sociological scholarship on work and family in the decades surrounding World War II, most notably in the writings of sociologist Talcott Parsons. Drawing on the work of Emile Durkheim (discussed in Chapter 2), Parsons and his colleagues (Parsons and Bales 1955; Parsons 1964) argued that domesticity and the gender division of labor on which it was based were especially well suited to the requirements of an industrial economy. In particular, he argued that a division of labor whereby men have responsibility for the instrumental tasks associated with being a wage earner and women are responsible for the expressive tasks of caring for children and providing emotional support enhanced both family solidarity and industrial society as a whole. In this view, highly segregated gender roles provided a structure that was "functional" for the social order, in that it minimized conflict and competition within the family unit and social system more broadly.

For Parsons the occupational system was "organized primarily in terms of universalistic criteria of performance and status within functionally specialized fields" (1964: 79). By emphasizing its impersonality and rationality, Parsons' conception of work was consistent with other sociological treatments of industrial capitalism extending back at least to Weber and Marx (see Chapter 2). Although the details differed in important ways, each contributed to a view of work as fundamentally distinct from other areas of life. For American sociologists in the first half of the twentieth century, however, Parsons' views were especially influential. Not only did he call attention to the distinctiveness of work, but he went further by explicitly contrasting and even favoring the distinction between the "instrumental" principles of work organization and the "expressive" realm of family life.

Parsons' view of the work and family relationship has been extensively criticized. His critics have pointed out that his view of a rigid gender division of labor as "functional" for society overlooked the ways in which such arrangements operated to the severe disadvantage of women, who were denied access to independent sources of income, power, and self-fulfillment in the wake of industrial capitalism. At the same time, we should not underestimate the influence

Parsons exerted on sociological treatments of work, family, and gender. As Kanter (1977a) observes, his views helped to generate a view of work and family as "separate spheres," thus limiting the ability of social scientists and policy makers to perceive the deep interconnections that actually exist between these two realms.

Disrupting Domesticity: Changes in Work and Family Life

These interconnections became increasingly evident during second half of the twentieth century, as the system of domesticity began to be modified in significant respects (Williams 2000). Most important, married women's massive influx into the paid labor market meant that women, as well as men, were expected to be "ideal workers." Because employed women continued to have primary responsibility for housework and children, however, they could not easily satisfy the obligations associated with a completely work-centered life. Men's ability to be "ideal workers" was also challenged by women's participation in the paid labor force. The slow disappearance of the full-time homemaker meant that fewer and fewer men had wives who were available to attend to all of the household obligations.

As we saw in Chapter 11, the vast majority of women and men today work for pay, and majorities of both sexes are employed full time. Families have also changed, as a majority of households containing married couples with children now include two wage earners. Over 50 percent of married mothers with children under 1 year of age are in the labor force (see Figure 14.1). In addition, higher divorce rates have resulted in larger numbers of single mothers in the labor force than ever before (Casper and Bianchi 2002). Finally, work itself has changed in important respects, as

FIGURE 14.1 Labor Force Participation Rates of Married Mothers by Age of Youngest Child, 1994–2005

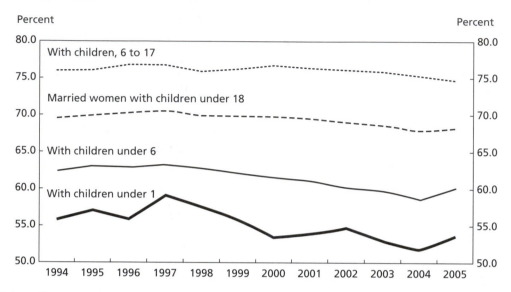

Source: Cohany, Sharon R. and Emy Sok. 2007. "Trends in Labor Force Participation of Married Mothers of Infants," *Monthly Labor Review* (February):10.

the post–World War II industrial economy gave way to one based on service.

Work Time, Family Time, and Work–Family Conflict

These developments created new challenges and opportunities for American workers and their families. Among the most important challenges has been the need to juggle the demands of both work and family. One way to understand this challenge is to examine the trends in hours worked for pay and at home.

Paid Work and Family Work

In *The Overworked American* (1991), Juliet Schor argued that employed Americans were working more hours than at any time since World II. Later

research refined Schor's claims. In particular, Jacobs and Gerson (2001) showed that the average number of hours worked for the labor force as a whole has not changed much over the past few decades, with women averaging 36 hours per week and men averaging about 42 hours. These averages are not the whole story, however. Jacobs and Gerson found that the workforce can be divided into two segments, with different patterns of work hours. At one end are college-educated managers and professionals, who average the longest work weeks. At the other extreme lie an increasing proportion of workers who average fewer than forty hours a week. These workers are likely to be found in sales and service jobs where part-time work is common. Hence, long work weeks are more likely to be found among some segments of the workforce than others.

These trends for individuals do not tell us all we need to know about the issue of work hours, however. People in dual-earner households with children or in single-parent households are likely to feel greater time pressures than those in households containing one wage earner, children, and a full-time homemaker. As Jacobs and Gerson (2001) note, even if the average worker is not putting in longer hours than in the past, the changed structure of American families may cause people to feel overworked. Their research showed that roughly half of both male and female workers surveyed in *The National Study of the Changing Workforce* said that they would like to work fewer hours. This suggests that people's feelings of overwork are widespread. Only a small minority (less than 20 percent) expressed a desire to work more.

Time pressures produced by the need to work more hours than one would like are exacerbated by what is happening in families. Both women and men have changed their patterns of household work over the last few decades. Women spend significantly fewer hours performing housework than in 1965, while men spend more hours than they did in the mid-1960s (Casper and Bianchi 2002). The gender gap in housework has decreased over time, especially in dual-earner households. This decrease stems primarily from steep declines in the number of hours women spend doing housework, not because men have begun to spend substantially more time engaged in these activities.

The hours each gender spends performing housework are influenced by the hours each devotes to paid employment and their relative incomes. Women who work for pay perform fewer hours of household work than full-time homemakers, and women employed part-time do less household work than those with full-time jobs. Women do less housework and men do more as the proportion of family income contributed by the woman increases (Spain and Bianchi 2000).

Household work, like paid work, is sex-segregated, with women and men each performing tasks typically associated with their gender (e.g., men perform outdoor tasks, such as mowing the lawn or working on the car, while women do cleaning and care for children) (Blair and Lichter 1991). Household tasks performed by men involve greater personal discretion than those women perform, are more likely to have a fixed beginning and end, and are more likely to involve a leisure component (Hochschild 1989). In addition, women perform almost 80 percent of all childcare (Robinson and Godbey 1997). The amount of care provided by mothers and fathers evens out somewhat as children age, but even among school-age children, mothers have more caregiving responsibilities than fathers.

Interestingly, while the number of hours women spend doing housework has declined over time, increases in women's labor force participation have not been associated with significant decreases in the amount of time mothers spend with their children (Bianchi 2000). Children—at least in some families—are also spending more time with their fathers than in previous generations. The net result of these changes is that parents who work for pay have not lessened their investments in their children, but rather are devoting large amounts of time to both sets of activities. Working mothers in particular seem to have sacrificed time spent doing other activities—including leisure and sleep, as well as housework—to create more time to spend with their children. This may

BOX 14.1 *On Work and Family: One CEO's View*

If there was ever a case of "Do as I say, not as I did," this is it. No one, myself included, would ever call me an authority on work-life balance. For 41 years, my operating principle was work hard, play hard and spend some time as a father.

It's clear that the balance I chose had consequences for the people around me at home and at the office. For instance, my kids were raised, largely alone, by their mother, Carolyn. And from my earliest days at GE, I used to show up at the office on Saturday mornings. Not coincidentally, my direct reports showed up too. Personally, I thought these weekend hours were a blast. We would mop up the workweek in a more relaxed way and shoot the breeze about sports. I never once asked anyone, "Is there someplace you would rather be—or need to be—for your family or favorite hobby or whatever?" The idea just didn't dawn on me that anyone would want to be anywhere but at work.

My defense, if there is one, is that those were the times. In the 1960s and '70s, all my direct reports were men. Many of those men were fathers, and fathers were different then. They did not, by and large, attend ballet recitals on Thursday afternoons or turn down job transfers because they didn't want to disrupt their kids' sports "careers." Most of their wives did not have jobs with their own competing demands. All that changed, of course.

I have dealt with dozens of work-life-balance situations and dilemmas as a manager, and hundreds more as the manager of managers. And over the past three years, I've heard from many people—bosses and employees—about the complex issue of work-life balance. I have a sense of how bosses think about the issue, whether they tell you or not. You may not like their perspective, but you have to face it. There's lip service about work-life balance, and then there's reality. To make the choices and take the actions that ultimately make sense for you, you need to understand that reality: your boss's top priority is competitiveness. Of course, he wants you to be happy, but only inasmuch as it helps the company win. In fact, if he is doing his job right, he is making your job so exciting that your personal life becomes a less compelling draw.

SOURCE: Welch, Jack with Suzy Welch, 2005. *Winning.* (Reprinted in *Newsweek,* April 4, 2005, p. 48).

explain in part why a significant proportion of workers would like to work fewer hours and why work–family conflict has become an important concern in the twenty-first century.

The Time Bind: Work and Family as "Reversed" Worlds?

To better illustrate the changing nature of work and family life in the United States, we turn to *The Time Bind* (1997), Arlie Hochschild's study of the work and family lives of women and men employed by a large U.S. corporation. Hochschild argues that work–family conflict caused by a shortage of time is a serious problem for working parents—mothers *and* fathers. Because of increased demands and rewards available to people in the paid workplace, families face a time deficit. As people spend more and more time at work, they are forced to be more efficient and time-conscious at home. In the process, work and family are experienced as "reversed worlds": work becomes a "haven" where people can relax and feel in control, while home becomes a workplace where people feel pressure and frustration. As she explains: "As the first shift (the workplace) takes more time, the second shift (at home) becomes more hurried and rationalized. The longer the workday at the office or plant, the more we feel pressed at home to hurry, to delegate, to delay, to forgo, to segment, to hyperorganize the precious remains of family time" (Hochschild 1997: 214–215). These pressures culminate in what she calls a "third shift—noticing, understanding, and coping with the emotional consequences of the compressed second shift" (Hochschild 1997: 215).

Both genders in Hochschild's study experienced the time bind and the difficulties of coping with "the third shift," although women's and men's experiences were by no means identical. Because women have primary responsibility for housework and childcare, the time bind was particularly problematic for women as they returned home to face the "second shift." By contrast, the men in Hochschild's study experienced somewhat different pressures. Because of the lingering expectations of the "good provider," it was hard for men to cut back on their work hours and take more time for family life. Many men she interviewed were reluctant to display concern for their families because they feared it would be costly at work, signaling to their employers that they were not committed workers. As Hochschild explains, "[t]raditionally, 'family man' meant a good provider, one who demonstrated his love of wife and children by toiling hard at the office or factory. In the modern workplace, however, 'family man' has taken on negative overtones, designating

a worker who isn't a serious player. The term now tacitly but powerfully calls into question a worker's masculinity" (1997: 132).

Hochschild's research on these issues is consistent with Larson, Richards, and Perry-Jenkins' (1994) study of employed parents. These researchers asked a sample of employed mothers and fathers to carry pagers for a week and report their emotional states at random intervals when signaled by the pager. These researchers found that women with children—particularly married women with children—experience a positive shift in mood as they moved from home to work, while men's emotional states improve as they moved from work to home.

Larson and his research team suggest that women are in better moods at work than at home because paid employment offers opportunities for social interaction and the ability to work more deliberately and in a less hurried way than at home. The employed mothers in their study did not enjoy housework, especially when it was not shared with a spouse. By contrast, employed fathers reported more positive emotional states at home than at work, a pattern Larson et al. (1994) attribute to fathers' tendency to feel constrained by their work obligations and to experience more freedom at home.

As we know, not all workers face the kind of time bind Hochschild described, as excessively long work hours are most likely to be found among college-educated professional and managerial workers (Jacobs and Gerson 2001). Nevertheless, because most two-parent households with children now contain two wage earners and single-parent households typically contain one employed adult, the time bind is a reality for many families. The problems it poses are compounded by the fact that "the rules of the road for working mothers and fathers are still being worked out" (Jacobs 1999: 1504). While mothers, fathers, and children have sought ways to cope with the time bind and the resulting "third shift," American workplaces are only beginning to address their workers' needs for a balanced life. As an institution, the workplace has been particularly slow to change, forcing individuals to adapt in ways that may not always be their choice.

The "Family-Friendly" Workplace?

Every year since 1986, *Working Mother* magazine has a published a list of the "Best Companies for Working Mothers." When the list began in 1986, the magazine identified only 30 companies that met its criteria for inclusion. This list included such companies as American Express, Apple Computer, General Motors, McDonald's, and Xerox Corporation. These companies earned their spots because they hired women for responsible positions and provided employee benefits designed to help working parents of both genders.

Fast-forward to 2006. The most recent "Best Companies" list included 100 companies, representing a wide variety of industries. For example, it included large financial institutions, such as Citigroup and American Express; retail establishments, such as Ikea; and computer companies, such as Microsoft, IBM, and Hewlett-Packard. All the companies that made the list offer a wide range of benefits, programs, and policies geared to working mothers (and fathers). For example, many companies on the list have policies that offer workers a flexible schedule or the possibility to telecommute. Some provide on-site childcare for employees or offer generous leaves for childbirth or adoption.

The companies on *Working Mother's* list were selected because their particular approach to work–family issues distinguished them from the crowd. They are not unique, however, in attending to their employees' work–family needs. Starting in about the mid-1980s, employers began to face growing pressures from their workers and from external groups, such as the government, the media, professions, and the public, to address work–family issues (Goodstein 1994). The source of these pressures should be easy to understand, given our earlier discussion about the rise of dual-earner families, the growing numbers of single parents, and other pressures on people's time and energy. As the labor market tightened in the 1990s, employers' interest in recruiting and retaining the best workers also played a role in their willingness to offer work–family benefits to some groups of employees.

Family-friendly policies encompass a range of different benefits and programs and can be broadly defined as "any benefit, working condition, or personnel policy that has been shown empirically to decrease job–family conflicts among working parents" (Glass and Fujimoto 1995: 382). Researchers often divide such policies into those having to do with flexibility in scheduling or place of work; paid or unpaid leaves to care for children or other family members; and dependent care policies, such as on-site child care, care subsidies, or referral services (Davis and Kalleberg 2006). According to surveys conducted by the Society for Human Resource Management (Burke, Esen, and Collison 2003), the top six family-friendly benefits included dependent care, flexible spending accounts, flextime, family leave (above required by law), telecommuting, compressed work week, and domestic partner benefits (for heterosexual couples).

Although more companies offer at least some of these benefits than in the past, most workers employed by U.S. companies do not have access to family-friendly benefits (Davis and Kalleberg 2006). Some firms are much more likely to offer these benefits than others, and some groups of employees within companies are more likely than other employees to have access to these policies. According to Deitch and Huffman:

> all else being equal, organizations with higher-salaried core employees, more opportunity for advancement within the organization, and greater employer investment in employee training were more generous in providing family-responsive as well as conventional fringe benefits. Increased sex segregation, either in the exclusion of women or a strong preference for hiring women, was associated with decreased provision of family benefits. (2001: 122)

In general, larger organizations are more likely to have the resources to offer these benefits than are those with fewer employees. More important, however, the greater visibility of large companies means that that they are more likely than smaller ones to face public pressure and scrutiny. Offering family-friendly policies helps these companies signal their concern for employees and their families, and these signals are good for recruiting top employees.

There is an economic payoff for companies that receive public recognition for their family-friendly policies. In a study of publicly traded firms appearing on *Working Mother*'s 100 Best Companies list between 1995 and 2002, Cascio and Young (2005) found that these firms outperformed the broader market benchmarks, measured in terms of financial returns and stock market performance. These authors suggest that "best" companies are better positioned to attract

and retain top employees. Consistent with this argument, other studies have shown that employers who provide work–life policies like flexibility benefits reap benefits in the form of higher employee commitment and organizational citizenship (Grover and Crooker 1995; Friedman and Greenhaus 2000; Lambert 2000). This research assumes that employee behavior is influenced by reciprocity norms: Employers provide benefits that employees need and want, and employees reciprocate by being better corporate citizens.

Workers' access to family-friendly policies depends not only on the size of their employer, but also on their particular occupation. Managerial and professional workers are more likely than other workers to have access to work–family policies and to take advantage of them (Glass and Estes 1997; Lambert 1999; Jacobs and Gerson 2004). Compared to other employees, these workers have more resources, such as advanced education and skills, high incomes, and strong work attachment (e.g., Secret 2000; Fredriksen-Goldsen and Scharlach 2001; Blair-Loy and Wharton 2002). These workers are also the most highly sought after by employers, who use family-friendly policies as a strategy to recruit and retain these desirable employees.

The vast majority of workers do not have access to family-friendly policies. This is especially true among employees making low hourly wages, who lack many of the resources that would enhance their bargaining power with and value to employers (Lambert and Haley-Lock 2004). Although firms that employ higher proportions of women in full-time positions are more likely than otherwise comparable firms to offer some kinds of family-friendly policies, many low-wage women workers do not have access to these policies. For example, Haley, Perry-Jenkins, and Armenia

(2001) found that women's access to work–family benefits was limited by such factors as working in a low paying or nonprofessional job, working part-time, having low organizational tenure, or working in a smaller establishment.

In addition, even when work–family benefits and policies are in place, employees' access to them is likely to be uneven. For example, Lambert and Haley-Lock (2004) found that many of the companies they studied had a 90-day waiting period for benefit use. Because lower-level jobs in these firms tended to have high turnover rates—a common feature of "dead-end" jobs—many workers never were able to take advantage of the firms' benefits package. Restricting benefits to full-time workers only is another way that companies limit workers' access to work–family benefits. In general, those most likely to need work–family policies the most thus may be least likely to have access to these policies.

Use of Work–Family Policies and the "Ideal Worker"

Even when work–family policies are available, workers may avoid using them out of a fear that this use will hurt their careers. This is especially likely to be the case among managers and professionals, who are expected to demonstrate commitment by working long hours and making work the central focus of their lives (Kanter 1977b; Schor 1991; Fried 1998). What Fried (1998: 39) calls an "overtime culture" can be seen in Perlow's (1997) research on engineers employed by a Fortune 100 company. The engineers she studied "...did everything they could to avoid using work/family policies because they feared the long-term career implications" (Perlow 1997: 228). Epstein, Seron, Oglensky, and Saute (1999)

found that lawyers who wanted to shift to part-time work were stigmatized as "time deviants," and this stigma limited the number of attorneys who desired and were able to negotiate reduced work loads. In a study of financial services managers and professionals, Blair-Loy and Wharton (2002) found that almost two thirds believed that taking an extended parental leave or setting limits on hours spent at work would harm their career.

Another recent study of these issues by Wayne and Cordeiro (2003) asked college students to assume the role of a manager and evaluate fictitious employee personnel records. Students were asked to assess the fictitious employees' levels of altruism or helpfulness at work and their expected compliance with organizational expectations (e.g., punctuality, regular attendance, following rules). Using an experimental design, the researchers created personnel records for women and men who had recently taken a family leave for the birth of a child, a child's illness, or the illness of a parent. The raters also evaluated the fictitious files of women and men who had not recently taken family leave.

The results showed that fictitious female employees who took a family leave for any reason were not viewed more negatively than female employees who did not take a family leave. By contrast, male employees who took a leave either for the birth of a child or to care for an elderly parent were seen as less altruistic than either other male employees or female employees who took leaves for similar reasons. Wayne and Cordeiro (2003) also found that male raters were more biased against men taking family leave for any reason than were female raters. Female raters evaluated men negatively only when they took leave for the birth of a child; men in these circumstances were seen less positively than women who took a leave for a similar reason and men who did not take a leave.

These findings illustrate how closely people's ideas about workers are tied to their conceptions of gender. Because women are expected to have family caregiving responsibilities, women who take leave are not viewed more negatively than other women. Men who take leave, on the other hand, are seen as "poorer organizational citizens" than men who do not (Wayne and Cordeiro 2003: 242), and these perceptions were held more strongly by male raters than women. Hence, while both men and women may still expect men's energies to be devoted more to breadwinning than family caregiving, men seem to be more committed to this belief than women.

Whether the perceptions of male and female leave-takers expressed by raters in an experimental study are shared by real managers evaluating real employees is an open question. Nevertheless, these studies underscore the powerful norms at work in most managerial and professional jobs. The "ideal worker," as defined by the gender system of domesticity, is able to be fully committed to the job and free from any domestic responsibilities.

In sum, as these findings show, while many companies have adopted some work–family policies or programs, they are less widespread than we might expect. Among lower-level workers, eligibility rules often restrict people's ability to take advantage of policies. In contrast, managers' and professionals' use is often limited by their fear of negative consequences. Work–family policies alone thus have not been a complete solution to the problem of work–family conflict for either group.

Care Work and the Price of Motherhood

Our discussion of work and family has, to this point, focused on the workplace and the "ideal worker." We now turn to the other side of the equation and consider issues of caregiving. As discussed in Chapter 9, the massive shift of services out of the household and into the market economy that took place during the second half of the twentieth century marked a major shift in the U.S. economy. The preparing and serving of food, caring for children and the elderly, and cleaning are but a few of such jobs that moved from home to the paid workplace. In recent years, the kinds of services that used to be performed in families and can now be purchased have expanded even more. At the broadest level, all of these activities are linked together by their ties to social reproduction, defined as "the array of activities and relationships involved in maintaining people both on a daily basis and intergenerationally" (Glenn 1992: 1). Many service jobs involve reproductive labor that has moved out of the household and into the market economy. These jobs, filled primarily by women in the paid labor market, are substitutes for the caregiving tasks historically performed by women in the home (Abel and Nelson 1990; England and Folbre 2000). In both settings, they involve activities performed directly for others' benefit or well-being.

England and Folbre (2000: 37) call this area of the economy "the care sector" (see also Meyer 2000). This sector includes jobs whose performance depends heavily on personal contact between the worker and the customer or client and involves workers showing concern for others. The care sector thus includes professions such as teachers or nurses, but also includes many low-paying and more routinized jobs where workers are involved in caring for children, the sick, students, or the elderly (see Chapter 9).

Research on the care sector has helped to highlight the "value" of care and the individual and social costs of undervaluing this labor (England and Folbre 1999; Crittenden 2001). For example, several studies have found that jobs requiring care pay less than otherwise comparable occupations where this is not required (England 1992; Kilbourne et al. 1994; England and Folbre 1999). In their research on this issue, England and colleagues define care work as "those occupations providing a service to people that helps develop their capabilities" (England 2005: 383). Controlling for numerous other factors (skill demands, educational requirements, etc.), they found that occupations involving care paid 5 to 15 percent less, on average, than other occupations. (Nursing, however, was an exception to this pattern and was not associated with any care penalty.) This care penalty has direct economic consequences for those who provide care—whether paid or unpaid—and it may have broader societal consequences in terms of its effects on people's willingness to perform this work.

Another line of research in this area focuses on the effects of parenthood on wages. These studies suggest that mothers, in particular, earn lower average wages than others, regardless of whether they are in a caring occupation or not (Waldfogel 1997; Crittenden 2001; Budig and England 2001). In one recent study of this issue, Correll, Benard, and Paik (2007) first conducted a laboratory experiment in which they asked paid undergraduate volunteers to rate a pair of equally qualified, same gender, same race job applicants who differed only on parental status.

Parental status was identified in a cover memo attached to each applicant's files. Parents were identified using such phrases as "Mother to John and Susan." The students participating in the experiment were told that they were helping an employer rank prospective job applicants. They then rated each fictitious candidate on a number of criteria, such as the person's perceived competence and commitment and other factors related to job qualifications and ability.

The results showed clear evidence of a motherhood penalty: Mothers were viewed as significantly less competent and less committed than nonmothers. Being a parent did not affect male applicants' ratings, however. Women without children were rated as more competent than men without children. The motherhood penalty was also seen in other areas. For example, study participants were asked to identify how many days an applicant could be late or leave early before they would no longer consider them for a position. Childless women and fathers were given more latitude in this area than mothers.

Correll and colleagues followed up their laboratory experiment with a real-world "audit" study, again focusing on motherhood's effects on the evaluation of job qualifications. They found that, like the college students in their laboratory experiment, real employers also penalize mothers. In particular, the results of the audit study showed that childless women received over twice as many "callbacks" from employers as equally qualified mothers. Fathers were called back at a slightly higher rate than nonfathers.

These studies of care work, the care sector, and the motherhood penalty provide another vantage point from which to consider the fate of domesticity in the twenty-first century. Recall that one aspect of this system, as Williams (2000) depicts it, is the expectation that women have the obligation to provide more care than men. This expectation may have weakened as women have entered the labor force, but it has not entirely disappeared. Moreover, as we have seen, women's caregiving obligations cause them to be devalued as paid workers, and caregiving itself is not rewarded to the same degree as other job characteristics.

Cross-National Differences in Work and Family

The forces transforming the American workplace during the latter half of the twentieth century were not unique. Virtually all industrialized economies saw increases in women's labor force participation and corresponding changes in the structure of families (Gornick, Meyers, and Ross 1998). In addition, during the last few decades, most economies experienced pressures to provide policies and programs aimed at supporting working families. Despite these broad similarities, however, industrial economies differ in many important respects. The United States, in particular, is an "outlier," running well ahead of most industrial economies in the amount of time people are spending at work, while lagging behind most other industrial economies in kinds of support it provides to working parents and their families.

Long work hours are more prevalent in the United States than in many European and other industrialized countries. In an in-depth comparison of work time across Canada, the United States, and eight European countries, Jacobs and Gerson (2004) found that, regardless of whether it is measured as weekly or annual hours, American workers put in more hours on the job than their European and Canadian counterparts. They found that American women, in particular, had the longest work weeks of any country in their study. Considering the combined hours worked by husbands and wives in dual-earner couples, American couples worked more hours than couples in other countries. What Fried has called the "overtime culture" thus is clearly most strongly expressed in the United States.

Though the United States leads the industrialized world in work hours, it falls behind many other industrialized countries in providing public support for working families. In the United States, the responsibility for integrating work and family life falls on the individual worker, his or her family, and, to some extent, the employer. There is much less governmental support for working families than is provided in many European countries (Van der Lippe and Van Dijk 2001). Government policies that can affect people's ability to balance work and family include regulations on work time, availability and regulation of part-time work, and policies relating to childcare and family leave.

Cross-national data on policies governing family leave provide evidence of key differences between the United States and other countries. The Family and Medical Leave Act (FMLA), signed into law by President Clinton in 1993, requires that employers having fifty or more workers provide up to twelve weeks of unpaid, job-protected leave per year to eligible employees. The leave can be used to care for a newborn, newly adopted, or foster child or to care for a relative with a serious medical condition. It can also be taken by an employee with a serious health condition.

This legislation is significant and has benefited many workers, but it has important

TABLE 14.1 Maternity, Paternity, and Parental Leaves in the OECD Countries, 1998–2002

Country	Duration of Child Birth Related Leave	Percentage of Wage Replaced	Country	Duration of Child Birth Related Leave	Percentage of Wage Replaced
Australia	1 year parental	Unpaid	Germany	14 weeks maternity including 6 weeks before birth +3 years parental child rearing leave full or part time up until child's 8th birthday	100% Flat rate Income-tested for 2 years; Unpaid for 3rd year
Austria	16 weeks maternity; 8 weeks before 8 weeks after birth (mandated) Parental leave replaced by child care allowance for 30 months one parent or 36 months if child care is shared by both parents. Previous employment requirement eliminated.	100% Flat rate Higher rate for single- and low-income parents	Greece	17 weeks maternity; 3.5 months parental leave for each parent	50% Unpaid
Belgium	15 weeks maternity; 3 months parental for each parent 3 days paternity	75–80%; Low flat rate benefit	Hungary	24 weeks maternity Childrearing leave up to child's 3rd birthday	70% Flat rate income-tested
Canada	17 weeks maternity 35 weeks parental, either parent or shared within first year. Unpaid family leave	55% 55%	Iceland	3 months each for mother and father and one parent can take an additional 3 months for 9 months parental leave in all. The 9-month leave may spread over the first 18 months after birth.	80%
Czech Republic	28 weeks maternity 37 weeks for multiple births or single mother Parental leave until child turns 3	69% Unpaid	Ireland	18 weeks maternity including up to 4 weeks before birth 14 weeks parental leave Maternity & parental leave cover adoption; 3 days paid family or emergency leave	70% Unpaid

Country	Policy	Rate
Denmark	18 weeks maternity including 4 weeks prebirth	90%
	10 weeks parents	60%
	2 weeks paternity	100%
	In addition, child care leave up to 52 weeks for either parent up to child's 8th birthday.	60%
Finland	18 weeks maternity	65%
	26 weeks parental	Flat rate
	Childrearing leave of absence until child is age 3, or can opt for home-care or child care allowances (under age 7). Guaranteed right to part-time work. Paternity– 18 days	
France	8 weeks maternity	100% for maternity & paternity leaves; Flat rate, income-tested. 80%
Italy	5 months maternity including 1 month prebirth	80%
	Additional 10 months parental leave, 20 months for multiple births Father applying for 3 month leave will be granted extra month. Unused parental leave can be taken until the child's 9th birthday.	30%
	Family (sick) leave–5 days year for children 3–8 yrs old.	Paid
Japan	14 weeks (6 pre- and 8 post-birth)	60%
	Additional year up to child's first birthday	Unpaid
Korea–South	8 weeks maternity	Unpaid

Sources: Kamerman, S.B. (2000). "Parental Leave Policies: An Essential Ingredient in Early Childhood Education and Care Policies," Social Policy Report, Ann Arbor, MI: Society for Research in Child Development; European Industrial Relations Observatory Online, http://www.eiro.eurofound.ie; Social Security Throughout the World, online, http://www-ssw.issa.int; Country Ministry sites. The Clearinghouse on International Developments in Child, Youth and Family Policies at Columbia University (http://www.childpolicyintl.org/issuebrief/issuebrief5table1.pdf)

limitations. Most notable is the fact the FMLA covers only about half of all U.S. workers (Moen and Roehling 2005). Provisions in the law pertaining to the criteria by which an employee is deemed "eligible" or that affect whether an employer is covered by the law exclude many workers. In contrast, "[o]f twenty-nine advanced industrialized countries in the Organizationa for Economic Cooperation and Development (OECD), only three, the United States, South Korea, and Austrialia, have no policy of mandatory paid maternity leave" (Moen and Roehling 2005: 163). Leave policies for the complete list of OECD countries are shown in Table 14.1.

Greater governmental support for working parents might be one solution to work–family conflict, but it is important to understand that no country has solved this problem completely or has done so in a fully gender equitable way. For example, countries that solve the problem of long work hours among dual-earner couples often accomplish this through policies that encourage part-time work by married women with children. Together, the couple devotes fewer hours to paid work, but women's economic dependence on men is increased and the level of occupational segregation by sex also tends to rise. On the other hand, gender equality—at least as measured by time spent in paid work—creates severe time pressures in families with two wage-earners. One important conclusion, then, to draw from cross-national research on work and family is that there are no simple policy solutions to this dilemma. Instead, as many researchers now argue, achieving integration between home and work will likely require a more fundamental rethinking of the structure and organization of workplaces and communities.

The Growth of Nonstandard Employment Contracts and the "24/7" Economy

The United States is in a period of economic and organizational restructuring and uncertainty (Cornfield, Campbell, and McCammon 2001). The workplace is changing, as are workers' jobs and career prospects. As we look toward the future, we need to consider how these issues will affect work and family relations in the years ahead.

Several observers have characterized U.S. employment relations as shifting from permanent, long-term ties between workers and employers to short-term, temporary ties (Kalleberg 2001). The primary outcome of this shift has been a dramatic increase in the "contingent" work force (Kalleberg and Schmidt 1996; Kalleberg 2001; see also Chapter 15). This segment of workers contains all who are not working regular, full-time jobs, such as those employed part-time (voluntary or involuntary), in temporary jobs, or working on a contractual basis. In 2001, just under one third of employed women and one quarter of employed men worked under a nonstandard employment contract (Mishel, Bernstein, and Boushey 2003).

Related to these developments is the rise of what Presser (2003) has called the "24/7" economy. In particular, she notes that the numbers of people working nonstandard schedules (e.g., evenings, nights, and/or weekends) is on the rise. Roughly one quarter of dual-earner married couples are "split-shift" couples. Among those with children under three, the number rises to one third. Among young, recently married dual-earner couples, one of every two is a split-shift couple (Presser 1998).

Nonstandard employment arrangements—including both nonstandard contracts and nonstandard schedules—are more common in some industries than others. Part-time and temporary jobs, in particular, are more common in the service sector (Kalleberg and Schmidt 1996). Workers with nonstandard schedules are also most likely to be found in the service sector—especially in personal service jobs (Presser 1998). Nonstandard workers are generally more likely to be found in lower-paying occupations and industries (Presser 2003; Mishel, Bernstein, and Boushey 2003). Compared to other employees, workers with nonstandard employment contracts have fewer opportunities for promotion and are generally less satisfied with their jobs than workers on standard contracts (Mishel, Bernstein, and Boushey 2003). Working a nonstandard schedule has been linked to a variety of negative physical and psychological problems, such as sleep disorders, stress, and depression (Fenwick and Tausig 2001). We discuss nonstandard employment in more detail in the next chapter.

A central issue for those interested in work and family is whether nonstandard work arrangements—in the form of either contingent jobs or nonstandard work schedules—provide workers with greater or fewer options for balancing work and family life. On one hand, some see the growth of nonstandard employment contracts as providing workers—particularly women—with the flexibility they need to integrate job and family demands. Part-time jobs are the type of nonstandard work most often viewed as an option for people seeking greater balance in their lives (Mishel, Bernstein, and Boushey 2003). In her study of mothers working the night shift Garey (1999: 139) found that some viewed this as a way to be " 'working mothers' who are 'stay-at-home' moms."

At the same time, there is little systematic evidence that women (or men) who need or want greater work–life balance are more likely than others to have nonstandard employment contracts or schedules or that these arrangements are truly beneficial in facilitating greater work–family balance. Women with nonstandard employment contracts are only slightly more likely to have children than other women, and such men are less likely to have children than other men (Mishel, Bernstein, and Boushey 2003). Moreover, many of these workers would prefer regular, full-time employment (Kalleberg and Schmidt 1996; Mischel, Bernstein, and Boushey 2003). As Kalleberg and Schmidt explain, the view "that employers created contingent work schedules in response to employee demand should not be overstated" (1996: 256).

Research on workers with nonstandard schedules yields similar conclusions in terms of their effects on work–family relations. As Presser (1998) explains, while women are more likely than men to cite family concerns as a reason for working a nonstandard schedule, both women and men are much more likely to work nonstandard schedules for involuntary rather than voluntary reasons. Moreover, evidence suggests that the consequences of working a nonstandard schedule for workers' family lives and relationships are mixed at best (Presser 1998, 2003). For example, split-shift couples have higher divorce rates and lower levels of marital quality than couples working standard schedules (Presser 1998). However, fathers in split-shift couples do more household work than other men and are the primary caregivers of their children when mothers are working (Presser 1998). These findings suggest that split-shift arrangements may be beneficial for children and families in some limited respects, but much more research is needed in this area.

The growing number of people with nonstandard employment contracts, who often work alongside more permanent, core workers, has created the beginnings of a two-tiered labor force (Kalleberg 2003). Along similar lines, Presser (1998) anticipates growing diversity in work schedules, especially among women. These divisions create work forces with very different interests vis-à-vis their employers' involvement in work and family life. For example, workers on nonstandard contracts are only weakly connected to firms and the workplace benefits they provide. In contrast, employees on standard contracts face even more intense demands on their loyalty and commitment.

The standard employment contract providing relatively permanent, full-time work has always been more available to white men than to other groups. These work arrangements, with their implied exchange of loyalty and hard work on the employees' part for secure employment and the prospect of mobility and wage growth on the part of employers, are consistent with domesticity's "ideal worker" norm. Women—especially those with children—were never viewed as ideal workers in the same way as men, and thus have always been less likely to obtain the jobs and rewards associated with stable, permanent work. Although nonstandard work schedules have increased for both genders, women with young children are expected to obtain a disproportionate share of new jobs organized in this way (Presser 1998). As global competition forces large employers to restructure their workplaces

and service employers continue to look for ways to cut their labor costs, workers are most likely to need jobs that are compatible with raising families. Yet some workers enjoy much greater access to work–family benefits than do others.

Although workers' access to "good" jobs has always differed, the workforce has grown more divided in recent years (Morris and Western 1999; Mishel, Bernstein, and Boushey 2003). As Levy (1998) notes, one difference from the past is that "the winners" in today's economy have a much greater influence on economic policies than in the past. While the divisions noted above are only one part of this polarization, they are important insofar as they signal a fundamental restructuring of work and employment. Even as employers, workers, and the public express greater concern about work–family balance, workers' access to jobs that make such accommodation possible grows increasingly more divided. In light of these changes, Lambert and Haley-Lock (2004: 186) call for an expanded definition of "work-life opportunities" to include job security, skill development, mobility into jobs that facilitate work-life balance, income stability and growth, flexibility and predictability in scheduling work effort, and benefits that support families as well as individual workers.

Conclusion

As women's and men's lives have changed, so too have work and family. Among the many social changes that accompanied industrialization was a growing separation between family and work and a corresponding understanding of women's and men's roles as distinct and separate. Cultural ideals and reality rarely align, however, and the new system of "domesticity" that emerged was undermined by economic and social changes that brought women into the labor force in large numbers.

One consequence of the increasing number of dual-earner households has been an increase in people's feelings of overwork and work–family conflict. Many women and men say that they would like to work fewer hours, and large numbers of both genders express interest in "family-friendly" policies offered by employers. Although some U.S. workplaces are changing in ways that enable workers to better balance their family and job demands, change has been slow and uneven, especially when compared to other industrial societies. In addition, policies themselves can only do so much to transform deeply entrenched cultural views of work and the "ideal worker." Reconciling the demands of work and family caregiving is likely to become even more challenging in the future as jobs and the economy attempt to keep up with global competition and technological change.

Chapter 15

❧

The New American Workplace

Employees today often face a bewildering set of shifts in every aspect of their jobs. Consider the impact of technology. These words are being written on a laptop, far removed from an office bureaucracy—an indication that cell phones, PCs, PDAs, Blackberry devices, and webcams now make it possible for employees to perform their jobs almost regardless of the time or place. This is of course a mixed blessing, as some organizations have begun to expect their workers to be available at all times of the day or night. Indeed, analysts like Jill Fraser (2002) have suggested that these technologies have tethered workers to their jobs, generating a "white collar sweatshop."

Yet technology is hardly the only source of change in the organization of people's jobs; social structural forces also play a vital role As was suggested in Chapter 14, new, "nonstandard" or insecure forms of employment have emerged that place workers in a far more precarious position than did permanent, stable jobs that offered benefits. Data reveal that temporary positions, part-time jobs, and jobs as independent contractors—types of work often called "contingent" jobs, reflecting their precarious nature—have grown much more rapidly than has the labor force overall. Although on occasion workers seek out such flexible employment—think of students, or parents with young children—data suggest that the majority of job holders in such categories would prefer more stable permanent jobs with real futures. As contingent work grows, customary notions of job security, of progression through a meaningful career, or of the enjoyment of ties with one's co-workers, all begin to sound quaint.

Change has gripped the jobs of even workers employed under "standard" work arrangements. Feeling pressure from international competitors, U.S. employers have increasingly adopted new forms of work organization, sometimes based on employee participation, to an unprecedented extent. Celebrated experiments at such American firms as Saturn, Southwest Airlines, Corning, Procter & Gamble, Xerox, and many other well-known firms—often following the example set by leading Japanese and Swedish firms—have helped to publicize systems for participative management, which promise to expand the worker's sense of autonomy and control. These new work systems are sometimes called "high-performance" or "high-commitment" work systems, for they hinge on the company's ability to foster a high level of commitment and identification among its employees. But the success of these systems often stands at odds with still other changes that economic competition has led employers to make: downsizing, large-scale layoffs, and efforts to outsource employment to local contractors or to sites located in other nations entirely. Thus at the very moment when many employers are asking more and more of their employees, they often provide significantly fewer of the job rewards that employees are most likely to seek (such as job security, provisions for health and retirement, and opportunities for advancement during a stable career).

Multiple forces are converging on the workplace, then, often in conflicting ways that invite uncertainty and anxiety. Sometimes these tensions break out into open conflict and debate. The students at Georgetown University in Washington, DC, recently conducted a hunger strike in support of custodial and housekeeping workers at their university to ensure that the workers would receive a living wage. Legal suits have been filed successfully against Microsoft, alleging that the software giant unfairly denied benefits and other rights to its "temporary" workers, some of whom had worked at the firm for decades. Some employees have alleged that "quality circle" teams and other systems for employee participation have in fact been used as company unions; in some cases, courts have agreed. Increasingly, economic decision makers have had to defend the outsourcing of American jobs, leading to an important debate about the factors currently undermining U.S. manufacturing in particular. Amid all these conflicting developments and organizational crosscurrents, it is no wonder that theorists have put forward dramatically different understandings of the workplace realities currently taking place.

In this chapter and the next, we examine the major changes currently unfolding at work

organizations in the United States and beyond, the better to understand and anticipate how the organization of work is likely to evolve under contemporary capitalism. In this chapter we focus on three distinct issues of interest to sociologists, managers, workers, and others concerned with the transformation of the American workplace. First, we examine trends affecting the occupational structure, chiefly through the growth and decline of various types of work. Second, we discuss the spread of "contingent" or nonstandard work arrangements, which alter the employment relationship as it has been traditionally understood. And third, we examine efforts to transform or humanize the centralized, bureaucratic structures that have persisted for so long. Making sense of these sources of workplace change—and familiarizing ourselves with the debates that have swirled around the question of the new American workplace—will put us in a better position to make sense of the risks and opportunities we are likely to face as workers and as citizens. In a sense, the debate about the new American workplace is really a debate about the kind of society in which we want to live, and the kind of people we aspire to be.

Trends in Occupational Growth: Some Evidence

One obvious source of change in the nature of the work people perform stems from shifts in the demand for labor. Some occupations have tended to shrink in size, whether in absolute numbers or relative to other occupations, while other occupations have tended to grow. Such trends are important to consider, since many social institutions must take account of such shifts. Educators, students, and employers, for example, need to be able to forecast changes in the need for workers in particular occupational groups. This is why the federal government uses a number of methods to track trends (both actual and projected) in employment by occupation.

Asked to name the occupations that account for the fastest growing groups of jobs in the contemporary setting, students often name such occupations as computer scientists and programmers, scientists and engineers, business consultants, or accounting, legal, and financial professionals. It's not difficult to see why. These occupations correspond to the occupational aspirations that many students hold. They often embody many widely discussed notions concerning the rise of a postindustrial society (see Chapters 2 and 9) and of a new, science-based "knowledge economy." The notion that underlies these latter views is that advanced capitalist societies rely less and less on *physical* inputs (such as manual labor or material resources) than on the *intellectual* capacities a given firm, region, or nation can command. In such a society, one might expect, an ever-smaller proportion of a nation's labor force is devoted to work with material objects. Now, this view holds, the occupations that are destined to grow most rapidly should be those that involve work on *symbolic* objects, such as computer programs, microchip designs, financial models, and even the human genome (see Bell 1973; Block 1990; Reich 1992; Powell and Snellman 2004). Indeed, one prominent author has spoken of "the rise of the creative class"—a growing category of designers, artists, writers, scientists, and other "knowledge workers" whose analytic and creative skills become the driving force of the new economy (Florida 2002).

What do recent occupational data suggest about such predictions? Figure 15.1 presents data that illustrate how the U.S. occupational structure has been changing since 1983, almost a quarter century. The bars in the graph show how much growth has occurred in each occupational category, using as the baseline the number of workers employed in each occupation in 1983. Since the overall labor force has grown by 44.9 percent, occupations that have increased by more than this percentage have been expanding their share of the labor force. Occupations that have grown, but more modestly than has the labor force as a whole, have thus been contracting in relative terms. An occupation with a negative percentage has been declining in absolute numbers even as the labor force has grown.

The figure reveals two points that are consistent with the argument of an expanding knowledge economy. First, the occupations that have expanded most rapidly in the last quarter century are the "management, business, and finance" occupations, along with "professional and related" occupations. In these job categories, the number of employees has grown by more than 75 percent, or half again as much as in the labor force as a whole. Although not shown in figure 15.1, the growth of these managerial and professional occupations has been especially rapid since the year 2000. Second, we do indeed see a sharp decline in the percent of the labor force engaged in "production operations." Indeed, this job category has barely expanded at all in absolute numbers even though the labor force has substantially grown. Perhaps most dramatic has been the decline of occupations in farming, fishing, and forestry, where the labor force has been shrinking in absolute numbers, and doing so for decades. These changes are all consistent with the notion that our occupational structure is more and more highly composed of mental or knowledge-intensive occupations.

FIGURE 15.1 Changes in the Occupational Composition of the U.S. Labor Force, 1983–2007.

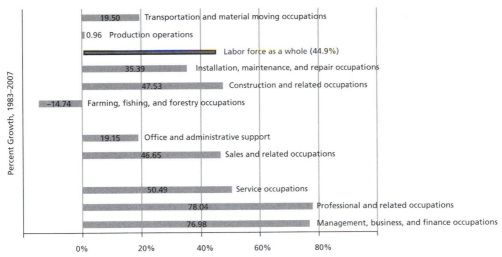

Source: U.S. Bureau of Labor Statistics, Current Population Statistics.

Yet in at least three respects, the data stand at odds with this notion of the knowledge economy. First, many manual occupations have either held steady as a proportion of the labor force or actually grown. This is the case not only with jobs involving "installation, maintenance, and repair" work, but also with work in the construction trades. These two job categories employed more than 15 million workers in 2007, a slightly larger proportion of the labor force than they made up in 1983. Second, many "mental" or white collar occupations (such as those in "office and administrative support") have declined in relative terms, showing some growth but at a level that lags well behind the growth of the labor force. Indeed, this category of office employment has declined in absolute numbers since the year 2000. Third, although service occupations have in fact grown more rapidly than the labor force overall, many of the largest and most rapidly expanding occupations in this category do not involve rewarding

positions in business or producer services, but rather more mundane jobs as health care aides, child care workers, and food preparation and fast food work. Clearly, if the occupational structure does give rise to an expanding stratum of "knowledge" workers, it also generates enduring and often growing levels of demand for workers whose jobs are completely different than prestigious professional work.

Much the same point emerges when we examine the federal government's labor force projections for the years 2006–2016. Table 15.1 presents the government's estimates of the levels of job growth that are likely to occur in the 25 occupations expected to generate the greatest number of new jobs in the coming years. Employment projections are of course somewhat uncertain, for economic crises, technological changes, and public policy choices cannot easily be foretold. Still, these projections do provide a reasonable portrait of the occupational shifts that

TABLE 15.1 Twenty-Five Leading Occupations with the Largest Job Growth, 2006–2016, by Income Quartile and Educational Requirements.

INCOME QUARTILE	OCCUPATION	PROJECTED JOB GROWTH (IN 000S)	PROJECTED SIZE IN 2016 (IN 000S)	EDUCATION OR TRAINING REQUIRED
Highest ($46,360 or more)	Registered Nurses	587	3,092	Associate degree
	Post-secondary teachers	382	2,054	Doctoral degree
	Software engineers	226	733	Bachelor's degree
	Accountants and auditors	226	1,500	Bachelor's degree
	Management analysts	149	827	Bachelor's degree plus work experience
	Total growth for quartile:	1,570		
Second ($30,600–46,300)	Exec Secretaries & Assistants	239	1,857	Work experience in related job
	Elementary school teachers	209	1,749	Bachelor's degree
	Truck drivers (heavy)	193	2,053	Moderate term on-the-job training
	Carpenters	150	1,612	Long term on-the-job training
	Total growth for quartile	791		
Third ($21,260–30,560)	Customer Service Rep.	545	2,747	Moderate on-the-job training
	Office clerks, general	404	3,604	Short-term on-the-job training
	Nursing aides and attendants	264	1,711	Post-secondary vocational award
	Accounting clerks	264	2,377	Moderate on-the-job training
	Landscaping workers	221	1,441	Short-term on-the-job training
	Receptionists and info. Clerks	202	1,375	Short-term on-the-job training
	Security Guards	175	1,216	Short-term on-the-job training
	Carpenters	150	1,612	Long term on-the-job training
	Total growth for quartile	2,225		
Fourth (up to $21,220)	Retail salespersons	557	5,034	Short-term on-the-job training
	Food preparation, incl. fast food	452	2,955	Short-term on-the-job training
	Personal and home care aides	389	1,156	Short-term on-the-job training
	Home health care aides	384	1,171	Short-term on-the-job training
	Janitors and cleaners	345	2,732	Short-term on-the-job training
	Waiters and waitresses	255	2,615	Short-term on-the-job training
	Child care workers	248	1,636	Short-term on-the-job training
	Maids and housekeeping cleaners	186	1,656	Short-term on-the-job training
	Total growth for quartile	2,816		
Total job growth, all quartiles		7,402		

Source: U.S. Bureau of Labor Statistics, Occupational Projections and Training Data, 2008–09 edition, Bulletin 2702.

are likely to occur. The question is what these projections suggest about the nature of the jobs that people are likely to hold in future years.

The table is organized into four different panels, according to the wage or salary levels which each job is likely to pay. Looking first at the bottom of the table, we see that these 25 jobs are projected to generate a total of 7.4 million jobs by 2016. Yet, as we see in the top panel of the table, only 1.5 million of these jobs are likely to offer pay in the highest quartile ($46,360 or more, in 2007 dollars). As the table shows, these five top-quartile occupations include management analysts, accountants and auditors, software engineers, college teachers, and registered nurses. Looking beyond these relatively favorable occupations, we see that roughly two-thirds of the jobs which these 25 occupations will generate will offer earnings that fall into the lowest and second lowest income quartiles, paying $30,560 or less. Of these 25 occupations, fully twenty require little more than a high school degree. Clearly, the great bulk of the new jobs coming on line in the near- and middle-term future are likely to bear little resemblance to the glamorous image often associated with the emerging knowledge or information economy.

Notably absent on the list of fast growing occupations are jobs in the manufacturing branches of the economy, whose share of the labor force has been declining, especially since 2000 (see chapter 16 on globalization). Yet when we consider the occupations that *are* expanding, and which employ workers in food preparation, landscaping, health care services, or truck driving—we see that many of these jobs involve substantial elements of manual work and are often performed under onerous conditions. Cooking and serving meals in commercial establishments,

moving patients from beds to gurneys, planting bushes at industrial office parks, or driving delivery trucks—these are all jobs that involve substantial physical effort and endurance, and sometimes expose workers to harsh or dangerous working environments. While such work may not epitomize the glamorous nature of work under the knowledge economy, they are quite clearly growing in size, suggesting that manual or "dirty" work is not so much disappearing as assuming new forms. What this implies for our society's opportunity structure has been much discussed among policy analysts, with some theorists increasingly speaking of an "hourglass economy"—one in which occupations in the middle seem to shrink in relative or even absolute terms. If true, such trends may introduce increasingly sharp social divisions and tensions into the society as a whole (Reich 1992; Harrison 1994).

It is important to point out that there is much that is uncertain about the shifting role of particular occupational groups. Whether manufacturing occupations will continue to decline, for example, is dependent on a number of influences that cannot be factored into any employment projection. Thus the number of manufacturing jobs performed in the United States is highly sensitive to U.S. financial, monetary, and trade policy. Apparel and textile employment, for example, has shown great fluctuation in the last several decades because of tariff and trade policies that have encouraged many companies to relocate production off shore. Likewise, the decision of Japanese and European automakers to build more and more of their cars in North America has partly stemmed from powerful political pressures and "domestic content" rules established by the U.S. government. Strategic concerns also come into play. Some analysts have pointed out that even the most highly advanced economies need to maintain a solid industrial base in machine production, metalworking, micro-electronics, energy production, durable goods, and chemicals if they are to sustain a position of economic, military, and financial strength and independence. These considerations suggest that occupational trends do not follow inevitable "iron laws" or a fixed progression through stages, but are subject to social and political contingencies, among which are public policies supported by the electorate itself.

The Changing Employment Relationship

Thus far we have discussed sources of workplace change that stem from shifting levels of demand for labor within one or another occupational category. But more is occurring than change in the *level* of demand for labor. Equally important are changes in the *nature* of demand—that is, the shifting nature of the employment relationship itself. Such changes have forced analysts—and employees—to rethink their most fundamental assumptions about what it means to be an employee under contemporary capitalism.

In many respects, these changes have reminded analysts that what most employees have taken for granted for many decades—the "standard" work arrangement, involving a stable and enduring tie between employer and employee, with decent pay and benefits—is actually a relatively recent construct. Given recent economic pressures, moreover, that construct is increasingly giving way to newer forms of employment that provide many benefits to the employer—greater flexibility in discharging workers, reduced pressures to provide expensive benefits, greater

protection against legal responsibilities—but which threaten to reduce the quality of employment that many job seekers can expect to enjoy.

Under the highly competitive conditions that existed during nineteenth-century capitalism, a large proportion of economic activity occurred through the mechanism of the market. Such market ties were highly dynamic and uncertain. As the need arose to coordinate markets on a national and even international basis, and as the advantages that flowed from economies of scale became clear, companies often found it beneficial to produce their own supplies, tools, and resources in-house, rather than buying them on the open market. In a word, firms began to "*internalize*" activities that had previously been performed and coordinated through market ties. This trend was also true for the labor on which firms relied. Instead of simply hiring mid-level managers or employees whenever positions became open—a market-based solution—during the early twentieth century firms began to construct institutions within their own boundaries that provided ongoing sources of skilled employees. By filling mid-level positions from below—that is, "promoting from within"—firms essentially constructed an *internalized* source of labor, much as they did with other strategic resources (Doeringer and Piore 1971; Edwards 1979).

The result, which developed momentum throughout the first three quarters of the twentieth century, was a system that social scientists have called "internal labor markets" (ILMs)—structures that governed the distribution of jobs among the firm's employees. From the employee's point of view, such arrangements provided a stable and orderly basis for one's career aspirations. Thus workers who were diligent and took their job responsibilities to heart could look forward to upward mobility within the firm and to a sense of accomplishment during the course of their working lives. From the point of view of the firm, ILMs also provided important benefits, for they provided material incentives for workers to acquire company-specific skills and to show their loyalty and commitment to a single firm. This convergence of interests led analysts to speak of a "social contract" at work. Although it probably never encompassed a majority of the labor force—minority workers and women only occasionally gained full admission to ILMs, as discussed in Chapters 11 and 12—it did provide an important source of stability and legitimacy and grew in strength during the years immediately after World War II.

Rapidly changing economic conditions have acted to undermine the prevalence of ILMs and with it the standard work arrangements that many employees have come to expect. Beginning during the late 1970s, a number of developments began to impose pressures on many U.S. firms, eventually compelling them to seek out ways of dismantling the internal labor markets they had spent a century building up. The energy crisis of the 1970s, the rising cost of labor (and especially of employee benefits), coupled with sharpening international competition and the weakening position of labor unions within U.S. society, all gave firms powerful incentives now to *externalize* their human resources—that is, to minimize the firm's obligations to its own employees. Rather than keeping large numbers of employees on the books, it became increasingly attractive for firms to contract out activities to outside suppliers. As the organizational sociologists Jeffrey Pfeffer and James Baron (1988: 269) put it, "work formerly conducted within the boundaries and under the administrative control of a single enterprise is parceled out to more specialized organizational entities"—that is, to *other* employers on the basis of a market arrangement. This trend, which gathered momentum throughout the 1980s and 1990s, has meant several things for the nature of the employment relationship within the United States.

For one thing, whole functions that used to be performed by employees of large, well-known corporations were now being hived off to outside suppliers. These new relationships took a number of different forms. In some cases, firms simply "outsourced" or contracted out various types of functions—not only janitorial services and security work, but also such professional jobs as marketing, legal services, communications, and human resources as well. Workers now performing these tasks were still permanent employees, but firms now "leased" their labor from an outside contractor instead of employing the workers outright. In other cases, firms opted to hire temporary workers, whether directly or through temporary employment agencies. Such "temps" hold a position that is legally and socially distinct from permanent employees, no matter how long the situation endures (Rubin 1995, 1996; Smith 2001), and often must wear specially colored badges denoting their different employment status. In still other cases, employers hired workers as independent consultants or contract employees, confining their obligations to the duration of a single project or time period. The underlying feature that these new forms of employment have in common is that each compels the employee to accept terms and conditions of employment that are much more contingent than before—that is, they no longer provide the certainty and stability that "jobs" had previously implied. The term "contingent worker" has become widely used by social scientists and policy analysts, and commonly refers to workers who are employed by temporary employment agencies, who hold jobs that are limited to a given duration, or who are involuntarily working part-time but would prefer full time employment.

There can be little doubt that the phenomenon of contingent work has indeed grown in recent decades. According to data from the Bureau of Labor Statistics, the number of jobs of all types increased by 53.7 percent during the years 1982 (just after a deep recession) to 1990—a period of sustained economic growth. The number of temporary jobs, however, increased at roughly four times that pace (210 percent). This growth in the ranks of temporary employment continued throughout the 1990s: Overall, the average number of temporary workers employed in the United States on any given day increased tenfold from 1970 to 1997, from a quarter of a million workers to fully 2.5 million temps. Data suggest that temporary work is no longer confined to holiday seasons or periods of economic uncertainty, when it may not make sense to hire permanent workers. Instead, more and more firms are incorporating temporary workers as stable and enduring features of their personnel systems. As Rubin (1995) puts it, ironically enough, "*temporary work has become a permanent feature of the American economy.*"

Part-time jobs also grew much more rapidly than did the economy as a whole, but in a manner that is itself interesting. Although some analysts suggest that the growth of part-time jobs reflects worker preferences, with workers increasingly opting to choose part-time jobs as a way of accommodating family life, the data suggest that this is not the whole story: The growth in part-time employment during the 1980s was confined to workers who actively sought *full-time* jobs, but could only locate jobs that offered part-time employment.

Studies conducted by both the U.S. Department of Labor and the American Management Association have pointed to a further trend. In an era of downsizing, when firms are seeking to shed employees, a significant number of workers are being rehired by their previous employers, performing the same duties as before, but now in much less secure and reward positions, whether as temporary workers, independent contractors, or "on-call" workers. Such workers may work alongside their old co-workers, conducting the same work and even sitting at the same desks as before. No longer full citizens of the firm, they also earn a significantly lower salary and often lack health insurance and retirement benefits. Their very presence may serve as a painful reminder of growing job instability even for workers who hold more permanent or standard work arrangements (Graham 1995; Di Tomaso 2001; Smith 2001a). Some researchers have drawn attention to the symbolic injuries that workers suffer because of their reliance on temporary employment. Kevin Henson's *Just a Temp* (1996) emphasized the multiple slights he endured while doing participant observation within office settings: He was surrounded by employees who rarely bothered to learn his name (but expected him to learn theirs) and who generally assumed that something was wrong with him if he was forced to rely on a temp agency for work. Often, his co-workers explained even the simplest of tasks to him in great detail, as if he were a person of limited intelligence. In a study called " 'Hey Why Don't You Wear a Shorter Skirt?' " Krasas-Rogers and Henson (1997) suggest that the relatively powerless work situation of female temps leaves them especially vulnerable to various forms of sexual harassment.

Although the growth of contingent labor is a relatively recent phenomenon, this trend has now garnered substantial attention from researchers of varying orientations. In 1993, the U.S. Congress held hearings on the growth of contingent work in order to assess the impact of this trend on the quality of employment in the United States. In August 1997, unionized members of the United Parcel Service conducted a strike that drew substantial public sympathy, inasmuch as a key issue in the work stoppage concerned the workers' struggle to set limits on the hiring of part-timers as a means of protecting the position of workers in permanent, full-time jobs. The research on contingent work supports a number of conclusions. First, although the initial wave of research tended to view contingent work in a simplified monolithic manner, there is increasing recognition that not all contingent jobs are alike, and that there is much greater diversity among nonstandard forms of employment than analysts recognized at first. Thus, highly educated workers who command valued skills in business services (technical experts, journalists or communications specialists, business consultants of various types) may actually benefit from the expansion of contingent forms of employment. As firms seek to outsource work previously done by full-time staff, such highly skilled agents can offer their services to many client firms at one and the same time. In this fashion, they can set their own hours, decide which projects to accept, and generally achieve much more control over their own work situations than traditional bureaucratic employment allowed—a development that some have described as "Free Agent Nation" (see Albert and Bradley 1997; Arthur and Rousseau 2001). Other analysts have celebrated this tendency for workers to broaden their horizons beyond the confines of a single firm, a development they refer to as the rise of the "boundaryless career"

(Arthur and Rousseau 2001). The point of such arguments is that it can be greatly misleading to paint all nonstandard forms of employment with the same brush.

Yet it would be equally misleading to suggest that most or even a substantial proportion of job seekers can hold such highly desirable positions within the labor market. Indeed, such instances seem to be more the exception than the norm. Using 1995 survey data, Kalleberg, Reskin, and Hudson (2000) explored the impact that employment in nonstandard jobs has on the job rewards that workers received. They found that workers holding one or another form of nonstandard employment—temporary jobs, part time work, "on-call" status, or a contract position—were significantly more likely to suffer a poor quality of employment—low wages, no health insurance or pensions, poor job security—than were workers in regular, full-time jobs. While 29.1 percent of all men in permanent, full-time jobs lacked health insurance, for example, fully 83.5 percent of their counterparts in part-time jobs reported lacking this important benefit. The point of the Kalleberg study and many others like it is that the expansion of contingent work has led to an overall but not uniform tendency toward more precarious conditions of employment for many employees, who are more exposed to the market than had been the case in the recent past.

The expansion of contingent work has had other effects as well, both for workers and for their employers. Several studies have begun to suggest that tensions and conflicts often develop in workplaces where permanent and temporary workers are employed alongside one another (Graham 1995; Smith 2001). In such situations, workers in regular, permanent jobs may feel threatened by those in less secure positions (fearing that their own positions may be redefined or redistributed to others). For their part, workers in temporary or other types of contingent jobs may feel unfairly excluded from important job rewards—according to Krasas Rogers (1995), temps often feel treated as "nonpersons," deprived even of the most basic forms of courtesy at work—even though they perform the same tasks as permanent workers and are equally qualified for such jobs. Given such organizational tensions, employers sometimes find that the use of contingent or nonstandard forms of employment is very much a mixed blessing in that it introduces levels of complexity they would very much prefer to avoid (Geary 1992).

Despite such hesitations, the use of contingent work has continued to spread throughout the U.S. economy, leading some analysts to suspect that it has only contributed to the polarized or "dualistic" conditions of employment discussed earlier in this chapter. Indeed, the British analyst John Atkinson (1985) argued that companies are increasingly adopting a form he dubbed the "flexible firm," in which job security and autonomy are increasingly reserved for a shrinking "core" of employees who perform functions that are central to the firm's mission. Employees performing other functions, by contrast, are peripheralized and subject to increasingly uncertain or contingent forms of employment. Although there is much debate about the applicability of the "flexible firm" (Vallas 1999), there is evidence to support such an approach. Thus, in their analysis of a survey of firms using temporary workers, Magnum, Mayall, and Nelson (1985) concluded that temps have come to serve as a kind of cushion or buffer, sheltering other, more secure workers against market uncertainties: "the more workers who are guaranteed

job security, the greater the number who will have to play the peripheral role to provide the necessary human resources buffer" (1985: 609). A later study by Barnett and Miner (1992) also found that upper-level workers within the firm tended to benefit from the employment of temporary workers, since the latter were usually prevented from competing for the most desirable jobs within the firm. What these studies suggest is that there is often a material basis underlying the tensions and resentments that develop among workers in distinct (standard/contingent) jobs—a development that may undermine the effort of firms to develop a collaborative, participative culture among all employees.

A last consideration that must be made concerning contingent work concerns the role of politics. If, as the bulk of the literature suggests, workers are increasingly finding it difficult to land jobs that offer the sort of security and benefits offered by the standard work arrangement, then the question becomes one of how U.S. society can adapt to this shift. If the workplace can no longer be viewed as the provider of social insurance benefits such as health care or retirement provisions, then how will such needs be met? The obvious answer would be through public policy—that is, through government supports of one sort or another. Yet clearly, the recent drift of public policy has been in the opposite direction—reducing, not increasing, public commitments to the nation's employees. Both corporations and our political institutions are adopting much the same policy of leaving workers to their own devices. So pronounced is this shift (and so great are the resulting anxieties) that analysts like Jacob Hacker (2006) have begun to speak of a "great risk shift"—that is, a ground trend in which uncertainties are shifted away from corporations and toward employees, whose income levels grow increasingly volatile and whose employment and retirement prospects are surrounded by instability. Whether this risk shift is a sustainable policy remains to be seen.

The Participatory Management Movement

A further source of workplace change—one that has received a great deal of discussion and debate—has been the effort to adopt more participative forms of management that expand the discretion of front-line employees.

In approaching this phenomenon, it is important to recall that efforts to humanize the work process have a long history. The coming of the factory system, as was discussed in Chapters 4 and 5, prompted much protest and collective action as workers struggled to change the harsh and often coercive regimes they faced during the late eighteenth and early nineteenth centuries. What resulted were not only laws limiting the length of the working day and the use of child labor, labor unions, and political parties representing factory workers (see Chapter 10). There also emerged producers' cooperatives, which sought to infuse an uplifting mission of human development into factory life. Later, in the wake of Taylorism and the rise of the assembly line, there again emerged widespread efforts to humanize the employment relationship, as in the "industrial betterment" movement that bred welfare capitalism (see Chapter 5). By the 1950s, such American managerial theorists as Frederick Herzberg and Douglas McGregor began to argue that the most widely used managerial methods—based as they were on Taylorism, hierarchy, and bureaucracy—not only undermined workers'

efforts to derive a sense of creativity and fulfillment at work, they also limited the achievement of organizational goals as well.

Until recently, few of these efforts to humanize the employment relationship left any enduring mark on the nature of work organizations. Although a handful of well-known experiments and surveys gained interest and curiosity among managerial audiences, they remained exceptions to the rule of centralized, bureaucratic hierarchies, which drew a sharp line between the managers and the managed.

All that began to change during the late 1970s and early 1980s. The reasons are complex, but most analysts point to the growth of sharp international competition (most notably, from Japan), the demands of new technologies, and the growing sense that more participative and flexible forms of work organizations were needed if firms were to respond quickly and effectively to rapidly changing consumer tastes. All these influences promoted the growing belief among senior managers that the old systems of management had reached their limits and that new organizational forms were needed to foster renewed economic growth.

Much of the ferment concerning new managerial practices in the United States took shape during the 1980s, when international competition from Europe and Japan exposed important points of vulnerability within U.S. production systems, undermining the taken-for-granted character of managerial orthodoxy at that time. Threatened with the erosion of U.S. competitiveness in key manufacturing industries such as automobile assembly, steel fabrication, machine tools, electronics, and semiconductors, U.S. firms and government policy makers were forced to take seriously many of the ideas that seemed to fuel the success of their competitors. There was an irony here: whereas in previous decades, foreign management teams had toured U.S. factories in an effort to learn how best to emulate American ingenuity, now the tables had been turned. Now it was the United States that sent management teams abroad in an effort to catch up with the competition. (Heckscher 1988, 1994; Appelbaum and Batt 1994; Cappelli and Neumark 2001). Thus the U.S. economy began to import from Japan not only manufactured products, but also the very models that were used in the manufacturing process itself.

During the early 1980s, much of the discussion centered on employee involvement and quality circles—two modest innovations that drew selectively on Japanese work practices and which sought merely to provide vehicles for worker consultation. By the end of the 1980s, however, Japanese and European influences had begun to leave a deeper impression on U.S. firms, leading to far-reaching efforts that took worker participation in new and more ambitious directions.

The Japanization of American Industry

Japan had itself drawn heavily on the U.S. statistician W. Edward Deming, whose work shaped the thinking of many Japanese managers in the years immediately following World War II. These were turbulent years for Japanese industry. Seeking to establish a domestic automobile industry during the late 1940s and early 1950s, Japanese firms such as Nissan and Toyota lacked the capital resources enjoyed by large U.S. firms. They also lacked the large customer base and the economies of scale that U.S. producers could achieve. Forced to innovate, Japanese manufacturers sought to adopt highly flexible production systems that required low levels of capital

investment and a highly demanding pace of work and which made no provisions for job security or worker representation. Yet Japanese workers—empowered by a U.S.-spawned constitution that gave them the right to organize on their own behalf—responded by insisting on the right to job security. After a series of widespread strikes at several of Japan's largest manufacturing firms during the 1950s, a new system of labor relations emerged that provided workers with a guarantee of permanent employment, in return for which workers were expected to demonstrate loyalty to the firm. The result involved what Womack, Jones, and Roos (1990) called the "lean" system of production, which many theorists believe was a critical ingredient in the dramatic industrial growth that Japan managed from 1960 to 1990 (see Dohse, Jurgens, and Malsch 1985).

Lean production was not the only model used by advocates of workplace change. Somewhat different models garnered attention in the Scandinavian countries and in parts of Germany and Italy, where the craft tradition of highly skilled workers had developed strong institutions and where strong apprenticeship systems were in place (Piore and Sabel 1984; Sabel and Zeitlin 1985, 1997; Berggren 1992). But the Japanese model exerted particular influence in the United States, as the rapid success of the Japanese automakers lent great prestige to their manufacturing systems. What emerged was a broad-based managerial movement in support of a series of innovations that spread rapidly from private manufacturing firms to governmental organizations.

Lean Production

Although formulations of lean theory varied, in retrospect four features seem critical. First, managers sought to eliminate all unproductive bureaucratic hierarchies, such as the separate layers of salaried staff who had previously been hired to oversee production workers and to maintain quality control. Eliminating jobs that were not directly productive often involved "delayering," or the effort to achieve dramatic reductions in supervisory staff. The notion here was that only workers who directly contributed to core production processes should be retained—a principle that dramatically reduced support staff of all kinds.

Second, the elimination of supervisory layers required that managers achieve high levels of commitment among all their employees, regardless of their rank. Thus, traditional distinctions between "managers" and "workers" had to be overcome; in Japanese-influenced plants, even the terms themselves began to lose favor, as workers were reconceptualized as "associates." The idea is that by winning full commitment to the firm, companies and other organizations can more fully take advantage of the knowledge and expertise that only front-line employees typically command. Breaking down the boundary between "us" and "them" is thus vital to the full utilization of the knowledge the firms needs to compete.

Third, in order to put worker commitment to use, managers increasingly introduced the practice of *kaizen*, team-based provisions for the sharing of ideas and innovations at the point of production itself. Such structures are more than recycled versions of the traditional suggestion box: in organizations that adopt *kaizen*, front-line employees assume direct responsibility for the continuous improvement of their own tools, work methods, and tasks. This is why one well-publicized automobile assembly plant was able to dramatically reduce the need for quality control and job design engineers: workers on the assembly line themselves assumed such tasks, rotating between work on the line and a separate position that involved the pursuit of organizational innovations advanced by employees themselves (Adler 1992).

Fourth, rather than maintaining on-site inventories of spare parts or large numbers of substitute employees—"buffers" that cushioned the production process against any disruptions in necessary supplies—lean production viewed such provisions as an undue waste of resources. What lean production advocated was a system of "just-in-time" delivery systems that carefully coordinated production schedules with the firm's network of suppliers. The result often dramatically reduced the need for space adjoining the direct production process. Achieving such close coordination with one's suppliers often required large firms to adopt a different relation to the smaller firms on which they relied. Rather than haggling over price and adopting a spot-market mentality (in which suppliers might be abandoned in order to pursue short term advantages), lean production invited firms to form strategic alliances with the smaller firms in their supply chain. Rather than simply dictating the terms of any transaction—a hierarchical approach that large U.S. firms had tended to adopt—lean production invited corporations to redefine their suppliers as partners who were worthy of a more collaborative approach. The result, once adopted, enabled firms to establish network ties to other firms, providing ready sources of production capacity and engineering expertise, in turn cutting the time needed to get new models to market (Adler 1992; Kenney and Florida 1993; Hackman and Wageman 1995; see also Dohse, Jurgens, and Malsch 1985; Berggren 1992).

Advocates of lean production argued that each of these elements complemented one another, forming an interlocking system that ensured the development of a collaborative form of work organization that was simply more productive—and more fulfilling—than the Taylorist methods on which production had been based. Thus, since many versions of lean production enabled assembly-line workers to stop production immediately if problems were detected—the "Andon" system, which used cords to slow or stop the assembly line—advocates argued that lean production was inherently participative: if management acted in ways that ran counter to the workers' preferences, then the production process could be brought to an immediate halt. In theory, then, lean production acted to ensure that the interests of management and workers converged. The result—again, in theory—was that the new form of work organization not only enhanced the quality and efficiency of production, but also rendered work more meaningful, thus freeing workers from the tyranny of mass production.

One of the most celebrated efforts to implement lean production is that of the Saturn Corporation, the joint effort between General Motors and Local 1853 of the United Automobile Workers (UAW), located in Spring Hill, Tennessee. This plant has adopted a system of team representation and joint management that seeks to achieve a dramatic shift in the social relations that governed the production process. Thus, workers in each department (or "module") belong to production teams, whose leaders play a critical role in plant operations. At Saturn, team leaders are elected by the team members themselves. Saturn has also developed a labor representation system that draws equally from the ranks of managerial and union-eligible employees. Thus in any given department, there are typically four employees

in leadership positions called "advisors"; two are drawn from management's side and two from the unionized workforce itself. Although such a system might seem to invite conflict, in practice it has worked quite smoothly. Studies of Saturn's innovations suggest that because the new system has brought the manual workforce into the management process, they are indeed more likely to share their production knowledge, to use their communication networks in the interests of the plant, and to develop humane leadership styles that gain the respect of the plant's employees (Rubinstein 2000; Kochan and Rubinstein 2001).

Many other such examples of workplace transformation might be cited. Thus, the New United Motor Manufacturing, Inc. (NUMMI) plant in Fremont, California—a joint venture between Toyota and GM—has instituted giant steps to institute lean production—in so doing transforming one of the worst performing manufacturing plants in all of North America into a highly competitive plant that cut the number of hours required to assemble a vehicle from 48.5 to 19.6. After only two years under the newly installed lean system, NUMMI began to rival Japanese plants in quality as well (Adler 1992). Xerox embarked on a similar path at significant numbers of its manufacturing establishments in the United States during the early 1980s, adopting a flatter and more egalitarian organizational structure that delegated greater autonomy to work groups on the shop floor. Systematic comparison of the traditionally organized and team-based plants revealed that the transformed workplaces registered significantly higher productivity and reduced waste (Cutcher-Gershenfeld 1991). Procter & Gamble has adopted a "technician" system at many of its forest products plants, seeking to abolish the distinction between managerial and hourly employees (Zuboff 1988). Southwest Airlines, a low-cost carrier that has adopted new strategies for competing with larger, full-fare airlines, has drawn on the participation of its employees as a source of flexibility and motivation, achieving levels of profitability that are the envy of more established airlines.

What makes these and other cases so important for the study of work is their shared claim: advanced capitalist societies have outgrown the old, mass production model of work organization. If firms are to achieve the kind of productive potential that economic competition now demands, management simply has no choice but to seek out ways of gaining the worker's full commitment to the goals of the firm. Doing so compels profit-seeking firms to institutionalize the new ethos of teamwork—and this, in turn, requires that management grant workers substantial degrees of involvement in decision-making processes at all levels of the firm.

These are bold, even sweeping claims. Critics often point out that such claims are hardly unprecedented among management thinkers, where fashion-driven approaches sometimes seem more the norm than the exception. What, then, does the evidence suggest about the advantages made possible by the new forms of work organization? In unpacking the evidence, three issues seem especially important to address.

Profits and Participation

One concerns the relation between adoption of worker participation systems and the performance of the firm. Recall that advocates have touted the new work practices as necessary for the success—even the survival—of the firm in an era of sharp international competition. Here, the evidence largely supports the claims of the advocates.

Not surprisingly, a wealth of data has now been gathered on the relation between adoption of employee participation and productivity and organizational performance more generally. While there is some disagreement in the literature, the great bulk of the research suggests that firms that make an overall commitment to implementing large-scale organizational change do indeed reap significant benefits relative to firms that do not make such changes, even after controlling for rival influences. Thus, careful studies of steel finishing plants (Ichniowski, Shaw, and Prennushi 1996), medical instruments manufacturing (Appelbaum et al. 2000), automobile assembly plants (Shaiken, Lopez, and Mankita 1997), and several other industries find that "high-performance" or "transformed" work organizations do indeed deliver greater levels of performance. Apparently, by engaging workers' commitment and identification, these instances of workplace transformation were able to keep downtime to a minimum, to improve product quality, and to find innovative approaches toward job design that might not otherwise have been found (Appelbaum et al. 2000; see also Cappelli and Neumark 2001). In the same vein, studies by Lawler, Mohrman, and Ledford (1992, 1995) and Osterman (1994) indicate that the pursuit of employee involvement is especially common among firms that have been strongly impacted by international competition and that produce goods for volatile product markets—a pattern that suggests that employers are in fact resorting to various forms of worker participation as a means of shoring up their ability to compete (see Osterman 1994; Lawler et al. 1995: 87–91).

If the linkage between team or lean systems and firm productivity does conform to advocates' claims, a number of points will require closer study in future research. One concerns the reasons why performance might be positively affected by the new work practices. As just noted, the most frequent explanation is that the expansion of worker discretion leads to higher levels of worker motivation and commitment, which in turn generates greater economic returns. Yet few studies have actually teased out the relations among these factors in ways that separate out fear of layoffs from more positive forms of motivation. (Thus the introduction of lean production into the NUMMI plant may have succeeded since the workers at the Fremont plant had been laid off for the two years preceding the plant reopening.) Moreover, there is good theoretical reason to believe that the adoption of innovations may enhance a company's financial returns—but for reasons that have nothing to do with greater efficiency as it is traditionally defined. The simple fact of adopting the latest managerial style and seeming to care about employee well-being may have a positive impact on the behavior of investors, customers, and government regulators, generating stronger financial returns without enhancing superiority (Meyer and Rowan 1977). Moreover, firms that adopt new work practices often enjoy a host of other advantages (newer technology, more favorable labor relations, better educated workers) over other sites, which is why they have been selected for innovative initiatives in the first place. Such advantages are in truth highly difficult to identify with confidence. Finally, the new work practices are often quite expensive, given management consulting fees, the salaries of human resource managers and facilitators (needed to introduce and support the new systems), as well as the pay that must go to support workers during extensive training in team principles. Such transition costs have not always been taken into account in research on the benefits of team systems.

A question that needs further research is why the new work practices succeed in some instances and fail in others. Some analysts contend that the key is to "bundle" organizational reforms to achieve a critical mass of change whose elements complement one another sufficiently well to achieve real, sustainable effects. For example, self-managed teams may accomplish little unless systematic provisions are in place for training and incentive systems encourage workers to engage the new work systems as well (MacDuffie 1995; Hunter, MacDuffe, and Doucet 2002). Note that this approach suggests that the key to success lies in the new *structures* that management chooses to adopt. An alternative view has emerged, however, which suggests that that the determining factor lies in the organizational *dynamics* set in motion during the change process, quite apart from the structures that management chooses to introduce. The notion here is that innovations that are introduced in a highly centralized manner, allowing for little local input—a "one-size-fits-all approach"—will tend to perpetuate the very hierarchies that workplace reform aims to transcend (see Thomas 1994; Vallas 2003c, 2006). This is not an idle debate, for precisely how to balance centralized versus local control is a key question of concern to decision makers and employees within large organizations of varying types. This is, in other words, the question of how democracy can be instituted at work.

The Prevalence of the Participative Model

A second question concerns the claim that the mass production model of work organization has now largely become obsolete. Analysts who make this claim often suggest that a far-reaching shift is underway that is reaching into all branches of the U.S. economy, and thus that the examples of Saturn, Xerox, and many other textbook cases are indeed making their mark on work organizations writ large. Here the evidence is complex and often somewhat mixed.

A sizable body of survey evidence has now been published that seeks to estimate the prevalence of the new work practices. The most revealing data here are the surveys of Fortune 1000 firms initiated by the Government Accounting Office in 1987 and then repeated during the 1990s (Lawler, Mohrman, and Ledford 1992, 1995; see also Appelbaum and Batt 1994; Osterman 1994). These data indicate that such employee involvement (EI) practices as job enrichment, self-directed or self-managed teams, quality circles, job rotation, "pay for knowledge," and total quality management (TQM) did find growing application within the largest American corporations during the late 1980s and continued to gain favor even through recessionary economic times during the early 1990s (Appelbaum and Batt 1994: 63–64). There is some evidence that the most ambitious efforts at change, however— those involving self-directed teams—have lost some support among senior managers, while other initiatives (TQM, quality circles, job rotation) have continued to spread.

For example, according to Lawler and colleagues, in 1987 only 27 percent of all Fortune 1,000 firms reported that as many as a fifth of their employees were involved in one or more of the new work practices. Yet only nine years later, fully 78 percent of such large firms had involved at least a minority of their workers in some form of participation. Using different methods, Osterman

(1994, 1999) studied U.S. workplaces with at least 50 employees and found a somewhat more optimistic pattern. In this study, completed in 1992, 40.5 percent of private sector establishments involved at least 50 percent of the employees in core occupations within two or more forms of workplace change. Between 1992 and 1997, interest in self-directed teams seemed to wane somewhat, but the appeal of other work practices continued to rise. Thus the use of "high-performance" work systems, based on continuous improvement and job rotation, roughly doubled in prevalence, rising from 26 to 55 percent of the workplaces in Osterman's sample. What these data suggest, then, is that although the adoption of the new organizational forms has continued to spread, the proportion of establishments that have adopted multiple forms of workplace change, and are genuinely "transformed," is relatively small. (Interestingly, research by Benders, Huijgen, and Pekruhl [2002] suggests that this fact remains true in much of Western Europe, save for the Scandinavian nations such as Sweden.) More commonly, firms have experimented with incremental shifts, involving varying proportions of their employees in efforts that received uneven levels of emphasis.

The question can therefore be asked: If, as suggested, firms do seem to benefit when they introduce the new forms of work organization, why have companies been so slow to adopt the new approaches? Why has the transformation of the workplace unfolded in so gradual and sporadic a way? Studies that have addressed this question serve to remind us that the nature of work is often shaped by influences quite apart from rational self-interest.

Thus, some analysts have found that the high-minded platitudes of participative work organizations are often stymied by resistance from occupational groups on the ground. Thus, technical experts often view their own knowledge as superior to that of the employees they oversee and resist efforts to base decision making on more participative grounds (Thomas 1994; Vallas and Beck 1996). Middle managers sometimes fear efforts to expand decision-making powers at the lower level, since the results create greater financial and organizational uncertainty (Zuboff 1988; Taplin 2001). In some cases, senior managers have so firmly embraced orientations and identities rooted in the past as to be ill equipped to adapt to the new approach (Schoenberger 1997). In still other cases, firms have encountered competing imperatives, such as the need to gain the confidence of powerful investors, who often favor firms that can boast high levels of technological and engineering sophistication. Finally, subordinate workers sometimes feel they have reason to suspect the motives of managerial initiatives, viewing team systems cynically, as constituting union-avoidance mechanisms (Fantasia et al. 1988) or as efforts to intensify their work situations in ways that might well produce job losses for themselves or their co-workers (Parker and Slaughter 1994). What these studies suggest, then, is that while the transformation of traditionally bureaucratic work organizations has made significant headway, the change has been relatively slow and the outcome by no means a simple or straightforward affair. Indeed, the elimination of bureaucracy often opens the way to a more precarious and unstable form of work organization in which the "new rules" become the object of ongoing negotiation.

Participation and Worker Perceptions

Most of the studies discussed in the previous sections have been broadly based aggregate accounts that provide a "telescopic" view of the spread of the new forms of work organization. More finely textured or "microscopic" studies provide a somewhat different view that is well suited to the effort to understand what workplace change means from the workers' point of view. Here, finally, we find even more complexity and uncertainty than on prior points.

Advocates of workplace change often suggest that systems such as "lean" production manage to synthesize the interests of management with those of lower-level employees. The key issue on this point is the assertion that team or lean systems tend to expand the discretion that front-line employees enjoy, and thus manage to restore the sense of meaning and control that the mass production approach had so often denied to lower-level employees.

Efforts to assess the validity of this last claim have been subject to much debate. Early studies, such as that of Womack, Jones, and Roos (1990), invited disagreement in that they were quick to draw conclusions about worker fulfillment on the basis of little or no empirical evidence (see Berggren 1992). Indeed, for much of the 1990s, research on the new work practices focused so heavily on its potential benefits for managerial goals (such as profits and productivity) as to neglect the question of how workplace change affected the situation of front-line employees themselves. This situation has begun to change in recent years, and we now have a fair-sized body of literature on how workers perceive and respond to the new forms of work organization. This literature indicates that participative work systems have a long way to go if they are to make the leap from rhetoric to reality.

Consider, for example, Laurie Graham's (1995) study of the workings of lean production as introduced at the Subaru-Isuzu plant in West

Lafayette, Indiana—a brand new plant started up in the early 1990s. Japanese transplants have been notoriously difficult to study, so Graham adopted the research strategy of covert participant observation: she applied for a job on the assembly line, concealing her motives as a social scientist, and worked alongside the company's workers ("associates") for the better part of a year. The company carefully selected its employees, using psychological tests and group exercises, and then trained its new associates in the ethos of lean production. Associates were encouraged to believe that they would have substantial discretion over the way they performed their jobs. Yet once production ramped up, team members' suggestions concerning tools and work methods were rarely taken into account, and *kaizen* sessions devolved into ceremonial exercises that few took seriously. The pace of work on the line grew increasingly intense, and associates came under strong pressure to keep the line moving no matter what. Associates began to experience rising numbers of repetitive motion disorders, requiring the wearing of wrist splints and often painful surgery (see Kenney and Florida 1993). The company showed little concern for such problems and sometimes even blamed its associates for their inability to keep up with the line. Eventually, associates began to conduct informal work stoppages as a way of gaining some control over their working conditions. The account that Graham's field work provides, then, involved a harsh managerial regime that bore little resemblance to the participative image that advocates of lean production so often propound. Indeed, in Graham's account, management seemed to use lean production as a mechanism with which to ensure the plant's nonunion operations.

If Graham's research was the only study that reached such conclusions, it might prompt little concern. Yet a number of studies have provided roughly parallel accounts. Thus, in his study of quality circles at a medical supply plant in New Mexico, Guillermo Grenier (1988) found that team systems provided management with a powerful method of labor control. Human resource personnel met regularly with team members, inviting them to engage in competition with other teams. Group sessions provided little opportunity for dissent and made many workers feel subject to a climate of intimidation. Since Grenier had initially been working as an intern for the human resource managers, he was privy to information that suggested that the company was indeed prone to view the team environment as a means of union avoidance. When a hard-fought organizing drive nonetheless broke out, Grenier felt compelled to go public with his knowledge and eventually received death threats for his trouble. The organizing drive narrowly failed amid accusations of unfair terminations and unfair labor practices, which only added to doubts about management's use of the team approach.

On the basis of studies such as this (see also Kunda 1991; Barker 1993; Taplin 1995; Milkman 1997), a number of theorists have begun to develop a more critical interpretation of the new work practices. In this critical view, team systems in effect provide companies with a new system of managerial control—and one that may be even more formidable than the old mass production paradigm, since the new regime targets not outward behavior but the organizational culture established among the workers themselves. The notion here is that team systems have a twofold nature: On the one hand, they invite workers to take responsibility for imposing discipline on one another and for enforcing productivity and quality norms—tasks that had previously been performed by supervisors. Meeting in situations that encourage a view of work as a shared endeavor, workers are increasingly exposed to managerial values and norms. On the other hand, workers are expected to work at an increasingly intensified pace, with peer pressure often goading workers to make production norms—a situation that has prompted some critics to portray lean production as a form of "management by stress" (Parker and Slaughter 1994).

Increasingly, researchers have unearthed findings that cast doubt on *both* the "empowerment" and "intensification" views of the new work practices. Thus, some researchers have pointed out that team systems need not undermine worker solidarity, but can instead lead down different paths (Hodson et al. 1993, 1994). In a series of case studies of office and factory workers, Vicki Smith (2001a) found that team systems were often actively embraced by workers— especially those in vulnerable positions in the labor market. Workers did so not because they were "taken in" by all the talk of empowerment, but because they viewed the new work practices as providing economically viable survival strategies. Thus, office workers with few corporate skills hoped to gain expertise in administrative practices, and factory workers hoped that an organizational make-over might provide greater security for their plant. Smith's point is that workers are not passive recipients of managerial initiatives; rather, workers actively respond to the new work systems in ways that enable them to adapt to the situations they confront.

Other studies, too, suggest that workers can in fact maintain substantial distance between managerial rhetoric and their own cultural norms. Thus, in his careful study of a prominent British banking corporation, John Weeks (2004) found a pervasive pattern of cynicism throughout the firm—he refers to a "culture of complaint"—in which employees commonly viewed the company's participative systems as often incompetent and frequently hypocritical. In Weeks's analysis, the management's efforts at reform provided a constant source of amusement for employees, who maintained significant elements of solidarity in muted *opposition* to the firm's management (Weeks 2004). Team systems have even been found to provide workers with informal resources that can help workers to *subvert* managerial control (Knights and McCabe 2000). Thus, one of this volume's authors found that factory workers sometimes used the solidarity and participative rhetoric that team systems provided as resources with which to gain leverage over the production process—a situation that management had sought to avoid (Vallas 2003b). This study suggested that when team systems succeed, they sometimes do so in spite of management's actions (not because of them).

Much more research on team systems is needed before their significance can be fully understood. It remains unclear, for example, whether corporate interest in such innovations has continued at the same level since the dot com recession. Arguably, corporations have begun to employ other, significantly harsher strategies— aggressive outsourcing of work to other countries, for example—as a means of maintaining their competitive position (see Chapter 16). Arguably, economic uncertainties and sharp competition have left firms loath to experiment with or invest in the new forms of work organization. Likewise, as evidence has emerged about the prevalence of a cynical approach toward team innovations, questions have emerged about the varying responses that workers adopt toward team systems and the effect their responses can have on the outcomes of workplace change.

Thus Collinson (2003) distinguishes three types of worker response to the uncertainties that team systems provoke. In the first, "deferential" type, employees respond to the changes that work requires of them by carefully conforming to the firm's demands—working harder and longer and otherwise trying to distinguish themselves in management's eyes. In the second, "resistant" type, Collinson refers to a more cynical or subversive response, in which workers actively distrust management and view team systems with manifest suspicion and distrust (see also Vallas 2006). In the third, "dramaturgical" type of response, employees seem to conform to managerial imperatives, but do so merely as a "front." That is, they strategically seek to make a strong impression, but without internalizing the managerial ethos. Their actions become increasingly strategic, in other words, rather than authentically felt. Whether other types of response are common, how each affects the outcome of change, and which organizational conditions prompt each type all remain important questions for further research.

Perhaps the most important question that needs to be addressed concerns the ways in which firms seek to coordinate the conflicting trends which this chapter has discussed—the rise of more polarized occupational structures, the growth of nonstandard and highly uncertain forms of employment, coupled with the demands for higher levels of employee commitment to the firm. A key question that many firms must confront is how they can expand their expectations of their employees even as they set about reducing the job rewards (not only pay increases but also job security, secure pensions, health benefits) that employees can expect (Rubin 1995, 1996;

Cappelli 1995; Vallas 1999). If a new social contract is developing at work, as some theorists suggest, it is a contract that seems more asymmetrical than before, in that employees are increasingly encouraged to perform at an ever-higher level even as they receive fewer rights in return. The business journalist Jill Fraser (2002) poses precisely this question and wonders how long corporations can pursue this contradictory approach without suffering an adverse response.

Of Mice, Men, and Mentalities

A final and perhaps most probing question to be addressed concerns the effects of workplace change on the workers' subjectivities—that is, their identities or selves. The question here is how the imperatives of the new work practices (or what some have called "fast capitalism") are likely to shape the employees exposed to them, and the emphasis it places on such things as teamwork, innovation, rapid and ceaseless change, and the need for flexibility in responding to market conditions. Two recent and highly popular books have sketched out the lines of this debate; the differences are worth considering in some depth.

Consider first the remarkably popular book, *Who Moved My Cheese?* (1998), written by Spencer Johnson, M.D. Johnson's book struck a popular chord in the corporate world and has been reissued many times, leading to widespread demand for seminars, workshops, and even a version of this book for teenagers. The book is written as a simple parable, in which a couple of mice—accustomed to a ready supply of cheese without question—suddenly confront a situation in which their source of food has simply disappeared. The parable is structured around two distinct forms of response to this crisis. One of the mice responds by simply behaving as he always has—searching down familiar corridors for his cheese, insisting that the food to which he is entitled will surely reappear. The other mouse is tempted by this strategy, but eventually rethinks his position and tries dramatically different survival strategies that take him far away from the familiar round of activities. In the end, of course, the more innovative rodent succeeds, locating a vein of cheese that enables him to survive (while also helping his former associate). He has learned his lesson, though, and will be sure never again to take it for granted that his basic survival needs will magically be met.

Johnson's parable might not be worthy of discussion here had it not met with such widespread interest. (In fact, one of the present authors encountered a senior plant manager who was so enthusiastic about the book that he ordered 2,300 copies of it, to be distributed to the entire plant workforce!) Its popularity stems from its ability to address the uncertainties that surround employees' jobs and career opportunities in an era of sudden economic change, and to do so in a straightforward and deceptively simple way. Yet what some may find worrisome about the book is precisely its lesson about the characteristics employees ought to adopt: unquestioning adaptation to economic conditions, a willingness to relinquish longstanding expectations and connections to the past, the importance of entrepreneurial thinking even on the part of subordinate employees, and an uncritical acceptance of simple, black and white choices. Johnson's narrative never allows its characters—who *do*, after all, seem capable of rational thought and speech—to ask *why* the cheese has moved, nor whether they might have the right to ask questions about their predicament. Its subtext, in short, seems to cut against the grain of the participative ethos that

firms have recently touted and to discourage critical thinking about workplace change—a message that carries certain dangers, especially in an era when the need for ethical concerns has been so clearly apparent.

A very different view of the relation between the new work practices and the self is developed by the sociologist Richard Sennett, whose book, *The Corrosion of Character* (1999) carries the subtitle "The Personal Consequences of the Work in the New Capitalism." Sennett's book (briefly discussed in Chapter 2) does not pretend to be based on rigorous social scientific methods. Instead, it develops a series of case studies that are chosen almost by happenstance: that of a friend who embarks on an especially revealing career departure, a support group comprised of IBM executives who have recently been laid off, and the experiences of a father and a son whose careers nicely track the transition from the bureaucratic world of stable employment to the newer world of flexible capitalism. As the title of his book suggests, Sennett's argument is that the newer forms of work organization have begun to uproot many of the social foundations on which people have based their sense of self. In a world where career ladders are being dismantled, where workers no longer have stable and enduring ties to their co-workers, and where workplace norms increasingly demand a superficial allegiance to the team ethos, Sennett's point is that employees begin to lose a sense of personal grounding. It may be possible for the leaders of multinational corporations to derive a heady sense of accomplishment from their strategic deal-making, but for the great bulk of the workforce, the culture of entrepreneurialism provides only a hollow basis on which to root one's personal identity. In Sennett's eyes, the new world of work is characterized by a certain hollowness or inauthenticity that deprives employees of the very yardsticks they used to judge the development of their own careers.

It is interesting to approach these two books using the typology introduced by Collinson, as discussed above. In a sense, Johnson encourages employees to adopt what Collinson has called the "deferential" response to organizational uncertainty, in which employees unquestioningly embrace the goals and methods which the new forms of work organization demand—working harder and longer, adapting to the organization's demands, showing that one is a team player. Sennett, on the other hand, sees this tendency as only too pervasive. In this view, the new forms of work organization invite not only such deference, but also Collinson's second, "dramaturgical" response, in which employees are compelled to act strategically, feigning allegiance to the firm when their only concern is for themselves. In a sense, Sennett's book is meant to invite a form of resistance—Collinson's third type—by fostering open debate and discussion about the effects the new work practices are likely to have, not only on our economy, but also on our very selves. In that respect, Sennett's message has much in common with the movement for workplace democracy.

Conclusion

This chapter began by pointing to the multiple strands of economic and organizational change that are converging in the contemporary workplace. It reviewed three such stands: shifts in demand for particular types of labor, changes in the employment relationship, and efforts to transcend the hierarchical pattern of industrial bureaucracy that mass production had involved.

Taken as a whole, what these changes portend is a complex and often contradictory set of developments that seem likely to ratchet up the level of uncertainty that labor force participants will face, both now and in the foreseeable future. They also seem likely to increase the level of social and economic inequality in the U.S. society, as highly qualified professionals and other experts enjoy increasing demand for their services, while less credentialed employees confront less advantageous conditions of employment. Such duality has also been encouraged by the erosion of the permanent or standard work arrangement, which draws an ever-sharper boundary between employees who are considered indispensable parts of the firm's "core" workforce and those who languish on its periphery. Such patterns may equip firms with greater flexibility in responding to market conditions, but they threaten to erode the sense of stability and security that workers have taken for granted for several generations. The labor market today has often been likened to participating in a high-wire act without any safety net in place. The risk of falling—being downsized, outsourced, or simply laid off—carries with it dangers that are as obvious as they are severe. Perhaps that is why self-help columns in the business sections of our newspapers so often advise workers to be on the lookout for signs of layoffs, and to be sure to maintain a fresh set of skills.

Such sources of uncertainty have combined with a very different source of change, involving corporate efforts to infuse the workplace with a more participative or self-directed ethos, through self-managed teams, high-performance work organizations, and other initiatives that promise to expand the discretion of front-line employees. Ironically, such new forms of work organization have for the most part been inspired by the Japanese example, whose success stemmed precisely from its ability to institutionalize a reciprocal relationship between the corporation and the employee: workers unstintingly committed to the enterprise, knowing that their place within the firm was secure and thus their own interests converged with the fate of the firm. A limitation that U.S. firms will have to deal with, it seems, is their inability to provide such reciprocity. The motivation on which worker participation depends cannot continue indefinitely as employees suffer an erosion of their job security, benefits, and career opportunities. Perhaps that is one reason the participative workplace has been so slow to emerge, and why cynicism has been so prevalent a response.

Chapter 16

Globalization and the American Workplace

During the years following World War II, the United States rose to a position of unrivaled economic dominance. So powerful were American firms such as General Motors, General Electric, and IBM that analysts could be forgiven for viewing the U.S. economy as an independent entity with little need to depend on foreign nations. Events soon showed this view to be superficial and misleading at best.

An initial sign was provided by the oil crisis of 1973–1974, which caused massive lines at gas stations and systems for the rationing of fuel (e.g., odd-even fill-up days). Japanese manufacturers began to make substantial inroads into markets previously controlled by U.S. automobile, steel, and electronics producers, emerging as major competitors by the early 1980s. The stock market crash of October 1987, which was sparked by the outbreak of financial crises in East Asia, revealed just how interdependent—and precarious—the global economy had become. And if any room for doubt remained, the rise of trade agreements such as the North American Free Trade Agreement (or NAFTA) accelerated the cross-border movement of capital, commodities, and production facilities, as U.S.-based firms (sometimes encouraged by big-box

retailers like Wal-Mart) increasingly relocated their manufacturing sites offshore.

Clearly, something dramatically new was unfolding on the world stage. The concept of "globalization," once solely the concern of the business press, exploded onto the front pages, most graphically at the Seattle meetings of the World Trade Organization in 1999. There, a novel coalition of environmentalists, human rights activists, and labor union members forcefully demanded changes in the trade policies that decision makers had pursued in the new, global economy (Klein 1999; Fiss and Hirsch 2005). These events inaugurated a far-reaching public debate about the nature and consequences of globalization for American and foreign workers alike.

And that debate has shown little sign of ending any time soon. Even the meaning of the concept "globalization" is contested, as theorists have staked out widely divergent perspectives on the nature and consequences of this development. Perhaps the dominant school of thought, especially among economists, has supported the movement toward unrestricted trade, arguing that the growth of cross-border economic activity delivers greater prosperity to all participants (Levitt 1983; Ohmae 1990; Bhagwati 2004a; Friedman 2006). A second, more critical approach suggests that unfettered globalization has had highly destructive effects. In this view, rampant globalization reduces the ability of democratic nations to control their own fates, undermining many workers' rights and weakening environmental protections (Held 1995; Tilly 1995). Other lines of debate concern the meaning of the cultural shifts that accompany globalization. Here, although many analysts agree that globalization tends to foster a convergence of cultural norms and beliefs, differences emerge: some thinkers find virtue in the rise of a global culture (to them, it signals increasing concerns for human rights), while other analysts bemoan the spread of market institutions across the face of the globe ("MacDomination"). One point on which virtually all analysts agree is this: the contours of the American economy—its ability to provide stable, rewarding jobs for all who seek them—increasingly rests on our ability to comprehend and address the challenges we confront in an increasingly global economy.

In this final chapter we address a series of questions centering on the globalization of work. We ask, in turn, such questions as the following. What *is* globalization, and how does it manifest itself in the current period? How has it transformed economic activity, and who seems to benefit (and conversely, which groups seem to lose)? What does it mean that the largest employer in the United States is now Wal-Mart, the massive retail corporation whose supply chains extend throughout the world, and whose low-wage strategy and organizational practices are the subject of so much political debate? Are the interests of U.S. workers necessarily at odds with those of workers in the developing world, or is it possible

to conceive of policies that would serve the interests of workers generally? Is globalization an irreversible trend that obeys laws beyond democratic control? Or is it responsive to social and political intervention in ways that might shape its trajectory in accordance with human choice? While answers to these questions often prove elusive, it is incumbent on us all to come to grips with the nature of what some have called an increasingly "borderless" world.

Dimensions of Globalization

Globalization involves much more than trade agreements, the outsourcing of jobs, or the rise of multinational corporations (important though these are). Although the term has acquired many meanings, at a minimum it refers to the extension of economic activities across national boundaries, yielding networks of production, exchange, and consumption that embed spatially dispersed regions of the world within a single, highly interwoven system. Involved in such an extension of cross-border activity is the transnational flow of not only such tangible things as capital goods, labor, or technology but also less tangible things such as cultural styles and fashions (for example, hip-hop music, sports, and styles of dress). Although definitions vary, what most approaches imply is that ours is a time in which *local* activities and events are increasingly bound up with far-flung *global* processes that are often rooted thousands of miles away (Giddens 1990: 64).

It is of course important to note that globalization is not entirely a new phenomenon. Indeed, sociologists studying the "world system" of capitalist economic activity trace the beginnings of a truly global economy to the 1500s (Wallerstein 1974), when the European conquest of the new world gave rise to a system of unequal exchange, in which the "core" societies of Western Europe achieved a position of dominance over the "periphery" of the less developed world (a matter discussed later in this chapter). More recently, analysts have pointed out that an enormous surge of international investment and trade occurred during the late nineteenth century in particular, leading up to the World War I years. Characteristic of this period was the "time-zoning of the world and the establishment of the international dateline; the near-global adoption of the Gregorian calendar and the adjustable seven-day week; and the establishment of international telegraphic and signaling codes," which were necessary conditions for global integration (Robertson, in Guillen 2001: 237).

Yet, if globalization has a long history, most analysts have come to agree that the contemporary era has greatly accelerated the broad movement toward transnational integration. An important question is why. The reasons most commonly given include developments in technology, political upheavals, the policies of international institutions, and shifts in economic policy within the developing world.

The importance of technology is clear. Improvements in transportation systems, logistics, the spread of new communications media, and especially the rapid spread of information technologies have all greatly reduced obstacles to the flow of goods, services, and information and eased the work of coordinating complex global networks, all of which has greatly facilitated cross-border economic transactions. This has enabled large corporations to shift production operations overseas, to pursue investments, and to assemble complex operational webs, often within low-wage economies that were not

previously practical. Increasingly, scanners at the cash registers of such upscale retail outlets as Bennetton and the Gap enable buyers to track trends in tastes and inventory levels, enabling factories to adjust their production schedules almost instantaneously.

A second factor is the end of the Cold War, which allowed international commerce to reach into realms of the world that had previously been closed to the West. Before, whole sectors of the developing world (Central America, Southeast Asia, Africa) had been caught up in a geo-political tug of war between the capitalist and communist powers. With the collapse of the Soviet Bloc, multinational corporations faced many fewer obstacles to direct foreign investment. A case in point is a country such as Vietnam, which had been embroiled in a worldwide struggle between colonial and capitalist powers (France and the United States), on the one hand, and their communist rivals (China, the Soviet Union), on the other. Now Vietnam has become an important field for direct foreign investment on the part of one Western corporation after another. Similar points can be made about many Eastern European countries, where geopolitical developments have also extended the sway of the capitalist economy much further than before.

A third, related factor has been a shift in economic policy on the part of the developing nations, many of which have moved away from "import substitution" strategies for economic development (in which trade barriers were erected to protect domestic industry) to "export-oriented" strategies (in which nations seek to develop by opening their economies to the global market). This shift has moved the Asian economies much more directly into the world capitalist system, beginning with the Asian Tigers (South Korea,

Taiwan, Singapore, and Malaysia) in the 1960s (Deyo 1989), and even more dramatically now in the case of China and India. By opening their borders to global capitalism, these nations have further widened the field on which global capitalism can operate, while also raising the level of global competition to an unprecedented degree.

A fourth and final factor stems from the policies adopted by such financial institutions as the International Monetary Fund (IMF) and the World Bank. These institutions were initially established after World War II as mechanisms that aimed to stabilize the world economy (in the case of the IMF) and to alleviate poverty within the least developed societies (in the case of the Bank). At the outset these institutions emphasized economic policies that sought to prevent a recurrence of worldwide economic crises such as occurred in the 1930s. Their policies were therefore designed to lend money, to provide technical assistance, and to stabilize the value of international currencies, in this way ensuring sufficient world demand for the products of the advanced industrial nations. Beginning in the late 1970s, however, the economic theories on which the IMF and World Bank relied underwent a dramatic change (Stiglitz 2002), and the mission of these institutions was reconceived as one of fostering the spread of market-based economic systems throughout all quarters of the world (Harvey 2005). As a result, developing nations seeking financial credits or development loans have been compelled to place their economies at the disposal of global markets, for example, by privatizing government functions, slashing public spending, and eliminating subsidies for essential goods like food and fuel (policies that were sometimes known as "structural adjustments," or sometimes as "shock therapy"). Although the

benefits of these policies have been much debated—economies that have resisted these structural adjustments have often outperformed those who complied (Harvey 2005)—their adoption has entangled the developing economies much more fully within the global capitalist economy, with foreign corporations often gaining dominant positions within local industries.

The combined result of these influences can be sensed in Figure 16.1, which shows shifts in total merchandise exports as a proportion of the gross domestic product (GDP; a rough indictor of trade in goods) for the world economy, Japan, and the United States since 1870. Although these data provide only one partial approximation of the globalization process, they reveal some interesting patterns. Increases in merchandise exports manifest two distinct waves—one that begins at the latter decades of the nineteenth century, lasting until the Great Depression of the 1930s, and a second that begins during the mid-1950s and continues sharply thereafter. Note that the second, post-1950 spike in exports was significantly steeper than the first, representing a nearly threefold increase in exports by 2000.

The data in Table 16.1 provide a more nuanced approach to the globalization of economic activity, displaying selected economic, financial, and social indicators within the most recent historical period. Here, we find evidence of how complex globalization tends to be, since its different facets develop in uneven and highly contradictory ways. Foreign trade (here defined as the combined total of imports and exports—that is, all cross-border transactions of goods) has indeed grown significantly during this 20-year period, increasing by roughly 25%. Foreign direct investment (involving the purchase or construction of business operations in foreign nations)

FIGURE 16.1 **Exports of merchandise as a percent of GDP for the world, the United States, and Japan, 1870–2000**

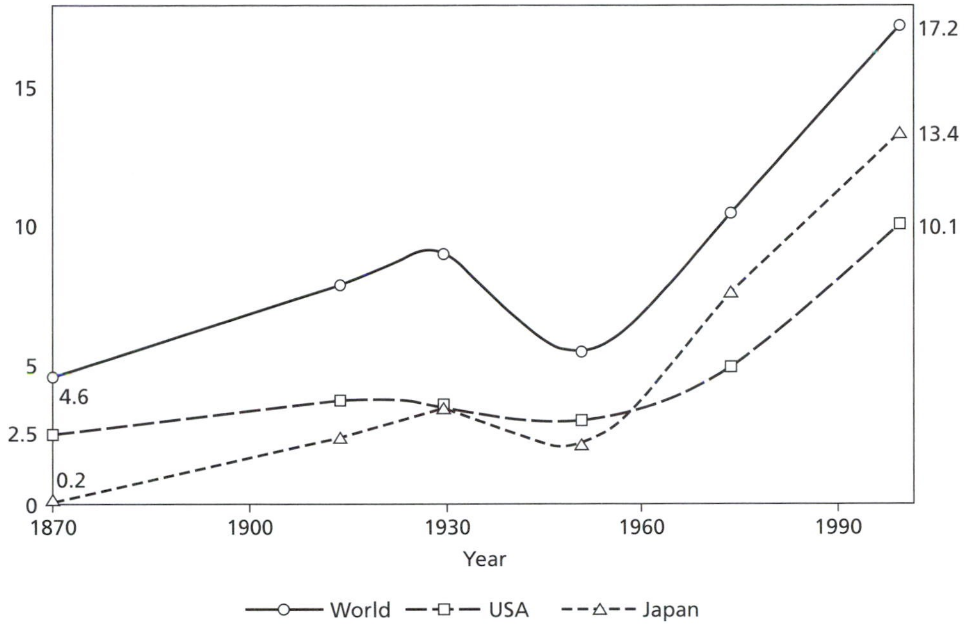

Source: From Maddison 2001.

has increased even more dramatically, especially within the developing world (where it has more than doubled as a proportion of GDP).

Even more remarkable has been the increase in financial activities, as currency transactions, the extension of credit and loans, and other kinds of banking transactions have all shown the steepest spikes. Note that the migration of people, whose movements are not nearly so freely permitted as are goods, has shown the smallest tendency to increase. This is an important point: While capital in its financial and monetary forms can be transferred anywhere in the world (and, increasingly, 24 hours a day), the movements of labor are much more constrained (partly by custom and, of course, by laws and sometimes by force). This means that globalization tends to make the relation between

large employers and workers increasingly asymmetrical: investors can easily relocate their capital, money, and stock ownership anywhere in the world, while workers are often rooted in a given locale. The greater mobility of capital and other financial assets has often enabled global businesses to impose harsh terms and conditions of employment on workers within particular regions, for workers often have few alternative means of survival to which they can turn.

The Meaning of Globalization for the American Worker

Thus far the data we have considered indicates that globalization as a structural trend does indeed characterize the contemporary period of

TABLE 16.1 Indicators of Economic, Financial, and Social Globalization, 1980–1998

INDICATORS	1980	1985	1990	1995	1998
A. Economic					
Inward foreign direct investment stock, % world GDP	4.6	6.5	8.0	10.1	11.7
Developed countries, % GDP	3.8	4.9	6.6	9.1	10.5
Developing countries, % GDP	4.3	8.2	8.5	15.4	16.6
Gross value added of foreign affiliates, % world GDP	—	5.2	6.4	6.3	7.8
Exports of foreign affiliates % total world exports	—	31.9	27.5	32.3	35.6
Exports + imports of goods, % world non-service GDP	72.7	68.1	76.0	87.5	92.1
Developed countries, % non-service GDP	76.6	72.1	81.8	90.1	95.1
Developing countries, % non-service GDP	60.9	54.6	55.0	77.3	83.2
Exports + imports of good & services, % world GDP	40.0	38.8	38.9	42.9	45.2
Developed countries, % GDP	40.2	39.4	38.3	41.2	43.8
Developing countries, % GDP	39.1	36.6	41.0	49.5	50.6
B. Financial					
Daily currency exchange turnover, % world GDP	0.7	1.3	3.8	5.6	6.8
Cross-border bank credit stock, % world GDP	13.9	19.9	34.3	33.1	—
Cross-border banking assets, % world GDP	13.7	19.9	28.1	28.5	—
C. Social & Political					
International tourist arrivals, % world population	3.5	6.7	8.6	9.9	—
Stock of international migrants, % world population	1.5	1.8	2.0	2.2	—
International calls, minutes per million $ world GDP	—	1,354	1,600	2,174	—
Internet hosts, number (thousands)	—	5	617	12,881	19,459
Nation-states with membership in the United Nations	157	157	159	184	184
International organizations, number	14,273	24,180	26,656	41,722	48,350

Source: Table adapted from Guillen 2001.

economic change. We have reviewed some of the reasons why globalization has accelerated so rapidly and how the global economy operates today. A key question then becomes how globalization impinges on the jobs and the well-being of workers employed within the United States.

The Debate over Outsourcing

One important line of analysis has emphasized the threat that "outsourcing" poses to the employment stability of the American worker. A point of conceptual clarification is in order here. "Outsourcing" can mean many things. It can refer, for example, simply to the subcontracting of work within the same national economy. Such a usage of the term often points to the decision by one company to purchase on the market goods or services that it previously produced for its own use. (A university that elects to rely on external catering or cleaning services rather than relying on its own employees can be said to have outsourced these operations to other firms.) By contrast, most of the debate and discussion has concerned a somewhat different and more specific phenomenon (occasionally called "offshoring"), which involves the substitution of foreign-made goods or services for those previously produced domestically. This *may* involve the outsourcing or subcontracting of work to another firm, but it may also involve the transfer of work to a foreign establishment that is owned and operated by a U.S.-based firm. Either way, the work is no longer performed domestically. In this section we will use the term outsourcing in this latter, "offshoring" sense.

Initially, discussion of the danger of outsourcing focused on the shipping of manufacturing work to less developed (and lower-wage) nations such as Mexico or South Korea. This reflected an important shift in economic policies on the part of many developing nations, as mentioned above: As poor countries sought to develop their economies by producing goods for export to the developed world rather than for their own consumption, the stage was set for multinational corporations to take advantage of this situation by outsourcing an increasing proportion of their production work to suppliers located within low-wage, less developed regions of the world. An example close to our own borders is that of Mexico, which sought to foster investment in its *maquiladoras*—specialized assembly plants located just south of the U.S. border, where taxation and trade policies favor industrial

exports. The *maquiladoras* typically import semi-finished products from abroad and then provide final assembly operations at very low cost. Passage of NAFTA in 1994 lent momentum to the *maquiladoras*, doubling their employment levels (from 460,000 in 1990 to 1.1 million by 2002). More recently, with the prodigious growth of China, the growth of export-oriented manufacturing platforms has been perceived by many as a clear and present danger for American manufacturing—and, in the view of some, for the American economy as a whole.

Many critics of globalization have pointed to this threat, often using emotional appeals to draw attention to the threats that offshoring poses to American workers. Good examples of this genre are Lou Dobbs's *Exporting America: How Corporate Greed is Shipping American Jobs Overseas* (2004) or Senator Byron Dorgan's (D-North Dakota) *Take This Job and Ship It* (2006). The latter book is typical of this genre in that it strikes a nationalist chord, viewing outsourcing as a kind of economic treason. Dorgan takes care to show how U.S. multinational corporations have shipped production of even the most iconic of American products—Levi-Strauss jeans, Huffy bicycles, Fig Newtons, Etch-a-Sketch toys, Fruit-of-the-Loom underwear—entirely overseas. The products are "American" only in the most hollow or symbolic sense. Dorgan (like several politicians in recent years) also stresses the perverse incentives established by U.S. tax policies, which actually reward firms for relocating production offshore. Dorgan's argument is that powerful corporations have in effect hijacked U.S. economic policy, using it to reward themselves even at the expense of the broad swath of American wage earners—indeed, at the expense of the nation's economic interests as a whole.

Increasingly, the debate over outsourcing has grown in intensity. Leading executives such as the CEO of Intel have been quoted as saying that American workers must now compete with their highly skilled counterparts in India, China, and Russia who can "do effectively any job that can be done in the United States" (Bhagwati 2004b). In fact, literature has emerged suggesting that the offshoring of work has begun to reach well beyond semi-skilled manufacturing jobs (its previous target). During the 1990s, for example, it became clear that firms were increasingly able to offshore not only routine customer service, sales, and technical support work—the now familiar call centers in Bangalore and other Indian cities—but to do so with highly skilled professional work. According to Thomas Friedman, the influential foreign policy commentator, U.S. hospitals have now begun to outsource the reading of CT scans to Indian doctors: Digitized versions of CT scans are transmitted electronically to India, and diagnoses arrive via email by the following morning. In his recent *The World Is Flat* (2006), Friedman reports that U.S. firms engage in similar practices with respect to accounting work—the preparation of tax returns is now often shipped overseas, unbeknownst to the client—and even to highly skilled design and engineering work as well. As he reports, Indian technology centers and industrial parks now rival those found in Silicon Valley, allowing U.S. firms to use electronic technologies to relocate much of their design work overseas, using the abundant supplies of English-speaking engineering talent that many Asian nations now boast, and at a substantially lower cost. A recent article in *The New York Times* (Timmons, 2008) finds that even mid-level financial management jobs—formerly, the core of lucrative careers on Wall Street—are

being shipped overseas, in a phenomenon which financial executives are calling "knowledge process outsourcing" (Timmons 2008: A1). Indeed, New York City financial institutions project that salaries and benefits are likely to decline by $18 billion in the single year from 2007 to 2008.

Interestingly, Friedman discusses many of the same phenomena as does Senator Dorgan, but interprets them in far more positive terms. While Dorgan sees outsourcing as inevitably harming the material interests of the American worker, Friedman instead draws the opposite conclusion: New technologies and free trade agreements promise to dismantle obstacles to international exchange, making possible an era of economic and cultural innovation that can benefit all of humanity, rather than elites within a few privileged nations. In this respect, Friedman is merely updating views that have been held by economists for nearly two centuries, beginning with the English economic theorist David Ricardo (1772–1823), whose famous theory of "comparative advantage" continues to provide the foundation for international trade policy. In this view, international trade enables nations to specialize in those production processes they perform most productively (whether because of geographic, cultural, or historical reasons). The result is a system of economic interdependence that enables all nations to utilize their labor and capital more fruitfully than would otherwise be the case.

Ricardo's theory remains highly influential for many elite policy makers, who often take its validity for granted. This, perhaps, is why Gregory Mankiw, President George W. Bush's head of the Council of Economic Advisors, thought nothing of publicly stating in 2004 (an election year) that the outsourcing of U.S. jobs is beneficial for the American economy and should

FIGURE 16.2 Trends in manufacturing employment in the United States, 1946–2003.

Source: Bivens, L. Josh, Robert Scott, and Christian Weller. 2003. "Mending Manufacturing." Briefing Paper #144. Washington D.C.: Economic Policy Institute.

be encouraged, since it lowered prices for firms and consumers and thereby stimulated economic growth. Because he was merely stating the conventional wisdom among economists and policy makers, he did not anticipate the flood of public outrage his comments provoked, which eventually compelled him to disavow his own remarks (Bumiller 2004). Clearly, Mankiw had naively walked into a political minefield.

What then do the data suggest about the actual impact of outsourcing? Although theoretical debates over the validity of Ricardo's doctrine cannot concern us here, a number of points must still be made. First, there can be little doubt that the American economy has been hemorrhaging manufacturing jobs in particular, and that many sectors of manufacturing are growing within the developing world. Instances in which U.S. firms shutter their domestic establishments and transfer production to a new, foreign facility are not hard to find, and indeed, since the late 1990s and continuing on throughout the first decade of this century, manufacturing jobs located in the United States have eroded quite sharply, both in absolute numbers and as a proportion of the nonfarm labor force (see Figure 16.2).

Second, economists generally agree that government policies encouraging increased trade, coupled with the growing economic strength of China, India, and other rapidly developing economies, have reduced the availability of good-paying manufacturing jobs in the United States. Still, several considerations prompt caution in approaching the debate.

For one thing, careful analysis suggests that the greatest share of the decline in manufacturing employment is not actually due to the export of jobs and free trade agreements, but rather to other causes rooted in the domestic economy, such as the spread of advanced technologies (which easily and cheaply automate less skilled operations), stock market–driven campaigns to downsize employment levels, a surge in mergers and acquisitions, and the inability of labor unions to combat many if not all of these developments. Indeed, even critical studies of free trade agreements such as those conducted by the Economic Policy Institute (Bivens 2006) suggest that during the early years of this century, only a fifth of the jobs lost in manufacturing could be attributed to the growing share of the market enjoyed by imported goods. Other analysts put this proportion even lower, at 12% (Baily and Lawrence 2004). Moreover, evidence suggests that the decline of manufacturing jobs is in fact a worldwide trend that even affects manufacturing employment in the developing world. Indeed, some analysts suggest that U.S. declines are occurring on much the same pace as in the global economy as a whole.

Moreover, many of the most widely reported projections regarding the future scale of outsourcing sound more frightening than they actually are. Thus, one influential projection by the corporate consulting firm McKinsey and Company projects that outsourcing will cost 3.3 million jobs over the next 15 years. But this projection, even if realized, would annually impact approximately two tenths of one percent of the actively employed workforce (Drezner 2004). Other trends seem even more important than the actual number of displaced manufacturing workers, such as how many and what kind of alternative jobs would be produced, how rewarding those new jobs are likely to be, and who is able to gain access to them. Finally, many analysts suggest that the job losses that are frequently projected

are not likely to occur. Often, when corporations experiment with the offshoring of jobs, they discover hidden disadvantages: consumers resist foreign customer service representatives. Managers find that offshoring tends to increase administrative complexity or generate cross-cultural conflicts within the firm. Companies find that offshoring of financial operations exposes the firm to risks in the misuse of customer information (as has plagued British telecommunications firms that shifted billing work to India). For these reasons, some analysts have concluded that the significance of outsourcing may lie precisely in the fears it generates rather than in economic realities. According to Cornell University researcher Kate Bronfenbrenner (1997), one of the most effective tactics that corporations now use to defeat union organizing efforts are threats of plant relocation—even when the firm making the threat is not in a position to engage in such outsourcing. The mere threat of outsourcing, in other words, may render workers powerless, despite its partly mythical nature.

There is further reason to be wary of the way the globalization debate has been framed in that it has tended to foster highly polarized, either/or approaches: *Either* one believes that outsourcing threatens the economic well-being of the American worker and the core of the U.S. economy, *or* one sees it as an unalloyed benefit. The former position is usually interpreted as implying an insistence on protectionism—the use of trade barriers to shelter U.S. firms and/or industries from foreign competition. The latter view, by contrast, embraces unfettered, free trade principles in ways that actually encourage the export of U.S. jobs. Yet clearly, something as complex as the workings of the global economy cannot be understood in such black-and-white terms. And indeed, a broad array of research has begun to emerge that indicates that the global dispersion of production facilities has highly complex and often quite disparate effects on the U.S. workforce: some strata and class groupings seem quite clearly to benefit, while others are seriously harmed. Moreover, the tendency seems clear that while outsourcing does not necessarily account for the largest number of job *losses*, it does have significant bearing on the job *rewards* (such as wages and working conditions) that various groups of workers can expect to enjoy, in turn ratcheting upward social and economic inequalities within the United States. With this point in mind, the next section of this chapter discusses the linkage between globalization and inequality at work.

Globalization and Structural Inequality at Work

As early as the early 1990s, a growing array of literature began to link the surge of economic inequality to the spatial dispersion of production facilities and to the rise of a new global economy. One of the most influential such studies was conducted by Robert Reich, former Secretary of Labor under the Clinton Administration and now a professor of economics and social policy at the University of California, Berkeley. In *The Work of Nations* (1992), Reich argued that a new type of economy was emerging, with sharply different consequences for workers according to their position in the system of production (see also Castells 1996).

Reich's argument makes points that are worth exploring in some depth. First, as firms have increasingly located their activities offshore, the bond between the firm and its presumptive "home" nation has become increasingly tenuous.

Large firms now operate on a worldwide basis as part of "global webs" that owe allegiance to no single nation. This means that efforts to further the nation's economic health by supporting corporate profits may no longer work, for corporations can use the resulting profits to bolster their foreign operations, providing little or no domestic benefit to their "home" country. This is why Reich concludes that there "are no *national* products or technologies, no national corporations, no national industries. There will no longer be national economies, at least as we have come to understand that concept. All that will remain rooted within national borders are the people who comprise a nation" (Reich 1992: 3).

And those people increasingly encounter sharply different fortunes as a result of the new global economy. The old economic order had been built on the mass production of goods in high volume. It therefore needed large numbers of mass production workers who could staff the nation's burgeoning factories. But now that firms operate within "global webs"—spatially dispersed production networks that outsource their operations on a worldwide basis—demand for labor (and the economic opportunity that such demand provided) has vastly changed. The economic fortunes of U.S. workers have therefore diverged more sharply than ever before.

Reich distinguishes three types of workers. "Routine production workers" are semi-skilled workers in mass production settings (as discussed in Chapter 6). Since workers in developing nations can increasingly perform this type of work—usually at dramatically lower wages than in the developed world—workers in this group suffer a dramatic deterioration in their wages and bargaining power when they retain their jobs at all. The second category of job that Reich observes—"in-person service workers"—involves tasks that require face-to-face contact and thus cannot, by their very nature, be exported. This group includes a diverse assortment of occupations—janitors, housekeepers, security guards, food service workers, and personal service workers generally—that require few credentials and are thus open to all job seekers (see Chapter 9). With the combination of two important trends—declining demand for routine production workers and the growth of the immigrant labor force—workers who perform in-person service work often encounter highly unfavorable labor market conditions—and harbor sharp resentment toward undocumented immigrants.

It is only the third group that Reich identifies—"symbolic analysts"—who derive material benefit from the new global economy. These are the much vaunted "knowledge workers" who are skilled at problem identifying, problem solving, and strategic brokering tasks. As the mass production of standardized goods and services gravitates toward the developing world, economic growth within the advanced capitalist nations comes to rely on the provision of more specialized products and services that only highly educated and credentialed experts can provide. Symbolic analysts find their expertise increasingly in demand, and enjoy ever-more advantageous conditions of employment.

In Reich's account, then, what the global economy produces are widening economic and social inequalities between the domestic winners and losers within the global economy, thus introducing far-reaching strains into American society. "No longer are Americans rising or falling together, as if in one large national boat. We are, increasingly, in different, smaller boats" (1992: 173)—and some of these boats are being swamped by unfavorable economic currents. Given these trends, workers in different categories no longer feel a sense of shared fate, and any conception of the common good begins to fade. Symbolic analysts increasingly disengage from public involvement, often retreating into gated communities that provide their own, private services far removed from those less fortunate than themselves (a development Reich calls "secession politics"). For their part, routine producers and in-person service workers respond to their increasing vulnerability by adopting an outlook that is driven by fear and suspicion, adopting nationalist and often anti-immigrant outlooks that, while understandable, fail to address the sources of their declining fortunes. The only antidote to this kind of thinking, Reich argues, is a proactive effort to adopt economic policies that would strengthen the only economic asset in our society that remains uniquely "national"—the productive capacities of our workforce itself.

Reich had no illusions that all workers could become symbolic analysts, but he did suggest that the competitive position of the U.S. economy increasingly rests on our ability to expand the pool of workers with strong analytical abilities. Only by enhancing the productive capacity of our nation's workforce can we increase the attractiveness of our nation's economy, thus ensuring the flow of capital investment that can provide good quality jobs to the nation's workforce. This is why he advocated economic policies aimed at strengthening the productive skills and knowledge our workforce can command.

A second line of analysis that is relevant here has sought to trace the connection between globalization and the occupational structures that emerge within the key metropolitan regions within the advanced capitalist societies. The most influential work in this vein has been conducted by the University of Chicago sociologist Saskia Sassen, author of the highly influential *The Global City* (2001). In her analysis, the globalization of economic activity creates a dynamic that revolves around two interrelated tendencies: the spatial dispersion of economic activities that firms maintain and the concentration of decision-making power that tends to occur within globally oriented firms and urban areas as well.

In Sassen's analysis, to be competitive, the largest and most powerful firms increasingly seek to disperse their operations around the world. Yet doing so greatly increases the complexity of the firm's work, generating an increased tendency for firms to concentrate their planning, coordination, and command operations within large metropolitan centers, for only these very large urban areas can provide the kinds of producer services on which globally dispersed operations now depend. In a sense, the global dispersion of production reduces demand for production work in the advanced capitalist nations, but compensates for this by generating demand for two different sorts of service work. On the one hand, it increases the need for high-wage *producer* services provided by experts in financial analysis, legal and accounting services, advertising, marketing and public relations, and design and engineering work, for all of these services are needed to coordinate and control globally dispersed investments and operations. (These are the "symbolic analysts" of which Reich has spoken.) On the other hand, there arise low-wage *personal* services in restaurant, hotel, entertainment, and other personal care occupations that cater to high-wage clientele in various sectors and capacities. Since the latter forms of service work are highly unstable and pay low wages, and since globally oriented firms and producer services bid

up the cost of real estate, what globalization produces is a dramatic polarization in the living conditions of workers living in cities that are most firmly embedded within the global economy. The centers of global commerce—London, New York, Tokyo, Frankfurt, Sao Paolo, Hong Kong—thus exhibit a tendency toward dualism, in which affluent professionals live within "core" areas near prestigious business and cultural districts, while marginalized populations grow in size, are often employed in "casualized" or informal sectors of the economy, and must either live within ghettoized areas or else commute very long distances for low-paying jobs. Reinforcing these trends is the tendency for the most privileged members of large cities to interact within communication networks that link them more strongly to the members of other global cities than to the local culture in which they physically reside. In a sense, Sassen's analysis suggests that the occupational polarization suggested in Chapter 15 is largely due to the nature of the global economy.

Manuel Castells, author of a far-reaching, three-volume analysis *The Rise of the Network Society* (1996, 2000), agrees with much of Sassen's emphasis, in that he finds much the same link between global dispersion and economic polarization within the advanced capitalist world. Castells suggests that with the rise of a global information society, there arise "mega-cities" that function as the engines of economic growth. These mega-cities serve as nodes within the global economy—they coordinate the economic activities of tens of millions of workers in a given region, but are themselves connected to global networks of commerce and communication. Indeed, Castells concludes that the stronger the commercial and technological "connections" between given urban areas and the global economy are, the more powerfully the city tends to "disconnect" or disenfranchise "local populations that are either functionally unnecessary or socially disruptive" (2000: 436). For Sassen, as for Castells, this tendency to "disconnect" or to marginalize large segments of the local populations is a general tendency of global cities, whether they are located within Mexico, China, Indonesia—or the U.S. "It is this distinctive feature of being globally connected and locally disconnected, physically and socially, that makes mega-cities a new urban form" (Castells 2000: 436). These sorts of developments, in fact, have led some theorists to speak of the "Brazilianization" of work within metropolitan regions of the advanced capitalist societies (Beck 2000)—that is, an erosion of the segment of the labor force that is employed in permanent, full-time work and a consequent increase in the proportion of workers that shifts uncertainly between informal or irregular forms of labor, self-employment, and other forms of uncertain employment.

Some analysts have drawn attention to difficulties in these formulations, in that at least some trends in the distribution of wealth and income seem to operate at odds with their predictions. Thus, for example, Reich predicts increasing levels of income and wealth on the part of a broad swath of educated professionals—his "symbolic analysts"—and yet, while their incomes have materially improved since 1975, the greatest increases in income have been enjoyed by a tiny stratum of wealthy investors—the top 1% of income earners—who wield not so much knowledge or expertise (as Reich has stressed) as shares of stock, investment capital, and inherited wealth. Other researchers have raised questions about trends in occupational growth, suggesting that much of the job growth within urban areas has rested

not in *producer* services (those Sassen stressed) but in *human* services—especially in education and health care—whose size reflects *political* decisions and public policy that are to an important degree independent of the global capitalist economy. In this connection it is important to note that the accelerated growth of capitalism within Asia has had *differential* effects on income inequality—growth has generated massive inequalities within China, to be sure, but not within Taiwan, Japan, or South Korea (Deyo 1989). Nor has capital accumulation within the European Union been accompanied by quite the same surge of inequality that has taken root within the United States and, to some extent, Great Britain. These differences point to the need for careful analysis of the local and political institutions that mediate global trends within particular regions, industries, and societies. The point recalls our discussion of the political context in which the Industrial Revolution began in Great Britain, as opposed to the United States (see Chapter 4).

These qualifications notwithstanding, few would deny that the globalization of economic activity has acted greatly to intensify social and economic inequalities within the United States. This should not be surprising. By its very nature, globalization tends to free economic entities—firms, pools of capital, highly educated executives and professionals—that are most mobile, whose latitude broadens relative to more locally rooted populations. Castells puts the point this way: "While capital is global, and core production networks are increasingly globalized, the bulk of labor is local. Only an elite specialty labor force, of great strategic importance, is truly globalized" (2000: 131). Again, the point here is that globalization reinforces the asymmetrical nature of the employment relation, as large corporations find it possible to operate on a worldwide landscape even as workers are confined to their local communities. How societies manage the resulting inequalities and tensions is a significant challenge virtually all nations must increasingly confront.

Studying Global Commodity Chains

One of the more fruitful ways to study globalization and the processes it unleashes has emerged among scholars studying capitalism on a world scale. This approach was first generated by Immanuel Wallerstein (1974), who developed a broad historical perspective toward the rise of Western economic dominance during the period following the European conquest of the new world. Founding what came to be known as "world systems" theory, this approach conceived of national economies as enmeshed within a global division of labor based on a system of unequal exchange. Economies within the *core* of the world system occupied the dominant position within the world system. Equipped with powerful military apparatuses, more advanced technologies, and means of transporting goods across large swaths of the globe, nations such as Spain, the Netherlands, and England at various times managed to dominate economic regions located on *the periphery* of the world system. The latter, peripheral regions (parts of Asia, Latin America, and Africa) found themselves merely supplying raw materials needed by the core economies, and often on highly disadvantageous terms. In between these two parts of the world system were nations lodged within the *semi-periphery*, which often supplied cheap labor and some manufactured goods to core nations and served as a kind of buffer between core and periphery. The boundaries of the semi-periphery are dynamic, composed as it is of nations moving

downward from the core (e.g., Spain after the fall of its Empire) or upward from the periphery to the semi-periphery (Mexico, South Korea, or Brazil).

The world systems approach made an important contribution in that it invited analysts to approach the workings of capitalism in broadly global and historical terms. Yet the approach tended to be so macro-structural in its approach as to lose sight of concrete economic activities. Seeking to address this problem, a growing number of scholars have developed an approach that retains the broadly global nature of world systems theory, but adopts an analytic strategy that can provide a fine-grained analysis of how concrete economic activities operate on a transnational basis. This approach, involving the analysis of *global commodity chains*, warrants careful attention here.

The concept of global commodity chains (GCCs) is easily understood. Any finished product that is familiar to you—this book, the computer you use, your cell phone, an article of clothing—represents the culmination of intricately interwoven webs of supply, production, and distribution networks that link the provision of raw materials through various stages in the production and assembly of parts, through the final packaging, distribution, and sale of the finished commodity. These complex chains of economic activity far transcend the boundaries of any given nation (let alone industry). Indeed, they increasingly reach across the globe and take different forms. Essentially, GCC research has sought to understand how transnational production and supply networks actually operate—that is, to understand the patterns that GCCs assume, the conditions that shape them, and the trends they exhibit over time. The body of knowledge that has resulted provides a unique way of understanding global economic activity and its impact on the work that people do within the various parts of the world economic system.

A key formulation in GCC analysis was provided by Gereffi (1994), who distinguished three dimensions of commodity chains. In his view, GCCs were characterized by (1) an input/output dimension (the technical structures used to add economic value at various points of the chain); (2) a territorial dimension (how "long" or "short" the chain is in space, and how globally dispersed its various operations are); and (3) a governance dimension (the power relations developed within the chain, shaping the division of labor and authority among its various agents). Since the last of these dimensions affects the share of profit and knowledge that flow to each part of the chain, it has attracted the bulk of the attention within the literature.

Gereffi and his colleagues have distinguished two broad types of global commodity chain (see Figure 16.2). *Producer-driven commodity chains* represent industrial or manufacturing networks in which control over the chain lies in the hands of the manufacturer. Examples include the production of automobiles, steel, aircraft, appliances, or electronics, all of which are capital-intensive manufacturing processes that only seldom allow newcomers to compete. Given such high barriers to entry (few people can establish a steel mill or a nuclear power plant), firms located at the center of producer-driven commodity chains are large multinational corporations with headquarters in the core of the world system. They can usually dictate economic terms and conditions to the suppliers that participate in the chain. A good example is General Motors, setting the terms that its parts suppliers must accept. This means

that the flow of profits and control over strategic design functions usually remain in the hands of the producer and not the suppliers they utilize.

Buyer-driven commodity chains—the second type of GCC—display very different characteristics. Here, control over the chain rests in the hands of firms that perform little of the manufacturing work. Instead, they perform functions that lie closer to the end-consumer, such as brand-name retailing, the provision of fashion-setting designs, or merchandising networks (e.g., chains of outlet stores). Firms that hold the most powerful positions within buyer-driven commodity chains include such retailers of branded or designer goods as Nike, Liz Claiborne, Donna Karan, and Ralph Lauren, as well as specialty retailers such as Benetton, the Gap, Banana Republic, or The Limited—and giant discount merchandisers like Target and especially Wal-Mart. These firms (sometimes dubbed "big buyers") typically operate no manufacturing operations, but instead establish elaborate chains of brokers, subcontractors, and other intermediaries, who in turn lease production time at factories dispersed throughout the world. What the big buyers control—knowledge about consumer demand, expertise in logistics, the ability to dominate retail markets—enables them to dictate the terms under which transactions will occur. (Winning a contract with a firm that supplies Wal-Mart or the Gap can involve an enormous infusion of revenue into the hands of small factory owners several levels down in a commodity chain.) This gives big buyers great *de facto* power over where production will occur, under what conditions, and at what levels of pay. Such power can have massive effects on the terms and conditions that exist within whole industries and geographical regions of the developed and developing world alike. As analysts have pointed out, the success of Wal-Mart has had major effects not only on the operations of the retailing industry, but also on supermarkets, appliance stores, and even longshoring as well.

Research on GCCs has examined the structure of numerous commodity chains, including shipbuilding, apparel, grain, footwear, wheat, sugar, coffee, and other foodstuffs (see Gereffi 1994, 2001; Korzeniewicz 1994; Bair 2005; Collins 2005). Although much remains to be known about the transformation of commodity chains during distinct periods and regions of the world economy, researchers have generally agreed on a number of conclusions. First, as less developed countries have been drawn into global capitalism, increasingly basing their economies on the production of goods for export to the developed world, commodity chains have grown increasingly lengthy—that is, they are extended across ever-further regions of the world. Nondurable consumer goods in particular are thus increasingly likely to be produced abroad, in widely dispersed locales that are linked to the developed world through complex production and supply networks. Such chains render it ever more difficult to maintain quality and even safety control, as has been evident in recent product safety scandals involving U.S. goods such as toys, pet food, and pharmaceutical products. This should not be surprising, given that aspects of the production process that that were previously located in adjacent spaces (even in the same plant or building) are increasingly dispersed around the globe.

Second, a general shift has occurred in the locus of control within commodity chains. As buyer-driven GCCs have taken hold, accounting for an expanding proportion of economic activity, many analysts have spoken of a historical reversal of the relation between industrial and commercial

businesses. Traditionally, manufacturing firms controlled the rhythms and operations of the economic system, either owning factories producing the parts and supplies they needed or else maintaining networks of suppliers whom they directly controlled. But now, it is marketing, retailing, and merchandising firms—the big buyers—who have gained the upper hand in many industries. Indeed, armed with sophisticated information systems and point-of-sale databases about consumer demand, merchandisers have reshaped the way in which production systems operate, leading some analysts to speak of a far-reaching "logistics revolution" affecting shipping, warehousing, supermarkets, and retail industries generally.

Although it remains in an early stage of its development, the GCC perspective has made several important contributions. For one thing, it encourages researchers to adopt a broader perspective than is possible using such traditional concepts as "industry" or "national economy." The GCC perspective points out that economic activity increasingly cuts across corporate, industrial, and national boundaries, linking raw materials, production facilities, and distribution networks with end-consumers through highly complex webs, or networks, which transcend the organizational structures on which we have customarily relied. Moreover, the GCC perspective draws attention to the complex connections that exist between consumers in the developed world and the many workers and merchants to whom they are connected. Using the GCC concept enables us to break down the distance between workers and consumers and to explore the ways in which economic activity is in fact bound up with events and activities that are spatially remote from us. We rarely think about such connections, even as we consume coffee grown in Sumatra or wear clothing made through the combined activities of workers located at multiple points around the globe. Advocates of human rights movements have rightfully suggested that we would do well to consider such ties.

For example, as producer-driven commodity chains have relied on intermediaries such as brokers and subcontractors, spaces have opened up in which even the most basic of human rights are increasingly placed at risk. Much attention has been given to the use of child labor in the production of apparel and footwear overseas, and associations that have been established to monitor worker rights must often develop complex datasets that trace commercial networks up and down various commodity chain. Yet economic activity now occurs at such a rapid pace, and less developed countries are often so difficult to monitor, that valid data are often impossible to maintain. Ironically, even labor-saving or digital devices such as laptops, PDAs, and cell phones routinely incorporate raw materials whose production uses unfree or even slave labor. This is true in the case of the mining of columbite-tantalite, sometimes called coltan, the great bulk of which stems from Rwanda and the Congo. It is not unusual for large multinational producers of cell phones, laptops, or video game machines to rely on sources of coltan controlled by armed militias using forced labor for their own enrichment, with the mining performed by adolescents working at the point of bayonets (Smith and Mantz 2006). The virtual world that we enjoy, in other words, has at its other end a rather different character, which raises ethical and sometimes even legal questions about the culpability of core producers whose commodity chains in fact rely on such unsavory forms of control.

The GCC perspective thus provides us with an important set of conceptual tools with which to understand the economic trends unfolding around us. By pointing to the spread of buyer-driven commodity chains, GCC analysis enables us to raise questions about the concentrated power of giant merchandisers such as Wal-Mart (whose commercial ties to China accounts for fully 1/10 of the U.S. trade deficit with that nation). Indeed, some analysts believe that Wal-Mart is so economically powerful that it now provides the template for work organization in the United States, in much the same way that Fordism did at the beginning of the twentieth century.

One final point should be made about the spread of GCCs. As buyer-driven commodity chains have taken root, and as they have succeeded in offshoring production to some of the poorer nations in the global economy, manufacturing work that has remained in the United States must increasingly conform to the pattern established abroad, especially as labor organizations have declined. The downward spiral that can affect wages and working conditions is particularly evident in the apparel industry, which has witnessed a resurgence of sweatshop conditions during the last twenty years (Ross 1997; Bonacich and Appelbaum 2000; Collins 2003).

A sweatshop can be defined as a workplace that routinely stands in violation of multiple standards established by law to protect worker safety and health, minimum wages, and other terms and conditions of employment (such as the hours of the working day, the right to periodic breaks, and so forth). Using this definition, in 1998 the U.S. Department of Labor has actually found that *most*—61 percent—of the apparel establishments in the city of Los Angeles exhibited these kinds of multiple violations, including nonpayment of minimum wages or overtime pay and violations of fair hours regulations. A year earlier, a survey completed of L.A. garment firms found that the great majority had significant deficiencies in worker safety and health, with 54 percent exhibiting the most serious (and dangerous) violations (Bonacich and Appelbaum 2000: 3). Similar patterns have been found in other large metropolitan areas. Indeed, in 1996, the U.S. Department of Labor estimated that between 40 and 60 percent of all registered garment establishments in the United States violate wage and overtime laws, with thousands of these workplaces exposing workers to highly unsafe conditions of employment (Collins 2003: 2).

The point here is not to engage in muckraking, or to emphasize the worst aspects of recent workplace trends. Rather, it is to draw attention to the fact that many production processes within our economy are increasingly forced to emulate patterns established in the poorest nations; that the ability of large designers and big buyers to rely on intermediaries (subcontractors) creates spaces in which workers' rights become more vulnerable; and that immigration from less developed nations swells the ranks of workers in the United States who are willing to take any job at any wage, affecting industries that previously afforded workers a measure of protection against sweatshop conditions. Left to their own devices, the workings of global commodity chains have multiple effects on U.S. workplaces, many of which have not been advantageous—or humane.

Conclusions: Shaping Globalization

One of the least helpful aspects of the debate over globalization has been the tendency of its defenders to view it as an irreversible trend that operates in accordance with laws all its own, independent of human intervention. Yet clearly, the argument can be made that while the world has grown increasingly interconnected (and is likely to continue to do so), the result of globalization can take many forms. Trade agreements, it is generally held, must contain important components that protect both labor and environmental standards. Federal and state laws provide corporations with their rights to incorporation and can establish certain basic standards as conditions of doing business. Indeed, even city governments have increasingly felt compelled to adopt resolutions mandating certain principles that must be met by all contractors and suppliers for city purchasing. Such actions have at times addressed questions of the living standards that must be met—and sometimes even mandated certain standards for contractors who operate plants overseas. The point here is that there is in fact much that *can* be done to humanize the globalization processes we have discussed in this chapter.

One such step involves changes that might be adopted by global financial operations such as the IMF and the World Bank. As we have seen, leading policy makers (such as the Nobel Prize–winning economist Joseph Stiglitz) have argued that much of the dogma that financial institutions use as the basis for their lending and regulatory policies actually impose substantial harm on the developing world. By imposing a theology of free trade—sometimes called "neo-liberalism"—these institutions not only make it hard for poor economies to develop in accordance with local needs and conditions. In addition, they close off open debate about the nature of free trade policies within the developed nations, encouraging people to view markets as sacred entities whose operations cannot be subject to human will. The result often operates to the disadvantage of workers living and working in the United States. Indeed, some trade analysts have suggested that free trade agreements can shape markets in ways that better serve the needs of workers in *both* the poor nations and the industrialized world. Thus, by linking the removal of trade barriers to provisions mandating verifiable protections for workers' rights, workers in the developed world would in theory enjoy material improvements in their working lives and workers in the industrialized nations would no longer have to compete with workers employed under unsustainable and immoral circumstances.

A second step that might be taken involves "living wage" campaigns advanced by local governmental bodies, often at the urging of labor and student groups and community-based organizations. Since neither the federal poverty threshold nor the minimum wage take into account regional variations in the cost of living, leaders within large metropolitan areas (where wages for full-time workers often fail to provide enough income to address housing costs) have increasingly felt compelled to establish locally attuned income needs that must be met by contractors seeking to do business with the local government. Such living wage campaigns have succeeded in St. Louis, St. Paul, Minneapolis, Boston, Oakland, Denver, Chicago, Cook County, New Orleans, Detroit, New York City, Long Island, Sacramento, San Francisco, and elsewhere (Reynolds 2003). Indeed, sometimes individual organizations are pressured to provide a living wage. This was the case in 2006, when students at Georgetown University in Washington, DC, conducted a hunger strike as a means of prompting their university to provide more reasonable levels of pay for the food service and janitorial staff who serve Georgetown students each day.

A third way of shaping globalization has emerged in the antisweatshop movement that swept across universities in the United States and abroad. Much of this movement began with the realization that many articles bearing university logos—t-shirts, caps, coffee mugs, and other souvenirs—were in fact being produced under conditions that involved the use of child labor, excessively long working days, beatings and firings for workers who protested, and so forth. In response, campuses organized on a national basis to establish the need for universities (and, often, merchandising firms) to certify that their products were produced in accordance with the most humane standards. Leaders of this movement have recently worked with U.S. labor organizations and the U.S. Congress to extend such an approach into the federal arena to ensure that "sweat-free" production is not dependent on corporate policy, but is a matter of federal law. With the support of the United   Steelworkers of America and some members of the U.S. Senate, legislation along these lines was introduced into the Congress in 2006, though passage (if it ever occurs) is still a long way off.

A final development that has emerged as a means of humanizing the globalization process concerns the spread of transnational movements in support of workers' human rights. National borders are formidable boundaries, and ethnic, racial, linguistic, and religious divisions often make it difficult for workers of different countries to form common cause even if they are employed by the same corporation. Yet the interesting point here is that communications and information technologies have increasingly exposed people to information, photographs, and video images of one another, in effect providing the basis for a greater sense of affiliation than existed in the last century. The tsunami that killed hundreds of thousands of Indonesians in 2005, for example, provoked an outpouring of sympathy and support from around the world. The unfree conditions of Burmese workers and Tibetan monks have prompted legal advocates and student organizations to provide support in various ways. An important question for the coming decade will be whether such instances of social and cultural globalization can catch up with the globalization of economic institutions. Time will tell.

References

Abbott, Andrew. 1988. *The System of Professions: An Essay on the Division of Expert Labor.* Chicago: University of Chicago Press.

Abel, Ellen K. and Margaret K. Nelson (Eds.). 1990. *Circles of Care: Work and Identity in Women's Lives.* Albany, NY: State University of New York Press.

Adler, Patricia A. and Peter Adler. 2004. *Paradise Laborers: Hotel Work in the Global Economy.* Ithaca, NY: ILR Press.

Adler, Paul. 1988. "Automation, Skill and the Future of Capitalism." *Berkeley Journal of Sociology* 22:42–56.

———. 1992. "The 'Learning Bureaucracy': New United Motor Manufacturing, Inc. Research." *Organizational Behavior* 15:111–194.

Albert, Steven and Keith Bradley. 1997. *Managing Knowledge: Experts, Agencies and Organisations.* New York: Cambridge University Press.

Albrecht, Karl and Ron Zemke. 1985. *Service America! Doing Business in the New Economy.* Homewood, IL: Dow-Jones Irwin.

Alvarez, Lizette and John M. Broder. "More and More, Women Risk All to Enter U.S." *New York Times*, January 10, A1, A23.

Ancona, Deborah G. and Caldwell, David F. 1992. "Demography and Design: Predictors of New Product Team Performance." *Organization Science* 3:321–341.

Anker, Richard. 1998. *Gender and Jobs: Sex Segregation of Occupations in the World.* Washington, D.C.: International Labor Organization.

Appelbaum, Eileen and Rosemary Batt. 1994. *The New American Workplace: Transforming Work Systems in the United States.* Ithaca, NY: ILR Press.

Appelbaum, Eileen, Thomas Bailey, P. Berg, and A. Kalleberg. 2000. *Manufacturing Advantage.* Ithaca, NY: Cornell University Press.

Applebaum, Herbert. 1992. *The Concept of Work: Ancient, Medieval and Modern.* Albany, NY: SUNY Press.

———. 1995. "The Concept of Work in Western Thought." Pp. 46–78 in *The Meanings of Work: Considerations for the 21st Century,* edited by Frederick C. Gamst. Albany, NY: SUNY Press.

Aronowitz, Stanley. 1973. *False Promises: The Shaping of American Working Class Consciousness.* New York: McGraw-Hill.

Arthur, Michael B. and Denise Rousseau. 2001. *The Boundaryless Career: A New Employment Principle for a New Organizational Era.* London: Oxford University Press.

Atkinson, John. 1985. "The Changing Corporation." Pp. 13–34 in *New Patterns of Work*, edited by D. Clutterbuck. London: Gower.

Atkinson, Paul, Amanda Coffey, Sara Delamont, John Lofland, and Lyn Lofland (Eds.). 2001. *Handbook of Ethnography*. Thousand Oaks, CA: Sage.

Babbie, Earl R. 2004. *The Practice of Social Research*, 10th ed. Belmont, CA: Wadsworth Publishing Company.

Baily, Martin N. and Robert Z. Lawrence. 2004. "What Happened to the Great US Jobs Machine? The Role of Trade and Electronic Offshoring." in *Paper on Economic Activity, V. 2.* Washington, DC: The Brookings Institution.

Bair, Jennifer. 2005. "Global Capitalism and Commodity Chains: Looking Back, Going Forward." *Competition and Change* 9:153–180.

Baldi, Stephanie and Debra B. McBrier. 1997. "Do the Determinants of Promotion Differ for Blacks and Whites?" *Work and Occupations* 24:478–97.

Baldwin, DeWitt C. Jr., Steven R. Daugherty, Ray Tsai, and Michael J. Scotti Jr. 2003. "A National Survey of Residents' Self-Reported Work Hours: Thinking Beyond Specialty." *Academic Medicine* 78:1154–1163.

Bantich, George. 2001. "Ford and the UAW." 2nd online volume of the E. C. Barksdale Memorial Essays in History (http://barksdale.uta.edu/journalvol2.htm).

Barker, James R. 1993. "Tightening the Iron Cage: Concertive Control in Self-Managing Teams." *Administrative Science Quarterly* 38:408–437.

Barley, Stephen R. and Gideon Kunda. 2001. "Bringing Work Back In." *Organization Science* 12:76–95.

Barnett, William P. and Anne S. Miner. 1992. "Standing on the Shoulders of Others: Career Interdependence in Job Mobility." *Administrative Science Quarterly* 37: 262–281.

Bates, Timothy Mason. 1997. *Race, Self-Employment, and Upward Mobility: An Illusive American Dream*. Baltimore, MD: Johns Hopkins University Press.

Baxter, Janeen and Erik Olin Wright. 2000. "The Glass Ceiling Hypothesis: A Comparative Study of the United States, Sweden, and Australia." *Gender & Society* 14:275–295.

Bayard, Kimberly, Judith Hellerstein, David Neumark, and Kenneth R. Troske. 2003. "New Evidence on Sex Segregation and Sex Differences in Wages from Matched Employee-Employer Data." *Journal of Labor Economics* 21:887–922.

Beck, Ulrich. 2000. Brave New World of Work. Cambridge: Polity.

Becker, Howard. 1967. "Whose Side Are We On?" *Social Problems* 14:239–247.

Belkin, Lisa. 2003. "The Opt-Out Revolution." *The New York Times Magazine*. October 26, 2003, pp. 43–85.

Bell, Daniel. 1947. "Adjusting Men to Machines." *Commentary* 3: 79–88.

———. 1973. *The Coming of Post-Industrial Society*. New York: Basic Books.

Bellas, Marcia L. 1999. "Emotional Labor in Academia: The Case of Professors." *Annals of the American Academy of Political and Social Science* 561:96–111.

Benders, J., F. Huijgen, and U. Pekruhl. 2002. "What Do We Know About the Incidence of Group Work (If Anything)?" *Personnel Review* 31:371–385.

Bendick, Marc, Charles W. Jackson, and Victor A. Reinso. 1994. "Measuring Employment Discrimination through Controlled

Experiments." *Review of Black Political Economy* 23:25–48.

Bendix, Rinehard. 1956. *Work and Authority in Industry.* Berkeley, CA: University of California Press.

Berggren, Christian. 1989. "New Production Concepts in Final Assembly—the Swedish Experience." Pp. 171–203 in *The Transformation of Work?*, edited by S. Wood. London: Unwin Hyman.

———. 1992. *Alternatives to Lean Production: Lessons from the Swedish Automobile Industry.* Ithaca, NY: ILR/Cornell University Press.

Berlin, Gorden and Andrew Sum. 1988. *Toward a More Perfect Union: Basic Skills, Poor Families, and Our Economic Future.* New York: Ford Foundation.

Bernhardt, Annette, Martina Morris, and Mark S. Handcock. 1995. "Women's Gains or Men's Losses: A Closer Look at the Shrinking Gender Gap in Earnings." *American Journal of Sociology* 101:302–328.

Bertrand, Marianne and Sendhil Mullainathan. 2004. "Are Emily and Greg More Employable Than Lakisha and Jamal? A Field Experiment on Labor Market Discrimination." *The American Economic Review* 94:991–1013.

Besen, Yasemin and Michael S. Kimmel. 2006. "At Sam's Club, No Girls Allowed: The Lived Experience of Sex Discrimination." *Equal Opportunities International* 25: 172–187.

Bhagwati, Jagdish. 2004a. *In Defense of Globalization.* New York: Oxford University Press.

———. 2004b. "Why Your Job Isn't Moving to Bangalore." *The New York Times*, 15 February, p. 11.

Bianchi, Suzanne M. 2000. "Maternal Employment and Time with Children: Dramatic Change or Surprising Continuity." *Demography* 37: 401–415.

Bianchi, Suzanne M., Melissa A. Milkie, Liana C. Sayer, and John P. Robinson. 2000. "Is Anyone Doing the Housework? Trends in the Gender Division of Household Labor." *Social Forces* 79:191–228.

Bielby, W. T. 2000. "Minimizing Workplace Gender and Racial Bias." *Contemporary Sociology.* 29:120–129.

Bivens, L. Josh. 2006. "Trade Deficits and Manufacturing Job Loss: Correlation and Causality." Washington DC: Economic Policy Institute. Briefing Paper #171.

Blair, Sampson Lee and D. T. Lichter. 1991. "Measuring the Division of Household Labor: Gender Segregation of Housework Among American Couples." *Journal of Family Issues* 12: 91–113.

Blair-Loy, Mary. 2003. *Competing Devotions: Career and Family among Women Executives.* Cambridge, MA: Harvard University Press.

Blair-Loy, Mary and Amy S. Wharton. 2002. "Employees' Use of Family-Responsive Policies and the Workplace Social Context." *Social Forces* 80:813–845.

Blakemore, Laurel C., Janette M. Hall, and J. Sybil Biermann. 2003. "Women in Surgical Residency Training Programs." *Journal of Bone and Joint Surgery* 85A: 2477–2480.

Blalock, Hubert M. 1967. Toward a Theory of Minority Group Relations. NY: Capricorn.

Blau, Francine D. and Lawrence Kahn. 1992. "The Gender Earnings Gap: Learning From International Comparisons." *American Economic Review, Papers and Proceedings* 82:533–538.

———. 2000. "Gender Differences in Pay." *Journal of Economic Literature* 14:75–99.

Blauner, Robert. 1964. *Alienation and Freedom: The Factory Worker and His Industry.* Chicago: University of Chicago Press.

Block, Fred. 1990. *Postindustrial Possibilities: A Critique of Economic Discourse.* Berkeley, CA: University of California Press.

Blumer, Herbert. 1958. "Race Prejudice as a Sense of Group Position." *Pacific Sociological Review* 1:3–7.

Boggs, Roderick, Joseph Sellers, and Marc Bendick, Jr. 1993. "Use of Testing in Civil Rights Enforcement". Pp. 345–376 in *Clear and Convincing Evidence: Measurement of Discrimination in America*, edited by M. Fix and R. Struyk. Washington, DC: Urban Institute Press.

Bonacich, Edna and Richard P. Appelbaum. 2000. *Behind the Label: Inequality in the Los Angeles Apparel Industry.* Berkeley, CA: University of California Press.

Borjas, George J. and Lawrence F. Katz. 2005. "The Evolution of the Mexican-Born Workforce in the United States." National Bureau of Economic Research, April 2005.

Bosk, Charles L. 1979. *Forgive and Remember: Managing Medical Failure.* Chicago: University of Chicago Press.

Boulis, Ann. 2004. "The Evolution of Gender and Motherhood in Contemporary Medicine." *Annals of the American Academy of Political and Social Science* 596:172–206.

Boushey, Heather. 2005. "Are Women Opting Out? Debunking the Myth." Center for Economic and Policy Research Briefing Paper, December 2005.

Bowles, Samuel and Herbert Gintis. 1974. *Schooling in Capitalist America: Educational Reform and the Contradictions of Economic Life.* New York: Basic Books.

Braddock, J. H. II and McPartland, James M. 1987. "How Minorities Continue to Be Excluded from Equal Employment Opportunities: Research on Labor Market and Institutional Barriers." *Journal of Social Issues* 43:5–39.

Braverman, Harry. 1974. *Labor and Monopoly Capital: The Degradation of Work in the Twentieth Century.* New York: Monthly Review Press.

Brinkley, Douglas. 2003. *Wheels for the World: Henry Fords, His Company, and a Century of Progress, 1903–2003.* New York: Viking.

Brint, Steven. 1994. *In an Age of Experts: The Changing Role of Professionals in Politics and Public Life.* Princeton, NJ: Princeton University Press.

———. 2001. "Professionals and the 'Knowledge Economy': Rethinking the Theory of Postindustrial Society." *Current Sociology* 49, 4(July): 101–32.

Brody, David. 1980. *Workers in Industrial America: Essays on the Twentieth Century Struggle.* New York: Oxford University Press.

Bronfenbrenner, Kate. 1997. "The Effect of Plant Closings and the Threat of Plant Closings on Worker Rights to Organize." Supplement to *Plant Closings and Workers Rights: A Report to the Council of Ministers by the Secretariat of the Commission for Labor Cooperation.* Dallas, TX: Bernan Press.

Budig, Michelle J. 2002. "Male Advantage and the Gender Composition of Jobs: Who Rides the Glass Escalator?" *Social Problems* 49:258–277.

Budig, Michelle J. and Paula England. 2001. "The Wage Penalty for Motherhood." *American Sociological Review* 66:204–225.

Bumiller, Elisabeth. 2004. "Bush Acts to Ease the Furor Over Jobs Shipped Abroad." *The New York Times* February 13. A21.

Burawoy, Michael. 1979. *Manufacturing Consent: Changes in the Labor Process under Monopoly Capitalism*. Chicago: University of Chicago Press.

———. 1985. *The Politics of Production: Factory Regimes Under Capitalism and Socialism*. London: Verso.

Burawoy, Michael, Joseph A. Blum, Sheba George, Zsuzsa Gille, Millie Thayer, Teresa Gowan, Lynne Haney, Maren Klawiter, Steven H. Lopez, and Sean Riain. 2000. *Global Ethnography: Forces, Connections, and Imaginations in a Postmodern World*. Berkeley: University of California Press.

Burke, Lisa, Evren Esen, and Jessica Collison. 2003. *Society for Human Resource Management 2003 Benefits Survey*. SHRM/SHRM Foundation, June 2003.

Burstein, P. and M. E. Edwards. 1994. "The Impact of Employment Discrimination Litigation on Racial Disparity in Earnings: Evidence and Unresolved Issues." *Law and Society Review* 28:79–111.

Calhoun, Craig. 1982. *The Question of Class Struggle*. Chicago: University of Chicago Press.

Cambois, E. 2004. "Careers and Mortality: Evidences on How Far Occupational Mobility Predicts Differentiated Risks." *Social Science and Medicine* 58:2545–2558.

Cappelli, Peter. 1995. "Rethinking Employment." *British Journal of Industrial Relations* 33:563–602.

Cappelli, Peter and David Neumark. 2001. "Do 'High-Performance' Work Practices Improve Establishment-Level Outcomes?" *Industrial and Labor Relations Review* 54:737–775.

Cascio, Wayne F. and Clifford Young. 2005. "Work-Family Balance: Does the Market Reward Firms that Respect it?" Pp. 49–63 in *From Work-Family Balance to Work-Family Interaction: Changing the Metaphor,* edited by D. F. Halpern and S. E. Murphy. Mahwah, NJ: Lawrence Erlbaum Associates.

Casper, Lynne M. and Suzanne M. Bianchi. 2002. *Continuity and Change in the American Family.* Thousand Oaks, CA: Sage Publications.

Cassell, Joan. 1991. *Expected Miracles: Surgeons at Work*. Philadelphia: Temple University Press.

Castells, Manuel. 1996. *The Rise of the Network Society,* Vol. 1. Malden, MA: Blackwell Publishing.

———. 2000. *End of the Millenium*. Malden, MA: Blackwell Publishing.

Catalyst. 2005. *Women 'Take Care,' Men 'Take Charge': Stereotyping of U.S. Business Leaders Exposed*. New York: Catalyst.

Catanzarite, Lisa. 2003. "Race-Gender Composition and Occupational Pay Degradation." *Social Problems* 50:14–37.

Center for Professional Responsibility. 2008. *Model Rules of Professional Conduct*. Chicago: American Bar Association.

Champlin, Dell and Eric Hake. 2006. "Immigration as Industrial Strategy in American Meatpacking." *Review of Political Economy* 18:49–70.

Chandler, Alfred D. 1977. *The Visible Hand: The Managerial Revolution in American Business*. Cambridge, MA: Belknap.

———. 1980. "The United States: Seedbed of Managerial Capitalism." Pp. 9–40 in *Managerial Hierarchies: Comparative Perspectives on the Rise of Modern Industrial Enterprises*, edited by Alfred D. Chandler and Herman Daems. Cambridge, MA: Harvard University Press.

Charles, Maria. 1992. "Accounting for Cross-National Variation in Occupational Sex Segregation." *American Sociological Review* 57:483–502.

Charles, Maria and David B. Grusky. 2004. *Occupational Ghettoes: The Worldwide Segregation of Women*. Stanford, CA: Stanford University Press.

Chatman, Jennifer A., J. Polzer, S. Barsade, and M. Neale. 1998. "Being Different Yet Feeling Similar: The Influence of Demographic Composition and Organizational Culture on Work Processes and Outcomes." *Administrative Science Quarterly* 43:749–780.

Chemers, Martin M., Stuart Oskamp, and Mark A. Costanzo. 1995. *Diversity in Organizations*. Thousand Oaks, CA: Sage Publications.

Cheng, Cliff (Ed.). 1996. *Masculinities in Organizations*. Thousand Oaks, CA: Sage.

Chinoy, Ely. 1955 [1992]. *Automobile Workers and the American Dream*. Urbana, IL: University of Illinois Press.

Cockburn, Cynthia. 1983. *Brothers*. London: Pluto.

Cognard-Black, Andrew J. 2004. "Will They Stay, or Will They Go? Sex-Atypical Work Among Token Men Who Teach." *The Sociological Quarterly* 45:113–139.

Cohany, Sharon R. and Emy Sok. 2007. "Trends in Labor Force Participation of Married Mothers of Infants." *Monthly Labor Review* (February): 9–16.

Cohen, Lisa E., Joseph P. Broschak, and Heather A. Haveman. 1998. "And Then There Were More? The Effect of Organizational Sex Composition on Hiring and Promotion of Managers." *American Sociological Review* 63:711–727.

Collins, Glenn. 2000. "Few Blacks Where Tips Are High; Racial Diversity Is Rare for Waiters in Elite Restaurants." *New York Times* May 30, 2000. B1.

Collins, J. L. 2003. *Threads: Gender, Labor, and Power in the Global Apparel Industry*. Chicago: University of Chicago Press.

———. 2005. "New Directions in Commodity Chain Analysis of Global Development processes." *Research in Rural Sociology and Development* 11:3–17.

Collins, Sharon. 1989. "The Marginalization of Black Executives." *Social Problems* 36:317–331.

———. 1997. *Black Corporate Employees: The Making and Breaking of a Black Middle Class*. Philadelphia: Temple University Press.

Collinson, David. 2003. "Identities and Insecurities: Selves at Work." *Organization* 10:527–547.

Cornfield, Dan B., Karen E. Campbell, and Holly J. McCammon (Eds.). 2001. *Working in Restructured Workplaces: Challenges and New Directions in the Sociology of Work*. Thousand Oaks, CA: Sage.

Correll, Shelley J. 2004. "Constraints into Preferences: Gender, Status, and Emerging Career Aspirations." *American Sociological Review* 69:93–113.

Correll, Shelley J., Stephen Benard, and In Paik. 2007. "Getting a Job: Is There a Motherhood Penalty?" *American Journal of Sociology* 112:1297–1338.

Cotter, David A., JoAnn DeFiore, Joan M. Hermsen, Brenda Marsteller Kowalewski, and Reeve Vanneman. 1995. "Occupational Gender Desegregation in the 1980s." *Work and Occupations* 22:3–21.

———. 1997. "All Women Benefit: The Macro-Level Effect of Occupational Integration." *American Sociological Review* 62:714–734.

Cotter, David A., Joan M. Hermsen, and Reeve Vanneman. 1999. "Systems of Gender, Race, and Class Inequality: Multilevel Analyses." *Social Forces* 78:433–460.

Cowan, Ruth Schwartz. 1983. *More Work for Mother: The Ironies of Household Technology from the Open Hearth to the Microwave.* New York: Basic Books.

Creighton Colin. 1996. "The Rise of the Male Breadwinner Family: A Reappraisal." *Society and History* 38:320–337.

Creswell, Julie. 2006. "How Suite It Isn't: A Dearth of Female Bosses." *New York Times,* December 17, p. B9.

Crittenden, Ann. 2001. *The Price of Motherhood.* New York: Henry Holt and Company.

Cuddy, Amy J.C., Susan T. Fiske, and Peter Glick. 2004. "When Professionals Become Mothers, Warmth Doesn't Cut the Ice." *The Journal of Social Issues* 60:701–719.

Cutcher-Gershenfeld, Joel. 1991. "The Impact on Economic Performance of a Transformation in Workplace Relations." *Industrial and Labor Relations Review* 44:241–260.

Dalton, Melville. 1959. *Men Who Manage: Fusions of Feeling and Theory in Administration.* New York: Wiley.

Darves, Bonnie. 2005. "Women in Medicine Force Change in Workplace Dynamics." *New England Journal of Medicine.* Boston, MA, NEJM Career Resources. http://www.nejmjobs.org/career-resources/women-in-medicine.aspx.

Davis, Amy E. and Arne L. Kalleberg. 2006. "Family-Friendly Organizations: Work and Family Programs in the 1990s." *Work and Occupations* 33:191–223.

Dawley, Alan. 1980. *Class and Community: The Industrial Revolution in Lynn.* Cambridge, MA: Harvard University Press.

de Grazia, Sebastian. 1994. *Of Time, Work and Leisure.* New York: Vintage.

Deitch, Cynthia H. and Matt L. Huffman. 2001. "Family-Responsive Benefits and the Two-Tiered Labor Market." Pp. 103–130 in *Working Families: The Transformation of the American Home,* edited by Rosanna Hertz and Nancy Marshall. Berkeley, CA: University of California Press.

Deyo, Frederick. 1989. *Beneath the Miracle: Labor Subordinator in the New Asian Industrialism.* Berkeley, CA: University of California Press.

Di Tomaso, Nancy 2001. "The Loose Coupling of Jobs: The Subcontracting of Everyone?" in *Sourcebook on Labor Markets: Evolving Structures and Processes,* edited by I. Berg and A. Kalleberg. New York: Plenum.

Dillman, Don. 2007. *Mail and Internet Surveys: The Tailored Design, Second Edition—2007 Update.* New York: John Wiley.

Dobbs, Lou. 2004. *Exporting America: How Corporate Greed Is Shipping American Jobs Overseas.* New York: Warner Business Books.

Docquier, Frédéric and Abdeslam Marfouk. 2006. "International Migration by Education Attainment, 1990–2000." Pp. 151–199 in *International Migration, Remittances, and the Brain Drain*, edited by Çaglar Ozden and Maurice Schiff. Washington, DC: International Bank for Reconstruction and Development.

Doeringer, P. B., and M. J. Piore. 1971. *Internal Labor Markets and Manpower Analysis.* Lexington, MA: D.C. Heath.

Dohm, Arlene and Lynn Shniper. 2007. "Occupational Employment Projections to 2016." *Monthly Labor Review* (November): 86–125.

Dohse, K., U. Jurgens, and T. Malsch. 1985. "From 'Fordism' to 'Toyotism'? The Social Organization of the Labor Process in the Japanese Automobile Industry." *Politics and Society* 14:115–146.

Donkin, Richard. 2001. *Blood, Sweat, and Tears: The Evolution of Work.* New York: Texere.

Donovan, Frances R. 1929. *The Saleslady.* Chicago: University of Chicago Press.

———. 1938. *The Schoolma'am.* New York: Frederick A. Stokes.

Dorgan, Byron L. 2006. *Take This Job and Ship It: How Corporate Greed and Brain Dead Politics Are Selling Out America.* New York: Macmillan.

Drezner, Daniel. 2004. "The Outsourcing Bogeyman." *Foreign Affairs* 83:3.

Dudley, Kathryn Marie. 1994. *The End of the Line: Lost Jobs, New Lives in Post-Industrial America.* Chicago: University of Chicago Press.

Durkheim, Emile. 1933 [1983]. *The Division of Labor in Society.* Translated by George Simpson. New York: Free Press.

Edelman, Lauren. 1990. "Legal Environments and Organizational Governance: The Expansion of Due Process in the American Workplace." *American Journal of Sociology* 95:1401–1440.

Edelman, Lauren B., Sally R. Fuller, and Iona Mara-Drita. 2001. "Diversity Rhetoric and the Managerialization of Law." *American Journal of Sociology* 106:1589–1641.

Edwards, Richard. 1979. *Contested Terrain: The Transformation of the Workplace in the Twentieth Century.* New York: Basic Books.

Ehrenreich, Barbara. 2001. *Nickel and Dimed: On (Not) Getting by in America.* New York: Metropolitan Books.

Ely, Robin J. and David A. Thomas. 2001. "Cultural Diversity at Work: The Effect of Diversity Perspectives and Diversity Processes." *Administrative Science Quarterly* 46:229–273.

Engels, Friedrich. 1993 [1845]. *The Condition of the Working Class in England.* Edited with an introduction by David McLellan. New York: Oxford.

England, Paula. 1992. *Comparable Worth: Theories and Evidence.* New York: Aldine de Gruyter.

———. 2005. "Emerging Theories of Care Work." *Annual Review of Sociology* 31:381–99.

England, Paula and Nancy Folbre. 1999. "The Cost of Caring." *Annals of the American Academy of Political and Social Science* 561:39–51.

———. 2000. Capitalism and the Erosion of Care. Pp. 29–48 in *Unconventional Wisdom: Alternative Perspectives on the New Economy,* edited by J. Madrick. New York: Century Foundation Press.

Epstein, Cynthia Fuchs. 1988. *Deceptive Distinctions: Sex, Gender, and the Social Order.* New Haven: Yale University Press.

———. 1993. *Women in Law.* Urbana, IL: University of Illinois Press.

Epstein, Cynthia Fuchs, Robert Saute, Bonnie Oglensky, and Martha Gever. 1995. "Glass Ceilings and Open Doors: Women's Achievement in the Legal Profession." *Fordham Law Review* 64:306–449.

Epstein, Cynthia Fuchs, Carroll Seron, Bonnie Oglensky, and Robert Saute. 1999. *The Part-Time Paradox.* New York and London: Routledge.

Erickson, Rebecca J. and Christian Ritter. 2001. "Emotional Labor, Burnout, and Inauthenticity: Does Gender Matter?" *Social Psychology Quarterly* 64:146–164.

Fantasia, Rick, Dan Clawson, and Gregory Graham. 1988. "A Critical View of Worker Participation" *American Industry Work and Occupations* 15:468–488.

Feagin, Joe. 1991. "The Continuing Significance of Race: Antiblack Discrimination in Public Places." *American Sociological Review* 56:101–116 .

Federal Glass Ceiling Commission. 1995. *Good for Business: Making Full Use of the Nation's*

Human Capital. A Fact-Finding Report for the US Department of Labor. GPO Printing Office: Washington DC.

Fenwick, Rudy and Mark Tausig. 2001. Scheduling Stress: Family and Health Outcomes of Shift Work and Schedule Control. *The American Behavioral Scientist* 44:1179–1199.

Fields, Dail L. 2002. *Taking the Measure of Work: A Guide to Validated Scales for Organizational Research and Diagnosis.* Thousand Oaks, CA: Sage.

Fine, Gary Alan. 1996. *Kitchens: The Culture of Restaurant Work.* Berkeley, CA: University of California Press.

Finlay, William. 1988. *Work on the Waterfront: Worker Power and Technological Change in a West Coast Port.* Philadelphia: Temple University Press.

Firlik, Katrina. 2006. *Another Day in the Frontal Lobe: A Brain Surgeon Exposes Life on the Inside.* New York: Random House.

Fiss, Peer C. and Paul M. Hirsch. 2005. "The Discourse of Globalization: Framing and Sensemaking of an Emerging Concept." *American Sociological Review* 70:29–52.

Fligstein, Neil. 1987. "The Intraorganizational Power Struggle: Rise of Finance Personnel to Top Leadership in Large Corporations, 1919–1979." *American Sociological Review* 52:44–59.

———. 1990. *The Transformation of Corporate Control.* New York: Cambridge University Press.

Florida, Richard. 2002. *The Rise of the Creative Class.* New York: Basic.

Form, William. 1976. *Blue Collar Stratification: Autoworkers in Four Countries.* Princeton, NJ: Princeton University Press.

Frankel, Alex. 2007. *Punching In: The Unauthorized Adventures of a Front-Line Employee.* New York: HarperCollins.

Fraser, Jill Andresky. 2002. *White Collar Sweatshop: The Deterioration of Work and Its Rewards in Corporate America.* New York: Norton.

Fredriksen-Goldsen, Karen, and Andrew Scharlach. 2001. *Families and Work: New Directions in the Twenty-First Century.* New York: Oxford University Press.

Freeman, Richard B. and James L. Medoff. 1984. *What Do Unons Do?* New York: Basic Books.

Freeman, Richard B. and Joel Rogers. 1999. *What Workers Want.* Ithaca, NY: ILR Press.

Freidson, Eliot. 1986. *Professional Powers: A Study of the Institutionalization of Formal Knowledge.* Chicago: University of Chicago Press.

———. 1994. *Professionalism Reborn: Theory, Prophecy, and Policy.* Chicago: University of Chicago Press.

Fried, Mindy. 1998. *Taking Time: Parental Leave Policy and Corporate Culture.* Philadelphia: Temple University Press.

Friedman, Stewart D. and Jeffrey H. Greenhaus. 2000. *Work and Family: Allies or Enemies?* New York: Oxford University Press.

Friedman, Thomas. 2006. *The World Is Flat: A Brief History of the Twenty-First Century.* New York: Farrar, Straus, and Giroux.

Fuegen, Kathleen, Monica Biernat, Elizabeth Haines, and Kay Deaux. 2004. "Mothers and Fathers in the Workplace: How Gender and Parental Status Influence Judgments of Job-Related Competence." *Journal of Social Issues* 60: 737–754.

Gallie, Duncan. 1978. *In Search of the New Working Class: Automation and Social Integration Within the Capitalist Enterprise.* New York: Cambridge University Press.

Gamst, Frederick. 1995. *Meanings of Work: Considerations for the Twenty-First Century.* Albany NY: SUNY Press.

Garey, Anita I. 1999. *Weaving Work and Motherhood.* Philadelphia: Temple University Press.

Gawande, Atul. 2002. *Complications: A Surgeon's Notes on an Imperfect Science.* New York: Metropolitan Books.

Geary, John F. 1992. "Employment Flexibility and Human Resource Management: The Case of Three American Electronics Plants." *Work, Employment and Society* 6: 251–270.

George, Jennifer M. and Gareth R. Jones. 1997. "Experiencing Work: Values, Attitudes, and Moods." *Human Relations* 50:393–416.

Gereffi, Gary. 1994. "The Organization of Buyer-Driven Global Commodity Chains: How US Retailers Shape Overseas Production Networks." Pp. 95–123 in *Commodity Chains and Global Capitalism*, edited by G. Gereffi and M. Korzeniewicz. Westport, CT: Greenwood.

———. 2001. "Beyond the Producer-Driven/Buyer-Driven Dichotomy: The Evolution of Global Value Chains in the Internet Era." Institute of Development Studies Bulletin 32:30–40.

Gerson, Kathleen. 1985. *Hard Choices: How Women Decide About Work, Career, and Motherhood.* Berkeley, CA: University of California Press.

Gibson, Campbell J. and Emily Lennon. 1999. "Historical Statistics on the Foreign-Born Population of the United States: 1850–1990." *Population Division Working Paper No. 29*, U.S. Bureau of the Census.

Giddens, Anthony. 1990. *The Consequences of Modernity.* Cambridge: Polity Press.

Gillespie, Richard. 1991. *Manufacturing Knowledge: A History of the Hawthorne Experiments.* New York: Cambridge University Press.

Glass, Jennifer L. and Sarah Beth Estes. 1997. "The Family Responsive Workplace." *Annual Review of Sociology* 23: 289–313.

Glass, Jennifer and T. Fujimoto. 1995. "Employer Characteristics and the Provision of Family Responsive Policies." *Work and Occupations* 22:380–411.

Glenn, Evelyn N. 1992. "From Servitude to Service Work: Historical Continuities in the Racial Division of Paid Reproductive Labor." *Signs* 18:1–43.

Goffman, Erving. 1959. *The Presentation of Self in Everyday Life.* New York: Doubleday Anchor.

Gold, Ray. 1952. "Janitors Versus Tenants: A Status-Income Dilemma." *American Journal of Sociology* 57:486–493.

Goldscheider, Frances K. and Linda J. Waite. 1991. *New Families, No Families? The Transformation of the American Home.* Berkeley, CA: University of California Press.

Goldstone, Jack. 2002. "Efflorescences and Economic Growth in World History: Rethinking the 'Rise of the West' and the Industrial Revolution." *Journal of World History* 13:323–389.

Gonos, George. 1997. "The Contest over 'Employer' Status in the Post-War U.S.: The Case of Temporary Help Firms." *Law and Society Review* 31:81–110.

Goodman, Bill and Reid Steadman. 2002. "Services: Business Demand Rivals Consumer Demand in Driving Job Growth." *Monthly Labor Review* (April):3–24.

Goodstein, Jerry. 1994. "Institutional Pressures and Strategic Responsiveness: Employer Involvement in Work-Family Issues." *Academy of Management Journal* 37:350–382.

Gorman, Elizabeth and Julie Kmec. 2009. "Hierarchical Rank and Women's Organizational Mobility: Glass Ceilings in Corporate Law Firms." *American Journal of Sociology.* Forthcoming.

Gornick, Janet, Marcia K. Meyers, and Katherine E. Ross. 1998. "Public Policies and the Employment of Mothers: A Cross-National Study." *Social Science Quarterly 79, 1:* 35–54.

Gose, Ben. 1998. "The Feminization of Veterinary Medicine." *Chronicle of Higher Education.* April 24, pp. A55–A56.

Gouldner, Alvin. 1954. *Patterns of Industrial Bureaucracy.* Glencoe, IL: The Free Press.

Gowan, Teresa. 2002. "American Untouchables: Homeless Scavengers in San Francisco's Underground Economy." Pp. 432–443 in *Working in America: Continuity, Conflict, and Change,* edited by Amy S. Wharton. New York: McGraw-Hill.

Graham, Laurie. 1995. *On the Line at Subaru-Isuzu.* Ithaca, NY: ILR/Cornell University Press.

Granovetter, Mark S. 1974. *Getting a Job.* Cambridge, MA: Harvard University Press.

Greenhouse, Steven. 2003a. "The Nation; Wal-Mart, Driving Workers and Supermarkets Crazy." *New York Times,* October 19 Section 4, p. 3.

———. 2003b. "Illegally in U.S., and Never a Day Off at Wal-Mart." *New York Times,* November 5, A1, A23.

———. 2004a. "Rewards of a 90-Hour Week: Poverty and Dirty Laundry." *New York Times,* May 31, B1, B4.

———. 2004b. "Local 226, 'the Culinary,' Makes Las Vegas the Land of the Living Wage." *New York Times,* June 3, A22.

———. 2005. "At a Small Shop in Colorado, Wal-Mart Beats a Union Once More." *New York Times,* February 26, A9.

Grenier, Guillermo. 1988. *Inhuman Relations: Quality Circles and Anti-Unionism in American Industry.* Philadelphia: Temple University Press.

Grey, Mark A. 1995. "Pork, Poultry, and Newcomers in Storm Lake, Iowa." Pp. 109–127 in *Any Way You Cut It: Meat Processing and Small Town America,* edited by Donald D. Stull, Michael J. Broadway, and David Griffith. Lawrence, KS: University Press of Kansas.

Griffith, Barbara S. 1988. *The Crisis of American Labor Operation Dixie and the Defeat of the CIO.* Philadelphia: Temple University Press.

Griffith, David. 1995. "*Hay Trabajo*: Poultry Processing, Rural Industrialization, and the Latinization of Low-Wage Labor." Pp. 129–152 in *Any Way You Cut It: Meat Processing and Small Town America,* edited by Donald D. Stull, Michael J. Broadway, and David Griffith. Lawrence, KS: University Press of Kansas.

Grover, S. L. and K. J. Crooker. 1995. " Who Appreciates Family-Responsive Human Resource Policies: The Impact of Family-Friendly Policies on the Organizational Attachment of Parents and Non-Parents." *Personnel Psychology* 48:271–288.

Grow, Brian. 2007. "Nardelli: Out at Home Depot: Behind the Flameout of Controversial CEO Bob Nardelli." *Business Week,* January 9. (http://www.msnbc.msn.com/id/16469224/).

Gubrium, Jaber. 2007. "Urban Ethnography of the 1920s Working Girl." *Gender, Work, and Organization* 14:232–258.

Guillen, Mauro F. 1994. *Models of Management: Work, Authority and Organization in a Comparative Perspective.* Chicago: University of Chicago Press.

———. 2001. "Is Globalization Civilizing, Destructive, or Feeble? A Critique of Five Key Debates in the Social Science Literature." *Annual Review of Sociology* 27:235–260.

Guion, Robert M. 1966. "Employment Testing and Discriminatory Hiring." *Industrial Relations* 5:20–37.

Hacker, Jacob. 2006. *The Great Risk Shift.* New York: Oxford.

Hackman, J. Richard and R. Wageman. 1995. "Total Quality Management: Empirical, Conceptual and Practical Issues." *Administrative Science Quarterly* 40:309–342.

Hagan, Jacqueline Maria. 2004. "Contextualizing Immigrant Labor Market Incorporation: Legal, Demographic, and Economic Dimensions." *Work and Occupations* 31:407–423.

Halberstam, David. 1986. *The Reckoning.* New York: Morrow.

Hales, Colin P. 1986. "What Do Managers Do? A Critical Review of the Evidence." *Journal of Management Studies* 23:88–115.

Haley, Heather-Lyn, Maureen Perry-Jenkins, and Amy Armenia. 2001. "Workplace Policies and the Psychological Well-Being of First-Time Parents: The Case of Working-Class Families." Pp. 227–250 in *Working Families: The Transformation of the American Home,* edited by Rosanna Hertz and Nancy Marshall. Berkeley, CA: University of California Press.

Halle, David. 1984. *America's Working Man: Work, Home, and Politics among Blue-Collar Property Owners.* Chicago: University of Chicago Press.

Hamilton, Darrick. 2006. "The Racial Composition of American Jobs." Pp 77–115 in *The State of Black America 2006: The Opportunity Compact.* New York: National Urban League.

Hamper, Ben. 1986. *Rivethead: Tales from the Assembly Line.* New York: Warner.

Haraven, Tamara K. 1990. "A Complex Relationship: Family Strategies and the Processes of Economic and Social Change." Pp. 215–244 in *Beyond the Marketplace: Rethinking Economy and Society,* edited by Roger Friedland and A.F. Robertson. New York: Aldine de Gruyter.

Harkness, Susan and Jane Waldfogel. 1999. "The Family Gap in Pay: Evidence from Seven Industrialized Countries." Centre for Analysis of Social Exclusion, London School of Economics. Working Paper No. 219 (November).

Harlow, Roxanna. 2003. "'Race Doesn't Matter But...': The Effect of Race on Professors' Experiences and Emotion Management in the Undergraduate College Classroom." *Social Psychology Quarterly* 66:348–464.

Harris, Craig. 2006. "Suit Says Costco Denies Women Promotions." *Seattle Post-Intelligencer,* Wednesday, November 15.

Harrison, Bennett. 1994. *Lean and Mean. The Changing Landscape of Corporate Power in the Age of Flexibility.* New York: Basic Books.

Hartman, G., I. Nicholas, A. Sorge, and M. Warner. 1983. "Computerized Machine Tools, Manpower Consequences and Skill Utilization: A Study of British and West German Manufacturing Firms." *British Journal of Industrial Relations* 21:221–231.

Hartmann, Heidi. 1975–76. "Capitalism, Patriarchy and Job Segregation by Sex." *Signs* 1:137–169.

Harvey, David. 2005. *A Brief History of Neo-Liberalism.* London: Oxford University Press.

Hecker, Daniel E. 2004. "Occupational Employment Projections to 2012." *Monthly Labor Review* (February):80–105.

Heckman, J. and Payner, B. 1989. "Determining the Impact of Federal Anti-Discrimination Policy on the Economic Status of Blacks: A Study of South Carolina." *American Economic Review* 79:138–177.

Heckman, James and Peter Siegelman. 1992. "The Urban Institute Audit Studies: Their Methods and Findings." In *Clear and Convincing Evidence*, edited by M. Fix and R. Struyk. Washington, DC: Urban Institute.

Heckscher, Charles. 1988. *The New Unionism: Employee Involvement in the Changing Corporation*. New York: Basic Books.

———. 1994. "Defining the Post-Bureaucratic Type." In *The Post-Bureaucratic Organization*, edited by Charles Heckscher and Anne Donnellon. Thousand Oaks, CA: Sage.

Heilman, Madeline E. 2001. "Description and Prescription: How Gender Stereotypes Prevent Women's Ascent Up the Organizational Ladder." *Journal of Social Issues.*57:657–674.

Heinz, John P. and Edward O. Laumann. 1982. *Chicago Lawyers: The Social Structure of the Bar.* New York: Russell Sage Foundation.

Held, David. 1995. *Democracy and the Global Order: From the Modern State to Cosmopolitan Governance.* Stanford, CA: Stanford University Press.

Henson, Kevin D. 1996. *Just a Temp.* Philadelphia: Temple University Press.

Henson, Kevin D. and Jackie Krasas Rogers. 2001. "Why Marcia You've Changed!" Male Clerical Temporary Workers Doing Masculinity in a Feminized Occupation." *Gender & Society* 15:218–238.

Hernández-León, Rubén and Víctor Zúñiga. 2000. "'Making Carpet by the Mile': The Emergence of a Mexican Immigrant Community in an Industrial Region of the U.S. Historic South." *Social Science Quarterly* 81:49–66.

Hirst, Paul Q. and Grahame Thompson. 1996. *Globalization in Question.* Cambridge, MA: Blackwell.

Hobsbawm, Eric. 1962. *The Age of Revolution: Europe 1789–1848.* New York: Vintage.

Hochschild, Arlie R. 1983. *The Managed Heart: The Commercialization of Human Feeling.* Berkeley, CA: University of California.

———. 1989. *The Second Shift: Working Parents and the Revolution at Home.* New York: Viking Penguin Inc.

———. 1997. *The Time Bind.* New York: Metropolitan Books.

Hochschild, Jennifer. 1999. "Affirmative Action as Culture War." Pp. 343–368 in *Cultural Territories of Race*, edited by M. Lamont. Chicago: University of Chicago Press.

Hodson, Randy. 1995. "Worker Resistance: An Underdeveloped Concept in the Sociology of Work." *Economic and Industrial Democracy* 16:79–110.

———. 2001. *Dignity at Work.* New York: Cambridge University Press.

Hodson, Randy, S. Welsh, S. Rieble, C. S. Jamison, and Sean Creighton. 1993. "Is Worker Solidarity Undermined by Autonomy and Participation? Patterns from the Ethnographic Literature." *American Sociological Review* 58:398–416.

Hodson, R., S. Creighton, C. S. Jamison, S. Rieble, and S. Welsh. 1994. "Loyalty to Whom? Workplace Participation and the Development of Consent." *Human Relations* 47:895–909

Horrell, Sara and Jane Humphries. 1995. "'The Exploitation of Little Children': Children's Work and the Family Economy in the British Industrial Revolution." *Explorations in Economic History* 32:19–95.

Hughes, E. C. 1946. "The Knitting of Racial Groups in Industry." *American Sociological Review* 11:512–519.

Humphrey, Ronald. 1985. "How work roles influence perception: Structural-cognitive processes and organizational behavior." *American Sociological Review* 50:242–252.

Humphries, Jane. 1977. "Class Struggle and the Persistence of the Working Class Family." *Cambridge Journal of Economics* 3:241–258.

Hunter, Larry W., John Paul Macduffe, and Lorna Doucet. 2002. "What Makes Teams Take? Employee Reactions to Works Reforms." *Industrial and Labor Relations Review* 55:448–472

Ibarra, Herminia. 1992. "Homophily and Differential Returns: Sex Differences in Network Structure and Access in an Advertising Firm." *Administrative Science Quarterly* 37:363–399.

———. 1993. "Personal Networks of Women and Minorities in Management: A Conceptual Overview." *Academy of Management Review* 18:56–87.

———. 1995. "Race, Opportunity, and Diversity of Social Circles in Managerial Networks." *Academy of Management Journal* 38:673–703.

Ichniowski, Casey, Kathryn Shaw, and Giovanna Prennushi. 1997. "The Effects of Human Resource Management Practices on Productivity: A Study of Steel Finishing Lines." *American Economic Review* 87:291–313.

Industrial Workers of the World. 1973. *Songs of the Workers*. Chicago: Industrial Workers of the World.

Inkeles, Alex and Peter Rossi. 1956. "National Comparisons of Occupational Prestige." *American Journal of Sociology* 61:329–339.

Jackall, Robert. 1988. *Moral Mazes: The World of Corporate Managers*. New York: Oxford University Press.

Jackman, Mary R. and Robert W. Jackman. 1983. *Class Awareness in the United States*. Berkeley, CA: University of California Press.

Jacobs, Jerry. 1989. *Revolving Doors: Sex Segregation and Women's Careers*. Stanford, CA: Stanford University Press.

Jacobs, Jerry A. 1999. "The Sex Segregation of Occupations: Prospects for the 21st Century." Pp. 125–141 in *Handbook of Gender and Work*, edited by Gary N. Powell. Thousand Oaks, CA: Sage.

Jacobs, Jerry A. and Kathleen Gerson. 2001. "Overworked Individuals or Overworked Families: Explaining Trends in Work, Leisure, and Family Time." *Work and Occupations* 28:40–63.

———. 2004. *The Time Divide*. Cambridge, MA: Harvard University Press.

Jacobs, Jerry A. and Suet T. Lim. 1992. "Trends in Occupational and Industrial Occupation by Sex in 56 Countries, 1960–80." *Work and Occupations* 19:450–486.

Jacoby, Sanford M. 1985. *Employing Bureaucracy: Managers, Unions, and the Transformation of Work in the 20th Century*. New York: Columbia University Press.

Johnson, Spencer. 1998. *Who Moved My Cheese? An Amazing Way to Deal with Change in Your Work and in Your Life*. New York: Penguin.

Juravich, Tom. 1985. *Chaos on the Shop Floor: A Worker's View of Quality, Productivity, and Management*. Philadelphia: Temple University Press.

Kalev, Alexandra, Erin Kelly, and Frank Dobbin. 2006. "Best Practices or Best Guesses? Assessing the Efficacy of Corporate Affirmative Action and Diversity Policies." *American Sociological Review* 71:589–617.

Kalleberg, Arne L. 2001. "The Advent of the Flexible Workplace: Implications for Theory and Research." Pp. 437–453 in *Working in Restructured Workplaces: Challenges and New Directions for the Sociology of Work*, edited by D. B. Cornfield, K. E. Campbell, and H. J. McCammon. Thousand Oaks, CA: Sage.

————. 2003. "Flexible Firms and Labor Market Segmentation: Effects of Workplace Restructuring on Jobs and Workers." *Work and Occupations* 30:154–175.

Kalleberg, Arne L. and Kathyrn Schmidt. 1996. "Contingent Employment in Organizations: Part-Time, Temporary, and Subcontracting Relations." Pp. 253–275 in *Organizations in America,* edited by A.L. Kalleberg, D. Knoke, P. V. Marsden, and J. L. Spaeth. Thousand Oaks, CA: Sage Publications.

Kalleberg, Arne L., David Knoke, Peter V. Marsden, and Joe L. Spaeth. 1994. "The National Organizations Study: An Introduction and Overview." *American Behavioral Scientist* 37:860–871.

Kalleberg, Arne L., Barbara F. Reskin, and Ken Hudson. 2000. "Bad Jobs in America: Standard and Nonstandard Employment Relations and Job Quality in the United States." *American Sociological Review* 65:256–278.

Kanter, Rosabeth Moss. 1977a. *Men and Women of the Corporation.* New York: Basic Books.

————. 1977b. *Work and Family in the United States: A Critical Review and Agenda for Research and Policy.* New York: Russell Sage Foundation.

Kaplan, Ilene M. 1988. "Women Who Go to Sea: Working in the Commercial Fishing Industry." *Journal of Contemporary Ethnography* 16:491–514.

Karasek R. 1979. "Job decision latitude, job demands and mental strain: Implications for job redesign." Administrative Science Quarterly 24:285–308.

Karasek, R. A. 1981. "Job Socialization and Job Strain: The Implications of Two Related Psychological Mechanisms for Job Design." Pp. 75–94 in *Working Life*, edited by B. Gardell and G. Johansson. New York: John Wiley & Sons.

Kaufman, Robert L. 2002. "Assessing Alternative Perspectives on Race and Sex Employment Segregation." *American Sociological Review* 67:547–572.

Kelley, Maryellen R. 1990. "New Process Technology, Job Design, and Work Organization: A Contingency Model." *American Sociological Review* 55:191–208.

Kenney, Martin and Richard Florida. 1993. *Beyond Mass Production: the Japanese System and Its Transfer to the U.S.* New York: Oxford University Press.

Kerr, Clark, John T. Dunlop, Frederick C. Harbison, and Charles A. Meyers.1960. *Industrialism and Industrial Man; The Problems of Labor and Management in Economic Growth.* Cambridge, MA: Harvard University Press.

Khurana, Rakesh. 2002. *Searching for a Corporate Savior: The Irrational Quest for Charismatic CEOs.* Princeton, NJ: Princeton University Press.

Kilbourne, Barbara S., Paula England, and Kurt Beron. 1994. "Effects of Individual, Occupational, and Industrial Characteristics on Earnings: Intersections of Race and Gender." *Social Forces* 72:1149–1176.

Kimeldorf, Howard. 1988. *Reds or Rackets? The Making of Radical and Conservative Unions on the Waterfront*. Berkeley, CA: University of California Press.

Klein, Naomi. 1999. *No Logo: Taking Aim at the Brand Bullies*. New York: Picador.

Kluegel, James R. 1978. "The Causes and Cost of Racial Exclusion from Job Authority." *American Sociological Review* 43, 3 (Jun.): 285–301.

Knight, Don, Craig L. Pearce, Ken G. Smith, and Judy D. Olian. 1999. "Top Management Team Diversity, Group Process, and Strategic Consensus." *Strategic Management Journal* 20:445–465.

Knights, David, and Darren McCabe. 2000. "'Ain't Misbehavin?' Opportunities for Resistance Under New Forms of 'Quality' Management." *Sociology* 34:421–436.

Kochan, Thomas and Saul Rubinstein. 2001. "Toward a Stakeholder Theory of the Firm: The Saturn Partnership." *Organization Science* 11, 4: 367–386.

Kohn, Melvin L. and Carmi Schooler. 1983. *Work and Personality: An Inquiry in the Impact of Social Stratification*. Norwood, NJ: Ablex Publishing Corporation.

Konrad, A. and F. Linnehan. 1995. "Formalized HRM Structures: Coordinating Equal Employment Opportunity or Concealing Organizational Practices?" *Academy of Management Journal* 38:787–820.

Kornblum, William. 1974. *Blue Collar Community*. Chicago: University of Chicago Press.

Kornhauser, Arthur. 1965. *Mental Health of the Industrial Worker: A Detroit Study*. New York: John Wiley & Sons.

Korzeniewicz, Miguel. 1994. "Commodity Chains and Marketing Strategies: Nike and the Global Athletic Foodwear Industry." Pp. 247–267 in *Commodity Chains and Global Capitalism*, edited by G. Gereffi and M. Korzeniewicz. Westport, CT: Greenwood Press.

Kotter, John P. 1982. "What Effective General Managers Really Do." *Harvard Business Review* 156–167.

Krasas Rogers, Jackie. 1995. "Just a Temp: Experience and Structure of Alienation in Temporary Clerical Employment." *Work and Occupations* 22:137–166.

———. 2000. *Temps: The Many Faces of the Changing Workplace*. Ithaca, NY: Cornell University Press.

Krasas Rogers, Jackie and Kevin D. Henson. 1997. "Hey, Why Don't You Wear a Shorter Skirt? Structural Vulnerability and the Organization of Sexual Harassment in Temporary Clerical Employment." *Gender and Society* 11:215–237.

Kunda, Gideon. 1991. *Engineering Culture: Control and Commitment in a High-Tech Corporation*. Philadelphia: Temple University Press.

Lambert, Susan J. 1999. "Lower-Wage Workers and the New Realities of Work and Family." *Annals of the American Academy of Political and Social Sciences* 562:174–190.

———. 2000. "Added Benefits: The Link Between Work-Life Benefits and Organizational Citizenship Behavior" *Academy of Management Journal* 43:801–815.

Lambert, Susan J. and Anna Haley-Lock. 2004. "The Organizational Stratification of Opportunities for Work-Life Balance." *Community, Work & Family* 7:179–195.

Lamont, Michele. 1992. *Money, Morals, and Manners: The Culture of the French and the American Upper-Middle Class*. Chicago: University of Chicago Press.

Landers, Renée M., James B. Rebitzer, and Lowell J. Taylor. 1996. "Rat Race Redux: Adverse Selection in the Determination of Work Hours in Law Firms." *American Economic Review* 86:329–348.

Larsen, Luke J. 2004. *The Foreign Born Population in the United States: 2003.* Current Population Reports, P20–551, U.S. Census Bureau, Washington, DC.

Larson, Magali Sarfatti. 1977. *The Rise of Professionalism: A Sociological Analysis.* Berkeley, CA: University of California Press.

Larson, Reed, Maryse H. Richards, and Maureen Perry-Jenkins. 1994. "Divergent Worlds: The Daily Emotional Experience of Mothers and Fathers in the Domestic and Public Spheres." *Journal of Personality and Social Psychology* 67:1034–1047.

Lawler, Edward, Susan Mohrman, and G. Ledford. 1992. *Employee Involvement and Total Quality Management: Practices and Results in Fortune 1000 Companies.* San Francisco: Jossey Bass.

———. 1995. *Creating High Performance Organizations: Practices and Results of Employee Involvement and Total Quality Management in Fortune 1000 Companies.* San Francisco: Jossey Bass.

LeDuff, Charles. 2000. "At a Slaughterhouse, Some Things Never Die: Who Kills, Who Cuts, Who Bosses Can Depend on Race." *New York Times,* 16 June, p. A1.

LeDuff, Charlie and Steven L. Greenhouse. 2004. "Grocery Workers Relieved, If Not Happy, at Strike's End." *New York Times,* February 28.A8.

Le Goff, Jacques. 1980. *Time, Work and Culture in the Middle Ages.* Chicago: University of Chicago Press.

Leidner, Robin. 1993. *Fast Food, Fast Talk: Service Work and the Routinization of Everyday Life.* Berkeley, CA: University of California Press.

Levitt, Theodore. 1983. "The Globalization of Markets." *Harvard Business Review* 61: 92–102.

Levy, Frank. 1998. *The New Dollars and Dreams.* New York: Russell Sage Foundation.

Lichtenstein, Nelson. 1987. *Labor's War at Home: The CIO in World War II.* New York: Cambridge University Press.

Lichtenstein, Richard, Jeffrey A Alexander, Kimberly Jinnett, and Esther Ullman. 1997. "Embedded Intergroup Relations in Interdisciplinary Teams: Effects on Perceptions of Levels of Team Integration." *Journal of Applied Behavioral Science* 33:413–434.

Lieberman, Seymour. 1956. "The effects of changes in roles on the attitudes of role occupants." *Human Relations* 9:385–402.

Light, Ivan. 1979. "Disadvantaged Minorities in Self-Employment." *International Journal of Comparative Sociology* 20:1–45.

List, John A. 2004. "The Nature and Extent of Discrimination in the Marketplace: Evidence from the Field." *Quarterly Journal of Economics* 119:49–89.

Littler, Craig and G. Salaman. 1982. "Bravermania and Beyond: Recent Theories of the Labour Process." *Sociology* 16:251–269.

Liu, John M., Paul M. Ong, and Carolyn Rosenstein. 1991. "Dual Chain Migration: Post-1965 Filipino Immigration to the United States." *International Migration Review* 25:487–513.

Lohr, Steve. 2006. "Academia Dissects the Service Sector, but Is It a Science?" *New York Times,* April 18, 2006, p. C1.

Lowell, B. Lindsay and Stefka Georgieva Gerova. 2004. "Immigrants and the Healthcare

Workforce: Profiles and Shortages." *Work and Occupations*: 31:474–498.

Ludmerer, Kenneth M. 1999. *Time to Heal: American Medical Education from the Turn of the Century to the Era of Managed Care.* New York: Oxford University Press.

Lynn, Michael, George M. Zinkhan, and Judy Harris. 1993. "Consumer Tipping: A Cross-Country Study." *Journal of Consumer Research* 20:478–488.

Macdonald, Cameron L. and Carmen Sirianni. 1996. The Service Society and the Changing Experience of Work. Pp. 1–26 in *Working in the Service Society*, edited by C. L. Macdonald and C. Sirianni. Philadelphia: Temple University Press.

MacDaffie, John Paul. 1995. "Human Resource Bundles and Manufacturing Performance: Organizational Logic and Flexible Production Systems in the World Auto Industry." *Industrial and Labor Relations Review* 48:197–222.

MacLeod, Jay. 1995. *Ain't No Makin' It: Aspirations and Attainment in a Low-Income Neighborhood.* Boulder, CO: Westview Press.

Maddison, A. 2001. *The World Economy: A Millennial Perspective.* Paris and Washington: Organisation for Economic Co-Operation and Development.

Magnum, Garth, Donald Mayall, and Kristen Nelson. 1985. "The Temporary Help Industry: A Response to the Dual Internal Labor Market." *Industrial and Labor Relations Review* 38:599–611.

Mahoney, James. 2004. "Comparative-Historical Methodology." *Annual Review of Sociology* 30:81–101.

Maier, Mark. 1999. "On the Gendered Sub-structure of Organization: Dimensions and Dilemmas of Corporate Masculinity." Pp. 69–93 in *Handbook of Gender and Work*, edited by Gary N. Powell. Thousand Oaks, CA: Sage.

Malone, Nolan, Kaari F. Baluja, Joseph M. Costanzo, and Cynthia J. Davis. 2003. *The Foreign Born Population: 2000.* C2KBR-34. Washington, DC: U.S. Census Bureau.

Marglin, Stephen A. 1974. "What Do Bosses Do? The Origins and Functions of Hierarchy in Capitalist Production." *Review of Radical Political Economics* 6:60–112.

Marsden, Peter. 1996. "The Staffing Process." Pp. 133–156 in *Organizations in America: Analyzing Their Structures and Human Resource Practices*, edited by A. L. Kalleberg, D. Knoke, P. V. Marsden, and J. L. Spaeth. Thousand Oaks, CA: Sage.

Martin, Susan Erlich. 1999. "Police Force or Police Service: Gender and Emotional Labor." *Annals of the American Academy of Political and Social Science* 561:111–126.

Marx, Karl. 1964 [1844]. *Economic and Philosophic Manuscripts of 1844.* Translated by Martin Milligan. New York: International Publishers.

———. 1977 [1867]. *Capital: A Critique of Political Economy. Volume One. The Capitalist Process of Production.* Introduced by Ernest Mandel. Translated by Ben Fowkes. New York: Vintage.

Maslach, Christina and Susan E. Jackson. 1981. "The Measurement of Experienced Burnout." *Journal of Occupational Behaviour* 2:99–113.

Massey, Douglas S., Jorge Durand, and Nolan J. Malone. 2002. *Beyond Smoke and Mirrors: Mexican Immigration in an Era of Economic Integration.* New York: Russell Sage Foundation.

Mather, Lynn M., Craig A. McEwen, and Richard J. Maiman. 2001. *Divorce Lawyers at Work: Varieties of Professionalism in Practice.* New York: Oxford University Press.

Mather, Mark. 2007. "Closing the Male–Female Labor Force Gap," Population Reference Bureau. (http://www.prb.org/Articles/2007/ClosingtheMaleFemaleLaborForceGap.aspx)

Maume, David J. 1999. "Glass Ceilings and Glass Escalators: Occupational Segregation and Race and Sex Differences in Managerial Promotions." *Work and Occupations* 26:483–509.

Mayer, Kathrin L. Hung S. Ho, and James E. Goodnight Jr. 2001. "Childbearing and Child Care in Surgery." *Archives of Surgery* 136:649–655.

Maynard, Micheline. 2005. "Foreign Makers, Settled in South, Pace Car Industry." *New York Times*, June 22, C1, C5.

Mayo, Elton. 1933. *The Human Problems of an Industrial Civilization.* New York: Macmillan.

McAlinden, Sean P. 2004. *The Meaning of the 2003 UAW-Automotive Pattern Agreement. A Research Report for the Auto Industry of the Future Program.* Ann Arbor, MI: Center for Automotive Research.

McGeehan, Patrick. 2004. "Discrimination on Wall Street? The Numbers Tell the Story." *New York Times*, July 14 C1.

McLaughlin, Emma and Nicola Kraus. 2003. *The Nanny Diaries: A Novel.* New York: St. Martin's Press.

McPherson, Miller, Lynn Smith-Lovin, and James Cook. 2001. "Birds of a Feather: Homphily in Social Networks." *Annual Review of Sociology* 27:415–444.

Meisenheimer, Joseph R. 1998. "The Services Industry in the 'Good' vs. 'Bad' Jobs Debate." *Monthly Labor Review* (February):22–47.

Meyer, J. and B. Rowan. 1977. "Institutional Organizations: Formal Structure as Myth and Ceremony." *American Journal of Sociology* 83:340–363.

Meyer, Madonna H. (Ed.). 2000. *Care Work.* New York: Routledge.

Meyer, Stephen Eric. 1981. *The Five Dollar Day: Labor Management and Social Control in the Ford Motor Company, 1908–1921.* Albany, NY: SUNY Press.

Meyerson, Harold. 2004. "Las Vegas as a Workers' Paradise." *The American Prospect* January 15, pp. 38–42.

Michels, Robert. 1962. *Political Parties; A Sociological Study of the Oligarchical Tendencies of Modern Democracy.* Translated by Eden and Cedar Paul. Introduction by Seymour Martin Lipset. New York: Collier Books.

Micklethwait, John and Adrian Wooldridge. 2003. *The Company: A Short History of a Revolutionary Idea.* New York: Modern Library.

Milkman, Ruth. 1987. *Gender at Work: The Dynamics of Job Segregation by Sex during World War II.* Urbana, IL: University of Illinois Press.

———. 1997. *Farewell to the Factory: Autoworkers in the Late Twentieth Century.* Berkeley, CA: University of California Press.

Mills, C. Wright. 1948. *The New Men of Power: America's Labor Leaders.* New York: Harcourt Brace.

———. 1951. *White Collar: The American Middle Classes.* New York: Oxford University Press.

———. 1985. *The Fall of the House of Labor.* New York: Cambridge University Press.

Mintzberg, Henry. 1973. *The Nature of Managerial Work.* New York: Harper & Row.

Mishel, Lawrence and Matthew Walters. 2003. "How Unions Help All Workers." Economic Policy Institute Briefing Paper #143.

Mishel, Lawrence, Jared Bernstein, and Heather Boushey. 2003. *The State of Working America, 2002–03*. Ithaca, NY: ILR Press.

Mishel, Lawrence, Jared Bernstein, and Sylvia Allegretto. 2007. *The State of Working America, 2007/2007*. Ithaca, NY: ILR Press, an imprint of Cornell University Press.

Moen, Phyllis and Patricia Roehling. 2005. *The Career Mystique: Cracks in the American Dream*. New York: Rowman & Littlefield.

Montgomery, David. 1979. *Workers' Control in America: Studies in the History of Work, Technology, and Labor Struggles*. New York: Cambridge University Press.

Morrill, Calvin. 1995. *The Executive Way: Conflict Management in Corporations*. Chicago: University of Chicago Press.

Morris, Martina and Bruce Western. 1999. "Inequality in Earnings at the Close of the Twentieth Century." *Annual Review of Sociology* 25:623–657.

Moss, Philip and Chris Tilly. 2001. *Stories Employers Tell: Race, Skill, and Hiring in America*. New York: Russell Sage.

Mouw, Ted. 2002. "Are Black Workers Missing the Connection? The Effect of Spatial Distance and Employee Referrals on Interfirm Racial Segregation." *Demography* 39:507–528.

National Labor Relations Board. 2006. *Seventy-First Annual Report of the National Labor Relations Board for the Fiscal Year Ended September 30, 2006*. Washington, DC: U.S. Government Printing Office.

National Women's Law Center. 2000. "Sex Discrimination in the American Workplace: Still a Fact of Life." July 17, 2000.

Nelson, Daniel. 1975. *Managers and Workers: Origins of the New Factory System in the United States*. Madison, WI: University of Wisconsin Press.

Nelson, Robert L. 1988. *Partners with Power: Social Transformation of the Large Law Firm*. Berkeley, CA: University of California Press.

Nelson, Robert L. and William P. Bridges. 1999. *Legalizing Gender Inequality*. New York: Cambridge University Press.

Neumark, D. 1996. "Sex Discrimination in the Restaurant Industry: An Audit Study." *Quarterly Journal of Economics* 111: 915–941.

Newman, Katherine S. 1999. *No Shame in My Game: The Working Poor in the Inner City*. New York: Russell Sage.

Noonan, Mary C. and Mary E. Corcoran. 2004. "The Mommy Track and Partnership: Temporary Delay or Dead End?" *Annals of the American Academy of Political and Social Science* 596:130–150.

O'Brien, Timothy L. 2006. "Why Do So Few Women Reach the Top of Big Law Firms?" *The New York Times*, March 19, Section 3, pp. 1,4.

Ohmae, Kenichi. 1990. *The Borderless World. Power and Strategy in the Interlinked Economy*. New York: Harper Business.

Orr, Julian E. 1996. *Talking about Machines: An Ethnography of a Modern Job*. Ithaca, NY: ILR Press.

Osterman, Paul. 1994. "How Common Is Workplace Transformation and Who Adopts It?" *Industrial and Labor Relations Review* 47:173–188.

———. 1999. *Securing Prosperity: The American Labor Market: How It Has Changed and What to Do about It*. Princeton, NJ: Princeton University Press.

Ouellet, Lawrence J. 1994. *Pedal to the Metal: The Work Lives of Truckers*. Philadelphia: Temple University Press.

Ovitt, George. 1986. *Technology and Culture.* New Brunswick, NJ: Rutgers University Press.

Owen-Smith, Jason. 2001. "Managing Laboratory Work through Skepticism: Processes of Evaluation and Control." *American Sociological Review* 66:427–452.

Pacific Coast Longshore Contract Document July 1, 2002 – July 1, 2008, Between the International Longshore and Warehouse Union and the Pacific Martime Assocation. 2002. Pp. 1–285.

Padavic, Irene and Barbara Reskin. 2002. *Women and Men at Work.* Thousand Oaks, CA: Pine Forge Press.

Palmore, Erdman 1971. "The Relative Importance of Social Factors in Predicting Longevity." Pp. 237–238 in *Prediction of Life Span*, edited by Erdman Palmore and Races C Jeffers. Lexington, MA: Lexington Press.

Parker, Mike and Jane Slaughter. 1994. *Working Smart: A Union Guide to Participation Programs and Re-Engineering.* Detroit: Labor Notes.

Parsons, Talcott. 1964. *Essays in Sociological Theory.* New York: The Free Press.

Parsons, Talcott and Robert F. Bales. 1955. *Family, Socialization and Interaction Process.* New York: The Free Press.

Passel, Jeffrey S. 2005. "Estimates of the Size and Characteristics of the Undocumented Population." *Pew Hispanic Center Report*, March 21 pp. 1–10.

Paules, Greta Foff. 1991. *Dishing It Out: Power and Resistance among Waitresses in a New Jersey Restaurant.* Philadelphia: Temple University Press.

Perlow, Leslie. 1997. *Finding Time: How Corporations, Individuals, and Families Can Benefit from New Work Practices.* Ithaca, NY: ILR Press.

Perrow, Charles. 1986. *Complex Organizations: A Critical Essay.* New York: Random House.

———. 2002. *Organizing America: Wealth, Power, and the Origins of Corporate Capitalism.* Princeton, NJ: Princeton University Press.

Petersen, Trond and Ishak Saporta. 2004. "The Opportunity Structure for Discrimination." *American Journal of Sociology* 109:852–902.

Pfeffer, Jeffery and James Baron. 1988. "Taking the Workers Back Out: Recent Trends in the Structuring of Employment." *Research in Organizational Behavior* 10:257–303.

Phillips, Julie A. and Douglas S. Massey. 2000. "Engines of Immigration: Stocks of Human and Social Capital in Mexico." *Social Science Quarterly* 81:33–48.

Pierce, Jennifer. 1995. *Gender Trials: Emotional Lives in Contemporary Law Firms.* Berkeley, CA: University of California Press.

Pilot, Michael J. 1999. "Occupational Outlook Handbook: A Review of 50 Years of Change." *Monthly Labor Review* (May):8–26.

Piore, Michael and Charles F. Sabel. 1984. *The Second Industrial Divide: Possibilities for Prosperity.* New York: Basic Books.

Polanyi, Karl. 1944. *The Great Transformation.* Boston: Beacon Press.

Pond, S. B. and P.D. Geyer. 1991. "Differences in the Relation between Job Satisfaction and Perceived Work Alternatives among Older and Younger Blue-Collar Workers." *Journal of Vocational Behavior* 39: 251–262.

Pontusson, Jonas. 2005. *Inequality and Prosperity: Social Europe vs. Liberal America.* Ithaca, NY: Cornell University Press.

Porter, Eduardo. 2006. "Japanese Cars, American Retirees." *New York Times*, May 19, C1, C5.

———. 2007. "More Than Ever, It Pays to Be the Top Executive." *New York Times*, May 25, A1, C7.

Portes. Alejandro and Robert L. Bach. 1985. *Latin Journey: Cuban and Mexican Immigrants in the United States*. Berkeley, CA: University of California Press.

Powell, Gary N. 1999. "Reflections on the Glass Ceiling: Recent Trends and Future Prospects." Pp. 325–345 in *Handbook of Gender and Work*, edited by Gary N. Powell. Thousand Oaks, CA: Sage.

Powell, Gary N. and Laura M. Graves. 1999. *Women and Men in Management*, 2nd ed. Thousand Oaks, CA: Sage.

Powell, Walter W. 1990. "Neither Market nor Hierarchy: Network Forms of Organization." *Research in Organizational Behavior* 12:295–336.

———. 2001. "The Capitalist Firm in the Twenty-First Century: Emerging Patterns in Western Enterprise." Pp. 33–68 in *The Twenty-First Century Firm,* edited by P. DiMaggio. Princeton, NJ: Princeton University Press.

Powell, Walter W. and Kaisa Snellman. 2004. "The Knowledge Economy." *Annual Review of Sociology* 30:199–220.

Powell, Walter W. Kenneth W. Koput, and Laurel Smith-Doerr. 1996. "Interorganizational Collaboration and the Locus of Innovation: Networks of Learning in Biotechnology." *Administrative Science Quarterly* 41:116-145.

Presser, Harriet B. 1998. "Toward a 24 Hour Economy: The U.S. Experience and Implications for Family." Pp. 39–48 in *Challenges for Work and Family in the Twenty-First Century*, edited by D. Vannoy and P. J. Dubeck. New York: Aldine de Gruyter.

———. 2003. *Working in a 24/7 Economy: Challenges for American Families*. New York: Russell Sage.

Quadagno, Jill. 1994. *The Color of Welfare: How Racism Undermined the War on Poverty*. New York: Oxford University Press.

Quinn, R.P. and L. G. Shepard. 1974. *The 1972–73 Quality of Employment Survey*. Ann Arbor: University of Michigan, Institute for Social Research.

Reich, Robert. 1992. *The Work of Nations: Preparing Ourselves for 21ˢᵗ Century Capitalism*. NY: Random House.

Reskin, Barbara F. 2003. "Including Mechanisms in Our Models of Ascriptive Inequality." *American Sociological Review* 68:1–21.

Reskin, Barbara F. and Heidi I. Hartmann. 1986. *Women's Work, Men's Work: Sex Segregation on the Job*. Washington, DC: National Academy Press.

Reskin, Barbara and Irene Padavic. 1994. *Women and Men at Work*. Thousand Oaks, CA: Pine Forge Press.

Reskin, Barbara F. and Patricia A. Roos. 1990. *Job Queues, Gender Queues: Explaining Women's Inroads into Male Occupations*. Philadelphia: Temple University Press.

Reskin, Barbara, Debra McBrier, and Julie Kmec, 1999. "The Determinants and Consequences of the Sex and Race Composition of Work Organizations." *Annual Review of Sociology* 25:335–61.

Reynolds, David. 2003. *Living Wage Campaigns: An Activist's Guide to Organizing a Movement for Economic Justice*. Detroit, MI: Labor Studies Center, Wayne State University.

Rice, R. W., D.A. Gentile, and D.B. McFarlin. 1991. "Facet Importance and Job Satisfaction." *Journal of Applied Psychology* 76: 31–39.

Richard, O. C. 2000. "Racial Diversity, Business Strategy, and Firm Performance: A

Resource-Based View." *Academy of Management Journal* 43:164–177.

Ritzer, George and David Walczak. 1988. "Rationalization and the Deprofessionalization of Physicians." *Social Forces* 67:1–22.

Rivlin, Gary. 2004. "Who's Afraid of China?" *New York Times*, December 19, Section 3, pp. 1, 4.

Robinson, Corre L., Tiffany Taylor, Donald Tomaskovic-Devey, Catherine Zimmer, and Matthew W. Irvin, Jr. 2005. "Studying Race or Ethnic and Sex Segregation at the Establishment Level." *Work and Occupations* 32:5–38.

Robinson, John P. and Geoffrey Godbey. 1997. *Time for Life: The Surprising Ways Americans Use Their Time.* University Park, PA: Pennsylvania State University Press.

Rodgers, Daniel T. 1974. *The Work Ethic in Industrial America, 1850–1920.* Chicago: University of Chicago Press.

Rodriguez, Nestor. 2004. "'Workers Wanted': Employer Recruitment of Immigrant Labor." *Work and Occupations* 31:453–473.

Roediger, David R. 1999. *The Wages of Whiteness: Race and the Making of the American Working Class.* New York: Verso.

Roethlisberger, F. J. and William J. Dickson. 1939. *Management and the Worker.* Cambridge, MA: Harvard University Press.

Rollins, Judith. 1985. *Between Women: Domestics and Their Employers.* Philadelphia: Temple University Press.

Roos, Patricia A. 1985. *Gender and Work: A Comparative Analysis of Industrial Societies.* Albany, NY: State University of New York Press.

Roos, Patricia A. and Mary Lizabeth Gatta. 1999. "The Gender Gap in Earnings: Trends, Explanations, and Prospects." Pp. 95–124 in *Handbook of Gender and Work*, edited by Gary N. Powell.. Thousand Oaks, CA: Sage.

Ross, Andrew (Ed.). 1997. *No Sweat: Fashion, Free Trade and the Rights of Garment Workers.* New York: Verso.

Rose, Sonya. 1992. *Limited Livelihoods: Gender and Class in Nineteenth-Century England.* Berkeley, CA: University of California Press.

Ross, Andrew. 1997. *No Sweat: Fashion, Free Trade, and the Rights of Garment Workers.* New York: Verso.

Roth, Louise Marie. 2004. "Engendering Inequality: Processes of Sex-Segregation on Wall Street." *Sociological Forum* 19:203–228.

———. 2006. *Selling Women Short: Gender and Money on Wall Street.* Princeton, NJ: Princeton University Press.

Rowe, Reba E. and William E. Snizek. 1995. "Gender Differences in Work Values." *Work and Occupations* 22:215–229.

Roy, Donald. 1959. "'Banana Time': Job Satisfaction and Informal Interaction." *Human Organization*: 18:158–168.

Royster, Deirdre A. 2003. *Race and the Invisible Hand: How White Networks Exclude Black Men from Blue-Collar Jobs.* Berkeley: University of California Press.

Rubin, Beth A. 1995. "Flexible Accumulation: The Decline of Contract and Social Transformation." *Research in Social Stratification and Mobility* 14:297–323.

———. 1996. *Shifts in the Social Contract: Understanding Change in American Society.* Thousand Oaks, CA: Pine Forge.

Rubinstein, Saul A. 2000. "The Impact of Co-Management on Quality Performance: The Case of the Saturn Corporation." *Industrial & Labor Relations Review* 53:197–218.

Sabel, Charles and Jonathan Zeitlin. 1985. "Historical Alternatives to Mass Production: Politics, Markets and Technology in Nineteenth Century Industrialization." *Past and Present* 108:133–176.

———. 1997. "Stories, Strategies, Structures: Rethinking Historical Alternatives to Mass Production" in *World of Possibilities: Flexibility and Mass Production in Western Industrialization,* edited by Charles Sabel and Jonathan Zeitlin. New York: Cambridge University Press.

Sandefur, Rebecca. 2001. "Work and Honor in the Law: Prestige and the Division of Lawyers' Labor." *American Sociological Review* 66:382–403.

Sassen, Sasskia. 2001. *The Global City: New York, London, Tokyo.* Princeton, NJ: Princeton University Press.

Saxenian, AnnaLee. 1994. *Regional Advantage: Culture & Competition in Silicon Valley & Route 128.* Cambridge, MA: Harvard University Press.

Sayles, Leonard R. 1964. *Managerial Behavior: Administration in Complex Organizations.* New York: McGraw-Hill.

Schaeffer, Nora Cate and Stanley Presser. 2003. "The Science of Asking Questions." *Annual Review of Sociology* 29:65–88.

Schneider, David. 2005. *The Psychology of Stereotyping.* New York: Guilford Press.

Schoenberger, Erica. 1997. *The Cultural Crisis of the Firm.* Cambridge: Blackwell.

Schor, Juliet B. 1991. *The Overworked American: The Unexpected Decline of Leisure.* New York: Basic Books.

Seccombe, Wally. 1986. "Patriarchy Stabilized: The Construction of the Male Breadwinner Norm in 19th Century Britain." *Social History* 2:45–65.

Secret, Mary. 2000. "Identifying the Family, Job, and Workplace Characteristics of Employees Who Use Work-Family Benefits." *Family Relations* 49:217–226.

Sennett, Richard. 1999. *The Corrosion of Character: The Personal Consequences of Work in the New Capitalism.* New York: Knopf.

Shaiken, H., Steven Lopez, and I. Mankita. 1997. "Two Routes to Team Production: Saturn and Chrysler Compared." *Industrial Relations* 36:17–45.

Sharpe, Erin K. 2005. "Going Above and Beyond: The Emotional Labor of Adventure Guides." *Journal of Leisure Research* 37: 29–50.

Shu, Xiaoling and Margaret Mooney Marini. 1998. "Gender-Related Change in Occupational Aspirations." *Sociology of Education* 71:44–68.

Simpson, Ida Harper. 1989. "The Sociology of Work: Where Have the Workers Gone?" *Social Forces* 67: 563–581.

Sloan, Alfred P. 1963. *My Years with General Motors.* Garden City, NY: Doubleday.

Smith, Adam. 1991 [1776]. *The Wealth of Nations: An Inquiry into the Nature and Causes of the Wealth of Nations.* Introduction by D. D. Raphael. New York: Knopf.

Smith, Allen C. III and Sherryl Kleinman. 1989. "Managing Emotions in Medical School: Students' Contacts with the Living and the Dead." *Social Psychology Quarterly* 52:56–69.

Smith, James H. and Jeffrey W. Mantz. 2006. "Do Cellular Phones Dream of Civil War? The Mystification of Production and the Consequences of Fetishim in the Eastern Congo." Pp 71–94 in *Inclusion and Exclusion in the Global Arena,* edited by M. Kirsch. New York: Routledge.

Smith, Ryan A. 1997. "Race, Income and Authority at Work: A Cross-Temporal Analysis of Black and White Men." *Social Problems* 44:19–37.

———. 2001. "Particularism in Control over Monetary Resources at Work: An Analysis of Racio-Ethnic Differences in the Authority outcomes of Black, White, and Latino Men." *Work and Occupations* 28:447–468.

———. 2002. "Race, Gender, and Authority in the Workplace: Theory and Research." *Annual Review of Sociology* 28:509–542.

Smith, Ryan A. and James R. Elliott. 2002. "Does Ethnic Concentration Influence Employees' Access to Authority? An Examination of Contemporary Urban Labor Markets." *Social Forces* 81:255–279.

Smith, Vicki. 1997. "New Forms of Work Organization." *Annual Review of Sociology* 23:315–339.

———. 2001a. *Crossing the Great Divide: Worker Risk and Opportunity in the New Economy.* Ithaca, NY: ILR Press.

———. 2001b. "Ethnographies of Work and the Work of Ethnographers." Pp. 220–233 in *Handbook of Ethnography*, edited by Paul Atkinson, Amanda Coffey, Sara Delamont, John Lofland, and Lyn Lofland. Thousand Oaks, CA: Sage.

Spain, Daphne and Susan Bianchi. 2000. *Balancing Act: Motherhood, Marriage, and Employment Among American Women.* New York: Russell Sage Foundation.

Spangler, Eve. 1986. *Lawyers for Hire: Salaried Professionals at Work.* New Haven, CT: Yale University Press.

Special Task Force to the Secretary of Health, Education, and Welfare 1973. *Work in America.* Cambridge, MA: MIT Press.

Spector, Paul E. 1997. *Job Satisfaction: Application, Assessment, Cause, and Consequences.* Thousand Oaks, CA: Sage.

Stark, David. 1980. "Struggle and the Transformation of the Labor Process: A Relational Approach." *Theory and Society* 9:89–130.

Steinberg, Ronnie J. and Deborah M. Figart. 1999. "Emotional Labor Since *The Managed Heart.*" *Annals of the American Academy of Political and Social Science* 561:8–27.

Stenross, Barbara and Sherryl Kleinman. 1989. "The Highs and Lows of Emotional Labor: Detectives' Encounters with Criminals and Victims." *Journal of Contemporary Ethnography* 17:435–452.

Stewart, Matthew. 2006. "The Management Myth." *The Atlantic Monthly*, June: 80–87.

Stewart, Rosemary. 1967. *Managers and Their Jobs.* Maidenhead: McGraw-Hill.

Stiglitz, Joseph. 2002. *Globalization and Its Discontents.* New York: W.W. Norton & Company.

Stouffer, Samuel A., Edward A. Suchman, Leland C. DeVinney, Shirley A. Star, and Robin M. Williams, Jr. 1949. *Studies in Social Psychology in World War II: The American Soldier.* Princeton, NJ: Princeton University Press.

Sutton, John R., Frank Dobbin, John Meyer, and W. Richard Scott. 1994. "The Legalization of the Workplace." *American Journal of Sociology* 99:944–971.

Sutton, Robert I. 1991. "Maintaining Norms About Expressed Emotions: The Case of Bill Collectors." *Administrative Science Quarterly* 36:245–268.

Sutton, Robert J. and Anat Rafaeli. 1988. "Untangling the Relationship Between

Displayed Emotions and Organizational Sales: The Case of Convenience Stores." *Academy of Management Journal* 31:461–487.

Sykes, Gresham M. 1958. *Society of Captives*. Princeton, NJ: Princeton University Press.

Tannen, Deborah. 1994. *Talking From 9 to 5*. New York: William Morrow.

Taplin, Ian M. 1995. "Flexible Production, Rigid Jobs: Lessons from the Clothing Industry." *Work and Occupations* 22: 412–438.

Taplin, Ian. 2001. "Managerial Resistance to High Performance Workplace Practices." *Research in the Sociology of Work* 10:1–23.

Taylor, Frederick W. 1911. *The Principles of Scientific Management*. New York: Norton.

Terkel, Studs. 1974. *Working*. New York: Pantheon Books.

Thomas, Robert J. 1994. *What Machines Can't Do: Politics and Technology in the Industrial Enterprise*. Berkeley: University of California Press.

Thompson, Edward Palmer. 1964. *The Making of the English Working Class*. New York: Pantheon Books.

Tienda, Marta and D. Lii. 1987. "Minority Concentration and Earnings Inequality: Blacks, Hispanics and Asians Compared." *American Journal of Sociology* 93:141–165.

Tienda, Marta and Rebeca Raijman. 2000. "Immigrants' Income Packaging and Invisible Labor Force Activity." *Social Science Quarterly* 81:291–310.

Tilly, Charles. 1995. "Globalization Threatens Labor's Rights." *International Labor and Working Class History* 47:1–23.

———. 1998. *Durable Inequality*. Berkeley, CA: University of California Press.

Timmons, Heather. 2008. "Cost-Cutting in New York, but a Boom in India." *New York Times*, August 11, p. A1.

Tomaskovic-Devey, Donald. 1993. *Gender and Racial Inequality at Work*. Ithaca, NY: ILR/ Cornell University Press.

Tomaskovic-Devey, Donald, Kevin Stainback, Tiffany Taylor, Catherine Zimmer, Corre Robinson, and Tricia McTague. "Documenting Desegregation: Degregation in American Workplaces by Race, Ethnicity, and Sex, 1966–2003. " *American Sociological Review* 71: 565–88.

Touraine, Alain. 1971. *The Post-Industrial Society*. New York: Random House.

Toussaint-Comeau, Maude. 2005. "Self-Employed Immigrants: An Analysis of Recent Data." *Chicago Fed Letter*, 213, April, pp. 1–4.

Townsend, Anthony and K. Dow Scott. 2001. "Team Racial Composition, Member Attitudes, and Performance: A Field Study." *Industrial Relations* 40:317–337.

Tsui, Anne S. and Barbara A. Gutek. 1999. *Demographic Differences in Organizations: Current Research and Future Directions*. Lanham, MD: Lexington Books.

Tsui, Anne S. and Charles. A. O'Reilly. 1989. "Beyond Simple Demographic Effects: The Importance of Racial Demography in Superior/Subordinate Dyads." *Academy of Management Journal* 32:402–423.

Uchitelle, Louis. 2008. "The Wage that Meant Middle Class." *New York Times*, April 20, Section 4, p. 3.

Uchitelle, Louis and N.R. Kleinfield. 1996. "On the Battlefields of Business, Millions of Casualties." *New York Times*, March 3, Section 1, pp. 1, 26, 28, 29.

U.S. Bureau of Labor Statistics. 2005. *Women in the Labor Force: A Databook*. Washington, DC: U.S. Department of Labor, Report 985.

———. 2007a. *Women in the Labor Force: A Databook*. Washington, DC: U.S. Department of Labor, Report 1002.

———. 2007b. *Employment and Earnings*. Vol. 54, No. 1, pp. 1–278.

———. 2007c. *Highlights of Women's Earnings in 2006*. September 2007, p. 4.

———. 2007d. *Occupational Outlook Handbook 2008–09 Edition*. Washington, DC: U.S. Department of Labor.

———. 2008. *Employment and Earnings*, Vol 55, No. 1, pp 1–320. Washington, DC: U.S. Department of Labor.

U.S. Census Bureau. 2006. "Statistical Abstract of the United States: 2004–2005." Washington, DC: U.S. Census Bureau.

———. 2008. *Statistical Abstract of the United States: 2008*. Washington, DC: U.S. Census Bureau.

U.S. Department of Education. 2005. *Postsecondary Institutions in the United States: Fall 2003 and Degrees and Other Awards Conferred: 2002–03*. National Center for Education Statistics (2005–154).

U.S. Department of Health, Education, and Welfare. 1973. *Work in America. Report of a Special Task Force to the Secretary of Health, Education and Welfare*. Cambridge MA: MIT Press.

U.S. Department of Labor. 1991. *Report on the Glass Ceiling Initiative*. Washington, DC: U.S. Department of Labor.

Uzzi, Brian. 1996. "The Sources and Consequences of Embeddedness for the Economic Performance of Organizations: The Network Effect." *American Sociological Review* 60:674–698.

———. 1997. "Social Structure and Competition in Interfirm Networks: The Paradox of Embeddedness." *Administrative Science Quarterly* 42:35–67.

Valenzuela Jr., Abel. 2001. "Day Labourers as Entrepreneurs?" *Journal of Ethnic and Migration Studies* 27:335–352.

Valenzuela Jr., Abel, Nik Theodore, Edwin Meléndez, and Ana Luz Gonzalez. 2006. "On the Corner: Day Labor in the United States." UCLA Center for the Study of Urban Poverty, January.

Vallas, Steven P. 1993. *Power in the Workplace: The Politics of Production at AT&T*. Albany, NY: State University of New York Press.

———. 1999. "Rethinking Post-Fordism: The Meanings of Workplace Flexibility." *Sociological Theory* 17:68–101.

———. 2003a. "The Adventures of Managerial Hegemony: Teamwork, Ideology, and Worker Resistance." *Social Problems* 50:204–225.

———. 2003b. "The 'Knitting of Racial Groups' Revisited: Re-Discovering the Color Line at Work." *Work and Occupations* 30:379–400.

———. 2003c. "Why Teamwork Fails: Obstacles to Workplace Change in Four Manufacturing Plants." *American Sociological Review* 68:223–250.

———. 2006. "Empowerment Redux: Structure, Agency, and the Re-Making of Managerial Authority." *American Journal of Sociology* 111:1677–1717.

Vallas, Steven P. and John P. Beck. 1996. "The Transformation of Work Revisited: The Limits of Flexibility in American Manufacturing." *Social Problems* 43:339–361.

Van den Berghe, Pierre L. 1967. *Race and Racism: A Comparative Perspective.* New York: John Wiley and Sons.

Van der Lippe, Tanja and Liset Van Dijk (Eds.). 2001. *Women's Employment in a Comparative Perspective.* New York: Aldine De Gruyter.

van Knippenberg, Daan, Carsten De Dreu, and Astrid C. Homan. 2004. "Work Group Diversity and Group Performance: An Integrative Model and Research Agenda." *Journal of Applied Psychology* 89:1008–1022.

Wadhwa, Vivek, AnnaLee Saxenian, Ben Rissing, and Gary Gereffi. 2007. "America's New Immigrant Entrepreneurs." Master of Engineering Management Program, Duke University and University of California-Berkeley School of Information. January 4.

Waldfogel, Jane. 1997. "The Effect of Children on Women's Wages." *American Sociological Review* 62:209–217.

Waldinger, Roger, Howard Aldrich, and Robin Ward. 1990. *Ethnic Entrepreneurs: Immigrant Business in Industrial Societies.* Newbury Park, CA: Sage Publications.

Waldinger, Roger and Michael I. Lichter. 2003. *How the Other Half Works: Immigration and the Social Organization of Labor.* Berkeley, CA: University of California Press.

Walker, Charles R. and Robert H. Guest. 1952. *The Man on the Assembly Line.* Cambridge: MA: Harvard University Press.

Wallerstein, Immanuel. 1974. *The Modern World System: Capitalist Agriculture and the Origins of the European World Economy in the Sixteenth Century.* New York: Academic Press.

Wallerstein, Michael and Bruce Western. 2000. "Unions in Decline? What Has Changed and Why." *Annual Review of Poltical Science* 3:355–377.

Waters, Mary C. and Tomás R. Jiménez. 2005. "Assessing Immigrant Assimilation: New Empirical and Theoretical Challenges." *Annual Review of Sociology* 31:105–125.

Wayne, Julie Holliday and Brian L.Cordeiro. 2003. "Who Is a Good Organizational Citizen? Social Perception of Male and Female Employees Who Use Family Leave." *Sex Roles* 49:233–246.

Weber, Max. [1905]/1949. "Objective Possibility and Adequate Causation in Historical Explanation." Pp. 164–188 in *The Methodology of the Social Sciences*, edited by Edward A. Shils and Henry A. Finch. Glencoe, IL: The Free Press.

———. 1968. *Economy and Society: An Outline of Interpretive Sociology.* Edited by Guenther Roth and Claus Wittich. Translated by Ephraim Fischoff and others. New York: Bedminster Press.

———. 1996. *The Protestant Ethic and the Spirit of Capitalism.* Translated by Talcott Parsons. Introduction by Randall Collins. Los Angeles: Roxbury Publishing Company.

Weeks, John. 2004. *Unpopular Culture: The Ritual of Complaint in a British Bank.* Chicago: University of Chicago Press.

Weisberger, Lauren. 2003. *The Devil Wears Prada.* New York: Random House, Inc.

Wellman David. 1995. *The Union Makes Us Strong: Radical Unionism on the San Francisco Waterfront.* New York: Cambridge University Press.

Wharton, Amy S. 1993. "The Affective Consequences of Service Work." *Work and Occupations* 20: 205–232.

Whyte, William Foote. 1948. *Human Relations in the Restaurant Industry.* New York: McGraw-Hill Book Company.

————. 1987. "From Human Relations to Organizational Behavior: Reflections on the Changing Scene." *Industrial and Labor Relations Review* 40, 4:487–500.

Whyte, William H. 1956. *The Organization Man.* New York: Simon and Schuster.

Wilensky, Harold. 1964. "The Professionalization of Everyone." *American Journal of Sociology* 70:137–158.

Williams, Christine L. 1989. *Gender Differences at Work.* Berkeley, CA: University of California.

————. 1992. "The Glass Escalator: Hidden Advantages for Men in the 'Female' Professions." *Social Problems* 39:253–267.

————. 1995. *Still a Man's World.* Berkeley: University of California.

————. 1998. "What's Gender Got to Do with It?" Pp. 141–147 in *Required Reading: Sociology's Most Influential Books*, edited by Dan Clawson. Amherst, MA: University of Massachusetts Press.

Williams, Joan C. 2000. *Unbending Gender: Why Work and Family Conflict and What to Do About It.* New York: Oxford University Press.

Williams, Joan C., Jessica Manvell, and Stephanie Bornstein. 2006. "'Opt Out' or Pushed Out?: How the Press Covers Work/Family Conflict." The Center for Work Life Law. San Francisco, CA: University of California Hastings College of the Law.

Williams, K.Y. and O'Reilly, C.A. 1998. "Demography and Diversity in Organization." *Research in Organizational Behavior* 20: 77–140.

Wilson, George. 1997. "Pathways to Power: Racial Differences in the Determinants of Job Authority." *Social Problems* 44:38–54.

Wilson, Sloan. 1955. *The Man in the Gray Flannel Suit.* New York: Simon & Schuster.

Wilson, William J. 1986. *The Truly Disadvantaged: The Inner City, the Underclass, and Public Policy.* Chicago: University of Chicago Press.

————. 1996. *When Work Disappears: The World of the New Urban Poor.* New York: Random House.

Winslow, Emily R., Michele C. Bowman, and Mary E. Klingensmith. 2004. "Surgeon Workhours in the Era of Limited Resident Workhours." *Journal of the American College of Surgeons* 198:111–117.

Womack, James P., Daniel T. Jones, and Daniel Roos. 1990. *The Machine That Changed the World.* New York: Rawson Associates.

Word, Carl O., Mark P. Zanna, and Joel Cooper. 1974. "The Non-Verbal Mediation of Self-Fulfilling Prophecies in Inter-Racial Interaction." *Journal of Experimental Social Psychology* 10:109–120.

Yoon, In-Jin. 1997. *On My Own: Korean Businesses and Race Relations in America.* Chicago: University of Chicago Press.

Zuboff, Shoshana. 1988. *In the Age of the Smart Machine.* New York: Basic Books.

Index

$\sim$